State Building in Latin America

State Building in Latin America diverges from existing scholarship in developing explanations both for why state-building efforts in the region emerged and for their success or failure. First, Latin American state leaders chose to attempt concerted state building only where they saw it as the means to political order and economic development. Fragmented regionalism led to the adoption of more laissez-faire ideas and the rejection of state building. With dominant urban centers, developmentalist ideas and state-building efforts took hold, but not all state-building projects succeeded. The second plank of the book's argument centers on strategies of bureaucratic appointment to explain this variation. Filling administrative ranks with local elites caused even concerted state-building efforts to flounder, while appointing outsiders to serve as administrators underpinned success. Relying on extensive archival evidence, the book traces how these factors shaped the differential development of education, taxation, and conscription in Chile, Colombia, Mexico, and Peru.

Hillel David Soifer is an assistant professor of political science at Temple University. His research has been published in journals such as *Comparative Political Studies*, *Studies in Comparative International Development*, and *Latin American Research Review*. He was awarded the 2013 Alexander George Award for Best Article by the Qualitative and Multi-Method Section of the American Political Science Association, and has served as the Peggy Rockefeller Visiting Scholar at the David Rockefeller Center for Latin American Studies at Harvard University.

State Building in Latin America

HILLEL DAVID SOIFER
Temple University

CAMBRIDGE
UNIVERSITY PRESS

32 Avenue of the Americas, New York NY 10013-2473, USA

Cambridge University Press is part of the University of Cambridge.

It furthers the University's mission by disseminating knowledge in the pursuit of education, learning and research at the highest international levels of excellence.

www.cambridge.org
Information on this title: www.cambridge.org/9781107107878

© Hillel David Soifer 2015

This publication is in copyright. Subject to statutory exception and to the provisions of relevant collective licensing agreements, no reproduction of any part may take place without the written permission of Cambridge University Press.

First published 2015

A catalogue record for this publication is available from the British Library

Library of Congress Cataloguing in Publication data
Soifer, Hillel David
State building in Latin America / Hillel David Soifer, Temple University.
    pages cm
ISBN 978-1-107-10787-8 (hardback)
1. Nation-building – Latin America.   2. Political development – Latin America.   I. Title.
JL966.S74   2015
320.98–dc23   2015004870

ISBN 978-1-107-10787-8 Hardback

Cambridge University Press has no responsibility for the persistence or accuracy of URLs for external or third-party internet websites referred to in this publication, and does not guarantee that any content on such websites is, or will remain, accurate or appropriate.

Contents

Acknowledgments	*page* ix
Abbreviations	xiii
Annual Official Government Publications Used, by Library/Archive Location	xv
Introduction: The Origins of State Capacity in Latin America	1
Two Questions	3
The Emergence of State-Building Projects	4
The Success of State-Building Projects	5
Studying Intra-Regional Variation	6
State Capacity: Concepts and Measures	9
State Capacity in Latin America: Historical Trends	11
Research Design: Thick Measures, Detailed Case Studies	15
Explaining Variation in State Capacity	17
The Emergence of State-Building Projects	17
Theorizing State-Building Failure	20
Applying the Argument	23
1 The Emergence of State-Building Projects	24
Geography and State Development	27
Size	29
Terrain	30
Urban Primacy, Regional Salience, and State Development	32
Chile	38
Mexico	39
Peru	40
Colombia	41
The Ideational Foundations of State-Building Projects	46
The Varied Content of Mid-Century Liberalism	46

v

	The State and Progress in Chile	48
	"Order" and "Progress" in Mexico	49
	The State and "Progress" in Peru	51
	Colombia's Anti-Statist Consensus	52
	Conclusion	55
2	**A Theory of State-Building Success and Failure**	59
	Administrative Institutions and the Outcomes of	
	State-Building Efforts	61
	Causal Mechanisms	62
	Scoring Cases on the Forms of Rule	65
	The Public Administration of State Building	82
	Patrimonialism	82
	Overlapping Bureaucratic Networks	83
	Technical Expertise	84
	Customary Law	85
	Conclusion	86
3	**Alternative Historical Explanations and Initial Conditions**	87
	Colonial Legacies	88
	Mechanisms of Colonial Impact	88
	The Bourbon Reforms: State Power at the Twilight of	
	Colonial Rule	89
	Foundational Wars, New States?	94
	Post-Independence Crisis	96
	Education	97
	Taxation	100
	Monopoly of Force	103
	Explaining State Administrative Appointment Practices	107
	Perceived Threats to Systemic Stability	108
	The Place of Traditional Authority in National Projects	116
	The Currency of Patronage	120
	Conclusion	123
4	**State Projects, Institutions, and Educational Development**	124
	Educational Development and State Power: Dimensions and	
	Indicators	126
	Indicators of Primary Schooling Provision	126
	Indicators of Control over Public Primary Schooling	126
	Comparative Development	127
	Provision	127
	Systematization	130
	Inspection	133
	Lack of Educational Initiative in Colombia	134
	A Structural Alternative: Inequality and Education Development	138
	Deployed Rule and State Power: The Development of School	
	Inspection in Chile	140

	Institutional Change and Education Development in Peru	143
	Explaining Cross-State Divergence in Mexican Education	147
	Statistical Analysis	148
	Sonora	154
	Michoacán	155
	Conclusion	156
5	Political Costs, Infrastructural Obstacles, and Tax State Development	158
	Operationalizing Tax State Development	160
	Tax Types	160
	Tax Burden	162
	Comparative Development	162
	Tax Types	163
	Tax Burden	172
	Explaining Variation in Tax Capacity	179
	Deciding to Tax: Resource Rents and Political Costs	179
	Implementing Taxation: Forms of Rule and Effective Administration	181
	Peru: Local State Agents and the Failure to Tax after the Guano Boom	181
	Chile: Deployed Rule and the Recovery of Taxation after the Nitrate Boom	186
	Federalism and Tax State Development in Colombia and Mexico	193
	Laissez-Faire Liberalism and Reluctance to Tax in Colombia	193
	Mexico: Deployed Rule and the Expansion of Federal Taxation	195
	Conclusion	200
6	Local Administration, Varieties of Conscription, and the Development of Coercive Capacity	202
	War and the State: Limits of the "Bellic" Approach	204
	The Capacity to Mobilize	206
	Chile	207
	Peru	209
	Colombia	211
	Mexico	214
	Local Officials and Military Recruitment	220
	Deployed Rule, Legal-Formal Conscription, and Chilean Military Effectiveness	222
	Mexico: Voluntary Enlistment and Legalistic Recruitment	224
	Delegated Rule and Peruvian Military Weakness	227
	The Absence of Systematic Recruitment Efforts in Colombia	229
	Conclusion	230

Conclusion | 232
   The Emergence and Outcomes of State-Building Efforts | 232
      Alternative Explanations | 234
   A Broader Perspective on Latin American State Building | 235
      Urban Primacy and the Origins of State-Building Projects | 235
      Forms of Rule and the Outcomes of State-Building Efforts | 246
   The End of the Liberal Era | 249
   Theorizing State Building | 252
      Bringing Ideas into State Development | 252
      Separating Emergence and Success | 255
      Causal Importance | 259
   Historical State Building and Contemporary "Nation Building" | 260

Works Cited | 263
Index | 291

Acknowledgments

I don't know why authors seem to leave the most important acknowledgments for last; in my case there is one person to whom clearly I owe the most. Annie has supported me, made me laugh, joined me on much-needed outings, challenged my ideas, and taught me about hers. Though this book would not have been completed without her, her impact goes far beyond that. I don't know what stroke of luck has allowed me to share my life with such a smart, warm, adventurous, and patient partner, but I count my blessings daily.

Sanity during the long road to completing this book was also maintained by the support and distraction of old friends near and (alas, too often) far, including Emma and Mike, Abbie and Willy, Steph and Mike, and Sean and Sam. I'd also like to thank Lance for always greeting me with a wagging tail and the eternal hope for a walk and a snack, and to acknowledge the distraction of political debates on email with Alex, David, and Matt. Academia has the wonderful quality of turning colleagues into friends. Some of my closest friendships – with Casey, Fiona, Mark, Will, Magda, Diana, and Shannon – date back to the beginning of graduate school, and it has been a real pleasure to have known these good people, their partners, and their families over the years. I'm also grateful to my family: my parents, my brother and his three great kids, and my in-laws Pam, Robbie, JP, Coley, and Lizzie, including even those individuals who asked when the book would be done every time we talked.

This book began as a dissertation supervised by Jorge Domínguez, Steven Levitsky, John Coatsworth, and Paul Pierson. My hope is that the final product on these pages shows just how much I got from their careful reading and helpful feedback even as it barely resembles that initial foray into these issues. I'm also grateful to various institutions at Harvard University for funding the dissertation research on which much of the book is based. Early in my research, I imposed myself on scholars in both Chile and Peru, who patiently answered my incoherent questions and steered me away from making even more fundamental errors. For their time and kindness, I thank Sol Serrano, Rafael Sagredo Baeza, Carlos Contreras, Patricia Ames, and Aldo Panfichi. Jen Tobin has (I believe) not read a word of this manuscript, but her company made my research in Lima more enjoyable.

Thanks to generous invitations from colleagues, I was able to present seminars on this project as it developed and to benefit from the feedback I received. In approximate chronological order, starting from the earliest (and probably painfully incoherent) version, I thank audiences at Dartmouth University, the Princeton Program on Latin American Studies, the University of Michigan, St. Antony's College of Oxford, SUNY-Stony Brook, Brown University, The College of New Jersey, CDDRL at Stanford University, the University of New Mexico, and Trinity College. I'd like to single out Eduardo Dargent and Juan Pablo Luna, who also provided welcome opportunities for me to present research related to this book at their institutions, to exchange ideas about our shared interests, and to benefit from their hospitality in Lima and Pirque. I look forward to continuing to work with both of these generous colleagues, and to returning the favor to the extent possible by welcoming them to our small town in New Jersey.

The advice, reading suggestions, comments, and criticisms of many friends and colleagues have shaped this book in important ways. I am grateful to Nancy Appelbaum, Michael Bernhard, Max Cameron, Giovanni Capoccia, John Carey, Ryan Carlin, Miguel Centeno, Sarah Chartock, Mark Copelovitch, Jorge Domínguez, Angelica Duran Martínez, Kent Eaton, Andres Estefane, Gustavo Flores-Macías, Daniel Gingerich, Agustina Giraudy, Paul Gootenberg, Ivan Jaksic, Rob Jansen, Diana Kapiszewski, Robert Karl, Alan Knight, Kendra Koivu, Marcus Kurtz, Mara Loveman, Lauren Morris MacLean, James Mahoney, Reo Matsuzaki, Conor O'Dwyer, Maritza Paredes, James Robinson, Joshua Rosenthal, Andrew Schrank, Gay Seidman, Dan Slater, Maya Tudor, Kurt Weyland, Nicholas Wheeler, Sean Yom, and Daniel Ziblatt.

For kind advice about the revision process, I thank Miguel Centeno, Steve Levitsky, Rachel Riedl, Rich Snyder, and Deborah Yashar. For the time they took to carefully read large portions of the manuscript (in most cases, when it was much longer than the version in your hands!) and for

Acknowledgments xi

their helpful comments, I thank Alisha Holland, Jamie Loxton, Rachel Riedl, Ryan Saylor, Erica Simmons, Prerna Singh, Dan Slater, Rich Snyder, Annie Stilz, and Alberto Vergara. A few generous souls – Steve Levitsky, Ryan Saylor, and especially Matthias vom Hau – have each seen more iterations of this project than I care to admit and than they might care to remember, yet each has patiently offered helpful and thorough comments on many different occasions. I'm truly lucky to have such colleagues.

Much of the writing of this book was accomplished during my time at Temple University, and I consider myself very lucky to share space and community on the fourth floor of Gladfelter Hall with such a smart and generous group of folks. I'm particularly grateful to Rich Deeg and Gary Mucciaroni who have served as wonderful department chairs during my time at Temple, to Sandra Suarez, Robin Kolodny, and Orfeo Fioretos for their wisdom and advice, and to Kevin Arceneaux, Sarah Bush, Ryan Vander Wielen, and Megan Mullin (even though she left us for warmer climes!) for joining me to get coffee, helping me explore Philadelphia, and otherwise being good company. Thanks, too, to Cassie Emmons and Travis Blemings for their careful research assistance.

Bates College was my first home in professional academia. I'd like to thank my colleagues there, especially John Baughman, Áslaug Asgeirsdottir, and Karen Melvin, for their friendship and for understanding my reasons for leaving. Before arriving at Temple, I also spent a year at Princeton University, where thanks to the generosity of the University Center for Human Values and the Politics Department, I was able to enjoy a semester to focus on my research. The final revisions on the book manuscript were completed during a year of leave funded by the Peggy Rockefeller Visiting Fellowship at the David Rockefeller Center for Latin American Studies at Harvard University, and I thank Merilee Grindle and Edwin Ortiz for their generosity and for welcoming me back into the community where I spent several years as a graduate student. Thanks to Rich Snyder, I spent much of that year in residence at Brown University, where the graduate students, visiting scholars, and faculty at CLACS and the Watson Institute helped make my time rewarding and intellectually stimulating. I thank Rich, the staff at the Watson Institute and the Center for Latin American and Caribbean Studies, and especially Kate Goldman for welcoming me to Providence.

Eric Crahan originally expressed interest in this manuscript many years ago, and he and Robert Dreesen shepherded it through the review process. I am grateful to both for their efficiency and their guidance. Robert in particular improved the book with his urging to leave out some extraneous material that was not ready for primetime. I'm also grateful to Liz Janetschek and the production team at Cambridge University Press for their efficiency and professionalism. The anonymous reviewers were careful and generous with their time, and I thank them for their comments on several iterations of the manuscript; though it took me a long time to address their comments, I am truly grateful for the additional work I was encouraged to do, and I'm confident that the book has improved as a result of their urgings. I, of course, bear exclusive responsibility for all of the errors it still contains.

Abbreviations

[Note that while I use a consistent label to refer to each publication over time, government reorganizations at various points in time in each country led to changes in ministerial names and portfolios.]

AE	Anuario Estadístico, Chile (Annual Statistical Extract, Chile)
CNR	Compañía Nacional de Recaudación, Peru (private firm with which the national government contracted for tax collection after 1902, as discussed in Chapter 5)
HEC	Estado Mayor General del Ejército (various years) *Historia del Ejército Chileno* (10 volumes) (Santiago: Colección Biblioteca Militar) (official history of the Chilean Army)
MED	Memoria del Ministerio de Instrucción Pública, Peru (Annual Report of the Ministry of Public Education, Peru)
MGOB	Memoria del Ministerio de Gobierno e Interior, Peru (Annual Report of the Ministry of Governance and the Interior, Peru)
MGUERRA	Memoria del Ministerio de Guerra, Peru (Annual Report of the War Ministry, Peru)
MHAC	Memoria del Ministerio de Hacienda, Chile (Annual Report of the Finance Ministry, Chile)
MILIMA	Memoria de la Dirección de Instrucción Pública del Departamento de Lima (Annual Report of the Directorate of Public Education, Department of Lima)
MINT	Memoria del Ministerio de Interior, Chile (Annual Report of the Interior Ministry, Chile)

MIP   Memoria del Ministerio de Justicia, Culto, e Instrucción Pública, Chile (Annual Report of the Justice, Religion, and Public Education Ministry, Chile)

Annual Official Government Publications Used, by Library/Archive Location

[Note this list does NOT include individual government documents accessed, which are cited as necessary in the text.]

CHILE

Archivo Nacional Histórico

Boletín de Leyes (various years)
Memoria del Ministerio de Guerra 1848, 1856–1858, 1860, 1868, 1873, 1875–1877, 1881, 1882, 1884, 1885
Memoria del Ministerio de Industria y Obras Públicas, 1891–1895
Memoria del Ministerio de Interior 1852, 1854, 1856, 1859, 1860, 1864–1866

Biblioteca Nacional

Anuario Estadístico de la República de Chile 1848–1858, 1861–1912
Memoria del Ministerio de Guerra 1887–1900
Memoria del Ministerio de Hacienda 1834–1836, 1839, 1884–1900
Memoria del Ministerio de Interior 1875–1878, 1880–1881, 1884–1902, 1904, 1908–1910
Memoria del Ministerio de Justicia, Culto, e Instrucción Pública 1840–1851, 1868–1900
Mensajes Presidenciales (various years)

PERU

Archivo Nacional

Memoria del Ministerio de Gobierno 1890, 1896, 1898, 1901, 1902, 1904, 1905, 1907, 1908, 1911, 1913

Memoria del Ministerio de Guerra 1874, 1889, 1890, 1893, 1897, 1900–1929.

Memoria del Ministerio de Instrucción Pública 1853, 1862, 1864, 1890–1893, 1896–1898, 1900–1910, 1912–1922

Instituto DeNegri

Memoria de la Dirección de Instrucción Pública del Departamento de Lima 1875

Memoria del Ministerio de Gobierno 1831, 1847, 1860, 1870, 1872, 1874, 1878, 1879, 1883, 1885, 1888, 1897, 1899, 1906, 1920, 1921

Memoria del Ministerio de Guerra 1829, 1845, 1853, 1870, 1872, 1879

Memoria del Ministerio de Hacienda 1828, 1849, 1851, 1853, 1862, 1864, 1867, 1868, 1874, 1876, 1878, 1879, 1885, 1886, 1890, 1892, 1896, 1903

Memoria del Ministerio de Instrucción Pública 1847, 1883

Mensajes Presidenciales, various years

Government Documents Collection, Harvard University

Censo Escolar 1902

Introduction

The Origins of State Capacity in Latin America

States are crucial to nearly every aspect of our lives. The ability of state institutions to effectively exert authority throughout the national territory underpins variation in access to economic opportunity, the provision of public goods, and the protection of legal rights. Yet in Latin America, variation in state capacity has only recently become an object of serious scrutiny. Much of our understanding of the state has come from studies of its origins in Europe, where a vigorous debate among scholars has generated extensive cumulation of knowledge in both theoretical and empirical terms.[1] This school of research has been complemented in recent years by a growing literature exploring the "failure" of some contemporary states to fulfill even their basic functions.[2]

This dual focus on the world's strongest and weakest states ignores much of the contemporary variation: no state in Latin America, for example, could be described as a Hobbesian Leviathan or a Scandinavian cradle-to-grave provider, nor is any as vestigial as those of Chad or Somalia. Yet within Latin America, state capacity varies quite widely across countries. Some countries, like Chile and Uruguay, provide basic public goods and security to their citizens, and are able to extract revenues and enforce laws. But illiteracy in Bolivia is about five times as high as in Uruguay. For every child not vaccinated in Chile, about ten go unvaccinated in Ecuador. While the 2011 census in Uruguay was administered effectively, the 2005 census in Peru was so flawed it had to be

---

[1] Among the many important contributions to this literature, some central works are Tilly (1975), Tilly (1992), Ertman (1997), Downing (1992), Spruyt (1994), and Gorski (2003).
[2] Herbst (2000); Bates (2008).

repeated two years later. The homicide rate in Venezuela is about ten times as high as that of Uruguay. How can we account for this variation in the state's ability to carry out a set of core functions?

Even more striking is the territorial unevenness in state capacity in the region's weaker states, which is concealed by national average measures of state capacity (Snyder 2001b). In Colombia, for example, the national literacy according to the 2005 census was 85.9 percent, but schooling only reached 60 percent of the residents of La Guajira, and 78.4 percent of the residents of Córdoba. By contrast, in Chile, which had a national literacy rate in 2002 of 87.5 percent, every province's literacy rate was more than 80 percent. In Bolivia, the national vaccination rate for children in 1997 was 74.1 percent, but at the department level, vaccination rates ranged from more than 95 percent in Chuquisaca to less than 50 percent in Pando.[3]

This subnational variation in the provision of basic services reflects a crucial aspect of stateness: the state's reach over territory and ability to implement its chosen policies. Today, Latin America's states share many features of institutional design, a certain degree of bureaucratic professionalism in the halls of ministries and executive agencies, and enjoy basic stability.[4] The most striking difference across states in the region is in the performance of basic functions, and in particular, in the reach of the state agencies that provide those functions over a territory.

The goal of this book is to explain why in some Latin American countries, state institutions reach across the national territory and operate with a degree of capacity, while in others, the state is vestigial and ineffective. Rather than assuming that contemporary variation has contemporary roots, I begin by examining the historical record. I show that contemporary rankings of countries on various aspects of state capacity are very strongly associated with their ranking in 1900. This finding resonates with a central aspect of the scholarship on state strength more generally: nearly all research on this question points to historical causes (such as war, colonial rule, or early institutional choices) to account for

---

[3] Data are from Instituto Nacional de Estadística de Bolivia, 1997 data on immunizations by province. I generate average immunization rate figures as follows: average the number of each of five types (Polio first and third dose, BCG, and DPT first and third dose) given in each province, and divide by the number of one-year-old residents (estimated as 2.9% of total population, based on population pyramid in 2007 census).

[4] Both Dargent (2015) and Gingerich (2013) show that bureaucratic professionalism and institutional capacity vary more across agencies within states than they do across states within Latin America. The same is not true for the state's performance of basic functions and its reach across its territory.

contemporary variation. Thus in devising a historical account of contemporary variation in state capacity, the argument advanced in this book falls in the mainstream of scholarship on state development.

But this book diverges from existing scholarship in an important way: I argue that we must explicitly separate the theoretical accounts of the factors that cause state-building efforts to *emerge* and the factors that lead to *success* or *failure*. Making this separation, the framework I develop charts three paths to contemporary outcomes: those in which state-building efforts never emerged, those in which state-building efforts failed, and those in which state-building efforts succeeded. As I discuss later, accounting for all three paths is necessary for a theoretically complete explanation of variation in state capacity. Most existing scholarship falls short of this goal because it tends to limit itself to explaining why state-building efforts emerge, and fails to theorize the set of causal factors underlying state-building success.

This book follows the evolution of the state in four Latin American countries during the Liberal era, running from the end of the post-independence crises in each to the early twentieth century. Colombia followed the first path described previously, and Peru the second: these are two logically distinct routes to contemporary state weakness.[5] I select Mexico and Chile as my two cases of successful state building because the many differences in historical, social, economic, and political terms between these cases help me to isolate the factors they had in common that were necessary for state-building efforts to succeed. These three trajectories leading to the outcomes of state strength and weakness account for variation in state capacity in Latin America, and are the topic of this book.

TWO QUESTIONS

The theory developed in this book is designed to answer the two key questions about the development of state capacity: What are the factors that cause state-building efforts to *emerge*? And what are the factors that lead to *success*? The answers I develop to these questions, which I preview in this brief discussion and present in Chapters 1 and 2, are shown in Figure 0.1.

---

[5] As discussed later, Peru saw some gains in state capacity during the Aristocratic Republic (1895–1919): the contrasting trajectories of state development during two historical periods in Peru helps isolate the factors necessary for state building to succeed.

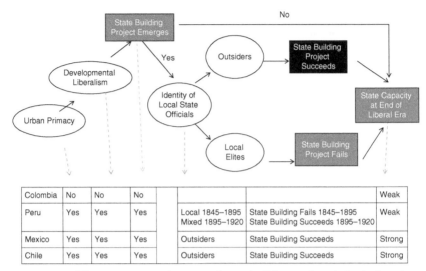

FIGURE 0.1. The emergence and success of state-building projects in Latin America.

The Emergence of State-Building Projects

The first puzzle is why state-building projects emerge. In the absence of the wars that force state leaders to mobilize resources and manpower or risk defeat and devastation, we cannot take for granted the decision to undertake major investments in extending the reach of state institutions. Here, I focus on the role of geography and broad ideas about development. I argue that in a climate of relative stability that emerged after the post-independence crisis eased, state leaders opted for state building if and when they saw it as a means to the developmental goals they sought – economic growth, social peace, and political stability.[6] Whether state building seemed propitious depended, in turn, on the nature of political and economic geography: where a single dominant urban core existed and development was seen in a center-periphery dynamic, an elite consensus about the importance of extending central authority for

---

[6] In pursuing state building as a means to seizing on an opportunity, I argue that Latin American state leaders acted more like Olsonian "stationary bandits" (Olson 1993) and that state building was largely proactive rather than emerging as a reaction to threats, whether internal or external. Internal threats do enter into the explanation for success and failure of state-building projects, as discussed later – where they were present, they affected the design of administrative institutions in ways that impacted state-building efforts – but I argue that they did not spur state-building efforts in Liberal-era Latin America.

Introduction

development could take hold. By contrast, where multiple regional centers each sat astride a distinct regional political economy, the construction of central state authority did not seem a propitious development strategy. This was so for two reasons: first, elites clashed because each region had distinct public good preferences. Second, where regions had self-contained economies and could generate sufficient economic production on their own to maintain and even increase standards of living without the need for national integration, visions of development centered on the promotion of regional progress, which did not depend on the extension of the authority of the central state.

As the left half of Figure 0.1 indicates, Colombia diverged from the other three cases at this point: its trajectory of state weakness across the century after independence can be explained by its polycentric economic geography. Fragmented into multiple regions, it saw the consolidation of a strikingly laissez-faire elite consensus that brought to power a series of efforts to pursue development by dismantling, rather than building, the state. In the other three cases, the broadly liberal consensus after mid-century had a developmental core, and concerted state-building efforts ensued.

The Success of State-Building Projects

But accounting for the emergence of state-building projects is insufficient to explain the variation we observe in state capacity. Among our cases, Peru saw major state-building efforts, yet its state is quite weak by regional standards. We need, therefore, an explanation for why only some state-building efforts succeed, and some fail. The failure of such efforts is not only a logical possibility but a historical reality, yet explaining why state-building efforts fail has been almost completely neglected by political scientists and historical sociologists. For more than three decades after 1845, state leaders in Peru presided over a concerted effort to extend the reach of the state across the national territory, and funded this effort with immense revenues from the guano monopoly the country enjoyed. Yet despite consistent policies and more than adequate spending, the results were minimal. How can we explain why state-building efforts succeeded in Mexico and Chile, but failed in Peru? In answering this question, the greater success of state building in Peru after 1895 provides an opportunity for contrast within a single country over time, in addition to the analytical leverage gained from analytical comparison.

Relying on both cross-national and within-nation comparison, I argue that the fate of state-building efforts depended on the design of the institutions of local administration that extended the state's reach into the national periphery. More specifically, I argue that state-building efforts failed where local elites were tasked with administering them, but saw more success where local administrators were outsiders in the communities in which they served. Two logics underpin this claim: I argue that local elites were both less invested in state building, and less accountable to their superiors in the national bureaucracy. In Peru, especially before 1895, state leaders delegated administration to local elites, and the result was that the state-building initiatives emanating from the center bore little fruit. By contrast, in Chile and Mexico, state leaders deployed bureaucratic outsiders across the national territory; this led to greater success in state building.

In combination, then, the account I develop for variation in state capacity in Latin America is causally complex in two senses. First, variation cannot be accounted for in a univariate model: it depends on ideational factors (and their geographic underpinnings) and the design of local administrative institutions. Second, these two sets of factors are not analytically equivalent independent variables: instead, the former set accounts for the emergence of state-building efforts, while the latter, causally relevant only where state-building efforts emerge, accounts for success and failure.

This book traces this account through the four cases highlighted in Figure 0.1. It is based on material in the voluminous collection of national and regional histories of these cases, and on extensive primary source research in archives of various government ministries. In the Conclusion, I use this framework to consider the state-building trajectories of other Latin American countries, showing that they can also be explained by this argument. I begin in this chapter by defining state capacity and collecting systematic data to substantiate the broad regional trajectories. I then develop the research design and describe what is to come in the chapters that follow, which focus on the four cases in detail.

STUDYING INTRA-REGIONAL VARIATION

Studies of state capacity in the developing world can be crudely sorted into two categories. A first set of works, such as Centeno (2002), explain why the states of a particular region differ from those in early modern Europe, and downplay or set aside the determinants of intra-regional

Introduction

variation. Although he does devote part of his account to explaining intra-regional variation in the capacity of African states, Herbst (2000), too, focuses on explaining why African states do not resemble those of Europe. These studies have made important contributions to our understanding of the limits to the scope of theories derived from European history, but in logical terms, regional characteristics cannot account for the intra-regional variation I seek to explain.

A second set of studies have set aside comparisons with Europe to focus on explaining intra-regional variation. Holding regional characteristics constant where possible, these works have sought to account for the distinct trajectories taken by individual countries. Slater (2010) and Vu (2010) explain the evolution of state-making in postwar Southeast Asia. Downing (1992), Ertman (1997), and Gorski (2003) identify differences among countries in early modern Europe that account for the distinct trajectories taken by their states within a broadly similar regional context marked by intensified military competition. Fernando López-Alves (2000) engages in the same sort of intra-regional comparison within Latin America. Like this book, he focuses on the nineteenth century as the crucial moment in which variation in state capacity emerged among Latin American countries. López-Álves argues that the nature of internal conflicts in the aftermath of independence was the crucial factor underlying variation in the subsequent evolution of states, although the ultimate goal of his study is to explain the type of regime that was consolidated. This book differs from his in two crucial ways. First, I argue that the crucial moment in which state building was possible occurred only after the post-independence conflicts came to a close and a modicum of stability emerged. Second, I do not explore regime dynamics at all in this book; my focus is on the power of states, independent of the regimes that rule them.

Kurtz (2013), Saylor (2012), and Paredes (2013) also explore intra-regional variation in state capacity within Latin America, although both Kurtz and Saylor also extend their argument to cases outside the region. Saylor and Paredes argue that commodity booms are windows of opportunity for state building, moments in which state capacity can be built if certain conditions hold. Both emphasize the nature of elite coalitions in explaining when commodity booms spur the state's creation of new public goods: Saylor argues that state building occurs in the context of commodity booms when insiders (members of the ruling coalition) seek new public goods in order to maximize their gains from commodity exports, or when booms benefit outsiders sufficiently to scare insiders into state building to lock in their distributional advantage. Paredes also emphasizes the divisions between existing elites and newly rising sectors that benefit from commodity revenues in preventing coordination around concerted, planned, state-building efforts.

Kurtz, too, focuses on relations among societal actors, but in addition to relations between elites, he argues that interest in state building on the part of rural elites depends on rural labor relations: where agrarian labor is marketized, he argues, elites will be more amenable to state building than when it is more akin to serfdom. My account differs from these important studies in two fundamental ways. First, whereas Kurtz and Saylor focus on the political motives for state building, I also unpack its administration. As I argue in more detail in Chapter 2, to explain the breadth of elite support for a state-building project is insufficient to account for variation in state capacity; a full theory of variation in state capacity must also explain the fate of the state-building projects that are undertaken, and that fate (as I show in this book) is determined by factors independent from those that determine the choice to build state capacity. Second, I see the motives behind state-building projects as shaped more by ideology and less by the narrow elite interests emphasized by all three authors. As I show in Chapter 1, the onset of state building was propelled not by narrow interests in the provision of particular public goods, but by a belief that increased state capacity would serve a broad range of interests in the long term.[7] I argue that state building was a *state* project rather than a sectoral or class project.

Explaining variation within a single region has both advantages and limitations. Restricting the analysis to Latin American cases truncates the range of state capacity being investigated. At first glance, this may be seen as a disadvantage in terms of generalizability. Yet the extent of intra-regional variation to be explained is still sizable, and it is quite striking, especially given that the cases shared similar (if not identical) experiences under Spanish colonial rule, similarly low levels of international war, and similar trajectories of integration into the global economy. Exploring this more fine-grained variation, which emerges in the presence

---

[7] As I discuss further in Chapter 1, this should not be misread as a claim that state leaders were benevolent rather than self-interested. I simply claim that their interests in stability and economic development, which would serve both their interests in generating legitimacy and a hold on power as well as broader societal interests, are not reducible to interests of particular social actors. Underlying, perhaps, my differences with Kurtz and Saylor's accounts is the fact that I attribute more autonomy to Latin American state leaders than do either of my interlocutors, who see the state as serving the interests of a ruling elite coalition. My position here echoes that of Mahoney (2001), who studies the Liberal era in Central America. This issue is discussed in Chapters 1 and 2.

of so many similarities in historical and structural conditions, allows us to identify causal factors that remain obscured in comparisons of cases with a wider range of scores on the dependent variable. Thus, this book eschews claims of global generality to focus on careful comparison and within-case analysis of a set of countries that diverge on the outcome of interest without representing extreme cases (Slater and Ziblatt 2013).

STATE CAPACITY: CONCEPTS AND MEASURES

Building on Michael Mann's concept of infrastructural power, the object of interest in this study is the state's ability to exercise control and implement policy choices throughout the territory it claims to govern.[8] Guillermo O'Donnell (1993) identified the importance of the spatial reach of state authority in a seminal article, which has formed the foundation of much concern about "stateness" in Latin America in the last two decades. Yet while many indices of state capacity exist, few capture this aspect of the state; few measure the territorial reach of state institutions, or the ability of the state to consistently and effectively perform a set of core basic functions throughout its realm.

Existing indices of state capacity are fraught with problems. This is particularly true of the industry of indicators of state weakness, state failure, and state fragility that has emerged in recent years. Among other problems, these datasets lack the historical data needed to trace state capacity over the long term, often rely on expert assessments rather than on objective data, and fail to make careful and transparent choices about conceptualization and scoring (Mata and Ziata 2009). As Kurtz and Schrank (2007) have shown, cross-national indicators of state capacity, such as the World Bank Governance Indicators, also suffer from problems of conceptual clarity and validity. The same is true of the Putterman Index of state antiquity, which has seen increasing usage in cross-national scholarship (Chanda and Putterman 2005).

Since even the most minimal core of state functions contains multiple dimensions, a single indicator of state capacity is too crude for all but the most general analyses. Thus single indicator measures of state capacity are also inappropriate for attempts to capture the overall concept (Hanson and Sigman 2011). This is true not only when the indicators are

---

[8] The concept of infrastructural power is first developed in Mann (1984). See Soifer and vom Hau (2008) and Soifer (2008) for a more detailed unpacking of this concept and approaches to its study. For stylistic reasons, I use the terms "state strength," "state power," and "state capacity" interchangeably throughout.

crude, like GDP per capita (Fearon and Laitin 2003) or state antiquity (Chanda and Putterman 2005), but even for indicators like road density (Herbst 2000) or the tax ratio, which tap a particular dimension of the state. In response to these concerns, I choose not to rely on existing indices or on single indicators of state capacity. Instead, my approach assesses state capacity by examining the presence of various state institutions across the national territory, and their systematization and efficacy in enforcing state authority. I focus on three categories of core functions of the state: the administration of a basic set of services (primary public education), the mobilization of manpower, and the extraction of revenue. These are, of course, closely related to Charles Tilly's (1975, 50) disaggregation of state power into regulatory, extractive, and coercive dimensions.[9] Because all states sought to perform these functions, assessing their performance on these dimensions captures the core content of Mann's concept of infrastructural power: the state's ability to implement its chosen policies. By focusing on these core functions, I ensure that my operationalization of state capacity does not conflate the state's strength with the scope of functions it performs (Fukuyama 2004).

Rather than capturing each of these three dimensions with a single indicator, I develop a more nuanced measurement scheme for each. These indicator-level measures are designed to capture the reach of state institutions over territory and their penetration of society, rather than just relying on national-level scores. They are also designed to measure as closely as possible the empirical *outputs* of the state, avoiding scoring based on the *de jure* content of legislation, the design of state institutions, or the outcomes of state policy.[10] The chapters that follow focus on a small number of cases and take a more nuanced approach to the measurement of state capacity, focusing on the service provision, extractive, and coercive dimensions in turn. The power of the state to provide and administer basic public services is assessed in the realm of primary public education. Chapter 4 evaluates the spatial spread of public primary schooling, as well as the systematization of education: textbook and curriculum standardization, teacher training, and the construction of centralized inspection and oversight. The extractive power of the state

---

[9] For a similar application of Tilly's three dimensions to measure state power, see Ziblatt (2006). Hanson and Sigman (2011) perform a factor analysis of more than thirty existing measures of state capacity and find that they cluster on the dimensions of extraction, administration, and coercion.

[10] On the trade-offs involved in using outputs, outcomes, and institutional design to measure state capacity, see Soifer (2008) and Fukuyama (2013).

Introduction

is assessed in the realm of taxation – Chapter 5 examines the tax burden per capita imposed on the population, and the types of taxes collected by the state, differentiated by the extent of spatial reach and administrative development needed for their assessment and collection.[11] The coercive dimension is assessed in Chapter 6, which examines military mobilization in response to internal and external threats, and the state's capacity to conscript in a consistent and reliable manner. Here, too, I focus on the spatial reach of conscription practices, which are associated with the extent to which the army can serve as a "school for the nation" by mixing conscripts from across the country within its ranks.

STATE CAPACITY IN LATIN AMERICA: HISTORICAL TRENDS

While the succeeding chapters examine the four cases using the detailed operationalization scheme described previously, I begin by using a somewhat less nuanced approach to map the broad trends in the development of state capacity across the region. Table 0.1 scores the ten major countries of South America and Mexico on various simple measures of state strength. The first two columns provide indicators of coercive capacity – military mobilization (measured as the average of the share of the population in the armed forces and military spending per capita) and the homicide rate.[12] The next two columns provide indicators of the provision of basic public goods – the literacy rate and the rate of provision to children under the age of one of immunizations for measles and DPT.[13] The final indicator used is road density, which captures the ability of state agents to penetrate the territory within a country's borders.[14]

---

[11] For reasons further explained in Soifer (2013a), I do not believe that the tax ratio (taxes/GDP) is a valid measure of state infrastructural power. Its numerator, the amount of taxes (or direct taxes) collected by the government, is often lowered by political considerations since governments choose not to tax as much as they can. As a result, the tax ratio always under-represents extractive capacity, which acts as an upper bound on taxation rather than shaping the level of taxation.

[12] Military mobilization is calculated for the decade 1990–1999 by averaging annual scores in that timespan for military spending per capita and military size per capita, both of which are drawn from the Correlates of War dataset. The homicide data come from Mainwaring and Scully (2010), Table 1.5, p. 32.

[13] Data for the literacy rate are drawn from Thorp (1998, 354) and are based on calculations of the illiterate percentage of the population above the age of fifteen. Vaccination data are drawn from the World Development Indicators.

[14] Road density data are drawn from the International Road Federation World Road Statistics, using data from as close to 1999 as possible.

TABLE O.1. *State capacity rankings, c.2000*

	Military*	Homicide rate	Literacy	Immunization	Rd dens.	Average**	St dev.
Argentina	6	3	2	5.5	8	5.42	2.27
Bolivia	8	9	11	9	11	9.67	1.53
Brazil	8	9	10	1	2	5.33	3.25
Chile	1.5	1	3	3	7	3.75	2.95
Colombia	6	10	5.5	7.5	5	6.50	1.50
Ecuador	5	5	7	11	4	6.00	2.65
Mexico	9	8	8	2	3	5.50	2.78
Paraguay	9	7	5.5	7.5	9	7.83	1.26
Peru	6	4	9	5.5	10	7.42	2.50
Uruguay	2	2	1	4	1	1.83	0.76
Venezuela	5.5	6	4	10	6	6.25	0.66

Ties are indicated by .5; for example, for literacy, Colombia and Paraguay tied for fifth and each receive a score of 5.5.
* "Military" is an average of the rankings for military participation ratio and military spending per capita, as defined in the text and using data from the *Correlates of War* project.
** The column for the average aggregates across dimensions of state capacity rather than across indicators. The first two columns relate to coercive capacity, the third and fourth to the provision of basic public goods, and the last to infrastructure provision. I therefore aggregate each dimension and average across them.

Introduction 13

TABLE 0.2. *State capacity rankings c.1900*

	Military*	Literacy	RR dens.	Census	Average	St dev.
Argentina	2.5	2	3	7	3.625	2.29
Bolivia	9	11	8	5	8.25	2.50
Brazil	7.5	4	5	3	4.875	1.93
Chile	1	3	4	1	2.25	1.50
Colombia	10	5	10	7	8	2.45
Ecuador	6	6	11	11	8.5	2.89
Mexico	8	9	2	7	6.5	3.11
Paraguay	4.5	7	9	9.5	7.5	2.27
Peru	9.5	10	6	9.5	8.75	1.85
Uruguay	2.5	1	1	3	1.875	1.03
Venezuela	5.5	6	7	3	5.375	1.70

Ties are indicated by .5; for example, for literacy, Colombia and Paraguay tied for fifth and each receive a score of 5.5.
* "Military" is an average of the rankings for military participation ratio and military spending per capita. It is calculated as the average of scores on each measure for each year with available data between 1900 and 1910.

When these rankings are averaged across each dimension, as shown in the rightmost column in the table, they conform quite well to our prior findings about intra-regional variation in state capacity: Uruguay and Chile score as the strongest states, with Brazil, Argentina, and Mexico lagging somewhat behind.[15] The weakest states are Peru, Bolivia, and Paraguay. This ranking of countries is quite similar to how they were arrayed nearly a century ago. Despite some significant data limitations and problems with comparability across countries, we can assemble a similar set of indicators for state capacity as of 1900 (See Table 0.2). Coercive capacity is captured by the same military mobilization measure used in Table 0.1. The literacy rate captures the provision of basic public services. Railroad density is used, like the road density measure in Table 0.1, to reflect the spatial reach of state agents and infrastructure. Finally, census implementation is used as an indicator of the state's overall ability to reach over the national territory and collect information about its residents. Drawing on data in Goyer and Domschke (1983),

---

[15] The Government Effectiveness and Rule of Law components of the World Bank Governance Indicators provide similar rankings as those in Table 0.1; I choose not to include them because of the conceptual and methodological concerns raised by Kurtz and Schrank (2007).

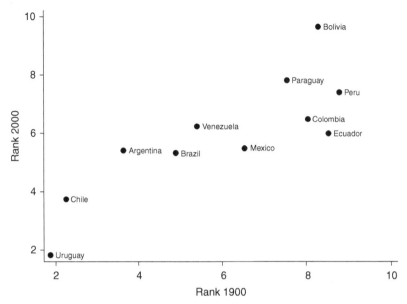

FIGURE 0.2. Persistence of rankings over time.
Data in this graph are drawn from the "Average" column in Tables 0.1 and 0.2.

I rank countries based on the number of censuses implemented between 1840 and 1920.[16]

Table 0.2 shows a clear gap between leaders and laggards in state capacity by 1900. Argentina, Uruguay, and Chile perform better than do the other countries on all dimensions, scoring in the top four of rankings for every measure. At the other end of the spectrum, Bolivia, Peru, Colombia, and Ecuador are among the weakest states in the region. Mexico, Brazil, Paraguay, and Venezuela fall in the middle of the pack.

A comparison of the rankings for 1900 and 2000 shows that they are very strongly correlated; the Pearson correlation of the two sets of rankings is 0.83. Figure 0.2, which arrays the rankings for 1900 and 2000, shows that the relative levels of state capacity across the region have remained strikingly stable over the past century. Perfect stability would place all countries on a line emanating at 45 degrees from

[16] Other sources produce slightly different numbers of censuses for certain countries; the overall rankings are unaffected by this. Scoring countries based on census iterations in different time periods (1820–1900, for example) also has little effect on the rankings. For a more detailed justification of the census as an indicator of state capacity, see Soifer (2013a).

the origin. Countries falling below the line, most notably Mexico, saw their ranking improve over the course of the twentieth century, while those located above the line (like Argentina) saw their ranking decline. Although there are some deviations from the line, the general pattern is one of striking stability over the past century: just as Mahoney (2010) has shown for social and economic development indicators, ordinal rankings of state capacity are also durable over the course of the twentieth century. Thus, the findings of this section point to the fact that relative levels of state capacity in 2000 are very well predicted by those in 1900. This implies that the origins of contemporary variation lie in the pre-1900 era. The stark historical continuities demonstrated in this discussion justify my turn to history to account for the divergence across countries in state capacity, and for my focus on the nineteenth century in the chapters that follow.

RESEARCH DESIGN: THICK MEASURES, DETAILED CASE STUDIES

Rather than approaching the explanation of this variation through time-series, cross-sectional quantitative analysis, I choose to investigate a smaller set of cases through detailed historical study. I do this for two reasons. First, as discussed previously, while the crude indicators deployed sketch broad trends, the concept of state capacity is not adequately captured in existing cross-national data. Nor can it be sufficiently precisely assessed through simple indicators that can be compiled into a dataset for cross-national analysis. Instead, I opt for the detailed study of the development of various dimensions of state capacity in a small number of cases. By exploring each of these dimensions separately, I trace the development of state capacity in a nuanced fashion. Although each state generally develops along similar trajectories for each dimension (as seen, for example, in the fairly low standard deviations across dimensions in Tables 0.1 and 0.2) this multi-faceted approach to state capacity allows me to identify instances of within-case variation, to highlight moments in which a given state performs well on one dimension but not others, and to leverage this variation for theory development and testing.

Secondly, as commonly argued by scholars who use case study methods, detailed investigations of small numbers of cases allow scholars to identify evidence of causality through process-tracing, a tool unavailable in cross-national regression analysis, which relies heavily on correlational evidence (George and Bennett 2005). The separate analysis of each dimension also allows me to better address alternative explanations by considering them where they are most likely to hold. Rather than evaluating an alternative explanation on a particular dimension of state capacity that I have chosen as my operationalization, a multi-dimensional operationalization of state capacity can be used to evaluate alternative explanations on their own most favored terrain. To the extent that these alternatives are shown to fall short precisely where scholars have staked their claim to explain state capacity, I have more convincingly identified their shortcomings. Thus, a multi-faceted conceptualization and measurement scheme for state capacity, in addition to better description, increases the analytical power of explanations for its development.

To account for the full range of state power outcomes in the region, and for a variety of different trajectories of state development, I select four cases for protracted investigation in the remainder of the book. The first cardinal rule of case selection in theory testing is to ensure that cases vary on the dependent variable. I select cases that follow the full set of trajectories outlined at the beginning of this book: Chile and Mexico's gains in state capacity, the state weakness of Colombia, and the case of Peru, which saw periods of both successful and failed state building.

As Table 0.3 shows, the variation in state strength across these cases is not correlated with a range of commonly cited alternative explanations, such as victory in war, intensity of colonial penetration, ethnic diversity or social inequality, and distortionary commodity booms. The fact that state-building outcomes do not align in expected ways with any of these factors suggests that we could reject them in studying the Latin American context. But instead of making that move in too hasty a manner, I grant these alternative explanations, which have great credence in the existing scholarship on state capacity, the respect that they merit and test each in detail in the empirical chapters to follow.

Based on this logic, I explore the role of colonial institutions, colonial legacies, and the nature of the independence conflict (in Chapter 3), the effects of colonial institutions and social inequality (in Chapter 4, which studies educational development), commodity booms (in Chapter 5 on extractive capacity), and the role of war (in Chapter 6 on coercive power) to show that even in the cases where they might be correlated with the outcome we expect, and even in examining the aspect of infrastructural power they are most likely to explain, they are not *causally connected*.[17] Thus I use within-case evidence, and not just cross-case comparison, to rule out alternative explanations.

[17] The relevant literature is discussed and cited in each of the empirical chapters.

Introduction

TABLE 0.3. *Cases and alternative explanations*

	Chile	Mexico	Peru	Colombia
State capacity c.1900	High	High	Low	Low
Victory in major war	Yes	No	No	No
Intensity of colonial penetration	Low	High	High	Low
Ethnic diversity	Low	High	High	Low
Commodity booms	Yes	No	Yes	Yes
Territorial System	Unitary	Federal	Unitary	Federal

Another important alternative explanation for varied levels of state capacity is geography. Chapter 1 investigates the causal role of a variety of geographic factors, identifying urban primacy as a necessary condition for the emergence of state-building projects, but showing that mountainousness, population density, national size, and complexity of terrain cannot account for variation in state capacity. Finally, each chapter illustrates cross-time variation in Peruvian state-building: some marked gains, particularly in the realm of education, were made during the Aristocratic Republic of 1895–1919. This cross-time variation illustrates the limitations of accounts that posit a time-invariant factor, such as geography, as the cause of state development.

EXPLAINING VARIATION IN STATE CAPACITY

The Emergence of State-Building Projects

The first question addressed in this book is why state-building projects are undertaken. The decision to invest political capital and huge amounts of money in extending state authority is theoretically important not only because leaders have other possible uses for these resources, but because extending state authority has fiscal and political costs beyond these direct outlays. One current of scholarship accounts for the onset of state building by identifying a threat to which state leaders respond by extending their authority. That threat can be external, as in the "bellic" school of state building that originated in studies of early modern Europe, or internal as in Slater's (2010) account of state building in Southeast Asia. A second view sees state building as a decision shaped purely by fiscal costs and benefits (Levi 1988; Herbst 2000). A third view looks for a social (usually class or sectoral) actor or coalition that benefits from the expansion of particular aspects of the state's writ, and attributes state-building policies to the influence of that actor (Waldner 1999; Anderson 1974; Spruyt 1994).

My approach to accounting for the emergence of state-building projects departs from these existing currents in several important ways. In contrast to the first view, I frame state building as a means of accessing opportunities, rather than only as a means of responding to threats. Threats, I argue, did not drive Latin American state building. As Miguel Centeno has shown, international wars were rare, and limited in scope in the region, and unlike in early modern Europe, state builders did not have to impose authority on society in order to avoid being wiped off the map. For Centeno, this explains why Latin America has weaker states than does Europe. But in trying to understand variation *among* Latin American states in the nineteenth century, the overall absence of war in the region cannot be helpful. Nor does variation across states in their involvement in war adequately account for variation in the onset of state building: Chile and Peru, for example, not only were each involved in two major nineteenth-century wars, but faced one another in both. And yet major differences in state capacity emerged. War-making, in short, did not spur state-building efforts in Latin America; nor did (as I discuss in Chapter 6) international threats falling short of war as Thies (2005) argues.

If international threats did not prod political elites into state-building initiatives, could domestic threats have played the same role? Slater (2010) argues that Southeast Asian state leaders undertook state-building efforts where the threats they faced from subaltern actors seemed particularly dire: contentious politics drove state building in the postwar era in that region. Yet the Latin American record looks quite different: state-building projects emerged not when internal threats were severe, but after a minimal level of order had been established and a modicum of political stability had emerged. In all four cases, as detailed in Chapter 3, the immediate aftermath of independence brought severe instability. In response, state leaders prioritized order – in the famous phrase appearing on the Chilean official coat of arms, they ruled "by reason or by force." State building – in the sense of the territorial extension and institutionalization of state administration – began only after order had been achieved.

Rather than emerging as a response to threats, I argue that state building emerged in pursuit of opportunities. State leaders leveraged moments of stability to develop long-term development projects. Thus, in contrast to the second, fiscally motivated, current of scholarship about state building, I show that the interests and decision-making calculus cannot be reduced to fiscal cost-benefit calculations. Instead, state leaders pursued long-term political stability. Where they believed that this required new roles for the state in promoting domestic and international trade, and in molding the population into citizens, they undertook concerted state building. State-building projects emerged where elites saw them as the means to goals they described as civilization, order, and progress, rather than in the direct pursuit of revenue. This explains why these projects included not only taxation, but also education and other dimensions of state capacity that fall outside the fiscal realm.[18]

Thus far I have argued that state building was neither driven by war nor reducible to the revenue imperative. It might seem, then, that I side with scholarship that sees state-building projects as serving the interests of dominant sectors in society, a view which has a long tradition in studies of state building (Anderson 1974; Waldner 1999; Saylor 2012). Yet the interests of dominant sectors do not provide a general account for why state-building projects emerged in some places but not others in mid-nineteenth-century Latin America. Although Saylor (2012) is correct to argue that satisfying the demands of exporting elites for public goods did spur the construction of state capacity at some moments, state-building projects also emerged in the absence of major exporting sectors – this was the case in Mexico, one of the cases I explore in detail. State-building projects also emerged in cases like Peru, where there was no dominant elite coalition driving state activity until the 1890s. Dominant-class arguments like that of Kurtz (2013) struggle to explain this case of prewar Peru, and mis-characterize it as one in which state building never emerged rather than its correct classification as a case in which a concerted state-building effort failed. Against this third view, I argue that state-building projects did not simply reflect the interests of particular class actors or the social composition of ruling coalitions. State building was a *state* project, not a class or sectoral project. My argument endows state leaders with a degree of autonomy in shaping not only goals for state policy, but in choosing the means by which those goals are to be pursued.

The determinant of whether the state was seen as the means to development was fundamentally ideational. Ideas explain why political elites

---

[18] Thus, whereas European state building saw a sequencing in the development of state functions, Latin America saw the simultaneous development of education, taxation, and coercive capacity. On the sequencing of state development in Europe, see Tilly (1992) and Weber (1976).

in different countries opted for different responses to the same opportunities. Where laissez-faire development visions dominated the political and intellectual arena, state leaders responded to identical opportunities by choosing not to undertake state building. State-building projects emerged only when state leaders held a set of statist liberal views and believed that the power of the state was needed to achieve economic development and political stability.

Finally, I account for the difference in ideology among cases, which shapes whether state-building efforts emerge, by bringing geography into the story. Against simple, cost-based accounts of geography's effect on state-building, I argue that urban primacy – the extent to which a country is dominated demographically and economically by a single urban center – affects the emergence of state-building projects through its effect on which ideas about development take hold. Only countries marked by high levels of urban primacy saw an elite consensus about state building. But where multiple cities aspired to national status, more laissez-faire views tended to emerge. Here, regional differences in public good preferences were more salient, which made consensus around a limited role for the state a least-bad solution to fiscal priorities. Because regions had self-contained economies, visions of development centered on the promotion of regional rather than national progress, which did not depend on the extension of the authority of the central state.

Thus, state-building emergence was shaped by geographic and ideational factors. Chapter 1 further develops this portion of the theoretical framework, and explains why state-building projects emerged in three of the cases but not in Colombia. The chapter argues that Colombia's polycentric political economy made the extension of central state authority seem less relevant to the development projects envisioned by political leaders than it did in Peru, Mexico, or Chile, and thus shaped the emergence of a more laissez-faire liberal consensus in that country. I trace the conversations among political elites and intellectuals about the role of the state in national development in each case, showing that all sought similar goals. But the Colombian consensus diverged in the overall reluctance to use state capacity in pursuit of development. This explains the absence of a state-building project in Colombia.

Theorizing State-Building Failure

The second puzzle of variation in state capacity is accounting for the success and failure of state-building efforts where they do emerge. This, as discussed further in Chapter 2, has been a question largely ignored in the existing scholarship.[19] That failed efforts by state leaders to extend control over territory within their borders are rarely theorized is surprising; we would expect attention to the question, in particular given contemporary events, which reveal how difficult state building is in Afghanistan, Iraq, Libya, and elsewhere.

In some studies, this failure to consider the possibility of state-building failure raises the specter of functionalism. Herbst (2000) simply disregards the issue, directly linking the cost-benefit calculations of state leaders to the outcomes of state capacity. Although he writes that "the viability of African states depends on leaders successfully meeting the challenges posed by their particular environment" (31), he never complicates the question of success. Instead, for Herbst, the cost structure posed by the environment shaped the varied inclination of state leaders, whether colonial or post-independence, to build state capacity. The weakness of many African states is seen as a strategic response to structural factors on the part of state leaders; it is the most efficient way to consolidate their hold on power. My point here is not to critique Herbst on empirical grounds; instead I seek to point out that the possibility of bad choices or poor implementation of their chosen policies by state leaders is something that his framework is unable to consider.

To my knowledge, the only existing study of state-building outcomes that incorporates an explanation for failed state-building efforts is Downing (1992).[20] Downing shows that Poland, despite encompassing as late as 1634 the largest territory in Europe, and its great wealth, failed to effectively mobilize in response to modernized military competition from Prussia, Russia, and Austria. This failure, and the partition that resulted, can be traced to the institutions that Poland inherited from its early modern era, which prevented any state-building effort from taking hold. The most famous of these, the *liberum veto*, allowed any single objection to stop the proceedings of the *sejm* (national council of nobles) until it could be resolved (Downing 1992, 140ff). Whereas Downing argues that Sweden and the Dutch Republic were able to fight major war without intensified taxation, and that England did not need to raise taxes because

---

[19] The work of Ian Lustick (1993) is a partial exception, although it focuses on failed efforts by states to incorporate new territories into their countries, rather than on failure to extend control over territory already formally within the state's jurisdiction. For a Latin American account of such an effort, see Skuban (2007).
[20] Failed state building is, of course, not the same thing as state failure, about which there is a robust scholarly debate.

it avoided war, he argues that Poland's state leaders tried but failed to increase state capacity in response to rising external threat.

My theoretical framework accounts for state-building failure as a route to state weakness in Chapter 2, which provides a theory of the success and failure of state-building projects. I argue that success depended on local administrative institutions, and in particular on whether or not the bureaucrats were prominent members of the local community. The relative weight of salary as a proportion of their income makes outsiders (that I call *deployed* bureaucrats) more responsive in general to the policy preferences of the central state than are local elites who hold identical positions. Additionally, their greater reliance on the institutions of the state as a source of legitimacy and power gives the deployed bureaucrats an *independent* interest (not shared by their local elite counterparts) in seeking increased state presence in their communities. Where state agents are deployed from outside the community, their interests more closely align with state builders than do the interests of local elites appointed to administrative posts. The result is a greater degree of collaboration with – and even promotion of – state-building efforts.

Chapter 2, then, accounts for success and failure by exploring the public administration of state building. It argues that only where state leaders opted to exclude local elites from administering the national periphery were their efforts to extend the reach of the state successful. This was the case in Mexico and Chile, and to a lesser extent in Peru after 1895. Chapter 3 traces the determinants of the choice to delegate administration to local elites, or to deploy bureaucrats, showing that it derived from a combination of historically contingent factors including the perceived threat of indigenous revolt, the specific content of liberal ideology, and the currency of patronage commonly used to bind political coalitions in a given case.

Chapter 3 also sets the stage for the empirical analysis of state-building emergence and success in the remainder of the book by describing the four cases in the decades prior to the onset of state building at mid-century. By showing that little difference marked the cases before the mid-nineteenth century, it provides evidence against alternative explanations for variation in state capacity centered on the nature of colonial administration or the conflicts of the independence era. I show that independence was followed by several decades of instability and state weakness in all four cases, as governments struggled to impose order, extract resources, and extend the reach of state institutions in unfavorable domestic and international climates. Only the mid-century emergence of economic stability allowed state leaders to turn to long-term development projects that would consolidate political stability and economic growth.

Applying the Argument

Chapters 4 through 6 trace the origins of variation in state capacity across the four cases. They explore the fate of the state-building efforts in Chile, Mexico, and Peru, showing how the choice of deployed administration was crucial for their success in the former two countries, and how delegation to local elites led to failed state-building efforts in Peru. The chapters also show absence of state-building efforts, and concomitant weakness, in Colombia. The chapters focus, as described previously, on education (Chapter 4), taxation (Chapter 5), and coercion (Chapter 6). Each chapter describes the trajectories each country took in terms of the relevant dimension of state power. It then shows how the form of administration shaped the outcome, and considers the causal power of a compelling alternative explanation that might be most likely to hold for that particular dimension of state capacity.

The Conclusion shows that the theoretical framework developed in the book can account for the trajectories of state development region-wide, and can also shed some light on the policy challenges of contemporary "nation-building." I also return to theoretical terrain, exploring the place of ideational and material factors, addressing issues of causal complexity and causal importance in theories of statebuilding, and showing the payoffs of the argument for scholarship on state development more generally.

1

The Emergence of State-Building Projects

This chapter explains why state-building projects emerged in some countries in post-independence Latin America but not in others. It thus provides the first central element of a theory of variation in state capacity; a theory of the fate of those state-building projects is the subject of Chapter 2. Existing scholarship simply assumes that the decision to undertake state building is determined by structural conditions that translate directly into incentives to increase state capacity. By contrast, I problematize the decision by political elites to undertake the concerted effort of building state institutions and extending their reach. In so doing, I show that the conditions prompting state building in some countries had no analogous effect in others. Given largely similar structural conditions, elites pursued the same ends of economic development and political stability with different means – in some cases, these means included state building, while in others, the means centered on minimizing state interference in private life.

I argue that the responses of political elites to the post-independence context were shaped by their distinct ideas about the role of the state in social transformation. Where elites came to believe that the state was the essential agent of "order and progress," they sought to increase its capacity. Where, by contrast, they saw the state as an obstacle to economic development and social peace, no state-building efforts emerged. The claim that ideas shaped whether political leaders chose to undertake state-building projects raises an important logical concern. The fundamental issue is one of causal depth: to say that ideas were the crucial independent variable explaining policy choice can be seen as tautological, since cause and effect fall so close together in logical terms. To alleviate

The Emergence of State-Building Projects

this concern, I preface the discussion of ideas by identifying the conditions that shaped the divergence in the content of the ideas that took hold across countries.

I argue that ideas about the place of the state in development efforts were shaped by the nature of political and economic geography. My account centers on a novel aspect of geography, unexplored by previous scholarship. I argue that urban primacy – the extent to which a country was dominated demographically and economically by a single urban center – affected the emergence of state-building projects. In countries marked by high levels of urban primacy, where a single dominant urban core existed and development was seen in a center-periphery dynamic, an elite consensus about the extension of central authority could take hold. By contrast, where multiple regional centers each sat astride a distinct regional political economy, the construction of central state authority did not seem a propitious development strategy. This was so for two reasons. First, elites clashed because each region had distinct public good preferences. Attempts to satisfy all parties were fiscally unsustainable, and this made a consensus around a limited role for the state more palatable than the conflict-prone alternatives. Second, where regions had self-contained economies and could generate sufficient economic production on their own to maintain and even increase standards of living without the need for national integration, visions of development centered on the promotion of regional progress, which did not depend on the extension of the authority of the central state.

Geographic explanations for state-development outcomes have tended to center on cost-based arguments, holding that size or terrain make the extension of state authority more costly.[1] Based on this cost-based conception of geography, scholars expect that state-building projects will see more success in smaller countries with less complex terrain – thus geography explains variation in the success of state-building projects. Another current of scholarship holds that leaders decide whether or not to pursue state building based on the costs imposed by geography and the fiscal gains from state building. My argument diverges from both of these positions. Against the first group, I show that geography affects the decision to undertake state-development projects but has no consistent impact on their success. Against the second group, however, I argue that geography shapes the decision to undertake state development not by influencing a cost-benefit fiscal calculation, but by shaping leaders' beliefs about

[1] Citations to the relevant literature appear later, where it is discussed in more detail.

whether the increase of central state authority will serve their broader goals of political order, social progress, and economic development.

The argument in full, then, unfolds as follows in this chapter. I first discuss alternative geography-based explanations for variation in state capacity, focusing on territorial size and characteristics of terrain. I show that the correlations between these factors and measures of state capacity are weak, and that they cannot account for the variation we observe in Latin America. By contrast, the statistical evidence for the claim that urban primacy is necessary for state capacity is much stronger.

Based on that finding, the second part of the chapter argues that urban primacy, or the absence of salient regionalism, is a necessary condition for the emergence of a consensus among national political elites that increasing central state authority is a promising development strategy. In its absence, regional divergences in public good preferences and the promotion of regional, rather than national, strategies generate an elite consensus around minimizing central state authority as a development strategy.

Third, I show that these distinct patterns of elite consensus – which I call statist and anti-statist or laissez-faire visions of development – shaped how political elites approached the common threats and opportunities they faced. Where statist views dominated, increasing state capacity was central to the development projects of state leaders. But in contexts where anti-statist views dominated, development projects had a strikingly minimal vision of the place of the state in political development. These patterns of elite consensus account for variation in the emergence of state-development projects after the mid-nineteenth century. Whether state building emerged during the liberal era had to do with the character of liberalism, as shaped by urban primacy.

In empirical terms, this chapter explains why, in the face of similar political, economic, and social conditions, a state-building project emerged in Chile, Mexico, and Peru, but not in Colombia. I show that Colombia was unique among the four cases in the presence of multiple salient regions, which had self-contained economies and sharply divergent public good preferences, especially when it came to the development of transportation infrastructure. By contrast, the other three countries were dominated by a single center and more closely resembled a single national economy. A center-periphery dynamic dominated political relationships across national territories and shaped the development of transport infrastructure in these cases, while regionalist tensions were muted. The chapter traces the impact of this geographic difference for the ways in which state leaders pursued their common goal of social pacification, economic development, and political stability, and confronted similar challenges to doing so.

GEOGRAPHY AND STATE DEVELOPMENT

Most scholarship on geography focuses on the costs of state-development efforts. Arguments about territorial size and terrain (whether jungle, mountains, or small-scale ruggedness) claim that each aspect of geography affects the cost of extending the reach of the state, and thus explains variation in the extent of state authority.[2] All else equal, the same investment in state building will produce fewer results where the geographic costs are higher. Herbst (2000) builds on these accounts in arguing that state leaders take the expected geography-induced costs into account in deciding whether or not to invest in state building. He argues that high geographic costs induce state leaders to choose not to undertake state building at all; thus, their rational calculation should lead to state building where conditions are favorable and to its absence where they are not.

By contrast, I show empirically that the correlations between these aspects of geography and levels (or rankings) of state capacity across Latin America are generally quite weak. The characteristics of territorial size, jungles, mountains, and small-scale ruggedness in our four cases do not line up well with the variation observed among them in state capacity. Thus, the argument that geography affects the success of state-building efforts by shaping the costs of administrative extension finds little support in Latin America. In response, I introduce a novel aspect of geography to the literature in showing that urban primacy is strongly associated with state capacity. To explain this association, I depart from existing cost-based frameworks, and argue that geography affects the decision to undertake state building rather than the success of state-building efforts. But this effect on the choice to undertake state building, importantly, does not operate through calculations about the cost of state building as suggested by Herbst (2000), but through a distinct set of mechanisms I elaborate. Cross-national evidence for the discussion that follows, covering the ten major South American countries and Mexico, appears in Tables 1.1 and 1.2.

---

[2] On the effect of jungles, see Albertus and Kaplan (2013). On mountainous terrain, see Fearon and Laitin (2003). The argument for small-scale ruggedness is made by Nunn and Puga (2012).

TABLE 1.1. *Geographic characteristics of major Latin American countries*

	Size (1000 sq km)	Ruggedness	Mountainous terrain %	Tropical forest %	HHI of elevation	HHI of climate zones	HHI of biomes	Primacy (year)	State strength 1900
Argentina	2,780	0.775	28.4	0	0.138	0.087	0.402	0.66 (1847)	3.625
Bolivia	1,099	0.853	35.9	59	0.220	0.190	0.245	0.46 (1858)	8.25
Brazil	8,515	0.24	3.1	60	0.198	0.183	0.455	0.73 (1866)	4.875
Chile	756	2.481	57.59	0	0.137	0.139	0.298	0.53 (1865)	2.25
Colombia	1,142	0.885	37.1	66	0.210	0.277	0.589	0.44 (1851)	8
Ecuador	256	1.278	38	56	0.164	0.215	0.623	0.47 (1885)	8.5
Mexico	1,964	1.732	31.2	19	0.192	0.119	0.282	0.45 (1850)	6.5
Paraguay	407	0.245	1.1	41	0.347	0.318	0.654	0.39 (1879)	7.5
Peru	1,285	1.347	47.6	51	0.182	0.226	0.505	0.6 (1876)	8.75
Uruguay	176	0.435	0	0	0.277	0.815	1.000	0.84 (1908)	1.875
Venezuela	912	0.634	21.3	75	0.160	0.344	0.356	0.39 (1874)	5.375

Cases were scored for all geographic characteristics using current rather than historical borders.

Sources:

Country size data as of 2008 from *CIA World Factbook* online.

Ruggedness scores are drawn from diegopuga.org/data/rugged as described in Nunn and Puga (2012).

Mountainousness scores are drawn from Fearon and Laitin (2003).

Tropical Forest % and HHI scores (Herfindahl-Hirschman Indices of Concentration) for Elevation, Climate Zones, and Biomes are calculated from data in CIESIN (2007).

Urban primacy score is the ratio of population of the largest city to the sum of the populations of a country's four largest cities. Data is taken from www.populstat.info for the earliest year after independence for which a country had population data for at least eight cities; the year for which primacy score is calculated is shown in parentheses.

State strength is the average ranking of each country on the state strength indicators (military mobilization, literacy, railroad density, and census administration) as of 1900, as described in the Introduction.

TABLE 1.2. *State capacity ranking and geography: region-wide correlations*

RANKS	State capacity	Military	Literacy rate	Railroad density	Census regularity
Elev	−0.150	−0.041	−0.099	−0.126	−0.198
Clim	0.338	0.247	0.374	0.214	0.224
Biomes	0.160	0.214	0.459	0.015	−0.179
Ruggedness	0.075	0.128	−0.136	0.161	0.083
Mountainousness	−0.230	−0.152	−0.304	−0.167	−0.096
Size	0.149	−0.190	0.156	0.215	0.268
Jungle	**−0.718**	**−0.730**	**−0.523**	**−0.759**	−0.239
Primacy	**0.607**	0.316	**0.584**	**0.649**	0.338

Calculated from geographic indicator data in Table 1.1, and tables measuring individual dimensions of state capacity in the Introduction. Positive correlations mean that a higher score for the geographic factor is associated with a stronger state. All correlations with absolute value greater than 0.5 are bolded. Results are little changed when numerical rather than ordinal measures of state capacity are used.

Size

Several arguments support the claim that smaller territories facilitate state development. First, larger territories are more costly to administer (Herbst 2000). Second, size of territory increases the transportation and information costs associated with representative government, and therefore the accountability that facilitates rulers' access to revenue (Stasavage 2011). All else equal, then, we might expect that governments overseeing smaller territories should come to be more effective.

The evidence linking territorial size and state building, however, is weak in the Latin American context. Impressionistically, we can see in Table 1.1 that the two smallest countries in the region (Uruguay and Ecuador) are the strongest state and the second weakest. More systematically, Table 1.2 (using the rankings for state capacity as of 1900, elaborated in the Introduction and size data from Table 1.1) shows that size is correlated with the overall state-development ranking at only 0.15, and not strongly correlated with rankings on individual dimensions of state capacity. Among our four cases, Mexico is by far the largest, with a territory about 50 percent larger than that of Peru, and yet it is one of the stronger states. If there is a relationship between size and state development, it is a tenuous one.

Terrain

Scholars have also often claimed that terrain poses challenges to state building and have identified several aspects of terrain that are said to matter. Mountainous terrain is said to be difficult for the state to penetrate, which explains why it acts as a facilitating condition for insurgency (Fearon and Laitin 2003). Jungles, too, have recently been said to have the same effect and thus increase the costs of state development. (Albertus and Kaplan 2013) Finally, terrain ruggedness – small-scale terrain irregularities as opposed to mountains – is said to make transportation and infrastructure development more costly and challenging (Nunn and Puga 2012).

Evidence for this relationship is again limited. Using the data in Table 1.1, Table 1.2 shows that mountainousness is correlated in the expected direction, but weakly, with all four dimensions of state development.[3] Ruggedness is very weakly correlated with state development at −0.08.[4] In addition to the weak overall relationship, we also see that while it is positively associated with some dimensions of state development (military mobilization, railroad development, and the census), ruggedness is negatively associated with the literacy rate. This is more evidence that the putative link between ruggedness and state capacity doesn't hold for Latin American cases, since its effect is only in the predicted direction for the aspect of state capacity it is least likely to affect. The jungle measure, by contrast to these, performs very well, with a correlation of −0.72 with state-development ranking overall, and similarly high correlations with railroad development (−0.76), literacy (−0.53), and military mobilization (−0.73).[5] The role of the Amazon basin, which includes large parts of our two weak state cases, is worth exploring further.

Looking at our four cases, we find scant evidence that the ruggedness and mountainousness aspects of terrain can explain variation in state

---

[3] Mountainousness is measured, using the data from Fearon and Laitin (2003), as the percentage of a country's terrain that is mountainous. This measure is calculated using contemporary rather than historical borders.
[4] Ruggedness scores are drawn from diegopuga.org/data/rugged as described in Nunn and Puga (2012). These, once again, use contemporary borders.
[5] Jungle scores for each country, following Albertus and Kaplan (2013) are measured as the percentage of the national territory (using contemporary rather than historical borders) falling in climatic zones 1–4 (tropical rain forest or tropical monsoon type, ground wet all year), using the PLACE II Dataset available at sedac.ciesin.columbia.edu/place (CIESIN 2007). Tables 1.1 and 1.2 also show HHI Indices for climatic zones and biomes, as suggested in Nunn and Puga (2012), but these are quite weakly correlated with all measures of state development.

development. Chile – our strongest state – has both the most mountainous and the most rugged terrain of our cases, and indeed of the region as a whole. While we might dismiss Chile's mountainousness score as an artifact of the fact that its border traces the spine of the Andes, ruggedness did increase the challenge of infrastructure development. Travel between Santiago and the coast at Valparaíso was so daunting that the route of fewer than 100 miles took days to cover (Saylor 2012, 307). Ruggedness posed daunting engineering challenges to the country's railroad builders, who had to fashion some of the largest railroad bridges to date in the annals of world engineering to cross the rough terrain of the southern heartland (Thomson and Angerstein 2000). Indeed, terrain posed such challenges to internal communication in Chile that a geographer of the 1940s described the country as an archipelago rather than a landmass (Loveman 2001, 10). And yet the Chilean state was strikingly powerful by comparison to the region as a whole, including, by the 1880s, much of the terrain south of the Bío Bío River that had never come under Spanish colonial control.

Little differentiates the other three cases, which score similarly on both of these measures of terrain. In all three, somewhat rugged terrain increased the costs of infrastructure development and communication, and mountains divided the country and hampered unification. This similarity, then, cannot explain the variation in state development – it cannot account for the fact that the Mexican state became substantially stronger than the other two by the end of the liberal era.

The presence of jungles seems a more likely direction for further investigation; whereas Chile has none, Peru and Colombia both have a majority of the national territory covered by tropical forest. Mexico falls in an intermediate category, with 19 percent of its territory covered by tropical forest. We can conclude from this discussion that while size, mountainousness, and ruggedness are unlikely candidates, the role of the Amazon (and of tropical forest more generally) in undermining state development is an issue that is worthy of further exploration. This is supported by the obvious difficulties posed by the jungle to infrastructure development, difficulties that caused travel between Lima and Iquitos, for example, to take "weeks if not months" (Pike 1967, 3) and which leave many towns in the Peruvian Amazon unconnected to the national road network even today.

Because the Amazon was scarcely populated and marginal in economic terms for much of the nineteenth century, the regions it spanned were of low priority to state leaders in both Colombia and Peru.[6] Yet the state in these two countries was equally weak in non-Amazonian regions; thus the presence of the Amazon cannot be sufficient to explain overall state weakness. Evidence of this can be seen, for example, in Chapter 4, where I show that education lagged not only in the Amazonian provinces of Peru and Colombia, but in the highlands as well. The cost of administrative extension into the Amazon is insufficient to account for why these states are weaker than those of Mexico and Chile.[7] This is confirmed by the fact that when rubber and oil booms made the Amazon an important site for states, they were unable to extend their reach to these territories (Yashar 2005).

Urban Primacy, Regional Salience, and State Development

If size and terrain cannot account for variation in the implementation of state-building projects, are there any aspects of geography that can? I argue that a population structure marked by urban primacy (the presence of a single dominant city) was necessary for state-building efforts in Latin America to emerge. This relationship holds because where urban primacy is present, state building – the extension of authority from the center to the periphery – is both more likely to be seen as a means to political and economic development, and less likely to be diluted by regionalist tensions.

Urban primacy has received little attention in political science scholarship. Instead, theories of state building begin from the presumption that it unfolds as the center extending its control over the national periphery.[8]

---

[6] There is an echo here of Herbst's argument about countries with large unpopulated regions; he would expect that because these regions lacked population that can be a source of revenue or a threat that needed to be controlled, the state had little incentive to extend its reach into them. Yet this would suggest that more resources were available for establishing effective state control outside the Amazon, and the observed weakness of the Peruvian and Colombian state in non-Amazonian regions casts doubt on this possibility. I am grateful to Richard Snyder for suggesting this line of argument.

[7] Were the object of study in this project subnational variation in the reach of the state in a single case, one might focus on the obstacles posed by the jungle to administrative extension. But given that national scores for state capacity diverge sharply even if the Amazonian regions are excluded from the analysis, one must focus attention on other variables.

[8] This approach characterizes a wide range of accounts of state building, including Weber (1976), Spruyt (1994), and Alesina and Spolaore (2005). Herbst (2000) is a partial exception in that he lumps size, terrain, and the presence of regional challengers together into the category of "difficult" political geographies. Much scholarship, including Herbst, conflates regionalism with ethnic diversity in linking regionalism to political conflict; by

But what about countries where there is no single center, but instead multiple spheres of influence that reach across sizable portions of the national territory? In these cases, where we cannot conceptualize the process of state building in terms of a center-periphery dichotomy, but instead as the knitting together of separate and salient regions, how is state building affected? I argue that, all else equal, the impetus to increase central state authority will be weaker in countries that have multiple salient regions with cities that have the potential to be centers of gravity for political centralization. I identify two mechanisms that make the absence of a single dominant center sufficient for state weakness in the absence of external motivations for state building.

The first mechanism relates to the likelihood that distinct regions will have divergent preferences about the location and type of public goods provided by the state. Location matters because willingness to contribute to public goods is likely to be correlated with proximity to them, which facilitates access to the benefits they generate (Alesina and Spolaore 2005). Given the scarcity of governmental resources, choices about where to locate state services will create high stakes conflict over basic state-building priorities.[9] As conflict over public good provision priorities intensifies, state building is diluted. Additionally, the presence of multiple urban centers often derives from the presence of distinct regional economies, each of which has elites with distinct preferences over the *types* of public goods the state is to provide. Rodríguez (1985) traces the turmoil that resulted from this conflict in nineteenth century Ecuador, where state building was undermined by regional tensions between Quito and Guayaquil that centered on the distinct policy preferences of each region's dominant economic sector. A similar dynamic can be found in the United States, which saw sectionalist tensions undermine state-building efforts both during and after the Civil War (Bensel (1984, 1990). Tensions between multiple salient regions over public good priorities contribute to political instability, and these tensions can only be resolved through compromises that satisfy actors from all regions (logrolling) and the resulting dilution of policy priorities, or through regionalist conflict, which may escalate to secession.

contrast I propose to examine the effects of purely spatial factors on state-development outcomes.
[9] Alesina and Spolaore (2005) argue that this dynamic might even generate conflict over the location of a capital city, since the seat of government generates a set of public goods as well as jobs. Thus, countries lacking urban primacy may even see conflict over the location of the capital city – we see this, for example, in Bolivia.

In the best case scenario, then, sufficiently high tensions over divergent public good preferences dilute state-building priorities.

The second mechanism relates to the fact that the absence of urban primacy is often accompanied by the presence of salient and self-sufficient regional economies. Where regional economies are self-enclosed and self-sufficient, the gains seen from overcoming regional tensions and knitting the country together are smaller.[10] In this context, centralization of authority is seen as less propitious for economic development, political stability, and social peace than policies that allow already salient regional economies and identities to flourish. The result is that development efforts, where they do emerge, unfold at the regional and local level, and the extension of national state authority is not seen as a means to "order and progress." In short, state building simply appears less important, all else equal, to political leaders. The salience of regionalism, then, may be compatible with robust local or regional political authority and indeed with local public good provision, but it is not a propitious context for the construction of national state power.

Measurement

To explore this proposed relationship between regionalism and state weakness, we need a measure of the economic and political importance of each region relative to the country as a whole. Because this importance is hard to measure, the crude but telling indicator of population is commonly used as a form of measure of the extent of urban primacy in a given country. To rule out the possibility that state development affects urban primacy – for example, by drawing population to the capital city – I measure primacy for the earliest post-independence date in each country for which I could find data on the population of at least eight cities.[11] The degree of urban primacy of a country refers to the concentration of a disproportionate share of its population in a single city, and there are standard measurement strategies for calculating national scores for the distribution of population. (Ades and Glaeser 1995; Zipf 1941) Most classically, one calculates a ratio of the

---

[10] This argument is not unrelated to that of Spruyt (1994) about how different forms of trade underpinned the emergence of distinct political institutions across early modern Europe.
[11] For the sake of consistency, all population data was drawn from the Populstat web database, available online at populstat.info, rather than from estimates by country specialists.

The Emergence of State-Building Projects

size of the largest city in a country to the sum of the four largest cities. The scores for each country shown in Table 1.2 use the standard measure; the results that follow are unchanged with alternative measures.

The standard measure of primacy divides the population of the largest city by the sum of that of the four largest, and the primacy score can vary between 0.25 (if the four cities are equal in size) to 1 (if the largest city contains the entire population of the country). In Latin America, urban primacy scores vary from Uruguay at 0.84 to Venezuela and Paraguay at 0.39. The regional average is 0.54, with a standard deviation of 0.15. Primacy, as seen in Table 1.2 is strongly correlated with state development, with a correlation coefficient of 0.61 with the overall ranking, and coefficients of 0.65 with the railroad development ranking, 0.58 with the literacy ranking, and about 0.3 with census iterations and military mobilization. Higher rates of urban primacy are associated with stronger states. This correlation remains robust even with the exclusion of Uruguay, which is an outlier in its high primacy score.

Yet given that I argue that urban primacy is causally *necessary but insufficient* for state development, it is not logically appropriate to assess the face validity of this relationship with simple correlations, as I have done in Table 1.2 for the other dimensions of state capacity. Instead, a scatter plot can be used to assess the face validity of claims of causal necessity. We should see, in the binary plots that follow, only low levels of state capacity when urban primacy is low. By contrast, at high levels of urban primacy, state-development scores can vary across the full range. If my claim about this causal relationship is correct, all points (or nearly all, given the possibility of outliers) should fall below the imaginary 45 degree line extending outward from the origin in each graph. Figure 1.1 shows scatter plots for five indicators of state capacity. All five charts confirm that only low levels of state capacity are found at low levels of urban primacy, while in countries with primarily urban distributions, values of state capacity from across the spectrum can be found. It is reasonable to propose, then, that the relationship between urban primacy and state capacity is worthy of further exploration.

The population-based measure of primacy, of course, lacks nuance for two reasons: first, it does not account for the distance between the cities included and thus the extent to which polycephaly reflects the presence of distinct regions – thus, for example Lima and Callao,

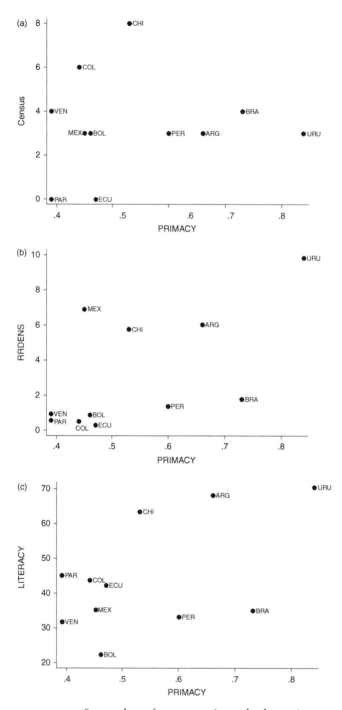

FIGURE 1.1. Scatterplots of state capacity and urban primacy.

The Emergence of State-Building Projects 37

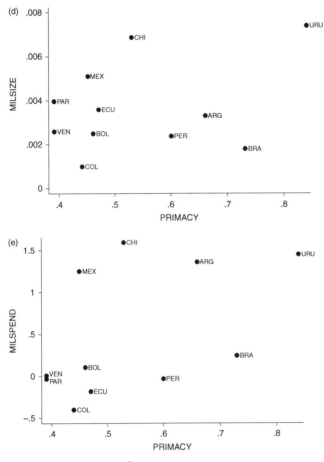

FIGURE I.I. *(continued)*

which abut but are jurisdictionally separate, are counted as distinct cities in Peru. As a result, scores for Peru are artificially depressed in this measurement strategy since the dominance of the capital city is understated when Callao is not counted as part of the Lima metropolis, and likewise for Buenos Aires and Argentina. Second, and likely more significant, this measure fails to fully capture the nature of regionalism that drives the political effects described previously. Thus, in investigating the role of primacy in state development in our four cases, we must explore the city network of each country and its regionalism in a more careful manner.

Urban Primacy in Our Cases

In Peru, Chile, and Mexico, the national territory was dominated by a single city. Although each country had peripheries not tightly linked to the urban core, regional tensions over public good priorities were limited, and all economically productive and politically salient areas were deeply embedded into the national economy with the capital at its center. This was not the case in Chile; therefore I discuss regional tensions and economic self-sufficiency in that case in more detail in the following section.

Chile

Chile's urban primacy score of 0.53 shows that Santiago was more than the size of the next three largest cities combined. Not only was Santiago by far the largest city, but the only other large center of population, Valparaíso, was nearby and deeply embedded in the capital's economic circuit. While Santiago and Valparaíso combined had nearly 200,000 residents, only four other cities had more than 10,000. Of these four, two (Talca and La Serena) were likewise firmly tied to Santiago in political and economic terms by the early nineteenth century. Not only did these regions provide grain to Santiago but they depended on production from the central valley around the capital to fulfill basic needs (Saylor 2012). The other two, Concepción and Copiapó, were the focal points of the country's northern and southern regions. Regional tensions were not completely absent in Chile: in the 1840s, southern landowners, for example, pressed the government for improved transportation, and mine owners in the north were negatively impacted by tax increases on copper exports, and infuriated by the refusal of the government to subsidize railroads from mines to ports (Saylor 2014, 61–62). These tensions were one spark in the short-lived civil wars of the 1850s, as both north and south sought greater regional fiscal autonomy and a more favorable allocation of governmental resources.

But with these brief exceptions, the political salience of regionalism was limited, and Santiago dominated. Deep ties between elites across rural and urban sectors, along with the consensus on economic openness, stemmed regionalism. Mine owners in the north, agriculturalists in the southern heartland and the central valley, and merchants in the capital and in Valparaíso had no deep divisions in trade preferences. While there was some dispute about infrastructure priorities and in particular railroad construction (Saylor 2012), the broad elite coalition that united

Santiago and its peripheries facilitated a concerted state-building project. The liberal-conservative "fusion" governments of the 1861–1891 era reflect this deep elite consensus (Scully 1992). The result was the construction of a railroad network that linked grain-producing regions to Santiago and Valparaíso; while this was not the most economically efficient path, it sufficed to satisfy producers while further reinforcing the hegemony of the capital and its port. As Bauer (1975, 65) shows, Valparaíso's flour exports as a share of the national total rose from 1 percent in the early 1850s to more than 52 percent by the late 1860s. Over time, the demographic centralization of Chile deepened, and the state building described in the chapters that follow unfolded as the extension of authority from the central valley into the national periphery.

Mexico

Mexico's raw score for urban primacy is quite low: data from the 1850 census generates a score of 0.45, or somewhat below that of Chile. Yet this understates the centrality of Mexico City in national life; its sizable contemporary importance was only reinforced by centuries of colonial history, and by the pre-colonial dominance of the Aztec empire centered on the same site (Hardoy 1967). Its 1850 population of 170,000 made it perhaps the largest city in Spanish America, and it was nearly twice the size of Guadalajara, the country's second city. None of the country's secondary cities was important enough to emerge as an alternative core of political power. The distribution of urbanization closely matched the classic primate pattern: secondary cities like Guadalajara, Puebla, Guanajuato, Colima, and Querétaro were located in the environs surrounding the capital and were deeply bound to it in both economic and political terms. By 1867, urban primacy had risen sharply to 0.53, which places Mexico on the same level as Chile; it would continue to rise thereafter.

Although Mexico's territory was immense by comparison to the other cases, even far-flung regions were tied to Mexico City rather than to alternative centers of authority. Veracruz, which controlled the vast majority of ocean-going trade, was deeply connected to the capital, and even sisal from the Yucatán traveled on small boats to the port of Veracruz to be loaded into large ships for export (Coatsworth 1981, 25). Railroad construction, the rise of cattle, and the recovery of mining tied the northern desert into Mexico City economically, as the north became a zone of transit between the United States and the capital. The deep tensions that made Mexican politics so unstable in the decades after independence, while fundamentally connected to disagreement over how much power the center should have, did not divide along regional lines. They pitted center (Mexico City and Veracruz) against periphery rather than regions against one another. Conflict was for control over an unquestioned center, and over the policies that would emanate from it, rather than between Mexico City and challengers for national power.

Peru

Peru's primacy score is the highest among the four cases. A skeptic might suggest this is an artifact of its calculation based on data from a later census, since population data from before 1876 is spotty. But data from earlier census iterations shows the dominance of Lima. Gootenberg's (1995) reconstruction of the 1827 census shows that Peru had a national population of slightly more than 1.5 million, of whom more than 10 percent lived in the department of Lima and its port of Callao. Centuries of colonial rule, which placed Lima and Callao at the center of not only national but continental life, reinforced its dominance. Although the highland province of Jauja, center of the mining industry, had a larger population than did Lima, it was deeply embedded in the capital's economic circuit as its production traveled by mule train down the Andes to exit the country from the port of Callao.

Initially, Peru did have a more salient regional cleavage than did either Mexico or Chile. This divide separated the southern highland region centered on Arequipa, which depended on free trade, from the protectionist regions of the north coast, central highlands, and Lima (Gootenberg 1989). Southern free traders were not powerful enough to seize power nationwide, but they made two concerted, although failed, attempts at secession in the 1830s. These were central to Peru's early post-independence instability, and Gootenberg argues that they "prevented the consolidation of a national state in Peru" in the 1830s (ibid., 44–45).

By the mid-1840s, this cleavage eroded dramatically for three reasons. The first was the victory of a pro–free trade coalition in Lima, which removed one of the core tensions between the two regions. Second, the onset of the guano boom after 1845 led to massive cuts in domestic taxation, which also diluted tensions as described in Chapter 5. Third, the center of gravity and population in the country shifted dramatically toward Lima, which grew sharply after mid-century. The result was that a center-periphery dynamic of Lima extending into the interior, rather than one of competition among regions, had firmly taken hold in the political

The Emergence of State-Building Projects 41

arena. In this way, a crucial facilitating condition for state development emerged by the mid-1840s in Peru.

Colombia

Although its raw score for urban primacy is quite similar to that of Mexico, Colombia's regional demography was in fact quite different from the other three cases. Colombia was a stark outlier in that it lacked a single predominant urban center.[12] The country's population was dispersed widely, as reflected in the fact that while Bogotá as of 1851 had just shy of 30,000 residents, thirty other municipalities had between 8,000 and 15,000. These medium-sized cities included regional centers like Popayán, Socorro, and Medellín. This meant that regions were, much more than those in the other countries, oriented around their central cities rather than linked to the national capital. As of 1870, Cundinamarca, Bogotá's state, ranked only fourth among Colombian states in population, behind Boyacá, Cauca, and Santander (Park 1985, 25). The city of Bogotá remained the same size in 1870 as it had been in the 1840s (Urrutia 2010, 8), as its share of national population fell over the course of the first fifty years after independence (Flórez and Romero 2010, 410).

This had two effects. First, instead of Bogotá dominating the country, it "had to share economic power with important rivals in other regions" (Safford and Palacios 2002, 9). The lack of dominance of Bogotá was perhaps reflected most clearly in a proposal debated during the 1863 Constitutional Convention to move the national capital to the state of Panama (Park 1985, 40). Second, because regional cities were large enough to absorb much of local economic production, trade within the country was limited. Palacios (2006, 5) describes Colombia as a "mosaic of isolated regions." Even plans to develop internal commerce as a means to economic development tended to focus on fairly local projects rather than ones that crossed regions (Rosenthal 2012, 125). There was simply no vision of Colombia as a national economic unit centered on Bogotá – this was reflected, for example, in Christie's argument that "there was little to draw [elites] automatically to the capital" (Christie 1979, 44).

What distinguishes Colombia from the other cases is not that these regions were separated by geographic obstacles – that describes significant

---

[12] Deas (1993, 207) argues that this is still the case today; indeed, contemporary urban primacy scores would still place Colombia far below the other cases in terms of the demographic dominance of its largest city.

portions of the territories of our other three cases. Instead, the key is that Colombia's regions both had distinct political economies and were economically self-sufficient. As a result, Colombia "differs from other countries of similar size in the deep imprint its regionalist sentiment has left on the pattern of national development" (Park 1985, 7). Because this "regionalist sentiment" was so powerful and so unique in comparative perspective, it needs to be explored more carefully. Later, I show that it underpinned the two mechanisms outlined previously that prevented the emergence of a state-building consensus. City size information for each case is shown in Table 1.3, 57.

Divergent Preferences across Colombia's Regions
Most scholars of Colombia portray it as divided into four salient regions – the Atlantic coast, Cauca, the Central Cordillera, and the Eastern Cordillera – during the first century after independence.[13] Because of their distinct political economies, Colombia's four salient regions had quite divergent preferences about public good priorities.[14] This was reflected most clearly in the divergent infrastructure improvements prioritized by each region[15] (Gallup et al. 2003, 90).

The Atlantic coast prioritized infrastructure development linking the region to the interior since that would increase the flows of exports through its ports of Cartagena, Barranquilla, and Santa Marta. The Central Cordillera (centered on the states of Antioquia and Tolima) and the Eastern Cordillera states of Cundinamarca, Boyacá, and Santander also prioritized transport on the Magdalena River that would allow mining and agricultural production to reach export markets.[16] But these co-partisans of improved Atlantic trade infrastructure were torn apart by severe disputes over the specifics of transport improvements. A fourth region, Cauca, diverged sharply. Here, transport to the Pacific port of Buenaventura was the central goal.

---

[13] The description in the succeeding paragraphs represents a consensus view among scholars, drawing most directly on Park (1985, 24–34).

[14] Posada-Carbó (1996, 3) argues that regional divisions in Colombia were fundamentally economic rather than about "subjective identity."

[15] Trade policy was also quite contentious; tariffs on imports burdened the interior almost exclusively. Regional tensions were paramount in tax policy debates, shaping both the initial 1850s decentralization and the mid-1870s demands for another round of decentralization (Junguito 2010, 68, 83).

[16] Santander's coffee and cacao was exported via the Venezuelan port of Maracaibo, which generated unique priorities for economic development.

The Emergence of State-Building Projects 43

Tensions were so high that "prominent Colombians were contemplating national dismemberment" in the late 1860s and early 1870s (Park 1985, 71–72). Most centrally, conflict revolved around proposals to improve links from highland production centers to the Magdalena River, since transport for the 150 miles between Bogotá and Honda, the capital's river port, cost more than shipping all the way from Honda to Liverpool (Safford and Palacios 2002, 13). Each potential route favored some parts of the states through which it would pass at the expense of others.[17] The coast and Cauca were horrified by the scale of funding entailed for a project that would not benefit them (Safford 1988, 53). This railroad was the central issue in the 1875 elections, and tension over the "feasibility and location" of railroad projects also spurred the 1876–1877 civil war (Safford 2010, 555).

A common means of defusing tensions was to fund enough projects to keep all important regional interests satisfied. While it reduced (but did not eliminate) conflict, this strategy drove budget deficits and diluted any concerted effort at infrastructure development (Junguito 2010, 91). Yet this type of logrolling was a consistent practice in Colombia throughout the second half of the nineteenth century. The 1864 Transport Law, for example, listed "fifteen projects deemed most worthy of federal aid" and was reformed in subsequent years to add yet more projects to the list (Park 1985, 65). The 1871 law listed twenty-eight priority projects, and this list, too, grew over time (ibid., 66). As deficits worsened, and major infrastructure projects fell incomplete, the national government was forced in the mid-1880s to make massive cuts in public works appropriations.

A second strategy was devolving public works decisions to the states. Devolution can be seen as far back as the 1836 Ley de Caminos, which distributed funds to provinces based on population as a way to avoid conflict over road priorities, and it was institutionalized under the 1863 constitution (Safford 2010, 531). As part of the settlement of the 1876–1877 civil war, funding was allocated to each state for transport projects it chose (Junguito 2010, 89). Despite a constitutional ban on the practice, states funded them through road taxes on goods in transit. This internal "tariff warfare," as described in contemporary press accounts, highlights the centrality of regional rather than national interests (quote from Park 1985, 253). Rather than a national development plan, Colombia saw a

---

[17] Before railroad technology became available, similar tensions stymied plans to connect the highlands to the Magdalena by the way of roads in both the colonial and early republican eras (Safford 2010, 530).

litany of state-level projects designed and implemented independently, as "interstate railroads were thus abandoned" (Park 1985, 157–158). This both reflected and reinforced the salience of its regional divisions.

Self-Sufficient Regions and the Locus of Development Efforts in Colombia

Because each of Colombia's regions had a large enough population and a diverse production profile, they were largely self-sufficient. As a result, the gains perceived from the potentially costly process of integration were quite limited, and there was no imperative to undertake an effort to overcome the regional tensions described previously. The fact that Colombia was "economically invertebrate" (Safford 1988, 53) made the payoffs from establishing a powerful state unclear, and made the path to development through the fostering of regional self-sufficiency seem plausible. As a result, "the integration of a national market, and therefore transportation improvement, may have been less fundamentally important to Colombians" than it was to political elites in our other cases (Safford 1988, 37). Instead, regions were tied into the world economy "without the presence and involvement of the central state" (Palacios 1980, ix).

Trade between Colombia's regions was minimal throughout the nineteenth century (Ramírez and Salazar 2010, 427). One exception was textiles from Santander, which did provide clothing in other states. But food and other basic commodities were rarely exchanged across regions (Safford 2010, 530). Even as the coffee export boom took off, peasants continued to grow food for local consumption, and larger haciendas cushioned against fluctuating coffee prices by producing food, sugar, and beef for local markets (Palacios 1980, 93–4).

Instead, regions evolved largely independent of one another in economic terms, and pursued economic policies chosen with regional rather than national imperatives in mind. One clear instance of this regionalist emphasis can be seen late in the nineteenth century, when a prominent politician in Antioquia spoke of the need to promote "industries producing goods which we unnecessarily bring from other states" (Park 1985, 254). He was not referring to the need to protect Colombian markets against imports from abroad, but Antioquian markets against imports from other Colombian states.

Colombia enjoyed a series of minor commodity booms over the course of the period under investigation, culminating with the much larger coffee booms. Because each boom was regionally concentrated, they drove a certain amount of infrastructure development in particular locations. Tobacco, for example, led to improvement of Magdalena River steam navigation. But none of these resulted in attempts to "promote other sorts of exports or promote regional integration by trade" (McGreevey 1971, 236). Even the coffee booms had limited effects on infrastructure: roads remained undeveloped, mules remained pivotal to getting coffee to export markets, and most of the coffee producing regions remained unconnected to the railroad network as late as 1920 (Palacios 1980, 12). The limited transport development that did occur linked each region to the external market, rather than unifying the country and its economy. Perhaps the starkest evidence of this absence of unification was the failure to coordinate track widths across regions. Even where multiple train lines intersected, goods could not easily pass from one region to another (Safford 2010, 563). The self-sufficiency of Colombia's regions led policy makers to see "order and progress" as goals to be pursued at the regional, rather than national, level.

Geography shaped state development in Latin America, then, because it affected the role for the state envisioned by political leaders when they sought to promote political order, economic progress, and social change. Where a country was characterized by a dominant urban center, linked to most of its populated and economically productive regions, the extension of the center's authority into the periphery seemed like a propitious development strategy. But where multiple cities stood astride regional economies and divided the country into salient zones, building central state capacity was hampered by conflict over public good priorities, and by the fact that it did not seem like a necessary step toward these goals.

These factors (regional tensions and self-sufficiency) explain not only the variation in the development of transportation infrastructure discussed previously. They also explain, as Chapters 4 to 6 illustrate, why a broader state-building project failed to emerge in liberal Colombia; why education, taxation, and conscription were not pursued in any systematic manner. The establishment of order and progress did not seem to Colombian political elites to depend on the imposition of central authority, nor could they agree on what that central authority, if empowered, should do. Instead, order and progress would come from creating political conditions that would encourage regional and individual initiative to flourish. The uniquely anti-statist liberalism of mid-century Colombia explains why a state-building project failed to emerge in that case, and thus accounts for the roots of Colombia's weak state.

THE IDEATIONAL FOUNDATIONS OF STATE-BUILDING PROJECTS

The remainder of this chapter digs more deeply into the role of ideas in the four cases, showing in more detail their causal weight in shaping state-building trajectories. Here I dig further into the mechanisms discussed previously that make urban primacy necessary for state building. I emphasize the divergence between Colombia and the other cases in the ideas held by political leaders about the policy instruments they would use to pursue political and economic development, and show that the content of this consensus links urban primacy to the divergence in state-building efforts between Colombia and the other cases.[18] Elsewhere, liberalism was more statist and a consensus around state building as a means to development emerged. But in Colombia, liberalism took a more anti-statist tone, and a consensus emerged around a laissez-faire development project. Thus urban primacy, by shaping the ideas of political elites about how to pursue development, determined whether state-building efforts emerged in mid-nineteenth-century Latin America. To complement the exploration of other dimensions of state capacity in Chapters 4 to 6, I highlight how this dynamic played out in the development of public transportation infrastructure in this section.

The Varied Content of Mid-Century Liberalism

Across the ideological spectrum in mid-century Latin America, a consensus emerged that political "order" had economic and social roots. Politicians believed that states should promote domestic and international trade as a means of economic "progress," requiring a new role for the state in the economy.[19] A broad consensus among political elites also held that the population needed to be molded into citizens that could participate in the "order" and "progress" being created. This implied state action to "civilize" the population. The consensus on this state

---

[18] My focus neither explains the content of ideas held by particular individuals, nor the dissemination of the ideas – those issues have been amply explored by the historians on whom I draw. Following Hall (1993) and Goldstein and Keohane (1993), I conceptualize ideas as policy instruments, or mental roadmaps.

[19] Against those who claim that the liberal reforms were an instance of state capture by exporting elites, I show that most (but not all) of these efforts involved an explicit attempt to increase the power of the state to penetrate society and effectively implement policies (Bushnell and Macaulay 1994, 191).

project cut across the liberal-conservative divide, which was the major cleavage of nineteenth-century politics. Both groups agreed, despite the heated debates on other fronts, that the state should actively promote "progress" within its borders. Conservatives generally accepted broadly liberal beliefs, with a particularly broad and stable consensus about the central role of primary product exports as the means to economic development (Mahoney 2001, 31; Hale 1989, 8). One important exception was church-state relations, which divided liberals and conservatives. Yet a focus on this small portion of the political agenda obscures the broader consensus that marked even Colombia and Mexico, where liberals were particularly anti-clerical and conflict over church-state relations particularly intense.

But positions on the policy means by which "development" should be pursued varied across countries in crucial ways, with Colombia a major outlier. In Chile and Peru, a consensus held that the state's ability to create "progress" and "civilization" depended on expanding its role through the national territory. The state, in their view, should promote "development" by fulfilling functions such as security provision, infrastructure development, and school construction. In Mexico, too, liberal reformers envisioned the state as a central actor in dramatic social transformation. In their view, the main obstacles to stability were the corporate power of the Church, and the social and economic stagnation of the indigenous population. They planned to build the power of the national state to overcome these obstacles. Thus, in these three cases, political power came into the hands of leaders who sought to expand the reach of the state as a means to "'order," "progress," and "civilization."

In Colombia, on the other hand, a consensus held that the state should promote development by minimizing its intervention, which would allow individual initiative and market incentives to create social change and economic development. Political elites in Colombia diverged from those elsewhere who saw state building as the means to those ends, seeing it instead as an obstacle to the individual initiative that would bring the progress they sought.

The following descriptions of the content of the liberal consensus in each country case highlight both the goals envisioned by leaders and ideologues, and the means by which they believed these goals should be pursued. The contrasting content of liberal ideas between the statist liberalism of Chile, Peru, and Mexico and the laissez-faire liberalism of Colombia, shaped by the divergences in political geography described previously, explains why state-development efforts only emerged in the former set of cases but not in the latter.

The State and Progress in Chile

Chilean political leaders sought to create social conditions that favored the expansion of primary product exports. The country's *Anuarios Estadísticos* and census publications, reflections of the vision of high-ranking state officials for their country's future, reflect the vision of "progress," "development," and "civilization" held by state officials and the audiences for their writings (Estefane Jaramillo 2004). In their constant comparative references to Europe, rather than to other countries in Latin America, the *Anuarios* clearly reflect the aspirations of state leaders. The Chilean political elite believed that expanding state authority and extending its reach into the national periphery was the most appropriate means for pursuing these goals (Silva 2008, chapter 1). Consensus on this program stretched across the entire ideological spectrum of the political class. Both the Portalian conservatives and the liberals who took power after the 1850s shared a desire to rationalize society (Loveman 1993, 330). Unlike their counterparts in both Mexico and Colombia, Chile's liberals accepted that the Church would continue to play a central role in society, including in education (Collier 2003, 115). This meant that state-building efforts were less conflictual, keeping the church and state as partners in the "civilizing" of a largely rural, poor society. A broad consensus also held that the state needed to undertake the infrastructural development necessary to end economic stagnation, including railroad development. (Thomson and Angerstein 2000) State building was at the core of the development project pursued by Chilean political elites.

As discussed further in Chapter 3, the state-building vision eventually expanded to include the territory controlled by the Araucana, across the southern frontier. With the wheat boom of mid-century, elites believed that Araucanía's fertile land and the easier mountain passes across the Andes to Argentina would allow wheat production for export to spread southward, generating revenue and economic stimulus if exploited with sufficient labor and capital. This spurred legal changes replacing corporate land rights with individual property rights. Indigenous refusal to follow these new legal norms made pacification a pre-condition for development (Pinto Rodríguez 2003). For the first time, "progress" became incompatible with indigenous autonomy, and the solution (on which

The Emergence of State-Building Projects

there was once again a broad – although not unanimous – consensus) was a massive state intervention to incorporate the indigenous population by assimilation, a process explicitly modeled on the reservations policy of the United States (Jones 1999). By the 1860s, state builders in Chile had ambitions to extend their control through the entire national territory, a massive expansion of the presence and weight of the state.

"Order" and "Progress" in Mexico

After its defeat by the United States and the devastation caused by the Yucatan Caste War, both liberals and conservatives were unsure of "the survival of Mexico as a nation" Hale (1989, 16). This forged a consensus among political elites that sweeping reforms involving increased state power were needed (Topik 1988, 121). But while the depth of the crisis spurred a consensus about the need for reforms, deep divisions remained about their content. The first attempt to increase state power as a means of exiting the crisis came during Santa Anna's last term (1853–1855). This conservative project was built around a radical centralization of public administration to generate order. Santa Anna's attempts at centralization and the imposition of a constitutional monarchy led to revolts by local elites. These revolts, once they succeeded in deposing Santa Anna in 1855, brought to power a group of liberals who had a very different prescription for curing Mexico's ills.[20] But divisions between liberals and conservatives about the content of reforms then spurred the greatest domestic conflict since independence: the Reform War of 1858–1861 and the subsequent French Intervention.

Yet in looking beyond the ideological differences with the conservatives they defeated, we can see that the liberal project continued an emphasis on state building. Liberals saw corporate privilege (of the church, the army, guilds, and Indian communities) as an obstacle to juridical uniformity, and thus to liberty. In response, they leveraged state power to dismantle these institutions and emphasized the expansion of central state authority as a means to these ends. Most scholarship has emphasized the anti-clerical component of the liberal project, which sparked the most intense resistance. But at its core, the liberal project intended to use the power of the state to create a "class of yeoman farmers in Mexico that

---

[20] Thus, "what began as a traditional barracks revolt ended up as full-scale conflict between disparate political ideologies" (Sinkin 1979, 34).

would serve as the basis for a stable and forward-looking economy and polity" (Haber 1989, 19).

Although it took a less confrontational tone in addressing traditional structures of power, the Porfirian regime that followed also sought to build an effective state to overcome the obstacles to economic development. The Porfiriato was the most classically positivist regime among our cases, particularly under the influence of the Científicos after 1892, who believed that economic development required state intervention to remove the obstacles of "crime, alcoholism, illiteracy, squalor, and disease" (Knight 1986, I, 23). The goal was to create "an educated populace, a democratic polity, and a commonwealth as civilized as those of Europe" and a propitious climate for the foreign investment that would bring economic development (Haber 1989, 22). A consensus among elites was that the country needed "more, better, responsible government" (Knight 1986, I, 30).

As in Peru and Chile, railroads were seen as a central plank of the activity that government should emphasize. Improved transport was seen as crucial for promoting economic development: "the country's elite viewed transport improvements in general and railroads in particular as the most important pre-requisite to progress" (Coatsworth 1981, 175). And state action to facilitate their construction was a consistent priority of the Porfiriato (1876–1910). Railroad building was perhaps more concerted in Mexico than in any of our other cases. Construction was a sizable enough effort, according to Coatsworth, to have a visible effect on unemployment and under-employment, and thus promote political stability in an indirect manner (ibid., 43). Because Mexico's economy did not center on commodity export, a truly nationwide network was needed to promote development, and during the Porfiriato, construction linked all of the country's most important regions to Mexico City, the United States border, and the port of Veracruz (ibid., 145).

Much as in Chile, Mexico saw a group of elites come to power in mid-century seeking to strengthen the state as a means to ending instability, economic stagnation, and social turmoil. Their state-building efforts bore some fruit, and were reinforced during the Porfiriato even as some of the strikingly anti-clerical content was diluted. Five decades of consistent state-building efforts that emphasized the centralization of civilian political authority and the extension of its control, overshadowing some inconsistencies in priorities, marked the late nineteenth century in Mexico (Topik 1988, 121).

The State and "Progress" in Peru

The guano export boom starting in the 1840s gave Peru's elites an opportune context for their developmental priorities. A broad consensus held that social and economic transformation depended on expanding administration and infrastructure.[21] State intervention would overcome obstacles to economic development by substituting for the lack of private capital, encouraging immigration, and better integrating the indigenous population into the market economy (Gootenberg 1993, 27ff). Ramón Castilla, the first guano-era president, focused on free trade and diversification into mining and agriculture. He emphasized boosting production in the heavily indigenous southern highlands as a way to give local elites an economic incentive to ally with the national government (Larson 2004, 150).

Peruvian elites (especially the Civilistas) saw railroads as fundamental to development and national unification. The most important case for railroad building as the means to "progress" appeared in the writings of Manuel Pardo, who founded the Civilista party, served as Finance Minister, and became president in the early 1870s.[22] In economic terms, Pardo argued that railroads would facilitate exports from the Andes. Railroads were also seen as a means to national "moral uplifting" as they accelerated "rural mobility, cultural contact, and thus enlightenment among peasants" (Gootenberg 1993, 87). Malinowski, the Polish engineer contracted for much of the railroad construction, claimed that train lines would resolve the fact that "two thirds of the country has yet to be made Peruvian" (91). Trains, the Civilistas believed, would help turn peasants into Peruvians. Railroads would also facilitate troop transport to the highlands for the suppression of revolts – this argument became more prominent after the Huancané revolt of 1866 (Larson 2004, 157–158). In many ways, then, railroad development was explicitly an effort to increase the state's infrastructural power. But the program of social transformation spread beyond railroads. For example, in implementing what Larson (2004, 159) describes as "the first state-directed civilizing project in the Indian sierra," the Pardo government of the early 1870s sought assimilation of the indigenous population via the spread of schooling into the highland regions and construction of roads linking more remote communities to the railroad.

---

[21] Gootenberg (1993), on which this discussion draws, explores the range of development projects envisioned in guano-era Peru.
[22] On Pardo's development vision, and his writings more broadly, see McEvoy (1994).

This first phase of state building was cut short by the fiscal collapse of the mid-1870s and the subsequent war with Chile; efforts would resume with the reestablishment of order after 1895. The war with Chile and the decade of chaos that followed, which included Chilean occupation, civil war, and a multitude of subaltern uprisings, hammered home to elites a sense of impending doom and the need for "national renovation" (Hale 1989, 275–276). The result was a strengthening of developmental efforts, centered on the construction of a more effective state, during the period known as the Aristocratic Republic (1895–1919). A nearly universal position among Peru's elites at this time was that a crucial step toward "order and progress" would involve state initiative in the construction of roads and railroads (Quiroz 1988, 52). Not only state-building politicians in Lima, but regional elites in the southern highlands viewed infrastructure as crucial for development (Jacobsen 1988, 158).

Tensions between local elites who sought state intervention for market access and state-building officials who had a broader vision of development that included education and increased taxation drove conflict during the Civilista era. These tensions constrained the success of this second phase of Peruvian state building, as described in detail in Chapters 4 to 6. With a gap during the years 1875–1895, when instability precluded any initiative on the part of the state, let alone quotidian policy initiatives, the Peruvian political class for the entire period between 1845 and 1920 sought the extension of state authority as the means to political stability, social peace, and economic development.

Colombia's Anti-Statist Consensus

As in the other cases, politicians influenced by broadly liberal views sought to transform Colombia after the mid-nineteenth century. Elites shared the views dominant in the other countries about the problems they faced, seeing ethno-cultural diversity, economic backwardness, and political instability as deeply connected (Jaramillo Uribe 1964). But unlike the other three cases, Colombian elites did not see state building as a means to those ends, and this would place this country on a distinct state-building trajectory.

The late 1830s War of the Supremes (which saw both subaltern mobilization and foreign incursion) highlighted for elites across the ideological spectrum the harm done by political instability (Safford 1991, 29; Earle 2000). In response, "Liberal and Conservative elites were united in a common concern: how to create out of ethnic and cultural diversity a new and purified white population on which 'true nationhood' could be built" (Larson 1999, 581). "Development" and "civilization" implied integrating the indigenous population politically, economically, and culturally into the broader society. In economic terms, elites believed that Colombia was hampered by its lack of both international trade and a domestic market (Safford 1988). These positions were largely unquestioned by broad segments of the Colombian elite, showing that across the board, elites sought the same outcomes of order and progress as in our other cases.

Where Colombian political thought diverged from the other cases was in the means it proposed. In the economic realm, elites espoused the elimination of state intervention in the domestic economy; this was "virtually a dogma" across the political spectrum from the 1840s to 1870 (Safford 1988, 36). In addressing political stability too, liberalism was taken to an extreme in a series of policy choices supported by both liberals and conservatives. The result of three decades of explicit fragmentation of national power, by 1880, was a strikingly impotent state.

Although factions of the liberal party had particularly doctrinaire stances on state intervention, most conservatives "were also economic liberals from the late 1840s through the 1870s" (ibid., 58). Upon coming to power in 1849, the liberal project of freeing individual incentives to allow market competition began. As described in Chapter 5, perhaps their most important initiative was the near-elimination of federal taxation. But the liberal project also included a transition to federalism that began with the 1853 constitution. A constitutional amendment allowed Panama to be a "self-governing entity" except for policy relating to self-defense and foreign relations (Bushnell and Macaulay 1994, 216). This led to analogous demands from other provinces, subsequently codified in the 1858 Constitution. The weakening of the federal system quickly spiraled out of control, as Cauca attempted to withdraw from the federation entirely in 1860.

After liberal victory in the 1860 Civil War that Cauca's withdrawal attempt triggered, the "heyday" of liberalism began (Park 1985, 1). The 1863 Constitution was described by Bushnell and Macaulay (1994, 217) as "in every respect ... the most advanced form of liberalism that any Latin American nation achieved (or was afflicted with) in the [nineteenth] century." As Chapter 6 explores in detail, this constitution allowed each state to control its own military, which fundamentally undermined the national state's monopoly of force. An 1867 ruling forced the national government to remain neutral in case of civil war within a state. This left the national government "virtually powerless" when state governments were threatened by rebellion (Delpar 1981, 13).

Under the 1863 Constitution, Colombia's states had an "existence independent of the nation," holding all powers not specifically delegated to the national government. Individual states operated independently in the international realm, signing treaties and exchanging diplomatic representatives (Park 1985, 43–44). The national government oversaw nothing more than foreign relations, national defense and trade policy, the regulation of weights and measures, and coinage. It shared responsibility with state governments for the postal system and public education (Delpar 1981, 12). Beyond these basic functions, all power was delegated to the states.

Many perceived a pervasive weakening of national feeling and a sense that national ties were fragile. Talk of "national dismemberment" became common (Park 1985, 71–72). A conservative newspaper in 1870 wrote that "the idea of national unity has been almost totally lost," and the fear of secession was endemic (ibid., 72–73). A brief and reluctant shift to re-centralization in the early 1870s was prompted by this sense that national collapse loomed. But after the 1876–1877 civil war, laissez-faire saw a resurgence. As described earlier, transportation spending was once again removed from the purview of the national government and decentralized to the states. The central government's power became even weaker in the first half of the 1880s. Miguel Samper, a prominent liberal, wrote in 1881 that Colombia resembled medieval Europe, with its states akin to feudal fiefdoms (Delpar 1981, 85). The situation was described as "organized anarchy" and observers commented that "national unity [did] not exist, except in name" (Park 1985, 207).

Although rhetoric changed a bit with the Regeneration (1886–1899), the fundamental anti-statism of Colombian development remained. Rafael Núñez, the driving force behind this centralizing reaction, believed that Colombia needed a process of national consolidation. In a statement that reveals his quasi-positivist conception of development, Núñez described the key to order as "scientific peace." The 1886 constitution, written in the aftermath of civil war by the victorious conservatives, was built on the belief that strong institutions (family, church, and state) "were needed to control men susceptible to evil passions and anti-social behavior" (Bergquist 1986, 16). One prominent means of control was the clause in the 1886 Constitution that (for the first time!) gave the national government a monopoly on the importation, manufacture, and possession of munitions (Park 1985, 265). But the emphasis on family and church as promoters of development, alongside the state, reveals the laissez-faire emphasis that continued to dominate the Colombian political sphere.

Concerted state action was still absent. In the realm of transport, for example, Núñez believed that construction simply required the creation of an attractive investment climate (Bergquist 1986, 222). One conservative president revealed the limited ambitions of the state by claiming that improved river transport "was in the hands of the heavenly powers" (cited in Posada-Carbó 1996, 157–158). Another, speaking even more broadly about the limited ambitions of the government, stated that he "should not be judged for the new bricks that [he] laid, but for the tremendous ruins that [he] avoided" (cited in Bushnell 1993, 164). This quote shows that the state continued to be seen primarily as an obstacle to development even as its positive role became evident, and even during nearly five decades of conservative rule. As Bushnell (1993, 160) writes, the state's activity under Núñez was "impressive only by Colombian standards."

Although the conservatives won the vast majority of elections between 1886 and 1930, they came to compromise with their liberal opponents. The decay of the intra-elite violence of the War of 1,000 Days into class-based guerrilla warfare taught elites on both sides that stable government could not emerge without the incorporation into policy the preferences of the losers (Bergquist 1986, 248; Safford and Palacios 2002, 266). Liberals came to believe that "some strengthening of central authority ... had in fact been necessary." (Bushnell 1993, 162) Conservatives, in turn, were amenable to a broadly liberal political economy because they had strikingly little interest in an activist state outside the realm of public works. Although the post-Regeneration Colombian state was not completely absent as it had been at the height of liberal control, it played little role in promoting development beyond some limited efforts to reduce transport costs. The consensus on "liberal political ideology, social conservatism, and pro-export economic policy" was far from an aggressive state-building agenda (Bergquist 1986, 261). The hegemony of anti-statist views in Colombia before 1930 underlay the lack of a concerted state-building project during the first century after independence, and differentiates it from the other three cases.

CONCLUSION

Ideas about the role of the state in development (the content of the liberal consensus – laissez-faire or developmentalist) influenced the commitment of state leaders to extend its authority. Arguments for the causal role of ideas, however, face two analytic challenges. One relates to the question of whether there are causal forces underlying the ideas that make the latter epiphenomenal – are ideas an intervening or independent variable? The second relates to the possibility that alternative factors actually create the outcome that I have attributed to ideas – is there an omitted variable lurking?

In dealing with the first challenge, I have argued in this chapter that ideas about the place of the state in development were shaped by urban primacy. Where a single center was absent, as in the Colombian case, interventionist state building did not seem to respond to the particular problems the country faced in the same way as it did in the other cases.[23] But what is the relationship between ideas (laissez-faire liberalism) and structure (polycentric urbanism) in Colombia, or in the other cases? Are these alternative explanations for the onset of state-building projects? I argue that this is not the case, since they operate together to explain why state-building efforts emerged in some countries but not in others. My claim, following the theoretical work of Sheri Berman and others, is that post-independence Latin America was a context where old ideologies were "slowly delegitimized" by the chaos engendered in the aftermath of independence (Berman 2001, 234; Gootenberg 1988, 80–84). In this common regional context where what Berman describes as a demand for ideas had emerged, "local political contexts" (11) determine the ideas that take hold in a given case. Laissez-faire ideas took hold in Colombia (while more interventionist ones took hold in the other cases) because they fit with the distinct political and economic context shaped by spatial factors. In a polycentric context where regional tensions over public good provision caused further strife, a laissez-faire liberal project seemed more plausible than the interventionist one that took hold elsewhere.

A skeptic of ideational accounts might suggest that urban primacy was the underlying cause and the content of liberalism at best the mechanism linking it to state building projects. But my argument is not that urban primacy explains which ideas emerged into the public sphere, or that laissez-faire ideas in Colombia were a direct reflection of regional interests. Instead, I claim that polycentric urbanism and the presence of salient regions helps to account for which ideas *took hold* among a broad segment of political elites, including actors both in the capital and in the

---

[23] I draw the language of ideas "responding to particular problems" from Berman (2001, 236).

TABLE 1.3. *Urban primacy in each case*

	Chile 1865	Colombia 1851	Mexico 1850	Peru 1876
Largest city	Santiago	Bogotá	Ciudad de México	Lima
	115,400	43,000	170,000	100,100
2nd largest city	Valparaíso	Popayán	Guadalajara	Callao
	70,400	20,000	90,000	34,500
3rd largest city	Talca	Socorro	Puebla	Huaraz
	17,900	20,000	64,600	17,000
4th largest city	Concepción	Medellín	Guanajuato	C. de Pasco
	14,000	14,000	49,000	13,000
National population	1,819,200	2,223,800	7,485,200	2,469,000
Primacy score	0.53	0.44	0.45	0.60

regions, but ideas shape the emergence of state-building projects. Thus, ideas do play an independent causal role in this framework, although their salience cannot be understood without reference to geography.

The second challenge relates to the relationship between ideas and interests; it proposes interest-based arguments as an alternative explanation. A more rationalist and perhaps more parsimonious account would link geography to state-development projects through an account of regional interests rather than through ideas. Indeed, my earlier account incorporates interests in identifying the divergence of public good preferences over regions, and the self-sufficiency of regional economies as the crucial consequences of the absence of urban primacy in Colombia. We might be concerned, then, that the account provided here could be reduced to a purely material one.

I want to suggest, however, two reasons why the role of ideas cannot be removed from the account of the origins of state-building projects. First, as discussed previously, laissez-faire and statist liberals shared common goals – all sought to generate political stability via economic development and social peace. Were they to differ on ends, we might be able to identify certain interests that were being served – this can be seen, for example, in the concurrent debate between free trade and protectionism in Latin America, which pitted sectoral and (in some countries) regional interests against one another (Gootenberg 1989). In the context of political development, however, the advocates of laissez-faire and statism did not align with particular sectoral or regional interests (Hale 1989; Bushnell and Macalay 1994). Instead, the debates among politicians and intellectuals were theoretical debates about the optimal role of the state. Second, and more centrally, the development projects and the political coalitions behind them that dominated each of these countries for decades at a time had a core ideological component that gave them coherence and legitimacy, and their "fantastic staying power" (Gootenberg 1988, 83). Liberal politicians appealed to potential allies and to voters not on the basis of specific interests and policy proposals, but on the basis of broad ideological visions. Ideas about order, progress, and development explain how a broad spectrum of political interests could coalesce around development projects; thus ideational factors are a central component of the emergence of state-building projects.

2

A Theory of State-Building Success and Failure

Regional evidence presented in the Introduction showed that a wide gap in state capacity between Latin American countries was present by 1900. The first part of an explanation for that variation, presented in Chapter 1, was a theory of the emergence of state-building efforts. The second part appears in this chapter, where I develop an account of the success and failure of state-building projects. My argument, evaluated in an examination of successful (Chile and Mexico), failed (pre-1895 Peru) and intermediate (post-1895 Peru) cases in Chapters 4 to 6, centers on the public administration of state-building efforts. I argue that state-building efforts failed where local elites were tasked with administering them in the national periphery, but saw more success where local administrators were outsiders in the communities in which they served.

I describe my account of success and failure as centering on the public-administration of state-building efforts because I argue that the determinants of state-building outcomes are found within the state, rather than in the resistance from societal actors.[1] Most scholarship on state building ignores the inner workings of the state and focuses on the relationship between state and society. One view takes state-building projects as serving the interests of segments of society, usually dominant sectors (Kurtz 2013; Spruyt 1994). A second view, tracing back to Charles Tilly's (1985) broad conception of "negotiation" as struggle

---

[1] Matthias vom Hau, in a series of contributions, has placed a similar emphasis on the intrastate determinants of state-building success and failure, with a focus on educational change and the transformation of nationalism. See vom Hau (2008, 2009) and Abbott et al. (2013).

between state and society over state control and getting new vigor in the work of Joel Migdal (1988) and James Scott (1998, 2009), presumes that state building is imposition on a recalcitrant society. The first view, which focuses on which social groups have their interests represented in state-building projects, tends to focus on the priorities of state leaders and takes for granted the success of their undertakings. The second, by contrast, is more relevant for our purposes, since resistance to the imposition of state-building efforts might explain their failure. But, as Chapter 4 on education shows most clearly, many aspects of state building are welcomed, rather than resisted by societal actors (Slater 2008). While the role of societal resistance in undermining state-development efforts may be important, scholarly accounts of the constraints on state building ignore dynamics internal to the state. Often, state-building efforts are supported, by broad sectors of society, but face resistance from within the state. This issue has been little explored by existing scholarship.

This chapter addresses this gap by developing a theory of the conditions under which local bureaucrats will act more or less effectively to implement state-building endeavors. There are several types of features of bureaucratic agencies that might determine the compliance and effectiveness of their rank and file. One is the professionalism, skill, or training of the bureaucrats – what we might call bureaucratic quality. A second set of features is the extent of oversight by central state agencies through overlapping networks of control or other characteristics of institutional design. A third, commonly cited by scholars of colonialism, relates to the extent of reliance on customary law at the local level within state institutions.

Finding no variation across my cases in these three elements of state bureaucracies, I focus instead on a different characteristic. In explaining variation in the success and failure of state-building efforts, I investigate the interests and incentives of these local bureaucrats themselves. I argue that variation in the relationship between bureaucrats and the communities in which they serve determines the variation in the benefits they perceive from state building, and therefore their inclination to enforce it and to pursue it in their appointed roles as state agents. I argue that this variation explains the success and failure of state-building efforts in Mexico, Peru (distinguishing between two historical periods with different outcomes), and Chile.

The first part of this chapter develops a distinction between two types of administrative appointments – those *delegated* to local elites, and

A Theory of State-Building Success and Failure 61

those filled with outsiders *deployed* into the community. I discuss the relationship between this and broader categories of administration such as direct and indirect rule, and develop two causal mechanisms linking deployment to more successful implementation of state-building projects. The second part of the chapter turns to coding the three cases on this independent variable – the type of administrative appointment that predominated in each. I also discuss evidence about bureaucratic professionalism, administrative oversight, and the use of customary law, showing no variation across cases in these aspects of their state administrations. I postpone a discussion of the origins of this institutional difference for the next chapter, where I also begin addressing possible alternative explanations for variation in state capacity. There I show that it cannot be attributed to preexisting variation in state capacity, and thus rule out the possibility of reverse causation.

ADMINISTRATIVE INSTITUTIONS AND THE OUTCOMES OF STATE-BUILDING EFFORTS

States are composed of networks of administration that extend over territory and penetrate society, reaching from the central bureaucracy into communities where the state seeks control. Particularly where technologies of communication, transportation, and administration are of poor quality, the national leadership must rely on representatives of some sort to carry out administrative functions throughout the national territory (Waldner 1999, 21ff). The central bureaucracy cannot eliminate the autonomy of those representatives, which derives from their discretion in the execution of their work, and from the logistical challenges to oversight by central bureaucrats who are their nominal superiors (Hechter 2000, 27). This autonomy becomes important when local officials have interests that diverge from those of their superiors.

The uneven implementation of state policies (including state-building efforts) is shaped by the incentives of local administrators (Lipsky 1980; Callaghy 1984). Where they can be induced to collaborate with their superiors in increasing the state's power in their bailiwicks, state-building efforts will succeed. But where the interests of local officials are not served by state-building efforts, they undermine or subvert these projects in their implementation.[2] Here, state building, even with a commitment

---

[2] Kaufman (1967) shows that bureaucracies can shape the interests (not just the institutional incentives) of their agents through recruitment, training, and other mechanisms.

from national leaders, is likely to fail. This was the factor that separated Peru from Mexico and Chile during the nineteenth century. It does not, however, account for state weakness in Colombia, where (for reasons explained in Chapter 1) a state-building project never emerged.

State administration was similar in many ways in Chile, Mexico, and Peru: all saw the use of prefectoralism in their appointment of authorities to oversee all government activities in a given region. And all three cases exercised a great deal of *de jure* centralization, which can be seen in the fact that local officials were regularly required to obtain permission from national agencies for a wide variety of actions (Hutchcroft 2000, 280). But administration in these cases, while similar in these and other ways, was characterized by a crucial difference: variation in the *identity of administrators* populating the national bureaucracy. As Hechter (2000, 27) writes, the state's agents "can be recruited from two quite different sources. Sometimes the ruler selects a culturally alien agent. ... At other times the traditional authority in the territory is selected as the central state's representative." Where the state relies (as in Hechter's first category) on local elites to administer in their territories, I label administration as *delegated rule*. These elites, including indigenous community leaders but most often large landowners, have a degree of private power in their communities. Alternatively, the state might fill its ranks with bureaucrats deployed from outside the community; Hechter's second category of "culturally alien agents." I call this model of administration *deployed rule* and refer in the discussion that follows to "outsiders" or "deployed officials." Hechter does not discuss whether this difference in the relationship between administrators and the local community can shape their commitment to state development. I argue that the distinction between deployed and delegated rule has fundamental implications for the fate of state-building projects, and identify two chains of causal logic underpinning that claim.

Causal Mechanisms

My key claim in this chapter is that this fairly subtle distinction between types of administrative institutions turns out to be crucial in underpinning the success and failure of state-building projects. Two mechanisms make state-building efforts less effective under delegated rule than under

---

But I find no evidence that administrative organs in nineteenth-century Latin America were able to exercise similar levels of control over their rank and file.

deployed rule. These mechanisms do not rely on the extent of formal hierarchy, qualifications (whether educational or otherwise), the *esprit de corps*, or other aspects of bureaucratic professionalization discussed later. Nor do they rely on the power of customary law in the hands of local elites, or the oversight capacity of the central state.[3] I show later that these are similar across country cases, and the causal logic I describe assumes that all these are held constant across deployed and delegated rule. Instead, these mechanisms work through the relationship between bureaucrats and the communities in which they serve, and derive from the *individual incentives* of the bureaucrats, which diverge depending on whether or not the bureaucrat is a prominent member of the local community.

Income and the Dynamics of Collaboration

The first mechanism that ties the collaboration of local state agents to the effective implementation of state-building efforts derives from their income. When state agents are deployed to communities from outside, they generate much of their income from access to their position.[4] These officials are therefore vulnerable to sanction by the national government: should performance be lacking, the central government can remove them from their post, depriving them of an important component of their income. This provides the central government with a certain degree of control over local officials.[5] We should therefore expect that deployed bureaucrats will be more likely to comply with edicts received from the national government. State-building initiatives, like any other edict sent

---

[3] I assume here that the oversight capacity of the central state is invariant under deployed and delegated rule. As discussed later, this assumption is reasonable in the cases under study, because all cases were characterized by overlapping networks of oversight within the bureaucracy, and because high-level bureaucrats (regional prefects) were always appointed from outside the community, meaning that at least some element of the bureaucracy operated outside local power networks.

[4] This income may come in the form of salary, or in the form of a share of revenues generated by the local government. Both forms of income were common in nineteenth-century Latin America. On the importance of the Latin American state as a source of income, see Veliz (1980).

[5] As discussed later, the lower rungs of territorial administration in both Chile and Peru were unsalaried positions seen as civic duty. This mechanism, then, would not apply to holders of those offices. Nevertheless, the effects of the income mechanisms should be seen through the actions of holders of offices in functional arms of the administration; these salaried actors play a major role in the state-building projects observed in Chapters 4 through 6. And the local power mechanism discussed later should apply to both salaried and unsalaried officials.

out from the capital, will be pursued more reliably by local bureaucrats under deployed rule.

In a system of delegated rule, positions in the local bureaucracy are given to local elites. In this context, even as they receive a government salary or access to profits from their office, officials continue to be able to generate much of their income from non-salary means such as landholding. These external sources of income make these officials less vulnerable to the sanctions of the national government. The fact that they have access to external sources of income makes them less likely, all else equal, to comply with the edicts of the national government by implementing the policies chosen by the central bureaucracy.[6]

Legitimacy, Local Power, and Shared Interests

In addition to the income mechanism, the other difference between deployed and delegated rule derives from the relationships between officials and the communities in which they serve. In their interactions with their communities, local bureaucrats must draw on various sorts of authority to achieve their goals. All have access to a certain degree of legal/rational authority from the very possession of their titles, but given that this is true of all officials, I set it aside for the purposes of this discussion. Other sources of authority can be *status-based* (deriving from their standing vis-à-vis the community) or *positional* (deriving from their position as state officials). Status-based authority derives from the prestige accorded to important members of the community, and from the private sources of power available to local elites. Positional authority derives most importantly from the fact that state officials' orders can be backed up with the power of the central state.

When a bureaucrat cannot rely on status-based authority, he has no option but to invest in building positional authority as he seeks to generate compliance from local society. Therefore, he will have more independent interest in increasing the state's rational-legal or coercive authority in the community where he serves, and in heightening the profile of the state in the local community. This creates an incentive for outsiders, absent for their delegated counterparts who have more access to status-based

---

[6] It should be noted that this income mechanism does not only apply to state-building efforts: the observable implication of the argument I put forward is that all types of policies instituted by the national government will see greater implementation at the local level by bureaucrats who depend on the national government for their income. Under deployed rule, I predict less administrative slippage between policy choice and implementation of all types of policy than under delegated rule.

authority, to pursue the increased penetration of the state into their communities. This increased penetration can serve to upgrade coercive power, to provide the public goods that win support from the community, or (in a longer-run manifestation of this mechanism) to shape identities and communities in ways that make them easier to control. In all these ways, the increased infrastructural power of the state has benefits that accrue to deployed bureaucrats much more than to their delegated counterparts.

The *independent interest* of local officials in increased state infrastructural power can lead them to champion its development by seeking to maximize the implementation of policies handed down from their superiors, and even by undertaking independent initiatives to press the central government for a greater emphasis on state building. Because both of these types of actions can be quite costly – whether due to conflict with social actors in the former instance, or with superiors and central offices in the latter – state officials will not undertake them unless they see an advantage to doing so. Thus, I argue that where deployed rule has been instituted, local officials will go beyond compliance with central efforts at state building to prodding the central state to increase its effective presence in their communities. Under delegated rule, state agents are indifferent, and even hostile, to state-building initiatives undertaken by the central state.[7]

Scoring Cases on the Forms of Rule

Assessing the type of administrative appointments that characterize a particular country's administration is complex, since these types of broad patterns emerge from the aggregation of a myriad of individual appointment decisions taken by executives and ministers, rather than from the product of a single explicit institutional choice. This has two implications for how cases can be coded. First, because state leaders rarely make any explicit statement about patterns of appointment, they must instead be imputed from the aggregation of individual appointment decisions. Second, it means that the patterns are probabilistic rather than deterministic: what we observe are tendencies rather than absolute rules. Thus, the

---

[7] Unlike the income mechanism described earlier, I do not expect the authority mechanism to be relevant to other kinds of policy: it is limited to those policies that increase the positional authority of local officials, those that increase the state's presence in their communities. For a similar argument to mine that traces how local elites appointed to local political and administrative posts undermined state-building efforts under U.S. colonial rule in the Philippines, see Hutchcroft (2000).

claim that a state leadership practices deployed rule does not imply that each and every appointment we examine must go to an outsider, nor does a coding of delegated rule imply that outsiders are completely absent. Instead, the comparison is of broad patterns of appointments in a case.

In assessing the bureaucratic model in place in each case, I draw on a variety of types of evidence. Most centrally, for Chile and Peru, I rely on evidence drawn from appointment decrees issued by the central government and printed in its official publication of record. I also draw on an analysis of several thousand entries in dictionaries of political biography from all three countries, as well as evidence gathered from both primary and secondary sources about individuals, particular agencies, and particular regions.

Decree Analysis

Methods: For the cases of Peru (both before and after 1895) and Chile, I draw on the analysis of hundreds of appointment decrees to examine the rates of reliance on deployed outsiders to fill bureaucratic posts throughout the national territory. These decrees are issued by agency heads, approved by the national executive, and published in each country's official government newspaper of record – *El Peruano* in Peru and *El Araucano*, which became *Diario Oficial* after 1876 in Chile. Unfortunately, an analogous source for Mexico does not exist and for that case we have to rely principally on the other, less direct, forms of evidence described later. I drew a random sample of years and analyzed each decree of appointment involving a bureaucratic posting.[8] Only two kinds of posts were excluded: the appointments of prefects (the highest ranking officials in the periphery) who were nearly always active-duty military officers, and those located within the capital city, since many of these posts were within the administrative headquarters rather than representing what Joel Migdal (2001) called the "local face" of the state. Thus, the dataset is limited to bureaucrats who were appointees in positions that had a direct role in implementing state policies at the local level.

I proceed as follows to code an appointment as an instance of delegated or deployed rule: each decree is examined for three pieces of information, of which the presence of any one is sufficient for concluding that

---

[8] The analysis of Peru used *El Peruano* for 1845, 1855, 1873, 1908 (January, February, November, and December), and 1912 (January–May). The Chilean analysis relies on *El Araucano* from 1846–1849, 1856–1857, 1862–1863, and 1869–1870, and the *Diario Oficial* for 1877. These years were randomly selected from among available years or rolls of microfilm; for the date ranges indicated, I reviewed each issue of the publication, and included every decree that contained enough information to be coded.

the appointment must have involved deployment. First, some decrees list the appointee's previous post in a different region of the country. Second, some decrees order that the relevant agency pay the costs of the appointee as he or she relocates across regions to take up a posting. Logically, each of these pieces of information signals deployed rule, since the appointee must have been an outsider either in the previous posting or in the new assignment. Third, some decrees explicitly state that the position was vacant because the previous occupant was transferred to a different region, meaning that the previous occupant must have been deployed. Any decree that contains one or more of these pieces of information is therefore coded as **clearly deployed**.

Coding was based on the largest subnational unit (department in Peru; province in Chile) in each country. This lowers the rate of appointments coded as deployed, since any move within a subnational unit (for example, from one district to another in a given Chilean province or Peruvian department) is not coded as "clearly deployed." Thus, even though the appointee may be an outsider in the local community to which they are sent, I do not consider this clear evidence of deployment unless the appointment crosses the boundaries of the largest subnational unit. This coding rule is designed to underestimate the rate of reliance on outsiders across all cases, and thus to bias against the cross-case variation I predict.

The analysis of decrees cannot provide information about the absolute rates of reliance on delegated and deployed rule, since the "clearly deployed" cases represent nothing more than a logical minimum of the overall instances of deployment. This is so because the vast majority of decrees provide no clear information for coding the type of administrative appointment. Many provide only the name of the appointee and no other information that allows us to determine whether or not the appointment was an instance of deployed rule. The percentage of all appointments that fall in the "clearly deployed" category as a share of all appointments must understate the extent of overall reliance on deployed rule, and we can't tell by how much it does so, since we cannot assume that decrees without information are a random sample of all decrees. We cannot, then, use the appointment decrees to calculate a figure for the share of all postings filled via deployed rule in a given case. Nor can we compare the rate of clearly deployed appointments to the rate of appointments that are clearly delegated: although some decrees do state that the appointee is a native of the community in which he or she is appointed, these instances occur only rarely (fewer than ten times out of the hundreds of decrees analyzed in each country case).

But we can draw comparisons across cases about the frequency of "clearly deployed" bureaucratic appointments, which can be used to assess the relative importance of deployed rule. This inference can be made so long as we believe that there is no difference across cases in the propensity of decrees to contain information about appointees and that the selection mechanism (the determinants of which decrees contain information about place of birth or location of previous office held) is similar across cases. An examination of the publications, and of the decrees, suggests that this is not a concern. The publications provide similar information about the day-to-day administration of various ministries, including appointment decrees, regulations, and statistics. There is no variation across countries or across time.

By comparing the relative prevalence of "clearly deployed" rule across cases, we can therefore draw conclusions about the relative prevalence of deployed rule in general. This, along with the other forms of evidence about forms of rule that follow, lets us code cases in a transparent manner. This coding, once again, is based not on an absolute figure of the extent of reliance on deployed or delegated rule, but on a comparison across cases of the proportion of all appointments that can clearly be coded as instances of deployed rule.

Findings: The findings of this analysis are that clearly deployed appointments are more than twice as common in Chile as in Peru before 1895. While the rate of clearly deployed appointments doubles in postwar Peru, it still remains somewhat below the Chilean rate. Of the 750 bureaucratic appointments examined in Chile, 19.5 percent were clearly filled via deployment, while in Peru before 1895, only 7.6 percent of the 471 appointments studied were filled in this manner. After 1895, the rate of clear deployment in Peru doubled to 16.3 percent of the 766 appointments identified in decrees. As discussed previously, we cannot conclude anything about the absolute rate of deployed rule in any of these cases. But by assuming that the "clearly deployed" rate is an undercounting of the overall rate of deployment in a consistent way across cases, we can observe that local and regional bureaucratic appointments in Chile were 2.5 times more likely to go to an outsider than they were in prewar Peru. This strongly suggests that Chile relied more heavily on deployed rule, while administration in prewar Peru relied more heavily on delegation to locals. That the rate of appointments that clearly went to outsiders more than doubled after 1895 in Peru strongly suggests a shift to greater reliance on deployed rule in Peru that distinguishes the Aristocratic Republic from earlier periods in Peruvian state development.

TABLE 2.1. *Clearly deployed appointments in Peru, 1845–1895*

Arena	Deployed	Total	% Deployed
Education	9	79	11.4
Customs and other fiscal	1	31	3.2
Courts	11	93	11.8
Roads/public works/engineering	6	20	30
Police/national guard	0	18	0
Subprefects, assistant prefects, and regional official staff	3	168	1.8
Mail	1	34	2.9
OVERALL TOTAL (includes other appointments)	36	471	7.6

Tables 2.1–2.3 break down the country-level data by sectors of state activity. Table 2.1 provides data on appointments in pre-1895 Peru. It shows that clearly deployed appointments fell largely into two categories: education (where 11.4 percent of appointments were clearly deployed) and courts (11.8 percent). Notably, even these rates, some of Peru's highest, are below the average in Chile. Nearly all other instances of clearly deployed rule in Peru were appointments to inspect roads, public works, and other engineering projects. The decrees themselves make clear that many of these were short-term missions to carry out a particular task on behalf of the national government (such as inspecting the construction on a particular bridge) rather than term or career appointments. With the exception of some limited service in schools and courts, then, the state appears to have relied on outsider appointments only quite infrequently.

Table 2.2 provides data on post-1895 Peru. It shows that while some facets of the bureaucracy saw real changes in appointment patterns, little change took place in others. The table shows that positions among the ranks of *jefes* at the provincial or departmental level (43.9 percent), and in the education (18.1 percent) and coercive (20.2 percent) apparati, were most likely to be filled through deployment, while deployment was non-existent in the courts, and rare (8.1 percent) among territorial appointees like governors, subprefects, and their staff.

This variation across state agencies is important, and will be discussed in more detail later, since it sheds light on the politics of administrative reform and patterns of state-building success after 1895. First, it shows an attempt by the state to layer new institutions dominated by deployed rule (the *jefes*) over existing ones (the governors and subprefects) that were

TABLE 2.2. *Clearly deployed appointments in Peru, post-1895*

Arena	Deployed	Total	% Deployed
Education	70	387	18.1
Customs and other fiscal	9	56	16.1
Courts	0	37	0
Roads/public works/engineering	3	17	17.6
Police/gendarmes/guardia civil	17	84	20.2
Public health	2	13	15.4
Jefes de provincia/dept	18	41	43.9
Subprefects, assistant prefects, and regional official staff	6	74	8.1
OVERALL TOTAL (includes other appointments)	125	766	16.3

TABLE 2.3. *Clearly deployed appointments in Chile*

Arena	Deployed	Total	% Deployed
Education	64	478	13.4
Customs and other fiscal	40	87	46.0
Courts	26	140	18.6
Roads/public works/engineering	2	4	50
Police/national guard	8	8	100
Public health	0	1	0
Governors, subprefects, and regional office staff	2	14	14.3
Mail and telegraph	7	18	38.9
OVERALL TOTAL (includes other appointments)	146	750	19.5

firmly in the hands of local elites. Second, as discussed further in Chapters 4 through 6, the patterns in the decrees reveal a willingness to challenge some aspects of elite interests (in the realm of education, for example) but not their core interests implicated in the revenue realm.

Table 2.3 shows the pattern of appointments in Chile. Here, the importance of deployed rule is especially clear. The customs agency (45.9 percent), policing (100 percent – but an N of only eight appointments) and telegraph and mail agencies (38.9 percent) saw high rates of deployed rule, while the rate was somewhat lower in the judicial (18.6 percent) and educational (13.4 percent) realms. Even these last two, realms in which deployed rule was less common in Chile, saw it used far more than in the highest-scoring realm of the pre-1895 Peruvian administration.

A Theory of State-Building Success and Failure 71

Evidence from Political Biographies

Methods: As a complement to the analysis of individual appointment decrees, and in particular to allow the coding of the Mexican case, for which appointment decrees were not available, I also examine evidence from an analysis of the patterns of appointments in the careers of all individuals included in the most prominent dictionaries of political biography for each country.[9] For each country's biographical dictionary, I reviewed every entry for mentions of a bureaucratic appointment outside the national capital.[10] I then compared the location of the administrative position to the place of birth and/or schooling for the individual.[11] Where the appointment was in the same subnational political unit (province, department, or state) as the place of birth or schooling, I coded the position as an instance of delegation. Otherwise, it was coded as an instance of deployed rule.[12] As in the decree coding earlier, coding was based on the largest subnational unit in each country, thus lowering the prevalence of deployed rule across the board.[13]

These sources were chosen because they represent the most systematic scholarly effort in each case to collect biographical information about government officials. Despite some differences, all three center on prominent individuals who served the state. Camp (1991) is most explicit about

---

[9] The sources for this analysis were Camp (1991) for Mexico, Milla Batres (1994) for Peru, and de Ramón (1999) for Chile.

[10] I include Mexican appointments between 1855 and 1910, Peruvian appointments between 1845 and 1920, and Chilean appointments from before 1910.

[11] Records without place of birth or education were dropped from the analysis.

[12] The use of place of education along with birthplace to define someone's place of origin also leads to an underestimation of deployed rule. This is true because, especially in the early post-independence period, secondary schools only existed in a small number of regional centers. As a result, I have coded as "delegated" appointments that fall within *either* the province of birth *or* the province of education, which inflates the count of delegated appointments. This especially affects coding in Chile, where (for example) nearly twenty appointments of teachers to the Liceo in Concepción were coded as delegated because appointees were educated at that institution – one of the few *liceos* in the entire southern half of the country – even though they were born and received primary school education in locations spread across the southern third of the country.

[13] A few additional caveats about this analysis are also in order. First, I exclude (as in the analysis of decrees) all positions in the top rung of the bureaucracy (prefects in Chile and Peru, and governors in Mexico) since in all three cases these appointments were commonly filled by deploying former or active-duty military officers. Second, I once again exclude all positions in the capital city and its province or department, since my interest is in how the design of the administrative apparatus affected the reach of the state into the national periphery. Third, I exclude all Chilean appointments before 1885 in the region seized from Peru and Bolivia in the War of the Pacific, and all appointments in Peru between 1879 and 1885, since anomalous factors may drive appointments by occupying forces. Fourth, I only include administrative positions, excluding all elected positions.

the criteria for inclusion, writing that his choices were based on "positional and reputational criteria and on the completeness and accuracy of information available" (xvii). In positional terms, individuals included had to hold a sufficiently high-ranking office in the executive, legislative, or judicial branch of government, or in the military or civil service, or to have been a major figure in one of Mexico's political parties. After compiling a list of some two thousand people who fit these criteria between 1884 and 1934, Camp dropped all individuals for whom information was lacking on three or more of his data categories. The approximately seven hundred individuals who remained comprise the full dataset he presents; he suggests that the results meet his goal of "portraying collectively" the leaders of Mexico's fundamental institutions (xviii).

De Ramón (1999) takes a similar approach to the case of Chile, seeking to include all individuals who held high-ranking posts in the three branches of government between 1875 and 1973. The source used for Peru, Milla Batres (1994), takes a slightly different approach. Rather than a dictionary of *political* biography, this is instead a historical dictionary. It includes both prominent individuals who never held government office (including writers, artists, and various socially prominent figures) as well as important events and other aspects of Peruvian history. The goal, as stated in the introduction, is to paint a portrait of the construction of Peru since the conquest by including a full range of prominent shapers of national history.

While the Chilean and Mexican sources select individuals to include based on explicit positional criteria, Milla Batres does not spell out such clear decision rules in the case of Peru. Nevertheless, all three volumes emphasize individuals who rose to positions of political or administrative prominence. Given our limited knowledge about the career trajectories of bureaucrats, we must allow for the possibility that access to such positions was affected by family background, wealth, or social prominence, and that these were not typical bureaucrats. Selection effects based on career trajectories, in other words, may exist.

The availability of biographical information also leads to selection effects in all three sources that bias the sample of bureaucrats included. Camp makes the size of the data problem clear in stating that two-thirds of his potential entries had to be dropped due to missing information. De Ramón goes further in talking explicitly about selection, writing that many officials who met the positional criteria, but who lacked complete biographical information, came from modest socioeconomic backgrounds (12). Because he, like his counterparts in the other countries,

TABLE 2.4. *Patterns of bureaucratic appointment based on biographical entries*

	Delegated	% of total	Deployed	% of total	Deployed % from decree analysis*
Chile	280	55.8%	222	44.2%	19.5%
Mexico	44	56.4%	34	43.6%	
Peru pre-1895	36	66.7%	18	33.3%	7.6%
Peru post-1895	15	50%	15	50%	16.3%

* Drawn from Tables 2.1–2.3.

relied heavily on genealogical records to compile biographical information, the figures included in the dictionaries tended to be descendants of prominent families rather than typical bureaucrats. One indication of this oversampling of elites can be seen in comparing the types of official positions mentioned in the biographical entries with those in the appointment decrees. The most common bureaucratic offices mentioned in dictionary entries were governor, subprefect, and (for Mexico) *jefe político*, while the analysis of all appointment decrees discussed earlier contained more appointments of lower-status bureaucrats like teachers. But the range of positions found in the biographic entries is quite broad: it includes many of those central to the administrative state, such as tax collector, school inspector, telegraph inspector, sanitation officer, and customs official.

Given that the same concerns about selection effects are present for all countries, we can safely make cross-national comparisons even if we cannot draw inferences about absolute rates of delegation and deployment. As in the analysis of decrees, we can draw conclusions from the analysis of biography entries about cross-national differences, but not inferences about absolute rates of delegation and deployment in any given case.

Findings: As shown in Table 2.4, the rates of deployed rule in Chile, Mexico, and Peru after 1895 were higher than that of Peru in the earlier period. These differences are statistically significant as well: a one-tailed *t*-test confirms that the sample of appointments in Peru before 1895 saw significantly more reliance on delegated rule than did the other cases, although the substantive differences between cases are fairly small.[14] Thus, we have further support for the claim that the pattern of administrative

---

[14] This difference, despite the small sample sizes, is significant at the .10 level for Chile and Peru after 1895, but not quite for Mexico (significance level is 0.11).

appointments was unique in this case. Additionally, a two-tailed *t*-test confirms that the extent of reliance on deployed rule was similarly important in the other three cases, suggesting that these patterns of administrative appointment had a great deal in common and that we should expect similar impact in their effect on state building in Mexico, Chile, and Peru after 1895.

Qualitative Evidence
In addition to these attempts to quantitatively assess broad patterns of appointment practices, a variety of qualitative evidence also sheds light on patterns of administrative appointments. This evidence is drawn from the official newspapers of record in Chile and Peru, other government documents, and a range of secondary sources that discuss appointment practices in particular agencies, administrations, or regions.

Chile: In making bureaucratic appointments at the regional and local level, Chilean state leaders tended not to select regional elites for these positions. Instead, local communities were penetrated by "powerful officials appointed directly by the president" (Valenzuela n.d., 3). The absence of bureaucrats among elite sectors of Chilean society was quite striking. Arnold Bauer, for example, studies several notable rural elite families, finding that while their ranks included a presidential candidate, congressional deputies, senators, bank presidents, mine owners, and a president of the national agricultural lobby (*Sociedad Nacional de Agricultura*), not a single bureaucratic post was held by a member of their ranks (Bauer 1975, 181ff). Maurice Zeitlin, similarly, collects biographical information on forty-four insurrectionary leaders in the 1851 and 1859 Civil Wars, who came from the country's economic elite (Zeitlin 1984; Table 2.1). He finds that only four were state officials: two military officers, and two judges. None had ever held any other appointed position in the regional bureaucracy. It was uncommon for social and economic elites to serve as cogs in the Chilean administrative machine, although they did more commonly hold offices in agency headquarters in Santiago.

We can also draw inference about the extent of central government control over local appointments from the instances in which officials requested to be sent to a particular location. In these cases, such as one of three vaccination officials requesting permission to work where his family lives (*Diario Oficial* March 17, 1877, p. 125), the request trickled up all the way to the minister of the interior himself. This, too, suggests that the central government held a great deal of control over appointments, rather than letting regional officials make appointment decisions.

Importantly, as I emphasize in Chapter 4, this absence of elites from the bureaucracy does not mean that these elites were weak. Indeed, Chilean elites were wealthier, and had *more* control over land and labor than did their counterparts in Peru (Bauer 1975; Saylor 2012). More to the point, they also held absolute sway over the country: top government positions like the presidency, congress, and ministerial portfolios were firmly in the hands of Chile's tightly knit oligarchy (Loveman 2001, 139). Elites, then, had total control over the rural areas, massive wealth, and a stranglehold on the "commanding heights" of the state. But they played little part in the bureaucracy through which the state administered its territory. Instead, the state administration at the local level was populated with state agents who arrived with no ties to the communities to which they were deployed to serve.

Peru 1845–1895: Colonial administration in Peru had relied on indigenous authorities to administer many parts of the country. After independence, the new republican administration chose to establish a new regional administrative apparatus and rely on non-Indian petty state officials.[15] These officials were almost exclusively local elites. The most important set of officials, the linchpins of administration at the local level who "linked" the hinterland with the regional and national state, were governors (Walker 1999, 137). Governors and their small office staff had tax collection as their central responsibility, but they also recruited soldiers, extracted supplies for the army in times of civil war, exercised surveillance over political opponents, and disseminated political information and propaganda on behalf of the government. In other words, they were the key agents of the state at the local level.

The importance of the governors can be seen in the fact that they, the subprefects, and other regional staff made up more than one-third of all bureaucratic appointments in the sample of decrees discussed earlier. That only three of the 168 regional official appointments in the *El Peruano* sample were clearly deployed strongly supports the claim that local elites held sway over these appointments. Contreras (2005, 118) describes the pattern quite clearly: while prefects and regional officials "belonged to a kind of caste of mobile public functionaries whose true home base was the army," governors "were local figures, chosen primarily for their knowledge of Spanish and also for their potential loyalty to the government of the day."

---

[15] Thurner (1997) describes the removal of chiefs as tribute collectors and their replacement with non-Indian officials in the Huaylas region.

In addition to the subprefects, the state-building governments of the guano era created a wide range of new positions at the local and regional level, such as public health inspectors and school officials (Jacobsen 1993, 147). Muecke (2004, 166) finds that tax collectors, school inspectors, teachers, district governors, and other officials were positions populated almost exclusively by local elites. Other accounts of this period agree. School inspectors, as discussed further in Chapter 4, were nearly universally residents of the local community. Rural security, too, was provided by corps of landowners organized into rural police (*El Peruano* July 12, 1873, p. 7). The 1856 national census was administered by commissions of local residents, who completed forms about their community and returned them to Lima (*El Peruano* October 6, 1855, p. 1). Similar procedures were also used to compile and update tax rolls. Thus, delegation to local notables dominated many aspects of administration in Peru.

This administrative arrangement was beneficial to local elites. Before the agricultural and mining booms that began in the 1890s, most elites were fairly poor, and relatively weak vis-à-vis their local communities.[16] Positions in regional administration were useful to these elites in consolidating their positions in local society and in power struggles at the local or regional level.[17] This could be done via the use of appointments to cement local alliances, or via the leverage provided by control of taxing or policing. It was because Peruvian elites were fairly weak that positions in the administration appealed to them.

The pattern of heavy reliance on delegation in Peru was reinforced by the high rate of refusal in the rare attempts where the national government *did* attempt to deploy a bureaucrat to a remote region. Refusals took the form of explicit rejection of a transfer or appointment, or more passively they sometimes manifested in the failure of an appointee to appear at a new posting.[18] This posed a severe challenge to the national government, which had to either punish the appointee for refusal, or compromise and keep them in a post close to home. Such cases included not only low-ranking officials but even those more senior, such as the judge fired for

---

[16] Evidence in Nugent (1997) for the Chachapoyas region, and in Thorp and Bertram (1978) for the country as a whole suggests that Peru's elites were fairly weak until the export booms of the 1890s.
[17] For examples of this pattern, see Nugent (1997, 34–35) and Taylor (2006, 57).
[18] For one of many examples of the latter, see *El Peruano* July 5, 1873, p. 17 for the discussion of the failure of a school director deployed to Puno to appear for the beginning of the school year.

refusing to relocate from Pasco to Ica (*El Peruano* March 22, 1845, p.1). Interestingly, claims of health as an obstacle to a posting were commonly deployed both by coastal residents seeking to avoid appointments in the Andes and by those unwilling to be sent to the coast from their highland homes. Health-based excuses were so common that government ministries began to demand and assess evidence for health-related appeals of appointments (*El Peruano* June 7, 1873, pp. 3–4).

Compromise between ministries and appointees was also common – attempts to deploy appointees to new regions often resulted in agreements allowing various appointees to swap jobs to head off the need to relocate. Indeed, much of the limited evidence of deployed rule that I *did* find in the Peruvian case took the form of local officials swapping jobs so that they could leave deployed postings and return to their homes. Much more often than in Chile, these requests for swaps seem to have been granted (see, among many other examples, *El Peruano* June 25, 1873, p. 11 and June 21, 1873, p. 11). In other words, local state agents in Peru seem to have resisted deployment in a way not seen in Chile, further reinforcing the dominance of delegated rule.

Resistance to deployment in the ranks of *médicos titulares* or regional medical officials is particularly interesting to note. Because most of these officials were army officers, I excluded them from the quantitative analysis of appointment decrees. Yet examining the appointment of medical officers – whether sent to respond to an epidemic or to oversee public health in a particular jurisdiction – reveals significant resistance to deployed rule. In 1873 alone, the records in *El Peruano* show eight instances of refusal of appointments. Given that 1873 saw only 38 medical officer appointments, and that most appointees were military officers, this is a strikingly high rate of refusal. Five of these refusals resulted in the cashiering of the officer, one in a resignation, one in failure to appear at a new post, and the eighth in a successful health-related appeal, which resulted in reassignment to a post open within the department in which the officer was currently posted.

Overall, we can conclude that deployed rule was fairly rare in Peru, and when it *was* implemented, it faced resistance from appointees, who seemed to prefer to remain in their home regions. But resistance by appointees only explains a certain amount of variation. Explicit evidence of delegation to local residents appears regularly in the record of Peruvian administration, and Lima's role in populating its administration was limited to rubber-stamping decisions made by local residents. At the local level, in many cases, the decrees indicate that only a single individual was even considered for the job in many cases, whereas decrees in Chile more commonly referred to the range of candidates considered for a position.

The result was that it was common to see local residents shifting across government agencies to take posts – much more common than in Chile. In 1873 alone, appointments in *El Peruano* include instances of a mail official being appointed subprefect (July 19, p. 10), a teacher getting a postal supervisor post (May 3, p. 13), and the aide of a prefect becoming a gendarme (July 12, p. 1). In one instance, a court official in Arequipa was appointed prefect – this indicates that even these positions, usually the exclusive purview of outside officials such as military officers, were filled by local residents in some cases (July 26, p. 4). Local residents, rather than outsiders with relevant skills and qualifications, were favored for a wide variety of positions across Peru during the guano era.

Peru after 1895: Appointment patterns after 1895 were markedly different than those in the preceding era. This can be seen in the quantitative analysis of decrees presented earlier, which showed that the rate of "clearly deployed" appointments more than doubled from that of the pre-1895 period. Moreover, this figure almost certainly represents an undercounting of the rate of deployed rule after 1895, since many more appointment decrees from this period include information stating that the previous occupant had been relocated to a post in a different location. Without information about the destinations of the former holders, I could not code those transfers as instances of clearly deployed rule. But this pattern – that so many positions were vacant due to the transfer of the previous officeholder to a position elsewhere – suggests that deployed rule must have been more common than the "clearly deployed" figure reported earlier indicates.

The Civilistas who came to power after 1895 undertook an explicit effort to cut local elites out of administration. This was motivated by their belief that the decentralization of the preceding Cáceres regime and the delegation common in the prewar period were responsible for Peru's developmental failures. But the Civilista project of administrative reform and state building sought to avoid directly challenging these powerful actors, as some short-lived postwar governments had done. Rather than taking the more politically difficult step of wresting control of existing offices away from local elites, the central state chose instead to layer a new set of positions above these offices, and to continue to appoint local elites as governors and subprefects while trying to undermine the extent of their authority. The most important element of the Civilista reforms was the creation of a new series of bureaucratic offices – the *jefes de provincia* and *jefes de departamento*, which would be populated with a class of "career politicians" (Nugent 1997, 48). Among appointments to these positions in the decrees analyzed earlier, nearly half were clearly deployed, a rate far higher than that for any other office. This practice created a new corps of regional and local bureaucrats, deployed from Lima, to sit alongside the subprefects and governors who continued to be drawn from among the local elites.

The practice of deployment during the Aristocratic Republic (1895–1919) expanded most where it did not directly challenge the interests of local elites. In addition to creating the *jefes*, we see that the state inserted outsiders into education and policing at a much higher rate than in the past, while deployment was completely absent from the courts, and from the officialdom that oversaw mining, irrigation, and river transport. The developments in schooling (discussed further in Chapter 4) were particularly striking: while school inspection at the local level remained in the hands of appointees from the local community, provincial and departmental inspection was systematically turned over to outsiders, who were rotated through different jurisdictions during their careers (MIP 1910, v.2, 35ff). This was a significant move toward deployed rule. On the other hand, since conscription remained in the hands of the subprefects and governors, and these positions continued to be overwhelmingly given to locals, this aspect of the state remained weak, as shown in Chapter 6.

The revenue realm was a more complicated story, as discussed in detail in Chapter 5. On the one hand, deployment increased among the ranks of the customs service as officers were rotated to limit fraud and smuggling. Given the state's heavy reliance on customs revenues, the reforms in that arena were crucial to its fiscal survival. On the other hand, the Civilista-era regimes made very few appointments at all in the realm of internal taxation. Learning from the conflict spurred by attempts to deploy tax commissioners in the late 1880s and "exclude local authorities from fiscal administration," the Civilistas abolished that office in 1893 and found a new strategy.[19] Rather than threaten the interests of local elites directly by deploying tax inspectors and collectors to the periphery, or continuing to rely on local elites to oversee tax collection, the Civilistas opted instead to contract tax collection to the private *Compañia Nacional de Recaudación* discussed in Chapter 5. Despite the hopes that privatization would eliminate the influence of local elites over collection, they retained

---

[19] On this conflict, see Contreras (2005, 120ff); quote from p.121.

appointments in this realm. First (as discussed in Chapter 5) the CNR relied on local elites to take up many positions in its ranks. Second, local tax rolls continued to be updated by commissions of local notables (see *El Peruano* January 10, 1912, p. 13 for the case of Contumazá). Thus, this shift had a smaller effect than state leaders intended.

The attempt to implement deployed rule can be seen in the statistical realm as well. Having come to realize that leaving data collection in the hands of local officials fundamentally undermined any chance of generating any systematic information, the state shifted toward more central control over these practices. This included the 1902 education census explored in Soifer (2012b), as well as other initiatives. For example, the 1903 census of the province of Lima, which was carried out by commissions of local notables, was deemed a failure, and scheduled in 1908 to be repeated by the Ministerio de Fomento (*El Peruano* February 27, 1908, p. 7). In a related initiative, the rise of labor unrest in the sugar regions on the north coast prompted the deployment of a series of inspectors from Lima who were charged with reporting on the roots of tensions – another example of the shift of the national government away from relying on local elites as it managed the challenges of governance.

Thus, the national government in the post-1895 period made an explicit effort to increase the incidence of deployed rule. Although national leaders wanted to cut local elites out of the administration, they were limited by political constraints in their ability to do so. The result was variation across arenas of administration. Some types of positions remained the exclusive domain of local elites. Others, such as educational offices, were transformed during these decades. The central state also created new organs of administration to indirectly undermine the hold of local elites over their communities, filling posts in these with outsiders as well. The result was a mixed pattern of administrative organization, a real change from the previous half century of delegation to local notables, but far from a complete shift to deployed rule.

Mexico: In Mexico, appointments in the federal bureaucracy were commonly filled through deployment. Although no collection of appointment decrees is available, the reports of historians about appointment practices are unanimous in supporting this assessment. Governors, who oversaw much local and regional administration, commonly were outsiders in the states where they served (Knight 1986, vol. 1, p. 17). The position saw high geographic mobility, as governors were commonly rotated among states (Haber 2003, 88–89). As governors built "bureaucratic machines loyal to themselves" at the state level, they often brought loyalists with them when they assumed leadership of a state (Perry 1978, 89). Thus, many of the appointments at the governors' disposal went to outsiders as well. For example, as discussed in Chapter 4, educational appointments remained in the hands of state governors, who often filled them via deployed rule.

Yet many aspects of administration remained under the control of the national government. This centralization increased over the course of the Porfiriato. Here, too, we can see the importance of deployed rule. The taxation administration, for example, as discussed in Chapter 5, was steadily centralized. A series of national-level tax corps – the *timbre* inspectors, the *visitadores*, and the *inspectores* – were deployed from Mexico City to administer taxes at the state level throughout the country. Thus, despite Mexico's federal institutions, the state-building era saw a steady increase of central control over bureaucratic appointment in many aspects of administration.

The same pattern of increasing central control over appointments in the periphery also unfolded at the municipal level. Porfirio Díaz created the position of *jefe político* as a means of exerting federal control at the municipal level. These officials were in charge of implementing a wide range of federal policies in their communities including conscription, as discussed in Chapter 6. The men appointed to these positions "were often from outside the state with few local ties" (Haber et al. 2003, 45). Appointment of outsiders "predominated" (Knight 1986, vol. 1, 27–28). The rise of the *jefes políticos* broke the monopoly of local control that had marked the early decades after independence (Chowning 1999, 10). Elites, in a relationship similar to that which we saw in Chile, often "accommodated themselves" to giving up political power at the local level in return for government policies that broadly aligned with their interests in economic development and security (Voss 1982, xv). Mexico saw little delegation of these positions at the fulcrum of local administration to local elites (Pittman 1989, 32).

Mexico was not as clear-cut a case of deployed rule as was Chile. We see variation across bureaucratic agencies and issue areas, as described briefly here, but also across regions. Bobrow-Strain (2007, 78–79), for example, shows that in Porfirian Chiapas "landowners themselves were called to serve as direct agents of state rule." These landowners not only actively resisted state-building efforts – (78) cites a landowner driving off his estate at gunpoint two fellow landowners serving as tax collectors – but also revealed their disinterest in broader development projects: landowners tried to bribe the governor of Chiapas to stop construction of a road connecting coffee and sugar estates to the national road network (65). Yet even in Chiapas, there were serious efforts by Porfirian officials to "challenge landowners' mediator position by extending the reaches of its legal system. ..." (78). The governor, an outsider, sought to use roads, census collection, and the intervention of bureaucrats and state agents to weaken the hold of landowners and impose the state's power despite their opposition. The uneven patchwork of administrative forms in Mexico explains the intermediate outcome of state development in that case; evidence presented in Chapters 4 to 6 highlights variation in state-building success across states and agencies in the Liberal and Porfirian eras.

THE PUBLIC ADMINISTRATION OF STATE BUILDING

Variation in several characteristics of the administrative apparatus of the state have been linked to its capacity in existing scholarship. Yet these aspects of public administration are similar in our cases, providing further evidence for the causal importance of the more subtle distinction discussed earlier – that between delegation to local officials or deployment of outsiders. This difference unfolded within very similar formal bureaucratic structures in each case, in cases with similarly low levels of bureaucratic professionalization, and in cases with similarly little entry of customary rule into bureaucratic practices.

Patrimonialism

One way in which the cases were similar was the absence of formal patrimonial office-holding, which (as Ertman [1997] and others have argued) was associated with state weakness in early modern Europe. This elimination of patrimonialism, as discussed further in Chapter 3, was a consequence of the Bourbon Reforms. Some characteristics of patrimonial offices did exist, especially in the realm of taxation: officials at times received a share of the revenues that passed through their hands in lieu of a salary, and some positions were filled by auction. These details of tax administration are discussed in Chapter 5. But in general, officials were appointed and removed from office by their superiors and thus patrimonial administration, in the sense of ownership of an office, had no place in Spanish America after the mid-eighteenth-century Bourbon Reforms discussed in Chapter 3. Instead, bureaucracies had a formal and complex

Overlapping Bureaucratic Networks

A second set of similarities relates to the network of bureaucratic institutions in each case. Mexico's federal system meant that its system diverged from the other two cases in some ways, but it was quite similar in terms of the presence of territorial administration overseen by the center, and the overlap of this network of state institutions with a set of functional institutions. In Mexico, as described in detail in the relevant case chapters, these functional institutions often operated at the state level of Mexico's federal system, while Chile and Peru were unitary systems.

In all cases, the national territory was divided into a territorial grid of various levels of subunits. Although these had different names, and varied in whether the territorial regime was federal or unitary, in all of the countries, local and regional administrative positions were filled via presidential appointment (whether directly or, in some branches of the Mexican administration, through appointment by presidential appointees). The appointment procedure for territorial administrators (intendants, governors, subdelegates, and inspectors in Chile; prefects, subprefects, governors, and deputy governors in Peru) was identical in Chile and Peru – appointments were made at higher levels in the territorial hierarchy on the recommendation of officials closer to the ground.[20]

In both countries, the two higher rungs of territorial administrators were salaried positions, and the office of intendant and prefect were commonly filled by former or current military officers, who composed what Contreras (2005, 118) describes as a "caste of mobile public functionaries whose true home base was the army." The offices of subdelegate and inspector in Chile and the analogous positions of governor and deputy governor in Peru were unsalaried. They were seen as part of the civic duty of citizens, and service was obligatory for those who did not qualify for exemptions based on age or holding another public office concurrently or previously. In addition to civic duty or sanction for not serving, these offices served two other purposes for their occupants. The first was as an entry into public service; citizens took these positions in the hopes

---

[20] On the Peruvian case, see Contreras (2005, 117ff); on the Chilean case see Vera (1886, 29).

of using them to gain access to paid offices in the future. The second, as described most clearly in Nugent (1997) for the Peruvian case, was as a means of exercising local power against rivals. In both Chile and Peru, elite dominance of localities was fairly weak, and competition among the locally wealthy unfolded to some extent through the manipulation of state institutions.

This regional apparatus overlapped with functional administrative institutions (most commonly ministries) headquartered in the national capital in realms of state activity such as education and conscription. In Chile, for example, the 1886 *Ley de Régimen Interior* made intendants responsible for overseeing state functions such as public health, security, public works, and education in their regions. Because both territorial and functional administrators reported to superiors and eventually to the capital, each class of state institutions could serve as a means of overseeing the other. This overlapping of state institutional responsibilities, because it is identical in both cases, cannot account for variation in the effectiveness of state institutions.

Technical Expertise

Nor can the technical qualifications of the rank and file, another way in which the cases were quite similar. In both Chile and Peru, the formal requirements for holding territorial administrative posts were quite few: appointees had only to be of a certain age (twenty-five if single; twenty-one if married in Chile), male, and able to read and write. The blind, deaf, mute, and those convicted of certain crimes were excluded from public service in the territorial administration. Even service in Chile's ministries had few official requirements (Urzúa Valenzuela 1970, 64ff) – candidates had to meet a minimum educational threshold and some basic skills (math or foreign languages, depending on the position) but little in the way of specific knowledge or training was required. In the 1890s, reformers like Valentin Letelier were still calling for a civil service reform that would list for the first time explicit knowledge/skill criteria for each position (Silva 2008, p. 45ff). There were some exceptions to this rule: for example, telegraph operators had to have completed the relevant course at the Instituto Nacional and to pass a series of examinations (*El Araucano* January 11, 1870, p. 4). But overall, administration in Liberal-era Latin America was far from a professional bureaucracy peopled with technical experts.

Customary Law

Scholars of colonial rule have focused on the extent of reliance on customary law as an axis of variation in administrative institutions (Young 1994; Lange 2009). Whereas direct rule is said to have integrated all members of African colonial society under European laws, indirect rule is said to have enforced customary authority, with the consequence of unifying traditional and customary authority in the community leader (Mamdani 1996). Scholars of Africa are divided about the contemporary impact of customary law – whereas Herbst (2000, 81) sees it as in practice insignificant, Lange (2009) shows that the divergence between direct and indirect rule in the British Empire underlies variation in the strength of the postcolonial state. But customary law did not play a similar role in Latin America, where the nature of the conquest ruled out reliance on traditional authority. Demographic collapse in its immediate aftermath, followed by centuries of exploitation in mining and agriculture, crippled traditional indigenous structures of authority (Coatsworth 2008). The resulting relationship between indigenous and national society was much more complex than the sharply defined group categories created by indirect rule in Africa (Mamdani 1996; Walker 1999, 11). As a result, even where indigenous authorities held sway over large portions of the population, states sought and succeeded in removing indigenous authorities as mediators in the state-society relationship.[21] Instead, they relied largely on non-indigenous mediators in a model that does not fit the category of indirect rule (Scarritt 2005, 35–37). Reliance on customary law was also precluded by the commitment of state leaders, even in the colonial era, to goals of "civilization" and "progress."[22] Colonial, rather than customary, law played a significant effort in state-indigenous relations even before independence (Walker 1999). Customary law never regained the place in official administration that it had lost before independence, as individualistic state-society relations replaced corporate rights. Unlike other

---

[21] The central aspect of state-indigenous relations was the tribute or head tax, assessed on the community as a whole with indigenous leaders responsible for its extraction. Its elimination in the mid-nineteenth century was part of a Liberal effort to dismantle the remaining structures of indirect rule (Thurner 1997; Larson 2004). These changes in taxation are explored in Chapter 5.

[22] Here I refer to a commitment dating back to the original "civilizing mission" of the conquest, which marked Spanish administration throughout the colonial era. Colonial authorities, even as they prioritized exploitation of resources both human and physical, sought with some success to stamp out customary law and practice, in favor of Christianity and Spanish legal practice.

postcolonial contexts, then, variation in Latin American state strength does not derive from a reliance on indirect rule and customary law.

CONCLUSION

This chapter has developed an institutional explanation for why state-building efforts succeed and fail. Whereas existing accounts of state building draw a direct link between incentives for state building and outcomes, I problematize the administrative challenges that state leaders face in seeking to impose control. Where state building was undertaken, it did not always succeed – and this is a crucial point missed by most existing scholarship. I trace the success and failure of these projects to dynamics internal to the state by focusing on the incentives of local administrators. Where these local officials have independent power in the communities in which they serve – power which derives from their status as local elites – they are less dependent on the state's power, and less likely to take an active role in implementing state-building policies. By contrast, where local officials are deployed into a community from outside, and depend on the state for income and standing, they have independent incentives to participate actively in state-building efforts. As I have shown in this chapter, Mexico and Chile saw deployed rule, as did Peru after 1895, while guano-era Peru saw delegated rule. These patterns of local administration align with the fate of state-building efforts: success in Mexico and Chile, as well as gains during the Aristocratic Republic (1895–1919) in Peru, as opposed to stagnation during the preceding guano years (1845–1895) in that country.

The result of this difference in administration is nothing less than the success and failure of the state-building efforts discussed in Chapters 4 to 6. There, I show that the composition of the administration accounts for variation in state-building outcomes in these cases better than do alternative explanations such as ethnic diversity, access to resource rents, and war. Before proceeding to the comparative analysis of different aspects of state capacity, Chapter 3 investigates the origins of delegated and deployed rule. It also addresses a set of alternative explanations for state-development outcomes that are based in historical differences between the cases.

3

Alternative Historical Explanations and Initial Conditions

My focus on the Liberal era as the key moment for state-building challenges accounts that highlight characteristics of earlier historical moments, such as colonialism and the independence era, as crucial in shaping state-development outcomes. This chapter begins by sketching the nature of colonial rule and the independence conflicts to show that these were not fundamental in shaping the states that emerged. Thus the first purpose of this chapter is to provide evidence that challenges alternative explanations for variation in state capacity based on earlier critical junctures.

The second purpose of this chapter is to explore the post-independence decades in all four countries, showing that their states were deeply weak, and political and economic crises severe, in these initial decades after independence. Only the emergence of a basic level of stability after about 1840 set the stage for mid-century leaders to turn to the projects of political development and social transformation that are the focus of the book. By showing that the states in the four cases were quite similar – similarly weak – as of about 1840, this chapter provides a baseline from which subsequent deviation on the outcome of interest can be assessed. Within this broad similarity, I also highlight a few differences in state capacity that predate the onset of concerted state building.

The third purpose of the chapter is to explain the choices of deployed and delegated rule shown in Chapter 2. Like any causal claim, my argument must withstand two threats to inference. The first is reverse causation, which would hold if preexisting levels of state capacity made states more likely to choose deployed rule. The second is the possibility of an omitted variable. This would hold if there were systematic differences between the cases that underlay the choices made by state leaders about populating their administration and also underlay the success and failure of state-building projects. The task, then, is to show that the form of rule is neither just an intervening variable nor an outcome of preexisting differences in state capacity. I address this in the final section of the chapter by explaining why state leaders in some countries chose deployed rule while others chose delegation to local elites.

COLONIAL LEGACIES

Mechanisms of Colonial Impact

Simple models that trace post-independence development to the extent of colonial penetration, like that of Palmer (1977), cannot account for the divergent outcomes in the colonial centers of Mexico and Peru, or for the divergence between Chile and Colombia, which were both colonial peripheries. Nor can more recent scholarship, which has focused on the nature of colonial rule rather than its intensity, account for variation in state capacity. One current of scholarship focuses on the economic institutions of colonial rule and how they shape trajectories of post-independence development (Acemoglu et al. 2001; 2002; Coatsworth 1998, 2008). Mahoney (2010) provides the most nuanced version of this account, showing that social and economic development in Spanish America were determined by the interaction of the type of colonial rule and its intensity. As the intensity of mercantilist colonialism increased, development suffered, while intensive liberal colonialism set off positive development trajectories. Mahoney also provides a more precise account of the causal mechanism linking colonial rule to development outcomes by showing how different patterns of colonial institutions distributed resources and differentially empowered collective actors. Yet Mahoney does not explain variation in *political* development. Indeed, by moving directly from the constellations of actors shaped by colonial institutions to development outcomes, Mahoney removes politics from his account altogether.

Among studies that focus more explicitly on the political effects of colonial institutions, Lange (2004, 2009) finds that, within the British Empire, direct rule is associated with positive outcomes in terms of political development. Yet the categories of direct and indirect rule do not apply in Spanish colonial America, where colonial institutions tended to "blur both categories" so this finding cannot be applied to our cases (Mahoney 2010, 23). Kohli traces the emergence of South Korea's strikingly effective

Colonialism and Independence 89

developmental state to the transformations enacted under Japanese colonial rule (1994, 2004). His study is valuable for our purposes because it focuses explicitly on the state's infrastructural power. Yet Latin America saw nothing resembling the Japanese colonization of South Korea; as Kohli acknowledges, the Japanese colonial state was both uniquely powerful and uniquely committed to the political transformation of the societies it controlled. Thus we are left with Young's (1994) more general claim that the hangover of political institutions into the republican era is crucial in explaining divergent development outcomes, but without a general theory that can link colonial and post-independence state power in Latin America.

Yet to convincingly set aside colonial state legacies, a brief exploration of the pre-indepedence era is warranted. The Bourbon Reforms provide a propitious context for examining the nature of the colonial state for two reasons. First, because they implanted identical institutions of colonial rule region-wide, the existence of the Bourbon Reforms belies theories that explain variation in development by focusing on the type of colonial institutions.[1] Second, because the Reforms took place on the very eve of independence, they reveal the nature of colonial institutions and their capacity at the twilight of colonial rule. The comparison that follows shows that Spanish administration was largely relatively weak; able to effectively implement its reforms only in Mexico. Thus neither the institutional character nor the capacity of the colonial state can explain variation in post-independence state capacity outcomes in Spanish America.

The Bourbon Reforms: State Power at the Twilight of Colonial Rule

The Bourbon Reforms are a case in which international threats promoted state building. Part of a pattern that unfolded simultaneously across the colonial world, these policies were an attempt to respond to international pressures by improving administration in the colonies, particularly in the realm of revenue extraction (Elliott 2006; Young 1994, 70). As such, the reforms had both institutional and policy components.[2]

---

[1] As described later, the Colombian case represents a partial exception to this general claim.
[2] Here I set aside another central component of the reforms – the expulsion of the Jesuits – to focus on those that relate to the state's penetration of society rather than its relationship with other structures of authority.

The centerpiece of the institutional component was an alteration of administrative organization: the creation of the intendancy as an appointed position designed to "weaken regional and local networks of interest and influence" (Stein 1981, 4). This model was introduced initially in the peripheral colonies in 1765 and thereafter in Peru (1784) and Mexico (1786). The establishment of intendancies was a means of rationalizing, systematizing, and centralizing political authority (Domínguez 1980, 71). For our purposes, the key policy component of the Bourbon Reforms was the effort to increase extraction from colonial society. The particular tax policies used varied somewhat across countries, but there was a general move to direct tax collection instead of the tax farming of the earlier colonial period, to more effective administration of state monopolies, and to greater imposition of direct taxes. Because these greater impositions prompted unrest, the Bourbon Reforms also involved an increase in the size of colonial militaries (Domínguez 1980). In all, the Bourbons attempted a "second conquest" of Spanish America (Lynch 1986, 7), and their success reveals the power of the colonial state. The discussion that follows evaluates the extent of institutional reform, increased extraction, and control of protest and threats to Spanish control in the last decades before independence in the four cases. I present the cases in order of what they reveal about the capacity of the colonial state – from weakest in Chile to strongest in Mexico, with Colombia and Peru (in that order) in the middle. This ordering shows quite clearly that variation in the extent of Spanish control cannot account for the state-building outcomes sketched in the Introduction. We see neither continuity nor a "reversal of fortune" in the development of state capacity (Acemoglu et al. 2002).

Chile

The fundamental purpose of the Bourbon Reforms was to increase the revenue that the Spanish Crown could extract from its colonies. Measured on this dimension, it becomes clear that the reforms' effect in Chile was limited at best. Before the reforms, the administration of the Chilean colony generated so little revenue for the crown that colonial administration depended on the *situado*, a sizable subsidy from Peruvian colonial revenues, to support its army and pay the salaries of administrators. The reformers eliminated the situado and established a tobacco monopoly to generate revenue. The reliance on a monopoly, rather than on the direct taxation imposed elsewhere by the Bourbons, and the inability to turn a profit from it (largely because of smuggling), reflect the limited extractive capacity of the colonial state in Chile.

Another indication of the weakness of the Chilean colonial state was reception of the administrative reforms. Because Chile was enjoying growing prosperity in the late eighteenth century, and because they created new administrative posts in Santiago which were largely filled by creoles, the Bourbon Reforms faced relatively little opposition from elites (Barbier 1980). And the reforms simply had little impact on the life of the broader population of the Chilean colony, revealing the weakness of the colonial state. Rather than leading to major revolts, as they did in Peru and Colombia where they impinged on local de facto autonomy, the Bourbon Reforms caused little disruption in Chile (Pinto Rodríguez 2003).

Colombia

Compared to most other parts of the Spanish Empire, colonial New Granada (the territory that would become Colombia) was "lightly governed" (Deas 1982, 293). The colonial state relied on four main sources of finance: the indigenous head tax, the *alcábala* or domestic transactions tax, customs revenue, and the tobacco monopoly. To supplement these, it relied on subsidies from the colonial centers of New Spain and Peru. Rather than institute new forms of taxes, the Bourbon administration sought to better collect those already on the books (McGreevey 1971, 25). Efforts to modernize taxation set off a series of revolts, of which the 1781 Comunero Rebellion was the largest. It culminated in a massive march on Bogotá by as many as twenty thousand, as rebels controlled one-third of the national territory. Colonial authorities had to rely on provincial militias to stem revolts in the absence of the army.

While the Comunero revolt was neither as bloody nor as long-lasting as Peru's Tupac Amarú revolt, it resulted in both coercive and concessionary responses from colonial authorities who feared endemic unrest (McFarlane 1984). The Bourbon state increased the number of troops in Bogotá, of which a majority were brought from Spain to ensure their loyalty. But it also backed away from efforts to transform the tax system in New Granada in order to placate the restive popular sectors. Finally, it opted not to institute the intendancy system, which allowed local elites to retain their positions in colonial administration[3] (McFarlane 1993). While the Bourbon Reforms were salient enough to spark revolt in New Granada, the fact that the colonial state was unable to impose its

---

[3] This is the one exception to the claim that colonial political institutions were invariant across the four cases.

preferred policies or administrative institutions reflects its lack of authority in this part of its empire.

Peru

The most notable impact of the Bourbon Reforms in Peru was an increase in taxation (Walker 1999, 122). This included an increase in the number of goods under state monopoly, such as gunpowder, tobacco, and playing cards as well as an increase in the head tax imposed on the indigenous population (Contreras and Cueto 1999, 80–84). Reformers installed customs houses and tax collectors even in the remote region of Puno, which was more than a week's travel time from Lima. The result is aptly summarized by Walker: the Bourbon Reforms "dramatically changed relations between Andean society and the state" in their initial phase (1999, 22).

The Tupac Amarú revolt of the 1780s, the most significant of a series of revolts that swept the heavily indigenous highlands, was a direct response.[4] The remainder of the colonial era was marked by state absence in the highlands, as the Spanish colonial administration "failed to reconquer the region after the defeat of the rebels" (Walker 1999, 13). In all, the evidence suggests that the Bourbon Reforms initially greatly increased the intensity with which the colonial Spanish state imposed its presence on the highlands, but that after the massive revolts this sparked, the state suffered a massive retreat which was not reversed before independence.[5] Thus, on the eve of independence, the Peruvian colonial state was just as weak as its Chilean and Colombian counterparts, and far weaker than the Spanish state in late colonial Mexico.

Mexico

In New Spain, the Bourbon Reforms resulted in increased internal taxation and a dramatically more powerful colonial administration as the new royal dynasty sought to replace the "old give and take of Habsburg rule" with greater centralization (Knight 2002, 240). Of the four cases under consideration, Mexico experienced the most intensive Spanish

---

[4] The causes of the Tupac Amarú rebellion are the subject of major debate among scholars. Whereas Mallon (1983, 47–48) and Jacobsen (1993, 45) attribute it to resistance to the economic impositions of the Bourbons, Walker (1999) and others see it as fundamentally proto-nationalist. Yet all agree that the Bourbon reforms were a key trigger.

[5] Mallon (1983, 48–49) characterizes the state as much more powerful in the silver mining regions of the central highlands, where an earlier uprising had led the state to heavily fortify the region. The remainder of the interior, however, saw significant retreat in the decades before independence.

presence during the colonial period, and this presence escalated during the Bourbon era.

The most striking manifestation of the strength of the Bourbon state was in taxation. The colonial state relied heavily on internal taxation rather than port taxes. High sales taxes on domestic commerce, the head tax on the indigenous population, and mining taxes made up the largest components of revenue (Chowning 1999, 47). In all, by 1790 residents of New Spain paid eighty-four categories of taxes (Tenenbaum 1986, 3). The amount of tax collected more than doubled from 1760 to 1790, with particularly large revenue increases coming from sales taxes, and from a tobacco monopoly created in 1766[6] (ibid., 4–5). Knight (2002, 246) describes late Bourbon New Spain as "an overtaxed and overgoverned society" – a description that could not apply to Chile, Colombia, or most regions of Peru.

The colonial state's strength was also reflected in its military might. Boasting in 1800 an army largely brought from Spain of nearly 10,000 as well as a militia composed of members of the upper sectors of colonial society that numbered greater than 22,000, the state was able to repress any unrest triggered by its exactions (Tenenbaum 1986, 2; Knight 2002, 252). Revolts in Guanajuato in 1767 (in response to the tobacco monopoly), and other, less severe uprisings in 1798 and 1804 (in response to financial impositions on the church) were met with intense repression (Tutino 1986, 107). The control of the state did waver at its northern frontier, where it exercised only limited oversight of its borders, and failed to effectively subdue indigenous unrest (Knight 2002, 253ff). In addition, the army, where Spanish soldiers served alongside forced conscripts, suffered from "demoralization and desertion" (253). But despite these limitations, the coercive apparatus of the Spanish crown, like its extractive power, was far more powerful in New Spain than anywhere else in mainland South America. The unique success of the Bourbon Reforms here is reflected in Domínguez's claim that they "brought unprecedented government control over the people" (1980, 74). Nothing of the kind could have been said about any of the other cases.

In all, the record of the Bourbon Reforms reveals the fact that the Spanish colonial state had a very weak hold on much of its American territory. In Chile, the colonial state had little impact on society, while in

---

[6] Unlike in Chile, where the tobacco monopoly generated little profit, it quickly became (despite, as in New Granada, facing some resistance) a significant revenue source in New Spain.

Colombia and (especially) Peru attempts to increase penetration through colonial reform efforts prompted massive unrest, which led to state retreat in the decades before independence. The intensity of colonial rule in Mexico was an exception. This pattern cannot account for the variation in state capacity observed as of 1900, which saw the states of Chile and Mexico as far stronger than those of either Peru or Colombia.

FOUNDATIONAL WARS, NEW STATES?

Nor can the nature of the wars for independence account for variation in state capacity. The independence conflicts in all four cases followed the same basic pattern. Overthrow of Spanish rule began with a sizable revolt by part of colonial society, which divided the colony into royalists and patriots as it succeeded in taking power and declaring independence.[7] This was followed by a reconquest by Spanish forces, after which brutal reprisals were committed against patriots and their supporters. Royalist forces held power for several years, but as their base of support narrowed, they were overthrown, often by patriot forces invading from outside the colony. In all cases, the conflicts failed to generate the national unity or the infrastructural and extractive capacity by which wars are said to make states, while inflicting massive economic and social costs on the newly independent societies. Thus, the independence conflicts founded independent countries, but not effective states to rule them.

In all four cases, the struggle over independence created deep divisions in society. In Mexico and Peru, the specter of class and ethnic conflict was raised from the moment independence appeared on the horizon. The war of Mexican independence began with the Hidalgo revolt of 1810, which started as protest against high food prices and rural labor market conditions, but quickly turned into "vengeance" by the poor against the landed elites (Tutino 1986, 129). In Peru, a wave of highland revolts after 1808 (highlighted by the 1814 Pumacahua rebellion in Cuzco) made elites wary of the risks of social upheaval that could accompany the independence conflict (Bonilla and Spalding 2001 [1972]). In both cases, the fear of lower-class revolt drove elites to the royalist cause initially, and made them reluctant to switch allegiance to the cause of independence. In Colombia and Chile, where the threat of indigenous revolt was lower, independence arrived more quickly. In both cases, divisions between

---

[7] In Mexico, as discussed in more detail later, the original revolt did not succeed in taking power.

royalists and patriots cut across class lines – in Colombia, these divisions meant that independence quickly deteriorated into civil war during the *Patria Boba*, as the period 1810–1816 is known (Domínguez 1980, 204). In all four cases, rather than a unifying force, the cause of independence deeply divided society. This division contributed to the ability of the Spanish state to hold on to the colonies for so long despite the damage it had suffered in the Napoleonic Wars. It also underlay the severe post-independence crises in each case.[8]

The decisive blows for independence (in all cases but Mexico) were struck by a patriot army composed mostly of foreign nationals. The result was that in no case did the mobilization of independence armies engender significant state building. San Martín's march over the Andes into Chile – in which Chilean units "played no real part" – led to the defeat of Spanish forces in 1818 (Collier and Sater 1996, 35). Both San Martín and later Bolívar led armies into Peru. San Martín was urged by Lima's elites to declare independence prematurely (royalist forces still controlled a majority of the national territory) in the hopes that his mainly indigenous troops – and the perceived threat they posed – would withdraw from the city (Lynch 1986, 179). Peruvian soldiers were present at the 1824 Battle of Ayacucho that culminated the independence conflict, but many fought on the royalist side. The two armies of independence commanded by Bolívar and San Martín were composed mostly of foreign troops, and the Peruvian troops that did join these forces were particularly prone to desertion, being relatively close to home (Bonilla 2001; Lynch 1986). The Bolivarian army that marched through the Llanos and over the Andes to defeat the Spanish at the 1819 Battle of Boyacá and liberate Colombia was composed of Venezuelan troops. It added Colombians – but only at gunpoint: forced conscription, particularly of slaves from the gold mines, was used to fill out the ranks. Only in Mexico was independence achieved without foreign intervention. But it came not due to massive domestic mobilization in support of the nationalist cause, but only after the collapse of Spanish forces, and by the decree of military leader Agustín Iturbide, who promptly crowned himself emperor. The foreign intervention and the internecine conflict that marked the independence period shows that these wars, which made the new Latin American countries

---

[8] This societal division casts doubt on the nationalism that is said (by Anderson [1983] and Padgen [1987]) to have fostered (or at least accompanied) the emergence of independence movements. For views that persuasively question the extent of this nationalism, see Hamnett (1977) and Adelman (2006).

in the sense of producing their independence, did not make states in the sense of effective and powerful governing entities.

POST-INDEPENDENCE CRISIS

After independence arrived, the new states had to reckon with continued fighting, and with the economic and social costs of the preceding decade of conflict. In Colombia and Chile, royalist holdouts engaged in guerrilla warfare in large swaths of the national territory. The *Guerra a Muerte* in southern Chile (described in more detail later in this chapter) devastated the economy's agricultural base, lasting until 1830 (Herr 2001). In Colombia, royalist guerrillas held on to the strategic region of Pasto until 1825, preventing direct access between Bogotá and Quito. In Peru, a massive rebellion in the Huanta region took up the royalist banner and established a quasi-state, collecting taxes, administering justice, and even mobilizing manpower for road and bridge repair (Méndez 2005).

No analogous regional rebellion plagued Mexico after independence, although this would change by the 1830s. Instead, the largest burden of the independence war in that country was the massive economic and social cost of the fighting: nearly 10 percent of the population was killed, mining declined by 75 percent, and agriculture and industry fell by similarly dramatic levels as a result of pillage and capital flight (Lynch 1986, 326). Peru and Chile suffered significant but lesser social and economic damage from the conflict; Colombia, on the other hand, suffered little when compared to these countries or to Venezuela (Bushnell 1993, 48–49). These economic costs were exacerbated as Spanish troops held on to key ports and coastal regions until the mid-1820s, including Callao in Peru, Veracruz in Mexico, and the island of Chiloé in Chile.

A final burden of the independence conflict was fiscal: rather than leading to the development of tax capacity, the necessities of the patriot cause led to loans (forced and foreign) and seizure of property, among other forms of emergency finance. This had long-term consequences in terms of capital flight, domestic and international debt, and political tensions as the new states were unable to make salary payments to the military or to civil servants (Bushnell 1954, 76ff). A particularly striking consequence was the sale of Chile's naval vessels to Argentina immediately after the end of the war. In Peru, the state's coffers were so empty that early years after independence saw no government domestic spending whatsoever (Tantaleán Arbulú 1983).

At the time of independence, then, states in all four countries were largely unable to exercise any significant authority over population and territory. This state weakness would persist for the next several decades, as Latin America entered a profound crisis marked by regime instability, economic stagnation, and social conflict (Halperín Donghi 1973). In these decades of crisis, the quest for order was paramount: state leaders were unable to turn to other policy projects until the fundamental instability that marked all four countries had been resolved. Only after order had been achieved – more or less at mid-century – did state leaders undertake the efforts at state development that are the subject of the next three chapters.

Before describing these efforts and explaining their success and failure, we must consider the initial conditions from which state development began. In so doing, an important alternative explanation – that Chile and Mexico already had stronger states than did Peru or Colombia, which made the efforts at state development more likely to succeed – can be dismissed. The evidence shows that in the immediate aftermath of independence, states in all four countries were weak: they were unable to effectively extract taxes from their populations, unable to provide security by preventing internal conflict, banditry, and other forms of violence, and played no role in the education of their populations. I briefly summarize the record of the strength of these aspects of the state for the four cases that follow, and highlight some exceptions to these broadly similar levels of weakness.

In showing that Chile and Mexico's states were no stronger than those of Colombia and Peru in the early decades after independence, this discussion casts doubts on claims that this variation predated the Liberal era. The similarly weak states found across all four cases also challenge an objection to the institutional argument I developed in Chapter 2. A skeptic might argue that the distinction between deployed and delegated rule is epiphenomenal because states varied in their capacity to deploy administrators to the interior, and thus the recourse to deployed rule reveals higher levels of state capacity. But this counterargument is debunked by evidence of the abject weakness of state institutions in cases where deployed rule would emerge, like that of Chile and Mexico.

Education

Although some schooling existed in each of the cases, it was vestigial at best. Public schools were rare outside the capital, standardization was absent, and in all cases private education providers played a larger role than did the state.

Chile
The first census of Chilean schools, carried out in January 1813, found only seven schools and 664 students in Santiago (Campos Harriet 1960, 12). By 1830, Santiago still had only twenty-six schools (only four of which were public) with a total enrollment of 1,723. There was little in the way of education elsewhere in the country, with the exception of a concentration of religious schools in Chiloé. (ibid., 16). The 1833 Constitution declared public education a "subject for preferential attention from the state." A flood of legislation appeared to confirm this, as convents and monasteries were required by law to open schools, and a series of decrees guaranteed free education, textbooks, and school materials to all children. Yet the national government devolved responsibility for education funding to municipalities, and its concrete actions were nearly nonexistent. The state of Chilean education was aptly summarized by Encina (vol. X, 310, cited in Campos Harriet 1960, 10): "the diligent efforts of governments to transform and extend the various branches of the education system represent ... a fireworks of laws, decrees, and measures which died before they touched reality or remained latent waiting for better times." This would change beginning in the 1840s, but before that date, public primary education in Chile was neither widely spread nor systematically organized.

Colombia
Colombian education foundered after independence. Like many other aspects of administration, it was devolved to the local level, where it was overseen by officials who "appeared to be indifferent to the state of education" (Loy 1971, 276). Finance was also a major issue, as municipal governments were unable to find the funds to open schools. The church played a major role in schooling, but even church schools were limited in number and poor in quality. In many provinces, enrollment and even the number of schools declined in the decades after independence. In Casanare, for example, the number of schools fell from nineteen to nine between 1839 and 1850, and the number of students from 285 to 223 (Rausch 1993, 69). In all, public schooling was at least as limited in Colombia as in the other countries in the early decades after independence.

Mexico

In Mexico, too, education development was slow before mid-century. Although national statistics are lacking, evidence suggests that public primary education was limited. For example, Tanck de Estrada (1977, 197) cites a figure of only thirteen public primary schools in Mexico City in 1838, with an enrollment of 1,240. Vaughan (1987) finds ten or fewer public schools in Puebla, an important regional center, at various points near mid-century.

Local jurisdictions and private actors, rather than the national government, dominated primary schooling. Municipalities retained much authority over primary education for much of the nineteenth century, although the legal locus of policymaking varied across states. No single standard for teachers existed even within states. Teacher qualifications were assessed based on an examination given by local officials and notables, and the criteria varied widely (Bazant 1998, 63). Although normal schools were opened in a variety of states, Staples (1992, 87) describes them as "ephemeral" and teacher training was far from systematized. More than any of the other cases explored in this study, private companies were central to primary education – in particular, the Compañia Lancasteriana. This organization was founded in 1822 by five prominent Mexico City residents, with the goal of bringing "modern" schooling to Mexico (Tanck de Estrada 1973). In 1842, the Santa Anna government placed all primary education in the country under its aegis, a role it maintained until 1845. Even after that point, private actors played a central role in teacher training. While education did grow slightly in the decades after independence, the lack of state intervention and oversight is striking.

Peru

Despite lofty goals – espoused, for example, in Article 184 of the 1823 Constitution, which called for opening a university in every department capital and a school in every town, and in the 1828 and 1834 constitution which guaranteed free education to all citizens – schooling in early republican Peru remained virtually nonexistent. Basadre (cited in Barrantes 1989, 69–70) cites primary schools in Lima and four other cities and three normal schools as the sum total of primary education in Peru in about 1840, and (as discussed in more detail in Chapter 4) in 1847 ten of the country's sixty-five provinces (and more than half of its 513 departments) contained not a single primary school. Thus, in terms of education, the Peruvian state in the early decades after independence had an extremely limited capacity to exercise control over its population.

Taxation

The weakness of the state's extractive capacity was particularly dramatic in Colombia and Mexico, although the states in Chile and Peru also underwent severe fiscal crises in the first two decades after independence. In none of the four cases was the state able to extract revenue from society in the form of direct taxes, nor even generate significant revenue from any source other than customs revenues. The only deviation from this overall pattern of state extractive weakness was the indigenous head tax in Peru, which revealed that the Peruvian state was able to impose some degree of extraction on some segment of its population.

Chile

During the first two decades after independence, government spending was financed largely with debt, although the government struggled at times to make payments to foreign and domestic creditors. By the mid-1830s, the state was able to generate some non-debt revenue, which came mainly from duties on imports and exports. It also relied on revenues from its monopolies on salt, tobacco, and playing cards, but collections from these sources were limited because of smuggling (MHAC 1835, 15–17). The tobacco monopoly was particularly troubled, suffering from a major corruption scandal in the late 1820s and failing to generate significant revenue. Although internal taxes were on the books, the state generated little revenue from them, finding the tithe (*diezmo*) hard to collect because it required the assessment of property, and the excise tax (*alcábala*) ineffective for revenue generation.[9] Other revenue sources such as stamps, official paper and seignorage generated negligible revenue. A real estate tax (the *catastro*) was introduced in 1834 in an effort to reduce reliance on customs duties and increase revenue, but its effects were limited. The Chilean state, in short, was unable to exercise sufficient authority over its population in order to extract taxes, reflecting its limited infrastructural power and forcing it to rely very heavily on revenues from foreign trade.

Colombia

Because of its limited export production and domestic commerce, and the long tradition of popular resistance to taxation, Colombia was "one of

---

[9] Mamalakis (1976, vol. 6, 213) suggests that the alcábala was eliminated with independence and only reintroduced in 1835, but the records of the Ministerio de Hacienda show evidence of its collection in earlier years.

the least taxable economies of Latin America" (Deas 1982, 292). The lack of commercial activity in the country led the state to limit taxation such as the *alcábala* tax on sales transactions for fear that it would discourage business development. Efforts to develop direct taxes during the Santander regime (1819–1826) foundered because of the lack of trained officials and the ease of evasion, and there was no significant progress made on this front over the next several decades (Bushnell 1954, 81ff). Without significant customs revenues, the state sought to fill its coffers with the salt, tobacco, and alcohol monopolies (in order of importance) that had been so unpopular in the colonial period. The head tax on the indigenous population failed to generate significant revenues before its elimination in 1832 (Deas 1982, 297–298). The limited revenue of the state is reflected in the fact that in 1835–1836, seignorage represented 29.9 percent of government revenues (McGreevey 1971, 40). Unable to tax internally, and without access to revenues from a flourishing export sector, the Colombian state was forced to turn to foreign loans, and to forced exactions of domestic wealth (Bushnell 1954, 112). In all, the Colombian state's extractive power was minimal for the first decades after independence.

Mexico

Having eliminated the Indian head tax immediately after independence in search of popularity, and having cut other domestic taxes to stimulate the recovery of business, early republican governments in Mexico had to find alternative sources of revenue. A tobacco monopoly and taxes on exports generated more than 50 percent of total government collections in all but one year between 1825 and 1835. Export taxes failed to generate the projected revenues, mostly because of the collapse of silver mining. They were assessed only in three ports, of which Veracruz was by far the most significant. Massive smuggling through other ports reduced revenue. Another limit on federal revenue was posed by weak federalism in the pre-1834 period: Tenenbaum estimates that 46 percent of tax revenue went into the coffers of individual states (1986, 23). Centralist administrations after 1834 did no better, also failing to develop domestic taxation (Voss 1982). Direct taxes, originally imposed on property and business during the 1836 Texas war, only generated between 3 and 17 percent of tax collections between 1836 and 1844, and once the costs of collection were deducted, the contribution to government revenue was minimal.[10]

---

[10] Unless noted, all figures in this paragraph come from Tenenbaum (1986).

Governments were forced to rely particularly heavily on short-term domestic loans with interest rates that sometimes reached 300 percent.[11] The providers of these loans, known as *agiotistas*, took over many state functions as a way to secure repayment, including road repair (in exchange for toll receipts), currency conversion, negotiation of foreign debt schedules, the postal service, and customs collections (Tenenbaum 1986). Although New Spain (as discussed previously) had seen effective taxation imposed by the colonial state, the collapse of this system during the independence conflict was not followed by a post-independence recovery. The first decades after independence saw a weak state, suffering from "pernicious financial anemia" and reliant on short-term loans and other forms of emergency finance (Knight 1992, 101).

Peru

The pattern of revenue sources in early republican Peru suggests that the state had a greater ability to extract taxes from its population than did states in the other cases. Yet its capacity should not be exaggerated: as in the other cases, short-term finance and customs revenues were crucial revenue sources. Short-term finance was generated by the sale of state bonds on future customs duties to the merchant class, as well as forced loans.[12] Customs revenues (including both import and export duties) comprised a large proportion of state revenue for the period before 1845 (Tantaleán Arbulú 1983, Appendix, Table 4). To the extent that the state relied on these two types of revenue, we can conclude that its reach over the national territory was limited, as it was in the other cases.

But the head tax on the indigenous population was also a major revenue source, and this did make Peru an outlier. Collection of this tax required a significant capacity to oversee and penetrate society. This tax, a fee imposed on each male of a certain age twice per year, was a legacy of the colonial era. Eliminated during the independence conflict as a way to win indigenous support for the patriot cause, it was reinstated in 1826 and remained one of the largest sources of projected government revenue until its elimination in 1854. For example, the 1831 budget estimated that the head tax would generate one-third of government

---

[11] Forced loans comprised another significant share of government revenues.
[12] The extent of reliance on short-term debt is the subject of debate among historians. Its role in state finance is emphasized by Gootenberg (1989, 104ff) and minimized by Klarén (2000, 138).

revenue (Gootenberg 1989, 101). Actual revenue collections, however, rarely matched these projections, demonstrating the limited ability of the state to extract revenue from the indigenous population.[13] Nevertheless, to the extent that the *contribución indígena* was collected, the Peruvian state demonstrated greater extractive capacity in the early decades after independence: it was the only one in which internal taxation was at all a significant imposition on the population, or a significant source of government revenue.

Monopoly of Force

In all four countries, the inability to tax in the early decades after independence was matched by an inability to impose order. All four cases saw states that were completely unable to exercise anything like a monopoly of coercion. The domestic disorder addressed here goes beyond common crime and insecurity to pose a challenge to the state's authority, showing that the problem of establishing order was paramount in the post-independence crisis.

Chile
In addition to the *Guerra a Muerte* that dragged on for years after independence, limits to the Chilean state's monopoly of force were highlighted by a massive wave of banditry that swept the southern half of the country. The Pincheira brothers led a band of outlaws fighting a guerrilla war against the Chilean state until 1832. Their raids extended as far as Mendoza, Argentina, and gripped the entire southern region (Herr 2001, 67ff). Their hold over such a vast territory made these bandits not only a regional menace but an obstacle to state organization and stability at the national level. Only with the capture of the last Pincheira in 1832 was a degree of order achieved.

Another obstacle to establishing order in the early decades after independence was that disputes among political elites often devolved into mass struggle. In the fighting between proponents of federalism and centralism that culminated in the Battle of Lircay in 1830, both factions, particularly federalists, "enlisted provincial troops, local peasants, and bandits to their causes" (ibid., 40). The state retained no

---

[13] A massive historiography debates the importance of the head tax for government revenues in early republican Peru, although all concede that it was a major imposition on highland society until its abolition. See Hünefeldt (1989) for a particularly skeptical view.

monopoly of force, and at times found an army (or at least individual officers and their units) unwilling to enforce the rule of law. The culmination of this trend was the military conspiracy of 1837, when Diego Portales, the country's most important political figure, was kidnapped and killed by a group of officers in the midst of the war against the Peru-Bolivian Confederation. Thus, the state's monopoly of force was challenged by both non-state actors and divisions within its coercive apparatus.

Colombia
Public order was "nearly impossible" to establish in Colombia during the decades after independence (McGreevey 1971, 87). Conflict was endemic through the 1820s, receding only in the 1830s and 1840s, which still saw significant conflict in approximately 10 percent of months and greater than 7,000 conflict deaths (ibid., Table 9). One attempt to limit the conflict was to keep the peacetime army small and thus defuse central-federal tensions, but this backfired as regional elites took advantage of the weakness of the central state to assert their claims to provincial autonomy. In response, as Posada-Carbó has argued for the case of the Caribbean provinces, the state often "had no choice but to rule with leniency" when confronted by regional elites claiming authority (1996, 28–29). When conflict emerged more along class and ethnic lines, the overwhelmed forces of the central state turned to provincial militias to reassert order. Although effective, these forces were "defending [local] property rather than [national] government" (Halperín Donghi 1973, 9). In all, the Colombian state after independence enjoyed nothing like a monopoly of force; it was more akin to a significant, and only sometimes dominant, actor in a fairly competitive protection market.

Mexico
Perhaps more than any of the other cases, the Mexican state's inability to exercise a monopoly of force led to dramatic instability over the course of the decades after independence. This time period was marked by wars of secession, waves of peasant revolts, and endemic banditry in many regions. Even Fowler, who seeks to minimize the impact of this violence, concedes that elites feared both loss of property and "social dissolution" (2000, 66). His chronology of unrest (72ff) in the years 1821–1857 finds episodes of political violence in every year, totaling at least 330 over the period. Of these, thirty-two resulted in at least twenty deaths, and twelve directly resulted in changes of government. This data suggests that the

Mexican state never enjoyed a monopoly of force in this entire period. It was only after mid-century that relative stability arrived.

Two secessionist incidents posed major domestic challenges to national integrity in the early years after independence; challenges more severe than those that emerged in any of the other cases. The first began when Texas declared independence shortly after the 1835 decision to enshrine centralism rather than federalism in the new constitution. Texan forces defeated local units of the Mexican army, as well as a punitive expedition led by Santa Anna himself, achieving and maintaining independence with the help of the United States. This help, of course, resulted in the Mexican-American War of 1846–1848, which saw Mexico lose a huge share of its territory.

Yucatecan autonomy movements, too, sought to separate the region from its *de jure* attachment to the Mexican state on many instances throughout the early decades of independence. For example, they issued their own constitution in 1841, created a flag, and declared Yucatán a sovereign nation (Reed 1964, 29). Mexican troops were defeated twice in their attempt to subdue restive regional elites. Yucatecan elites were only willing to place the region under national sovereignty when they had exhausted every alternative means of defeating the Maya rebels of the Caste War. Even after formal sovereignty returned, the state's hold over the region remained tenuous at best.

Order was also challenged by nearly constant peasant revolts.[14] In addition to causing localized economic damage and loss of life, these peasant revolts often "provoked or merged with larger regional movements" (Coatsworth 1988, 55). This peasant unrest, joined with and facilitated by elite political conflicts, was a major factor in the political instability of the early republican period. Perhaps the most serious of these revolts was the Caste War of the Yucatán.[15] Both fed by and contributing to state weakness, peasant revolts would remain a feature of Mexico for the whole of the nineteenth century (Katz 1988, 9).

Peru

The limitations of the state's monopoly of force at independence were quite severe in Peru. Long after the Spanish left the interior, and even

---

[14] For an overview of these revolts, see Coatsworth (1988).
[15] Although this conflict divided Yucatecan society on ethnic lines, Tutino (1986, 250–252) highlights the fact that in its causes and process it closely resembled peasant revolts elsewhere in Mexico.

after their 1826 abandonment of the fortress of Callao, highland communities continued to claim allegiance to the Spanish crown and refused to recognize independence. The most severe episode of this resistance took place in Uchuraccay, a community in the highland province of Huanta[16] (Méndez 2005). Over several years in the 1820s, rebels created a "regional government of sorts run by its own laws and ruled by its own authorities" (156). They were able to administer justice, mobilize manpower for road and bridge repair, and even deploy tax collectors across a wide region to generate revenue from local landowners. As a result, the Peruvian state was unable to exercise any control whatsoever in this region, and although the movement was defeated, the state never penetrated deeply enough into the rural areas to capture many of its leaders. The Huanta rebellion was unique only in the breadth of its challenge to the state: many other regions of the country saw revolts, unrest, and the inability of the state to maintain order. Security was a major issue, for example, in the mining regions of the central highlands, where mule trains carrying minerals to the port of Callao were often attacked.

The state's ability to establish a monopoly of force was limited because of the nature of the army. Rather than a national force, Peru's army was a poorly cohesive agglomeration of forces controlled separately by regional caudillos. The presence of multiple regional armies in the country led to constant conflict. There were, for example, at least seventeen revolts and conspiracies between 1829 and 1833. To prosecute these struggles, both regional caudillos and the national state were willing to rely on irregular forces of peasants, conscripted by force or (less often) with promises of shares in the spoils of victory. These troops were poorly trained, unequipped, and prone to desert. Thus, the early republican army in Peru, divided and reliant on conscripts, struggled to establish order in the country, and faced severe challenges from non-state actors. Indeed, until the guano boom of the 1840s, achieving order would be the paramount concern of governments in Lima.

The most important finding here is of an overall pattern of similar state weakness in the aftermath of independence. But a few differences can be seen: the Peruvian state was something of a positive outlier in its extractive capacity, and the Mexican state was something of a negative outlier

---

[16] Uchuraccay would become a beacon of the failure of the Peruvian state in the 1980s, when its residents murdered eight journalists in the apparent belief that they were members of the *Sendero Luminoso* guerrilla forces. Méndez (2005) argues that the roots of the state's absence in this region are fundamentally historical.

Colonialism and Independence

in terms of public order. If the overall similarity across cases shows that the great gap in state capacity only emerged after mid-century, these few differences show that legacies of the colonial era are not likely candidates for explaining it.

EXPLAINING STATE ADMINISTRATIVE APPOINTMENT PRACTICES

If the post-independence context was so similar across the cases, what were the origins of the divergent administrative practices shown in Chapter 2? Why do we see the reliance on delegation to local elites so much more often in some cases than in others? Without an answer to this question, the correlational evidence linking deployed rule and state-building success cannot be interpreted as supporting the claim that deployed rule *causes* state-building success.[17]

Although appointment decisions were made on a case-by-case basis, three factors shaped the thinking of decision makers, leading them to rely to a greater or lesser extent on delegation. State leaders knew that deployed rule would ensure more effective government. But this knowledge could not be translated into institutional choice, since appointment decisions were shaped by the context in which they were made. Three aspects of the context mattered in shaping the choices of administrative appointment in these cases. First was the perception that revolts by the lower classes and indigenous populations posed a systemic threat to the stability of the national state. Where this *perceived threat* was absent, leaders could simply choose deployed rule. Where this threat was present, state leaders would nevertheless take what they saw as a risk and turn to deployed rule if they believed that their development projects depended on undermining local elites. The place of traditional elites in their *vision of development*, in other words, was the second crucial factor. Third, where leaders feared upheaval from subaltern revolt, and were willing to ally with local elites, the *currency of patronage* used to cement this alliance mattered. Where local elites were incorporated into ruling coalitions through political offices, deployed rule was possible because state leaders could reserve administrative positions for their appointees. But

---

[17] It is important, for the purposes of assessing concerns about reverse causation, to emphasize that the outcome of interest in this book is the state's ability to effectively implement policies across its national territory. Thus evidence that some other aspect of state "strength" (which is a broad umbrella concept used in many divergent ways) facilitates deployed rule is a direct threat to my argument only to the extent that the two aspects of state strength are closely related.

TABLE 3.1. *Explaining the emergence of deployed and delegated rule*

	Chile	Liberal Mexico	Post-1895 Peru	Porfirian Mexico	Guano-Era Peru
Subaltern threat to systemic stability?	No	Yes	Yes	Yes	Yes
Traditional elite power seen as compatible with development project?		No	No	Yes	Yes
Elite support bought via political patronage?				No	Yes
Outcome	Deployed	Deployed	Deployed	Deployed	Delegated

This table shows that the three factors are *individually necessary and jointly sufficient* to explain the choice of delegated rule. Unless all three were present, the outcome was deployed rule.

where coalitions were cemented with administrative posts, leaders had no choice but to opt for delegated rule. These three factors, as scored for the cases, are arrayed in Table 3.1, which shows the logic of the discussion that follows.

Perceived Threats to Systemic Stability

Where state leaders feared that revolt by rural subaltern populations would be truly destabilizing, they needed powerful allies at the local level, and this led them to fortify their ties to local elites. A likely option for state leaders was to incorporate local elites into the bureaucracy – i.e., by establishing delegated rule. Delegation would build an alliance between the central state and these elites, reducing the chances of elite defection that could turn subaltern unrest into regional rebellion. Administrative positions would also strengthen the hand of local elites in responding to unrest in their communities by adding the legitimacy that came with office-holding to their reservoir of local authority. State leaders had to consider forgoing the benefits of deployed rule when they needed to buttress the power of elites who would help maintain order and social hierarchy at the local level. On the other hand, where this fear was absent and state leaders considered the political context to be fairly stable, they saw no reason to adopt delegated rule. Thus, the absence of a threat of

Colonialism and Independence 109

systemic unrest (as in Chile) was sufficient to induce state leaders to opt for deployed rule. Where this fear was intense, leaders' choices depended on the other factors discussed later.

Chile

As Chilean national leaders built their bureaucracy during the second half of the nineteenth century, they did so without any fear of systemic upheaval. To some degree, this belief was based on the historical record. In Chile, no major insurgency colored the late colonial period, and the independence conflict cut across social divisions in the country, rather than polarizing them. Although it was an internecine conflict, it did not include a major uprising by the rural poor as it had in Mexico, nor did it divide elites as deeply as did the independence conflict in Peru. But crucially, this perception that national institutions were not threatened by subaltern uprisings took hold despite two types of significant upheaval: massive waves of banditry in the southern heartland, and waves of conflict with the Mapuche indigenous population on the as-yet unclosed southern frontier. Chile was far from calm in the first half century after independence, but unrest and violence did not scare state leaders enough to affect their institutional design choices.

The most dramatic manifestation of violence was nearly a decade of guerrilla war after the final declaration of independence in Santiago. This war, known as the *Guerra a Muerte* (War to the Death), was first fought by Mapuche communities who were concerned with the changes that independence might bring to the *entente* they had developed with the Spanish colonial state, and then by bandits, most notably the Pincheira brothers, in an alliance with a Mapuche subgroup (Bengoa 1985).

More generally, Chile's countryside was assailed by massive waves of crime against persons, property, and state institutions throughout the mid-nineteenth century; reports by government officials from the first decades after independence refer to a great deal of banditry. But this was never seen as a threat to the national state but solely as a threat to local order and economic stability. Police were scarce outside urban areas, and the army was often called into duty to combat these depredations, which were most severe in the south. As Bengoa (1999, 154) described, the "state of the south" was not consolidated to the same extent as the "state of the center," as state leaders focused on the booming mining regions of the north. Through much of the mid-nineteenth century, there were years in which one could not travel between Talca and Chillan, or through the province of Aconcagua, because of bandits (Monteverde 1999). Insecurity in this region intensified in the aftermath of the 1859 Revolution, when members of the defeated forces took to the hills to wage a campaign of guerrilla warfare against the Chilean state, and made "pillage" and armed robbery common in various parts of the country, mainly the southern agricultural regions between Santiago and the Mapuche frontier (MINT 1860, 19). The rural regions of the province of Talca, for example, were "notorious" as the refuge for bandits who plagued landowners and small communities in the surrounding area (MINT 1865, Vol. II, 137).

Yet despite this clear lack of calm in much of the country, elites in Santiago didn't fear for national stability. Even the *Guerra a Muerte*, which swept large sections of the southern heartland for a full decade, did not scare state elites, despite the fact that recent commentators have described it as a threat to national stability (Bengoa 1985). This conflict was seen not as a case of an oppressed group, but as a problem of public order where the state confronted "traitors who broke established rules of conduct and therefore needed to be eliminated."[18] Officials in Santiago were confident that extirpating individual bandit leaders would eliminate the source of the conflict. This conflict, in short, was seen as episodic, rather than endemic.[19]

Tensions with the Mapuche, too, were seen in the same light. Chile is often erroneously lumped in with Argentina as an ethnically homogeneous "European fragment" in which the indigenous population, already small, was eliminated. And we might imagine that homogeneity might account for this perception of relative security among Chilean elites. But this was not the case – Chile was far more ethnically complex than was Argentina, and relations between the state and the indigenous population were tense. Most important for our purposes was the Chilean state's complicated relationship with the Mapuche community, which occupied territory on the southern frontier that the Chilean state had never effectively penetrated. The Mapuche and the state had a long entente (since about 1640) on the unfinished frontier dating back to the early colonial era, and thus the waves of unrest described previously were seen as continuity in a fluid and complex relationship (Pinto Rodríguez 2003, 31ff). Until the mid-nineteenth century, the Mapuche were seen as fundamentally Chilean. O'Higgins and other independence-era leaders had talked of the Mapuche (and other indigenous communities) as citizens of the new republic rather

---

[18] Herr (2001, 92) cites this language in state documents of the time.
[19] I borrow the language of episodic and endemic conflict from Slater (2010) who argues that only the latter will drive the emergence of state-building coalitions.

than as a separate ethnic group, and until the mid-nineteenth century "the dominant view was that Araucanía formed part of the national territory and that the Mapuche, although a different nation, should form part of the broad national brotherhood" (ibid., 87).

The rise of liberal-positivist ideas in the 1840s began to alter this view, emphasizing that the lack of legal uniformity that allowed the Mapuche to govern themselves under long-outdated colonial laws was a threat to equality. The Mapuche decision to side with the rebels in the failed 1851 Revolution provided the pretext of a "threat" that could motivate occupation by land speculators supported by the state, but this threat was more a justification than a real concern (Pinto Rodríguez 2003, 151ff). The assimilation policy that followed was driven largely by economic changes rather than by the perception that the indigenous posed a fundamental threat to the state or to social order.[20] The expansion of the Chilean agricultural economy and of state institutions into the territories occupied by the Mapuche prompted serious unrest on the southern border. The insecurity was highest in three waves: an "almost total uprising of the mapuches" (Bengoa 1999, 169) coincident with the 1859 Civil War, a major insurrection in 1868–1869, and another uprising that began in 1881.[21]

The first significant wave of unrest in the region began with the participation of many bands of Mapuche in the 1859 Civil War.[22] The "guerilla war" this prompted lasted until the end of 1861, and the army was "unable to do anything but resist some of the attacks" (Ruiz-Esquide 2000, 123). The effects of the violence cut a broad swath through the southern frontier: the important town of Los Angeles (as well as other communities) had to be abandoned, and every Chilean settlement south of the Bio-Bio was destroyed. Ruiz-Esquide (2000, 128) claims that 35,000 cows, 50,000 sheep, and 5,000 horses were lost, as well as more than 1 million pesos of damage to agricultural production. This was the

---

[20] The efficacy of the post-1860s assimilation effort, although beyond the scope of this project, reveals the strength of the Chilean state. Until a certain degree of indigenous mobilization in the last several decades (Mallon 2005), the limited salience of indigenous identity in Chile reveals a state that (as in Eugen Weber's [1978] landmark study of France) was able to assert control over its population and impose homogeneity on its national community.

[21] HEC 7, 265–266 refers to another such wave of banditry during the 1891 Civil War and its aftermath, although it seems to have been less severe.

[22] The participation of indigenous groups on both sides of this conflict mirrored the pattern of the less significant fighting during the 1851 Civil War.

most significant outbreak of violence in southern Chile since the Pincheira revolts three decades earlier.

The increased southward pressure of Chilean agriculture prompted a second major wave of violence in 1868–1869.[23] Indigenous communities amassed a force of about 6,000 to attack settlers, a force much larger than the Chilean army presence in the region of some 1,400 men. This prompted a harsh response from the Chilean army. In late 1868 and early 1869, Chilean army units of 100 to 1,200 soldiers carried out twenty-one expeditions against Mapuche communities, killing more than 200, injuring a similar number, taking nearly 100 prisoners, and capturing more than 12,000 animals (which were sold to pay for the operations) at the cost of thirty-five killed soldiers.

The third wave of violence on the southern frontier coincided with the War of the Pacific, which saw the deployment of the Army of the South to Peru and its replacement with less effective National Guard units from the communities of Angol, Malleco, Tijeral, and Curaco (HEC 4, 279). This opportune context fostered a wave of Mapuche uprisings in 1881 and 1882, which escalated to include the cutting of telegraph lines and attacks on many Chilean settlements. Chile responded with a determination to achieve the final pacification of the region. This final conflict involved thousands of troops recently returned from the fighting in Peru, and culminated with the capture of Villarica in 1883.

Yet despite decades of violence, contention, and massive military campaigns on the southern frontier, and despite the fact that the Mapuche conflict was seen as endemic, it was not perceived as a threat to Chilean state stability. Pinto Rodríguez (2003, 84–85) shows that presidents came into office concerned about it, but it became less of a policy priority (as reflected in public speeches) over the course of their terms. The equanimity with which this conflict was viewed may have had geographic roots. There was no sense that the Mapuche were interested in, or capable of, marching on Santiago, or that the conflict could spread northward to important population centers. Indeed, the location of the conflict moved steadily further from the national center over time as the frontier expanded southward. It posed no direct threats to elites in the capital, or to any significant portion of the wealthy sectors of Chilean society, who

---

[23] My discussion of this wave of fighting draws on the detailed account in Esquide-Ruiz (2000, 194ff), which summarizes the findings of Bengoa and other scholars as well as primary source accounts of the violence.

lived far from the frontier.[24] This equanimity also had ideational roots – as liberal positivism took hold in Chile, it brought a belief that progress would obviate the ethnic divisions over time, bringing a natural end to fighting.

The important thing for our purposes, however, is that political elites' perception of systemic stability existed despite rather intense unrest in the south. This perception did *not* derive from the fact that the Chilean state already enjoyed effective control over its national territory. It derived, instead, from the belief that unrest and violence in the south posed no endemic and unmanageable threat. Because Chilean state leaders did not perceive the same degree of social unrest and political instability as did their Mexican and Peruvian counterparts, the choice to rely on deployed rule, which promised reliably loyal bureaucrats, was an easy one. This alone, then, was sufficient to determine the institutional outcome of deployed rule in Chile.

Mexico

Nineteenth-century state leaders in Mexico, by contrast, perceived major threats from peasant unrest. These views were shaped both by memories of revolts past and by major indigenous revolts in the present. The Mexican independence struggle was the "most plebeian of the Spanish American revolutions," marked by a massive lower-class uprising that threatened to eliminate elite control (Halperín 1973, 4). The memory of the independence-era Hidalgo rebellion lived on in the minds of state leaders, and its salience was reinforced by active indigenous unrest that persisted long after the independence era.

The most salient instance of indigenous uprising was undoubtedly the "Caste War" of the Yucatan, but early republican Mexico also saw violence by indigenous populations along the northern border and in the mountain regions of central Mexico (Bazant 1991). Indeed, early republican Mexico saw nearly constant peasant revolts (Coatsworth 1988). Beyond causing localized economic damage and loss of life, these peasant revolts often "provoked or merged with larger regional movements" (Coatsworth 1988, 55). Rebellions by indigenous and peasant communities remained endemic well into the Porfiriato, including the Yaqui Rebellion of 1896 (DeHart 1984) and a major revolt in Chihuahua in 1891 (Vanderwood 1998).

---

[24] Bauer (1975), in his survey of rural life in Chile's central valley during the nineteenth century, never mentions the issue.

The salience of conflict involving lower classes dampened political conflict between elites, which emerged only when "social subversion" was no longer an imminent danger (Bazant 1991, 27). The fear of revolts among elites can be seen in their political behavior. Most dramatically, it was revealed in the reluctance of Liberals and Conservatives to rally Mexico's massive indigenous peasantry to their cause throughout their decades of intra-elite conflict. Only the war against the French led elites to risk unrest by calling on the lower classes to join the struggle – and "again, once organized, the popular movements did not show signs of subsiding quickly" (Katz 1991, 53).

Peru

As in Mexico, the specter of systemic revolt loomed large in the minds of Peruvian state leaders. Memories of the Tupac Amaru revolt of the 1780s "served as an example of what could happen" (Davies 1970, 4). Independence era rebellions in Cuzco and elsewhere also reminded leaders of the unrest that appeared constantly latent in highland regions. Upsurges of contention from below seemed to emerge whenever gaps opened in national stability, whether during the Bourbon Reforms, the independence era, moments of elite conflict, or (most notably) the period of Chilean occupation that followed the War of the Pacific. The fear of another Tupac Amaru revolt persisted even during the period of "remarkable indigenous quiescence" that lasted from the unrest in the aftermath of the independence struggle to the Huancané rebellion of 1866 (Gootenberg 1993, 199).

When significant violence of any kind did break out, it was consistently seen by large sectors of Lima officialdom through the lens of "caste wars," "Indian massacres," and "racial terror." The 1885 Atusparia rebellion, the largest since independence, reignited these fears first instilled by the Tupac Amaru revolt and "left an indelible mark of dread on elite consciousness" (Thurner 1997, 103). Elsewhere in the highlands, landowners "constantly feared attacks" (Jacobsen 1993, 327), and were thus reluctant to mobilize the indigenous population.[25]

When considering policies that impinged on the indigenous population – most notably taxation and forced labor – officials were constantly sensitive to the threat of revolt. Indeed, the insights of historians

---

[25] Elites did mobilize indigenous communities in episodes of domestic conflict in post-independence Huanta and some parts of the Central Highland (Méndez 2005; Mallon 1983, 48–49).

Colonialism and Independence 115

such as Thurner and Mallon about negotiation between the state and subalterns find particular resonance in highland Peru. This fear also led to the surveillance and control of the indigenous population by local and national officials, including careful observation of popular participation in festivals in Cuzco (Walker 1999, 179ff). Passports for domestic travel were required of the indigenous population until 1851 (Davies 1970, 28).

Fear also underlay the projects pursued by guano-era state leaders and their Civilista analogs: in addition to prosperity, the goal of development efforts was a transformation of the "savage" indigenous population, to turn them from a threat and economic deadweight into productive members of a "civilized" and "modern" society. While the thinking of state leaders often emphasized the need to protect and incorporate the indigenous population, the threat posed by this group was omnipresent in their calculations.[26] The threat of indigenous unrest, in other words, was just as salient in the minds of Peruvian leaders as it was among their Mexican counterparts. In both countries, leaders had to weigh the stability of social hierarchies against the establishment of reliably loyal bureaucracies. Yet while Peruvian and Mexican leaders faced the identical dilemma, they responded differently.

A skeptical reader might argue that the perception of threat was related to demography – the size of the indigenous population, in a more parsimonious argument than the one I develop, might explain administrative choice. After all, Chile did have a smaller and more geographically isolated indigenous population than did the other countries. But even if we grant this claim, the demographic argument cannot account for the difference in form of rule between Mexico and Peru, which had different forms of rule despite similarly sized indigenous populations. Nor can it account for change over time in Peru. The choice of institutions of state administration is not simply reducible to demographic factors.

Nor is deployed rule, as one might expect, a function of preexisting levels of state capacity. Indeed, there are several reasons to doubt this claim of reverse causation. First, as the earlier parts of this chapter showed, the Chilean state was fundamentally weak in the decades after independence, differing little from the other cases. Second, the historical record shows serious unrest in Chile, but this unrest did not translate into elite fear. Third, the Mexican state was particularly weak in terms of coercive capacity, but (for reasons discussed later) its leaders

---

[26] Thus Gootenberg's claim of a "national amnesia" about the indigenous population during the guano era seems a bit overstated (1993, 199–200).

opted for deployed rule. Finally, deployed rule was introduced in Peru after 1895 in a moment of state crisis far more severe than any of the guano-era moments, an outcome that cannot be explained by preexisting state capacity.

The Place of Traditional Authority in National Projects

Where indigenous populations and lower classes did pose a fundamental threat to stability, state leaders confronted a complex tradeoff. In Mexico and Peru, state leaders had to choose between deployed rule, which had the risk of undercutting local elites and facilitating mass uprising, and delegated rule, which weakened state power by diluting the implementation of state policies. State leaders were swayed toward delegation or deployment depending on two factors. The first, discussed here, was the place of traditional elites in the ideological views of national leaders. Where state leaders' view of the means to "order" and "progress" saw traditional elites as a central obstacle, they were unwilling to ally with them. But where local elites were not seen as a threat to the transformations sought by state leaders, an alliance based on administrative delegation was possible.

Because early and late state-builders in Mexico and Peru saw local and regional elites differently, here I periodize the discussion into two eras in each country. In Liberal Mexico (1857–1876) and Civilista Peru (1895–1919), state leaders believed that development *depended on* undermining local elites; to ally with them would undo a core element of their state-building efforts. Despite their fears of unrest, they were unwilling to ally with local elites, choosing instead to risk revolt and supplant them in pursuit of what they saw to be long-term development projects. By contrast, state leaders during the Mexican Porfiriato (1876–1910) and the guano era (1845–1879) in Peru did not see traditional elites as an obstacle to their visions of development, and thus they were willing to consider delegation as a solution to the unrest they feared.

Anti-Traditional Ideology in Liberal Mexico (1857–1876)

During the Restored Republic, tensions between Liberal state leaders and traditional elites were significant. Although they were also fixated on the power of the church and the communal landholding institutions of Indian communities, Liberals believed that transforming Mexico required eliminating the hacienda, replacing it with small landholders, to create the rural social conditions for economic modernization (Sinkin 1979,

25; Haber 1989, 19). During deliberations at the 1857 Constitutional Congress, many politicians decried the power of caudillos, and the document that emerged included many clauses that challenged the power of local elites (ibid., 67–68). It was clear after 1857 that the full flourishing of the Liberal project would depend on reducing the authority of provincial elites. This "antielite rhetoric" worsened relations between Liberals and elites, even as many elites "approved of key elements of the Liberal program" (Chowning 1999, 245).

Sinkin argues that the Liberals initially "sought the total destruction" of the local power of provincial elites (1979, 97). The radical rhetoric of Liberal leaders, and their threatening actions, left elites disenchanted with politics and "drove many of them to the political sidelines" during the Liberal era (Chowning 1999, 246). Liberal land reforms inflicted major costs on longtime, cash-poor landowners by replacing the church with private creditors (Chowning 1999, 271–273). Liberals "most approved" of haciendas "that were being worked intensively by owners or renters willing to experiment with new crops and new activities, buy new equipment, and invest large sums in increasing production" (ibid., 237). There, practices were not characteristic of traditional landowners.

Liberals did come to need many local powerholders, including traditional landowners, as allies in the Reform War and the subsequent struggle against the French Intervention. The decade of conflict that followed the proclamation of the 1857 Constitution made Liberals "almost totally dependent on the good will and military expertise of these local chiefs" (Sinkin 1979, 105). Thus, although "the ultimate goal of the Reform program was the destruction of the traditional caudillo system of politics," Liberals were forced to temper their transformationist zeal and ally with traditional elites. As Hale (1989, 22) pithily states, "liberalism ceased [after 1867] to become a combative ideology." Indeed, by the end of the Restored Republic, elites and liberals had mended their relationship. Liberals emphasized "relatively uncontroversial, indeed greatly desirable projects from the elite point of view" such as material improvements, tax reductions, and the abolition of Indian communities, and many economic elites aligned themselves firmly in the Liberal camp (Chowning 1999, 304). This version of liberalism was "discursively inclusive" (ibid., 332) and moderate in comparison to the pre-reform version.

During the period of Liberal rule, then, state leaders believed that their state-building project depended on the weakening of traditional authority. This made them reluctant to delegate administration to local caudillos. Direct threats to their hold on power forced the Liberals to ally with these opponents of their project in order to defeat the French and consolidate power. But crucially, even as this alliance endured through the Restored Republic, state leaders sought ways to weaken the local power monopolies of caudillos, and they made significant progress by 1876. This focus on weakening traditional elites made Liberal leaders in Mexico reluctant to rely on delegated rule despite their concerns about systemic stability. This was sufficient to explain why they tended to opt for deployed rule.

The Absence of Ideology in Porfirian Mexico (1877–1910)
Unlike the Liberals he succeeded, Porfirio Díaz did not see economic elites as an obstacle to the change he sought in Mexico. In turn, elites supported the "order and progress liberalism" that Díaz promised to bring (Chowning 1999, 305). Justo Sierra and other Porfirian political thinkers believed that economic elites, who had a stake in the decisions made by the government, should be involved in it (Hale 1989). Unlike their Liberal predecessors, these self-styled "Conservative Liberals" (also known as *científicos*) believed that elites were a "great potential force" for stability (ibid., 35). Thus while two prominent Liberals in 1893 decried the "tyranny of the upper classes" (Hale 1989, 117), Díaz was assiduously building ties with elites who controlled state and local politics. Although the state intervened little if at all in providing social policy, it engaged in what Haber (1989, 23) describes as extensive government intervention to benefit the powerful. As Chowning shows, elites were happy to be courted by the regime, although they remained outside the formal political arena (1999, 334–335).

The Liberals had been reluctantly pulled to focus on practicality as opposed to grand ideas. But Porfirio Díaz represented "the end of ideology." As Knight writes, he "displayed more appetite for power than adherence to principle" (1986, I, 15). Thus he had no commitments to grand social transformation that precluded alliances with local powerholders. Ideology, then, played no crucial role in determining the form of local administration during the Porfiriato. State leaders were willing to cement security by allying with local elites, although this did not (for reasons explained later) lead to delegated rule.

Accomodationist Ideology in Guano-Era Peru (1845–1875)
Because state leaders during the guano era in Peru did not see local elites as an obstacle to development, they did not find it inappropriate to rely

on them to represent the state in the national periphery.[27] Gootenberg finds that they developed a project of "traditional modernization" (1993, 8) that was practical and flexible rather than ideological. None of the thinkers he discusses – which include many important members of the guano-era political class such as Manuel Pardo – saw rural elites as an obstacle to development. Many (including Pardo) believed that guano wealth provided an opportunity to transform society precisely by improving the economic condition of these oligarchs through the promotion of non-guano exports.[28] This project of regional developmentalism would draw the country together, bringing local elites into alliance with the state and repairing the breaches of regionalist tensions from the pre-guano era. (Larson 2004, 150) Elites in the central and southern highlands were a particular focus of this effort.

In political terms, the Civilista project of the 1860s and 1870s "was an attempt to extend the fundamental accord that existed [among the bourgeoisie] to notables throughout the country." (Muecke 2004, 37) Indeed, Pardo's party organization and campaign for the 1872 presidential election created a national community of notables, integrating "regional and provincial elites" into the state. (ibid., 38) The 1873 decentralization was a demonstration of this development model. As Muecke (38) describes, it gave "the provincial elites a free rein in their districts." Because their vision of development did not depend on weakening the local authority of traditional elites, state leaders in Peru were willing to rely on these notables as local and regional administrators.

Anti-Traditional Ideology in Postwar Peru (1895–1919)

Horrified by the loss in war to Chile and the tumult that followed, the Civilistas were determined to take a different approach to national reconstruction than that of their predecessors. The Cáceres government of the immediate postwar period had sought political stability and fiscal recovery via radical decentralization that empowered local elites. The consequences, both in fiscal terms and in terms of stability, were strikingly negative, as highlighted by the weakness of the state during this period shown in Chapters 4–6. The Civilistas concluded from this experience that decentralization was a fundamentally flawed administrative model, and that the empowering of local elites had also undermined

---

[27] In the same vein, Peruvian liberals also incorporated church and Indian communal structures in their visions of progress and social transformation (Muecke 2004, 13).
[28] Pardo's "national project" is similarly described in McEvoy (1994).

state-development efforts during the prewar period. The crisis of the preceding decades forged a broad consensus that Peru needed drastic changes in order to survive as a nation, and that "the country had squandered seventy years of independent existence" (Contreras and Cueto 1999, 142–143). Thus, they were determined to chart a new course.

For Piérola and the Civilistas, national reconstruction depended on the removal of local elites from positions of authority and the establishment of centralized administration.[29] Although centralization was in part an ad hoc response to the failures of administrative and fiscal decentralization and to the weakening of local elites during the preceding decades, its central place in the Civilista governing program was a consequence of their ideological commitment to national transformation through state building (Contreras 2001). Thus, an explicit plank of Civilista administration was an effort to weaken the hold of local elites over the peripheral regions of the country. State leaders saw the power of local elites as problematic in two senses. First, it allowed these elites to abuse the indigenous population, which contributed to unrest (Mallon 1983). Second, local elites were seen as ineffective administrators by contrast to the educated coastal core of the Civilista coalition, a view buttressed by the failures of education development, tax collection, and the suppression of revolts in the postwar period (Thurner 1997). The view that empowering local elites was an obstacle to state development led to an effort to eliminate delegated rule. Instead, the Civilistas explicitly sought to transform Peru's administration with the imposition of deployed rule where they could.

Thus in post-1895 Peru and Liberal Mexico, deployed rule emerged because of beliefs that traditional elites were an obstacle to political development and stability. But in Porfirian Mexico and guano-era Peru, the choice of form of rule was not fully accounted for by the factors discussed thus far. To account for the different patterns in these cases, we need to examine the nature of patronage.

The Currency of Patronage

The third and final factor shaping the choice of deployed or delegated rule was the nature of patronage used to incorporate local elites into ruling coalitions. Where political positions were the currency of coalition

---

[29] Civilista concerns about local power monopolies were centered on the highlands regions that had seen the most unrest in preceding decades. Less concern was expressed about the power of local elites in the north coast regions from which most Civilistas were drawn.

building, elites could be incorporated through seats in elected office. This allowed state leaders to cement alliances with local elites and ameliorate their fears of revolt, while still allowing administration to be populated in a manner likely to produce more effective governance. Porfirian Mexico followed this pattern, leading to deployed rule. But where the currency of patronage was administrative office, those positions were given to local elites, and were not available for deployed rule. Alliances in guano-era Peru were cemented with administrative appointments, and this (along with the two factors discussed previously) explains why delegated rule was adopted in that case alone among those studied in this book.

Political and Federal Patronage in Mexico

Mexican state leaders had access to three patronage options in wooing elites to their coalitions: regional and local power in Mexico's federal system, elected office in the national government, and appointments to the national bureaucracy. Both Liberal and Porfirian state leaders used only the first two to build ruling coalitions. Few positions in the national bureaucracy were used to buy elite loyalty, and this allowed the national state to fill its administration with deployed rule because the need for patronage had already been satisfied.

The most important mode of incorporation of elites into the ruling coalition took place through elected office (Knight 1986, I, 20). The central axis of Restored Republic politics was ins against outs, and the positions at stake were largely political. Perry (1978) argues that the political machine built by Juárez and his successors in Mexico revolved around elected offices. The introduction of the Senate in 1874 was one example of Liberal efforts to use elected office to win over elites: it "provided fifty well-paid sinecures to be distributed among hand-picked partisans" (Perry 1978, 183). Díaz continued this pattern: he ensured elite access to most national political positions (Camp 1995, 173ff). The centrality of political office in state-elite relations in Mexico can be seen most clearly in the salience of the slogan of "no re-election." As Perry (1978, 187) traces, this slogan came into use in 1867 because elites such as Porfirio Díaz resented exclusion from the Liberal political machine.

Another means of incorporating elites was state-level patronage. Both Liberals and Porfirio Díaz faced opposition from local and regional-level elites. To co-opt these *caudillos* and *hacendados*, national leaders often appointed them as governors (Perry 1978, 5–6). The governor had control over state-level bureaucratic appointments (ibid., 97). Importantly, however, governors themselves were often deployed to states where they had few local ties. While they built local bureaucratic machines, state executives owed much of their power to the president rather than to local society. Thus, elites were rewarded for supporting the regime, but in a way that removed them from their local bases. Knight estimates that 70 percent of Díaz-era gubernatorial appointments were "presidential favorites imported into alien states where their prime allegiance was to their president and maker rather than to their provincial subjects" (1986, I, 17). Pittman (1989) provides a detailed account of tensions around the deployment of a governor in Morelos. Conflict between the governor and local elites revolved around administrative appointments, as governors, too, used deployed rule to consolidate authority against the large landowners in the state (pp. 32, 39–40, 122–123).

Thus, Mexican political machines encompassed elected office at the national level and many subnational positions. But many subnational administrative positions were filled via deployment, and positions in the national bureaucracy were less commonly allocated to local elites. This allowed Porfirian state leaders to both fill the ranks of the bureaucracy through deployed rule, and to combine robust ties with elites and the pursuit of administrative efficiency.

Administrative Patronage in Peru

National politicians in Peru relied on administrative patronage, drawing local elites into their coalitions by distributing bureaucratic offices and reserving political appointments for Lima-based elites. Economic elites multiplied their success by investing in political coalitions, receiving in return access to administrative positions (Jacobsen 1993, 332). Politicians built networks of support in their local and regional constituencies by ensuring the appointment of local elites to administrative offices at the local and regional level (ibid., 239–240). Indeed, Nugent (1997, 47–48) claims that elected office was only valuable insofar as it provided access to control over administrative appointments.

By contrast to the composition of the administration, the composition of political office-holders incorporated few regional elites. Residency requirements for elected office were limited, and politicians often were elected from multiple jurisdictions in the course of their careers (Peloso 1999). As Muecke's study of the 1868 and 1872 elections shows, the Civilista party leadership excluded regional elites: it was "composed entirely of Lima residents who claimed to represent the interests of the entire country" (Muecke 2004, 65–66). Party statutes "impeded the integration of the regional elites into the national executive" (67). The centralized and hierarchical nature of the party made local and regional party officers subject to national offices, giving those outside the national junta little power. Because they sought to dominate elected office, political party leaders chose not to use access to those positions as they built their coalitions. The resulting reliance on administrative patronage is the final element in accounting for the adoption of delegated rule in guano-era Peru.

CONCLUSION

Before proceeding to the coming chapters, which provide a comparative analysis of state building in the four cases, it is worth reinforcing what we've learned so far. First, this chapter has shown that Latin or American states in general were quite weak at independence, and little changed in the first few decades after colonial rule ended. The evaluations of three dimensions of state capacity across four countries in the third part of this chapter showed striking similarities, with partial exceptions appearing in the greater extractive capacity of the Peruvian state (through the institution of the head tax) and the lower level of security provided by the Mexican state in comparative perspective. The overall similarity cannot explain subsequent variation in state capacity, nor can the two outliers.

Second, there are no differences in state capacity across cases in the colonial or independence-era trajectories that line up with subsequent variation. Without claiming that these four cases are identical, this chapter has shown that they entered the mid-nineteenth century as similar, and this similarity is especially striking given the degree of variation that emerged over the succeeding decades. Variation did not emerge until after 1840; our search for its origins in the Liberal era that began several decades after independence unfolds in the next three chapters.

4

State Projects, Institutions, and Educational Development

As the first part of this chapter shows, our four cases display wide variation in the development of public primary education. The spread and systematization of public primary education in Chile and in some (but not all) of Mexico's states far outstripped that in Peru and Colombia. This reflects a divergence in the state's ability to incorporate citizens into public schools and to control educational content, and this variation provides an opportunity to test the explanation for the origins of state capacity developed in the first two chapters against an alternative view (sketched in the second section of the chapter) that prioritizes social diversity and economic inequality as the fundamental causes of limited progress in schooling. I do so in the remainder of the chapter by drawing on a combination of within-case process-tracing, cross-temporal comparison, and within-case statistical analysis.

I find that the failure of educational development in Colombia can be traced to the lack of interest by state leaders in its spread or systematization. While education was seen as crucial to the country's development, a broad range of political elites believed it best to leave its installation in the hands of local government, the church, or private actors. Just as in the dimensions of Colombian state building explored in Chapters 5 and 6, there was no effort to increase the state's control of education. This confirms the argument developed in Chapter 1 tracing Colombian state weakness to the absence of a state-building project.

Efforts to build public educational systems in the other three cases succeeded and foundered depending on the form of administration, as theorized in Chapter 2. When Chilean state leaders sought to increase the provision of schools, and to shape the content and conduct of education, they were able to do so because their policies were implemented by deployed bureaucrats. Moreover, the case study of the development of Chilean school inspection shows that these deployed bureaucrats went beyond implementing policies that systematized education: these local agents of the state pushed the central state to increase its oversight and penetration of the primary school classroom, and thus, for their own purposes, drove Chilean state building. This supports the claim, put forward in Chapter 2, that deployed bureaucrats have an *independent* interest in state building.

The Peruvian case also provides within-case evidence showing that deployed rule is crucial for the success of state-development efforts. The development of Peruvian education divides into two periods: one of stagnation of national government efforts (1845–1895) and one of striking success (1895–1915). After fifty years of thwarted efforts at educational development, a shift to educational administration through deployed rule led to dramatic gains in the public primary school system after 1895, even as social conditions made educational development *less* likely.

Social conditions have formed the basis of the most compelling existing arguments for variation in educational development. Scholars have claimed that the economic inequality engendered by plantation agriculture or mining, and the social inequality associated with the presence of a large indigenous population, have kept national governments in the hands of actors (the wealthy) who oppose educational development because of its redistributive properties. The result, these scholars claim, is that the development of primary schooling is negatively correlated with inequality and social diversity. The switch in forms of administration in Peru after 1895 provides an opportunity to assess the relative weight of this structural argument and my institutional alternative. If, as I find, the fate of educational development alters sharply with institutional change, this should lead us to favor the role of administrative institutions in mediating the ability of elites to block state-building efforts.

Mexico, too, provides a propitious climate for testing these claims. Because educational policy was in the hands of the states in Mexico's federal system, we can examine cross-state variation in trajectories of the growth of the school system. I present statistical evidence that shows the limited effect of social diversity (the indigenous proportion of the population) and urbanization to explain the diverging cross-state trajectories in Mexican educational development. In a paired comparison of two states that have similar proportions of rural and indigenous population, I show that the divergence in educational development can be explained by the institutions of local administration, by the preponderance of local elites in administrative positions in the stagnating case of Michoacán, and by their replacement with deployed bureaucrats in Sonora, which saw sharp growth in schooling during the second half of the nineteenth century.

Before I proceed to those tasks, however, I begin the chapter by describing the aspects of primary public schooling to be explored in this chapter, and by presenting a succinct comparison of the trajectories followed in the four cases.

EDUCATIONAL DEVELOPMENT AND STATE POWER: DIMENSIONS AND INDICATORS

The development of public primary education in the four cases can be compared along two dimensions: the provision of public schooling, and state control over the classroom. I use both qualitative and quantitative data to assess various indicators of each.

Indicators of Primary Schooling Provision

Using data from both primary and secondary sources, I measure the growth of schooling by examining trends in the **number of public schools,** the **number of teachers,** and the size of the student body (both **enrollment** and **attendance.**) In addition to national-level data, I examine the extent of territorial inequality in the provision of education. I focus on **regional variation** and the extent of **urban bias** in schooling. To assess the former, I examine the extent of concentration of schooling in some regions of the country. The latter is evaluated by comparing the provision of schools per capita across urban and rural areas.[1]

Indicators of Control over Public Primary Schooling

A more complete picture of the development of state power is obtained by combining data on provision with an investigation of the extent of state oversight of the content of education. To do so, I examine three aspects of the systematization of public primary schooling: **teacher training, textbook and curriculum standardization,** and the **development of an inspectorate.** Teacher academies, which provided both pedagogical training and

---

[1] Both of these indicators rely on subnational data, which is marred by uneven quality. Nevertheless, the findings are indicative of broader trends.

Educational Development

inculcation, were efforts to overcome poor teacher quality and heterogeneity of instruction, which were crucial obstacles to educational development. Where the state designed and enforced a standard curriculum, and oversaw the content and distribution of texts, it directly shaped the content of education, reflecting its growing infrastructural power. Perhaps most importantly, as school inspectors visiting classrooms reported back to the capital about the content and provision of education wherever they went, the central state could assess the extent of implementation of its policies, and exercise oversight and control. Together, these aspects of public primary education reflect its systematization and control, and thus, combined with the extent of educational provision, shed light on this aspect of the state's infrastructural power.

COMPARATIVE DEVELOPMENT

Before proceeding to the case studies, I provide in this section a summary of the comparative development of the provision and systematization of public primary schooling in the four cases. As Table 4.1 shows, the cases exhibited striking variation: educational development in Chile far outstripped that of Peru and Colombia, while Mexico represents an intermediate case, characterized by more subnational variation than in any of the other cases.

Provision

The first difference between the cases can be seen in the rate of schooling and enrollment growth during the late-nineteenth and early-twentieth centuries.[2] Chile saw an increase in the number of primary schools from 276 in 1853 to 2,716 in 1910, a rate which far outpaced the growth of population. Mexico, too, saw school provision grow faster than population: while the number of schools rose sharply from 2,424 in 1857 to 12,068 in 1908, population only doubled during the same period. By contrast, school growth in Colombia and Peru, which proceeded more slowly, lagged behind population growth well into the twentieth century. Variation in enrollment rates can be seen in the second row of Table 4.1,

---

[2] The data summarized in Table 4.1 and the succeeding paragraphs were compiled from a variety of primary and secondary sources, including but not limited to those cited elsewhere in the accompanying text.

TABLE 4.1. *Educational development in four Latin American countries*

	Chile	Mexico	Colombia	Peru
Schooling growth	1853–1910: c.900%	1857–1908: c.400%	1835–1905: c.300%	1847–1897: c.300% 1897–1921: c.200%
Enrollment, as % of population, 1900*	6.4	5.3	2.6	2.5
Regional variation of schools per capita	Low	High state-level variation (see detailed discussion in text)	Moderate	High, but declining after 1897
Urban bias in schooling growth	Low	Moderate	High	High, but declining after 1897
Size of teacher training system	Large	Moderate	Small	Small, but growing after 1895
Textbook distribution	High	Low	Low	Low before 1905; growing thereafter
Curriculum standards**	Detailed	National: at subject level; state-level standardization varies	None	Subject level after 1872
Inspection	Fully regimented (see discussion in text)	Moderate by 1910 but effectiveness varied by state	Limited to non-existent	Limited before 1890; moderate by 1908

* Data from Newland (1994).
** In this row, "detailed" refers to curriculum standards at the level of individual lessons; "subject-level" refers to standards about the content to be covered in each school year.

which draws on data from Newland (1994) to show a sharp divergence across the four cases by 1900.

This divergence persists when we turn to the regional unevenness of schooling – the extent to which school provision and enrollment vary across subnational units. In Chile, schooling was equally provided throughout the country. In fact, schooling grew more quickly between 1865 and 1910 in regions outside Santiago than in the capital. Mexico, where educational development was largely in the hands of subnational authorities, saw significant cross-state variation in enrollment rates. While school provision stagnated in states like Morelos, Campeche, and Guerrero between 1878 and 1907, it more than doubled in eight others (Estadísticas Sociales del Porfiriato (1956), pp. 42ff). Colombia, too, saw large variation across its federal subunits, but even high performers among Colombian subnational units saw relatively low levels of schooling: as late as 1922, none had more than 11 percent of the population enrolled in school (Helg 1987, 37).

Peru saw a sharp transition in territorial inequality before and after 1895. In 1862, Lima had about 50 percent more schools per school-age population than did the remainder of the country. By 1897, school provision had nearly doubled in Lima, while it fell by nearly 50 percent in the rest of the country to about one-fifth of the Lima rate. Growth in schooling before 1897, then, was concentrated in Lima. Between 1897 and 1921, by contrast, school provision per capita declined in Lima while it increased in the rest of the country – although at a slower pace in the heavily indigenous southern highland regions.[3]

Similar patterns can be observed when the urban bias of educational provision is addressed. Here, too, Chile remains an outlier: school provision per capita rose in nearly every department between 1874 and 1909. The unweighted average of schools per 1,000 residents in eighty-one departments rose from 0.6 to 0.9, a 50 percent increase.[4] This is strong evidence that school provision in Chile increased nationwide, growing even in departments with small, mainly rural populations.[5] Urban schools, by

---

[3] The claims in this paragraph are based on my calculations from school provision and census data.
[4] This analysis includes every department with available data for both 1874 and 1909. These years were chosen from the few with departmental education figures because both fall close to years of national census administration, allowing better estimates of schooling rates. The difference of the two means is statistically significant at $p < .05$.
[5] Even as schools spread into small towns and rural villages, it did continue to exclude remote rural populations (Serrano 1995–1996, 462). Nevertheless, the spread of schooling in Chile was far broader than in the other cases.

contrast, were massively over-represented in Colombia's school system. Helg (1987, 48–49) claims that in 1931, while 82 percent of Colombia's population was rural, only 52.2 percent of schools were located outside urban areas. The rural schools that did exist were far from beacons of learning, as they were lacking in comparison to urban schools. Most centrally, they provided only three years of schooling as opposed to the six provided in urban primary schools (Silva Olarte 1989, 76).

In Mexico too, urban areas saw greater school provision than did rural areas – but the extent of this bias (as of 1910) varied across Mexico's states. The territory of Baja California (where education was administered by the federal government) and Tamaulipas actually favored rural areas in school provision, but these were the only exceptions to a general pattern of bias toward urban schools. Nevertheless, schools had spread into rural areas by a significant extent: the available evidence (from Bazant 1993, 91 and 94) supports Vaughan's rejection of claims that "no rural schools existed at the time of the Revolution" (1982, 49).

As with the more general patterns of educational development, Peru is a tale of two distinct phases. In 1897, after fifty years of failed national policies, only eight of the country's eighty-seven provinces – none of which were rural areas – had more than one school per 1,000 school age children. By 1921, only eight provinces remained *below* this level. The initial striking urban bias of school provision was eroded sharply, although not eliminated entirely, during the Aristocratic Republic.

Systematization

As we move from the provision of schooling to its standardization and systematization, the gap between the cases remains apparent. It can be seen clearly in the development of teacher training. Here, too, Chile was a leader. Between 1867 and 1875, nearly 150 normal school graduates joined the ranks of public school teachers, bringing the proportion of teachers who had been trained in the country's pedagogical academies to 37 percent by 1875. A variety of policies (including earmarked scholarships, retention bonuses, salary increases, and moving subsidies) were in place to retain trained teachers, and to encourage them to take jobs at schools throughout the country.[6] Colombia's record of teacher training was poor: although nine normal schools were established in 1872, they

---

[6] For more detail on these, and citations to government documents describing the programs and their achievements, see Soifer (2009, 168–170) and Egaña Baraona (2000).

produced relatively few teachers (Loy 1971, 286–287). State oversight over teacher training was absent; it contracted the operation of the pedagogical academies to the Church in 1892 (Silva Olarte 1989, 81–82). As of 1931, fewer than one in four teachers had any certification, and the rate in rural areas was 7.5 percent (Obregón et al. 1999, vol. 2, p. 556).

Peru had an equally meager record of teacher training. The men's teacher training academy in Lima produced two graduates between 1859 and 1869, and closed again in 1877, returning to operation only in 1905 (Barrantes 1989, 79). After 1905, teacher training began to take hold, as 49 graduates of the Lima academy were serving in public schools by 1909, and several more normal schools had opened by 1915. Yet the vast majority of Peruvian teachers continued to lack pedagogical training, and many had little more than a primary school education.

Systematizing teacher training was a subject of great debate in Mexico. Liberals questioned whether imposing training requirements for teachers would interfere with the freedom to exercise professions, which was a touchstone of Liberal values (Cosio Villegas 1956, 537ff). Once these debates were resolved in favor of standardization early in the Porfiriato, progress was dramatic. The first normal school in the Federal District opened in 1880. Some states had moved more quickly than had the national government: according to Galván de Terrazas (1985, 174), normal schools existed in San Luis Potosí, Zacatecas, Guanajuato, Nuevo León, and Sinaloa before 1874. By 1910, Mexico had 45 normal schools with more than 2,000 students, up from seventy-two in 1878, and approximately one in four teachers nationwide had normal school degrees (Vásquez de Knauth 1970, 59; Vaughan 1982, 63).

Textbook standardization and distribution was another element in the systematization of primary schools. Here, too, Chile saw much greater development during the period under study. By the 1860s, the Chilean government was distributing hundreds of thousands of texts, providing between four and eleven texts per student over the subsequent decade.[7] The state was also heavily involved in overseeing the content of texts (Woll 1975). After 1877, sealed-bid auctions were held for national contracts on school materials including furniture, paper, and ink, which could then be allocated according to national government priorities (MIP 1877,

---

[7] This figure is based on data from various ministerial *Memorias* that show the number of books distributed by province. For seven fiscal years between 1868–1877 for which data is available, the average number of primary school textbooks distributed nationwide was more than 190,000.

35). Alongside these developments, Chilean officials developed a detailed primary school curriculum, which was so precise that (as discussed later) it was standardized down to the individual lesson.

Colombia remained at the opposite extreme, as it never declared a particular text to be mandatory or official. A small number of school materials, including texts and maps, were distributed after the 1870 school reform (Loy 1971, 287). By 1921, the national government was distributing materials ranging from chalk to catechisms (19,899 copies), reading, history, and math textbooks (in smaller numbers), and 2,000 copies of the national anthem (Helg 1987, 55). Compared to Chile – and even to Peru – these numbers are paltry. A national curriculum was never set: the content and organization of instruction remained at the departmental level. The only consistency in teaching came in the realm of religion, where practice was set by the church, not the state.

In Peru, teachers had free rein over texts before 1891, when usage was standardized at the province level. It would only be standardized at the national level after 1895. To be approved, texts had to use the metric system, use Peruvian examples whenever possible, and use maps that reflected the country's international claims (MIP 1897, 27ff). The Pardo administration (1904–1909) undertook the first efforts to standardize textbooks, opening contests for a new reader, and distributing copies of the winning entry widely. By 1909, the Peruvian government distributed textbooks at a limited level: an average of 22.8 texts per thousand residents to schools throughout the country.[8] Peruvian policymakers only systematized primary education at the subject level after 1900, and never developed a program of history instruction, limiting the extent to which the classroom inculcated national values.

Mexican state builders were concerned with the "heterogeneity of habits" that they saw as the cause of the country's social turmoil. But, as Bazant (1993, 23) discusses, their primary focus was making primary schooling free, obligatory, and secular as a way to make Mexican society uniform. As a result, little effort to standardize or distribute texts was made before the Porfiriato. The 1861 education law called for the use of the Liberal constitution as a reading text in primary schools, and that Mexican history be taught (Vásquez de Knauth 1970, 61–62). Further national standardization was debated, but textbook policy emerged at the state level (Covarrubias 1993; Bazant 1993, 54ff). This aspect of

---

[8] This figure is based on my calculation from enrollment and distribution data in MED 1909, 398–399.

Educational Development

education development remained quite limited at the end of the Porfiriato, as texts were lacking in many parts of the country (Vaughan 1982, 62). The standardization of curriculum at the national level was hotly debated at the third national pedagogical conference in 1891, and by the end of the Porfiriato, the "basic structure of primary schooling" was in place (Díaz Zermeño 1979, 63–64).

Inspection

The inspection of the day-to-day operation of primary schools by trained officials who report to the national education ministry was the linchpin of control over primary education. Here the divergences between the cases are particularly stark. And because inspection is so central to the state's infrastructural power – its ability to implement policy – differences in this dimension are particularly significant. Here Chile is a dramatic outlier. As discussed in detail later, it had by the 1890s a fully regimented inspection system that visited essentially every public school in the country, reporting back to Santiago on the nature of schooling.

Colombia only established a vestigial inspection system with the Uribe education reform of 1903. Unlike the professionalized system in Chile, inspection in Colombia was carried out by local elites (including the parish priest), and its function was blurred with teacher training. Evidence about the effectiveness of Colombian inspection is fragmentary. Helg (1987, 60–61) finds it to be uneven: its frequency varied from once per month to once per year, and that in some areas, it was carried out by self-reporting on the part of teachers.

Peru, too, saw limited inspection capacity during the nineteenth century, as the system in place relied heavily on self-reporting by teachers (see, for example, MILIMA 1875, pp. 4–6). Primary school inspection was established only in 1891 – but inspectors only covered about half the country, and visited schools about once per semester (MED 1891, xxxviii and 192). Oversight capacity, as discussed in detail later, increased sharply after 1895, culminating in the 1902 *Censo Escolar*. By 1907, a regimented inspection system was in place, and state oversight capacity increased sharply thereafter.

Mexican schools saw a general "trend" toward systematization and centralization of control under Liberal governments (Vaughan 1987, 59). By the 1850s, most states had created inspection systems of varying quality, which oversaw the administration of primary schools (Staples 1998, 53–54). The 1888 education law gave the national government the right to inspect municipal schools, and by 1896 the Federal District had a regimented inspection system. As with other aspects of education development, national government policies diffused to the states, and by 1910, inspection had spread through the whole country (Bazant 1993, 48). Its nature varied by state: in México state, it relied heavily on self-reporting by teachers, as inspectors only visited schools that self-reported "anomalies" (Bazant 1998, 65). Overall, by 1910, inspection was "skeletal and embryonic," as national systematization continued to be limited, and performance at the state level varied (Vaughan 1982, 60).

In all, we can reach three conclusions about the patterns of state development across the cases. First, Chile and (to a lesser extent) Mexico had more developed public primary education systems than did Peru or Colombia. Second, Peru saw a dramatic shift in fortunes, as education development initiatives that stagnated between 1845 and 1895 bore fruit for two decades thereafter. Third, Mexico was marked by striking patterns of subnational variation, as schooling grew much more rapidly in some of its states than in others. The rest of this chapter turns to accounting for this cross-national, cross-time (in Peru) and subnational (in Mexico) variation, showing that it is best explained by the two-part argument about the origins and outcomes of state-building efforts I outlined in Chapters 1 and 2.

LACK OF EDUCATIONAL INITIATIVE IN COLOMBIA

Even in comparison to a laggard like Peru, Colombia saw little education development before 1930. Indeed, Ramírez and Tellez (2007, 475) show that as late as 1950, only about 8 percent of the country's population was enrolled in school. The failure of Colombian primary education development was also reflected in the absence of any standardization or oversight by the national government. Although fiscal constraints played a role, the limited growth of education was a direct reflection of the lack of commitment by state leaders throughout the period 1830–1930 to building a universal, systematized education system.

The most striking reflection of this half-hearted commitment to education development can be seen in the interpretation of universal schooling by politicians and education policy makers. The notion of universalism in Colombia focused on making exclusion from schools (chiefly on financial grounds) illegal rather than on making schooling mandatory. Education was seen primarily as a family responsibility, and the state's role was to provide a context in which its citizens could choose to meet this responsibility (Hanson 1986, 30). Even as education was declared the "basis and foundation of representative government" and knowledge the root of freedom, efforts to establish primary education saw the state's role as limited to removing barriers to private initiative in school-building efforts rather than active involvement in building public schools.[9] Schooling became obligatory for the first time only with the passage of the 1863 constitution and the subsequent 1870 education reform, and this would be reversed in fairly short order, as described later (Silva Olarte 1989, 63). Strikingly, however, the Hilario López government that presided over these reforms focused on weakening the role of the church in schooling, and chose not to increase state education provision. Instead officials hoped that the requirement that all children enroll in school would lead to the opening of secular private schools (Helg 1987, 23).

These policies, which led to some growth in enrollment during the 1870s, were reversed in 1886 when the new constitution made education "free but not obligatory" (Article 41). This policy was motivated by the belief that mandatory education would obstruct the free market in schooling.[10] Proponents believed that education should be the work of private actors, and that the state should intervene only when private interest was lacking (Silva Olarte 1989, 67). Indeed, Helg (1987, 28) argues that political elites in the Regeneración era viewed the state as having no ambit over moral issues, and therefore believed that it had no right to intervene actively in education. The 1903 education reform, a product of Antioquia elites, gave up on creating a nationally unified primary education system, focusing instead on secondary schools at the national level while ceding control of primary schools to the departments. Liberal proposals in the 1920s to make education mandatory (while allowing parents to choose between public and private schools) were defeated, meaning that as of 1930, primary schooling was still optional rather than mandatory in most of Colombia.

In part, the failure of the Colombian state to institute mandatory schooling reflects pressure from church officials, who were strongly opposed to mandatory primary schooling even when they were guaranteed control over the content of the curriculum and the classroom.[11]

---

[9] The quote appears in Báez Osorio (2006, 26) and is attributed to the Congreso Nacional of 1821.
[10] The fact that this logic was put forward by Conservatives shows the breadth of the laissez-faire consensus in Colombia described in Chapter 1.
[11] For example, in 1872 the Archbishop of Popayán threatened to excommunicate altogether any Catholic who attended public schools (Silva Olarte 1989, 65).

Indeed, the challenges that the church perceived to its hegemony over Colombian schools were pivotal in triggering the 1876 civil war. Throughout the first century after independence, the church retained a great amount of influence over education. At times, this was the result of the failure of the state to build primary schools, leaving a void filled by religious schools. Even when it did not directly operate schools, the church often funded them (Báez Osorio 2006, 34). In practice, local priests often served on the municipal inspection councils, placing them in a position of oversight over public schools, particularly in smaller communities (Obregón et al. 1999, vol. 1, p. 379). The 1887 Concordato restoring relations with the Vatican prohibited the state from intervening in church schools, and it gave the church the power to intervene in public schooling. After this time, the state continued to fund education while ceding control over it to the church (Lebot 1978, 125). Many schools were run by Catholic priests and church officials (Silva Olarte 1989, 73–74). This meant not only that the church oversaw the content of religious education, and incorporated the study of Catholic doctrine and practice into the curriculum, but that the church unilaterally imposed texts in other courses as well, and operated the country's normal schools after 1892 (ibid., 81–82). The control of education was particularly dominant in the frontier regions, where the preponderance of political power was ceded to the church (Rausch 1993). But church control reached far beyond this territory, leading Lebot (1978, 125) to argue that the 1887 Concordato "turned Colombia once again into a country of missions as in the 16th and 17th centuries."

Yet the power of the church cannot fully explain the failure to institute mandatory schooling. Instead, it is a *consequence* of the failure of state building. In Peru and Chile, too, as we will see, the church had significant influence over education policy, curricular content, and other aspects of instruction. The central place of religious instruction in primary education was unquestioned in all the cases except Mexico. Throughout Latin America, the church operated many schools in the early decades after independence – in fact, post-independence laws in all four countries required religious organizations to operate schools. But over time in Chile and Peru, the direct operation of schools by religious orders was phased out and replaced by public administration of a school system deeply infused with Catholic values. In Colombia, the fact that the church operated the nominally public school system throughout the nineteenth century reflects the unique disinclination of Colombian state leaders to build a public bureaucracy.

This disinclination derived from the Colombian consensus about the place of the state in bringing "order, progress, and development": the state's role was seen to be limited to removing obstacles to private initiative. Just as in other countries, education was seen as a necessary piece of development efforts. But in Colombia, state officials were satisfied with policies that *encouraged* residents to enroll in school, rather than *requiring* them to do so. Unlike any of the other cases, political elites in Colombia never made a concerted effort to build a national school system.

Even when national leaders sought to increase school provision, they placed financing and administration in the hands of local and regional officials. The policies of the 1903 education reform were typical in this light: the national government mandated that schools be provided, and committed itself to paying for school materials such as textbooks and paper. But it placed responsibility for teacher selection, and for teacher salaries, on the departments, and the financing for school buildings on the municipal governments (Helg 1987, 103). Left free to design education policy as they saw fit, and responsible for paying for schooling, departmental and municipal governments commonly dragged their feet, and "limited themselves to the law" (ibid; 48). At other times, state governments went so far as "rejecting" national policy (Silva Olarte 1989, 65). The result was low school provision nearly everywhere in Colombia, with only scattered outliers.

Alongside the low levels of provision, the Colombian state also failed to undertake oversight and systematization efforts. This, too, reflected its lack of interest in using primary schools to penetrate and transform society and build a national community. Instead of nation-building or the inculcation of "Colombian-ness" among the population, schools were seen as a means of providing skills for economic activity (Ramírez and Tellez 2007, 464).

In all, the limited development of Colombia's education system is striking in comparative perspective. But more notable is that the Colombian state never undertook a project of education development. While political leaders of all stripes valued schooling as a necessary component of modernization and progress, they never undertook a systematic effort to build public schools, monitor the quality of education, or standardize the school system. The Colombian state lagged far behind its counterparts in education development throughout the first century after independence, a reflection of its lack of commitment to increasing its control over society and territory.

A STRUCTURAL ALTERNATIVE: INEQUALITY AND EDUCATION DEVELOPMENT

The other three cases – Chile, Peru, and Mexico – diverged from Colombia in that all saw state-building efforts in the education realm throughout the nineteenth century. Yet as described previously, the fruit of those efforts varied. In the remainder of this chapter, I weigh two possible explanations for this variation, putting the institutional account developed in Chapter 2 against a structural account common in the literature on education development.[12]

This structural account begins from the fact that public education spending redistributes wealth by creating economic opportunities for the lower classes, paid for by taxes which fall more heavily on the wealthy even if they are regressive in nature (Mariscal and Sokoloff 2000, 159; Ansell 2010). As inequality increases, then, the burden of taxation to fund education development falls on the rich in a more concentrated fashion, making them less willing to support education development.[13] This means that we should expect the growth of public primary schooling to be negatively associated with inequality. Moreover, because social actors shape political institutions to protect their interests, inequality should be associated with suffrage restrictions (Engerman and Sokoloff 1997). These limits on participation limit the ability of the poor to organize and press for education development in the political arena.

In this view, successful education development requires "great equality or homogeneity among the population [that] led over time to more democratic political institutions, to more investment in public goods and infrastructure, and to institutions that offered relatively broad access to economic opportunities" (Engerman and Sokoloff 2002, 4). Where society is largely equal and homogeneous in preferences – as in the northern United States or Canada during the early decades after independence – education development is said to have resulted from the initiative of local communities, in which the burden of funding education is evenly distributed. But in Latin America, where both economic inequality and ethnic

---

[12] Because of the central place of Kenneth Sokoloff in developing this argument, I refer to it later as the Sokoloff hypothesis. It was developed by Sokoloff and his collaborators in Mariscal and Sokoloff (2000) and Engerman and Sokoloff (1997, 2002). A slightly different argument, which emphasizes the exogenous origins of institutions rather than tracing them directly to the degree of inequality, has been made by John Coatsworth (1998, 2008).

[13] The logic here builds on the Meltzer and Richard (1981) model of taxation and redistribution.

diversity were higher during the nineteenth century, the Sokoloff argument would not expect local promotion of education.

In Latin America, where local inequality was high, the Sokoloff hypothesis expects that the initiative for education development would only come from national governments. But it expects that initiative to emerge only in societies that were fairly equal and homogeneous at the national level. Mariscal and Sokoloff (2000) find a negative correlation between the indigenous composition of the population and the provision of education. They conclude that the relatively low social inequality of societies without large indigenous or slave populations promoted the construction of democratic institutions (or at least low barriers to suffrage) that favored the development of education.

If this argument is to hold, we should expect that national political elites would be more likely to seek to supply education in societies where social homogeneity was low. We will see, however, that this was not the case: in both Peru and Mexico, where indigenous populations were large and social inequality high, state leaders made efforts to develop public primary education. The roots of variation are not in the choices made by state leaders, but in the extent to which they were able to effectively convert policy initiatives into outcomes. This failure to account for the determinants of the success of state-building efforts is a crucial limitation of the Sokoloff argument, and of other arguments that draw direct connections between the motivations of state leaders and the outcomes of state capacity.

The evidence presented later challenges this view. It shows that state leaders in Chile, Mexico, and Peru all sought to build primary education systems. The extent of implementation varied with the form of administration: where school building and oversight were delegated to local elites, as in some parts of Mexico, and in Peru before 1895, these state-building efforts foundered. But when states relied on deployed rule and sent bureaucrats out to implement education reform, their efforts were more successful. It is this variation, and not the preferences of elites about public school development, that explains the divergence across cases. Across all cases, the historical record shows that economic elites continued to oppose the taxation and spending that accompanied education development. In the racist language and thought of the time period, they wondered whether the indigenous population could be educated, and whether that education would serve any purpose. But where they had no influence over policy implementation, their opposition to education reform was left on the margins and school building continued. This institutional divergence, and underlying structural conditions, explains why Chile saw precocious school building, despite high social and economic inequality.[14] It also better explains the sharp change in the trajectory of Peruvian education development before and after 1895. Finally, the nature of administration, and not economic and social inequality, better explains the variation in education development across Mexico's states.

DEPLOYED RULE AND STATE POWER: THE DEVELOPMENT OF SCHOOL INSPECTION IN CHILE

Explanations for education development in Chile have focused on several factors: most prominently, the role of individual leaders and the broad elite consensus about education among its political elites, Chile's homogeneity relative to its neighbors, and societal demands for education.[15] While these factors all played a significant role in education development, an examination of the origins of school inspection reveals another central factor: the actions of Chilean bureaucrats in pursuing the development of an effective system of oversight of schools in the communities in which they served. Inspection represented the backbone of state-controlled primary schooling. The development of the inspection system, which reinforced the control of state officials over the school system, was the product of the establishment of deployed rule. We cannot understand the growing systematization of Chilean primary education, or its nationwide spread, without taking into account the role played by deployed local bureaucrats in pressing the state for more effective oversight of schooling.[16]

In the late 1860s, national education officials expressed repeated concern about the fact that the system relied on a few inspectors who had huge territories to cover (MIP 1869, 53). In response to these concerns,

---

[14] Mariscal and Sokoloff (2000, 197) claim that inequality was relatively low in Chile in regional perspective. They approximate inequality by measuring the rate of suffrage and the proportion of the population identified as indigenous. It is true that on both of these indicators, Chile seems more equal than many other Latin American countries. But accounts of rural life in nineteenth-century Chile (such as Bauer 1975) suggest that economic and social inequality was very high.

[15] The importance of the elite consensus and individual leaders is highlighted by Yeager (2005) and Britton (1994), while (as discussed earlier) Engerman and Sokoloff (2002) and Mariscal and Sokoloff (2000) see homogeneity and low inequality as crucial. Cruz (2002) authored one of the few studies of the societal demand for schooling in Chile, although Molina and Palmer (2004) see this as central in their study of Costa Rica.

[16] This section is based on Soifer (2009), which explores the development of Chilean school inspection in more detail.

the Education Ministry decreed on June 3, 1868 the creation of commissions of local notables to oversee education. These emerged by 1871 in big cities such as Santiago and Valparaíso, in local centers such as Vallenar and Freirina in the north and Angeles and Ligua in the south, and in a few small towns, most notably in Chiloé, and efforts were made to create commissions in other communities (MIP 1871). The commission members' lack of knowledge or training about education quickly became apparent as an Achilles' heel of their effectiveness. An 1869 visit by a special inspector to some of the provinces in the center of the country found that the only local commission that was effective was that of Caupolicán – and it was no coincidence that this commission was also unique in being headed by the department governor (*El Araucano* 1869, 4).

Local bureaucrats regularly expressed concern about these commissions to their superiors in Santiago. Their concerns revolved around two issues: (1) effective oversight of education and (2) disputes over who had the authority to hire and fire teachers. The complaints of local officials trickled up through the bureaucracy, and bureaucrats at the national level confronted evidence of the limitations of local commissions. The 1869 special inspector's report urged the bureaucrats in Santiago to rely more on the opinion of local officials, as the success of the project of education development was "entirely in their hands" (*El Araucano* 1869, 2–3). By the mid-1870s it was generally acknowledged within the education bureaucracy that these commissions were a total failure (see, e.g., MIP 1875, 214).

The authority to hire and fire teachers was a significant bone of contention. The commissions of local notables were seen as overstepping their bounds by taking on this role, and in the context of their acknowledged ineffectiveness, this jurisdictional conflict turned the national bureaucracy against the inspections. By the mid-1870s the government sought to establish a more effective system of oversight, but this effort was stymied for the remainder of the decade as a result of the severe economic crisis. This crisis saw the creation of a *protector de escuela*, a single overseer for each school (MIP 1877, 38–39), but this was a temporary measure during the time of penury.

As the economic crisis lessened during the War of the Pacific, pressures for the development of inspection mounted. The ministry was pressed by inspectors themselves to increase the number of inspectors and to equalize the number of schools each had to cover (MIP 1882, 127ff). By 1883, there were twenty-three inspectors, including one for the new territories of Antofagasta and Tarapacá, which had been taken from Bolivia and Peru during the War of the Pacific. At this point, the last local commissions were eliminated and school inspection turned over entirely to the professional inspectorate, which increased effective control over schools throughout the national territory, including the regions newly conquered in the war.

The criticisms of local state agents were effective in pressing the national government to professionalize the education system. But why were local officials so concerned with the quality of inspection? Their statements of concern about the quality of education cannot be taken at face value, as these reflect their attempts to couch their demands in terms that they thought would appeal to their audience. Instead, we can suggest two motives that drove local officials to seek to increase the presence and power of the professional inspectorate. First, local state agents saw professional inspectors as allies in a project of education development. Egaña Baraona (2000, 235ff) shows that the two types of bureaucrats collaborated on raising funds for schools from citizens, and on increasing school attendance. Increasing the provision and quality of education was a way for state officials to satisfy the communities in which they served. State agents were besieged with demands for increased school provision and school quality, demands they passed on to the national bureaucracy. Providing schools and overseeing the quality of education was a way to deliver concrete results to the communities in which they served. Because they were appointed by the president or ministries, local officials were not accountable to the communities. But their ability to provide services in response to their demands increased their legitimacy, and improved their relationships with these communities. Under deployed rule, local state agents could thus benefit from state strength, which motivated them to pursue its development.

Second, local state agents saw education development as a means of inculcating the youth of their district with national identity and civilization. Local officials were so interested in education development that they regularly took it upon themselves to regulate all aspects of schools within their jurisdictions, and they had to be restrained by the education law of 1883, which gave authority over local education to the inspectorate and limited local officials to appeals to the inspector general. The development of professional inspection was one front in a struggle for increased state presence in society, state presence that local officials sought because it would transform society in ways that increased their control.

Educational Development

Thus, while the central education bureaucracy sought to maximize its control of education by pushing inspection outward from the capital, local state agents criticized the type of inspection first introduced. By arguing that local commissions were ineffective and overstepped their bounds, state agents convinced the Education Ministry of the need to reform the system. Had these agents not been so critical of the local commissions, they likely would have been retained. At the time, the priorities of the central education bureaucracy (as reflected in their memorias and budgets) were increasing the number of schools in underserved areas of the country (mainly rural areas) and improving teacher quality. The pressures of local state agents placed the regimentation of school inspection on the national agenda, and the transformation of the inspection system that resulted was fundamental in increasing state control of education. Tracing the development of education inspection shows that economic factors alone cannot explain this growth of state control, although the recovery from economic crisis did allow funds for increased professionalization. Actions of officials in Santiago cannot be seen in a vacuum, as they made policy choices relying on and responding to the reports they received from the state agents in the periphery.

Education was one of the fronts on which deployed officials pushed for an expanded state role in their communities, and the ability of the Chilean state to penetrate and shape society on a national level through the school system developed as a result of their efforts. Thus, the success of state efforts to develop Chilean schooling depended on the actions of local officials in a system of deployed rule who pushed the central state to intensify and centralize the oversight of the country's schools.

INSTITUTIONAL CHANGE AND EDUCATION DEVELOPMENT IN PERU

Peru is a particularly propitious case in which to evaluate the power of the institutional explanation, because the administration of public primary education varied sharply over time. From 1845 to 1895, during the state-building efforts of the guano era and its aftermath, Peru relied heavily on local elites in a system of delegated rule. Despite a consensus among policymakers (Contreras 1996) that advances in education were necessary to achieve national integration and prosperity, and large investments in schooling facilitated by the huge guano revenues the state enjoyed for 25 years (Tantaleán Arbulú 1983, Appendix Table 4; Hunt 1984), few schools were built outside Lima, and the quality of education remained low. Systematization was so lacking even in the capital city that an 1872 government report described educational "disorder" as "complete," writing that "each teacher teaches what they want, and to whom they want, the school year ends when they see fit, and the length of vacation is only measured by the teacher's will or love for their job" (MED 1872, 6). By contrast, after 1895, even as economic changes strengthened local elites, the governments of the Aristocratic Republic bypassed them in placing education administration in the hands of deployed bureaucrats. The effects of this change are striking, providing compelling evidence for the limitations of the structural account that centers on elite preferences and social inequality. Unlike their predecessors, the governments of the Aristocratic Republic (1895–1919) established deployed rule in the realm of primary education.

The decision to shift from delegation of administration to a system of deployed rule resulted from several factors. First, the War of the Pacific drastically weakened local elites in highland regions, breaking their "rural hegemony" (Contreras and Cueto 1999, 145). Peruvian governments had long relied on traditional elites to maintain stability in the interior of the country, but these elites were overwhelmed by the extent of rural unrest (Mallon 1995; Thurner 1997). Disturbed by the level of chaos under the Cáceres government that followed the end of the war, a broad coalition emerged behind the Piérola government that succeeded him. At the center of this coalition was a new coastal elite, mainly invested in sugar plantations, and a new class of industrialists, miners, and merchants who gained power as exports grew (Thorp and Bertram 1978). The experience of turmoil under Cáceres raised the specter that economic recovery would be threatened by the lack of control over rural areas. Chastened by the poor performance of delegated rule, Piérola's government began a shift to deployed rule. This shift quickly led to increased state reach into the highlands, and for much of the period 1895–1915, steady progress in education was seen.

The Civilista project of education development sparked resistance from highland elites, who regained strength as the rural economy recovered from war. Elite resistance to deployed rule derived from the threat it posed to their efforts to restore hegemony over the rural population. But in the realm of education, resistance also resulted from elite distaste for educating Peru's indigenous population. Pamphlets, newspaper articles, and other sources reveal disbelief that the indigenous population could be educated or effectively integrated into a "modern" Peru. One example appears in the writings of Alejandro Deustua, who argued that the indigenous community "lacked all culture and had no notion of nationality." He wondered what effect education could have on those who, to him, "were not yet people, who did not know how to live like people, and had not managed to differentiate themselves from the animals" (Montero 1990, 85–87). Deustua was far from alone in this view – it was regularly expressed in the pages of *El Comercio* and other elite media. Many elites, to whom oversight of education policy had been delegated over the past fifty years, held the view that the indigenous population under their purview could not, and should not, be educated (Muecke 2004, 181). These attitudes had underpinned the failure of education development under delegated rule, and they led to tension as the central state undertook education development through deployed administration after 1895.

The first steps taken by Piérola were a series of national education inspections ordered in 1897 and 1898. For the first time, inspectors were deployed from Lima to the provinces. The difference from earlier inspections was dramatic: inspectors began to file reports that highlighted the shortcomings of the education system and criticized the actions of local government in the realm of education. Most strikingly for the central government, inspectors noted that many communities lacked schools altogether: for example, the inspector found that children in the border town of Desaguadero crossed into Bolivia to attend school there.[17] A commission on school hygiene, formed in 1899, also delivered stark findings, describing the conditions in rural schools as not only "unhealthy" but "homicidal" (MED 1900). The complete disarray of schooling, revealed in these overwhelmingly negative reports, led the national government to take control of education development.

As a prelude to this effort, Piérola's government undertook an education census in 1902, the first assessment of education at a national level since the 1876 census.[18] Despite some resistance from local officials, greater than 90 percent of the population and 75 percent of the national territory were covered by this census (Contreras 2004, 243). The results showed no progress in education since 1876. In response to these sobering findings, the Piérola government and its successors undertook massive efforts to expand education. From 1897 to 1920, the number of

---

[17] This anecdote appears in the MED 1898, p. 424. The general claims in this paragraph about the content of this new wave of inspectors' reports is based on a comparison of the reports appearing in all twenty-nine available annual ministerial *Memorias* over the period 1864–1919, as well as various reports of regional officials from the same time period.

[18] For a detailed study of this census, see Soifer (2013b).

primary schools in the country nearly quadrupled from 852 to 3,338.[19] Enrollment doubled as well, reaching more than 120,000. This growth far outpaced the growth of population, and was truly national, as schools per capita increased throughout the country, unlike in earlier periods where school construction was focused in Lima.

The Pardo government (1904–1909) complemented expanded provision by focusing on the content of textbooks. A contest opened on May 9, 1905 to write a reader for primary school students that would be "truly Peruvian," and by 1907 more than 150,000 copies of the winner were printed and distributed (MED 1905, pp. xlvi, 877–878, 904ff; MED 1906, xxxii; MED 1907, 644–649). In all, the education ministry distributed more than twenty-two books per 1,000 residents nationwide in 1908, and implemented a curriculum designed to inculcate students with knowledge of Peruvian geography and history (including the Inca heritage, the colonial period, the independence conflict, and the republican era) as well as moral, physical, and military education. Moral education was designed to transmit the "principal duties" of man to students: cleanliness, work, temperance, school attendance, honor, honesty, courage, savings, payment of taxes, electoral duties, and military service (MED 1902, 670–671; MED 1905, 905–906). These efforts to use schooling to unify the population under the national banner represented a direct response to the chaos of the 1880s and early 1890s, and were seen as the means to the "civilization of the indigenous and by that route their incorporation into the Peruvian nation."[20]

The Civilista governments were pioneers in the deployment of education officials from Lima to the nation's interior. The effects of this new policy were dramatic in terms of increased education provision and state oversight. Local elites, however, remained hostile to education development. But the shift to deployed rule eliminated the opportunity they had to dilute its implementation. Instead, their hostility revealed itself in active resistance to education officials deployed to their communities, which at times turned violent (see, for example, Jacobsen 1993, 212). A more sweeping limitation of education development turned on the fact that "despite its increased authority and reach, the central government nevertheless continued to rely on the regional power of the *gamonales* [rural elites] to keep order in the provinces" (Klarén 2000, 218). With

---

[19] The figures that appear here are collected from various annual ministerial reports.
[20] This quote is drawn from a 1901 statement by Pedro Cisneros, president of the Supreme Court of the Department of Ancash, cited in Contreras (1996).

increased rural unrest after 1915, national governments developed closer ties with local elites, and ceded ground on education. This can be seen in the disappearance of systematic inspection reports from the archives of the Ministry of Education after this time, and in the return of annual ministerial reports to their old focus on policy design rather than on the shortcomings of implementation.

Despite this retreat, the Civilista government shift to deployed rule underlay a dramatic increase in the state's provision of education, oversight of its quality, and control of its content. Thus, the form of rule shaped both the gains and the limitations in education development during the Aristocratic Republic (1895–1919) in Peru. Despite the fact that elite preferences did not change during this period, their influence varied with the institutional design of local administration. While delegated rule allowed elites to dilute education development, the deployed rule implemented during this period limited their ability to do so, and this allowed the central state to substantially increase this aspect of the state's power.

EXPLAINING CROSS-STATE DIVERGENCE IN MEXICAN EDUCATION

Patterns of local administration also explain cross-state variation in Mexico. Policy design and implementation was largely left to the states in Mexico's federal system. The fact that states set their own education policy even for much of the Porfiriato makes this an ideal site to assess the relative power of institutional and structural factors in explaining the variation in education development.

The national government began to intervene in education only after the Liberals came to power: a series of regulations issued after 1861 gave it influence over schooling in the Federal District and territories, serving as the model for similar consolidations in many Mexican states. By the 1890s, many states had stripped municipalities of control over primary schooling, and the national government did so in the Federal District in 1896. Despite the fact that policy was not formally coordinated across states, there was a great deal of diffusion as states adopted policies similar to those introduced by the national government in the Federal District.

Yet similar policies produced widely divergent results. The statistical analysis that follows uses state-level data on the composition of the population and education development to show that social inequality did not determine the development of schooling in Mexico. Neither the proportion of the population identified as indigenous, nor the extent of urbanization (used as a proxy for the repressive labor relations and social inequality often associated with large-scale agriculture) has the effect that the Sokoloff hypothesis would predict on literacy, primary education spending, or enrollment during the Porfiriato. A subsequent paired comparison of education development in Michoacán and Sonora shows that where state governments delegated administrative offices to local elites, education development lagged. By contrast, where bureaucrats were deployed from outside the state, and had independent reasons to seek education development, schooling thrived even in a context of high social and economic inequality.

Statistical Analysis

The dependent variables are various measures of education development, most of which are available for twenty-seven of Mexico's thirty-one states. (See Table 4.2 for descriptive statistics.) The central independent variables are the level of urbanization (drawn from Bazant 1993, 94) and the proportion of the population identified as indigenous in the 1895 census.[21]

Table 4.3 reports the results from six OLS regression analyses of the effects of urbanization and social diversity on education provision by state during the Porfiriato. Model 1 examines the determinants of enrollment growth between 1874 and 1907. While spending growth is the most significant contributor to enrollment growth, urbanization also has a significant effect – although, surprisingly for the arguments of economic historians discussed earlier, *lower* urbanization is associated with more rapid enrollment growth. Model 2 repeats the analysis in Model 1 while adding enrollment levels in 1875 and state and municipal revenues in 1907 to the analysis. Here, urbanization remains significant and signed in the unexpected (negative) direction. In neither model does the proportion of the population that is identified as indigenous have a significant effect.

Model 3 assesses the determinants of literacy rates in 1910. Here, three factors are significant: urbanization, school enrollment rates in 1907, and the proportion of the population that is identified as indigenous in 1895.

---

[21] The 1895 census provides data on the proportion of the population that spoke indigenous languages. This is, of course, a problematic way to conceptualize identity – in particular because literacy in Spanish is itself a way to assess education development – but it is the best available data. Repeating the analysis with data from the 1921 census produces very similar results (not shown here) to those presented here, in terms of both significance and size of effects.

TABLE 4.2. *Description of variables, Mexican state education*

Name	Units	N	Mean	St. dev.	Min	Max	Source
Indig. pop. 1895	Proportion	30	0.144	0.181	0	0.703	Estadísticas Sociales
Indig. pop. 1921	Proportion	31	0.256	0.176	0.01	0.69	AE 1930
Urbanization	Percentage	29	28.438	14.071	10.69	87.32	Bazant 1993, 94
Public school enrollment 1875	Proportion of school age pop.	28	0.226	0.121	0.07	0.54	Covarrubias 1993, my calculations*
Public school enrollment 1907		27	0.249	0.086	0.12	0.43	Vaughan 1982, 44
Enrollment growth	As % of 1874 level	27	179.744	181.661	−0.9	838	Vaughan 1982, 44
Literacy 1910	Percentage	27	20.285	8.38	3.52	38.9	Vaughan 1982, 44
Primary ed. spending 1874	Pesos per capita	27	0.174	0.097	0.02	0.38	Vaughan 1982, 42
Primary ed. spending 1907		27	0.503	0.284	0.12	1.12	Vaughan 1982, 42
Spending growth	As % of 1874 level	27	446.667	953.602	18	4800	Vaughan 1982, 42
Revenues 1907	Pesos per capita	27	3.994	2.300	1.25	11.51	Vaughan 1982, 42

* Calculated by assuming that 20% of total population was of school age.

TABLE 4.3. *Regression results, state-level education provision in Mexico*

	Model 1		Model 2		Model 3		Model 4		Model 5		Model 6	
DV	Enrollment growth		Enrollment growth		Literacy 1910		Enrollment 1907		Enrollment 1907		Spending 1907	
Constant	245.015***	69.581	272.688***	87.562	1.296	5.353	0.217***	0.053	0.099**	0.044	0.194*	0.105
Indigenous	−80.419	116.464	−175.248	118.908	−12.648*	6.986	−0.039	0.092	−0.061	0.064	−0.436**	0.171
Urbanization	−4.662*	2.575	−5.132**	2.441	0.298**	0.133	−0.002	0.002	−0.001	0.001	−0.003	0.004
Enrollment 1875			−273.555	187.37					0.448***	0.091		
Spending growth	0.159***	0.023	0.132***	0.025								
1907 revenues			17.827*	10.008	−0.396	0.981	−0.002	0.012	0.008	0.009	0.113***	0.014
Enrollment 1907					21.613	16.145						
Spending 1907					18.476**	8.099	0.189*	0.099	0.111	0.071		
Spending 1874												
# obs	27		27		27		27		27		27	
F	16.56		12.18		7.71		3.47		10.62		21.9	
Prob>F	0.0000		0.0000		0.0003		0.0243		0.0000		0.0000	
R-squared	0.6835		0.7436		0.6474		0.3866		0.7165		0.7407	
Adj R squared	0.6423		0.6826		0.5635		0.2751		0.649		0.7068	

* Significant at 90%.
** Significant at 95%.
*** Significant at 99%.

Urbanization – unlike in Models 1 and 2 – has a positive effect on literacy. At first glance, the statistically significant finding for the effect of the indigenous population appears to support the Sokoloff model. But the data on indigenous population is based on linguistic categorization, which makes it particularly likely to be related to this measure of education development, and thus this finding's import is limited.

Models 4 and 5 examine the determinants of school enrollment in 1907. Model 4 examines the effect of social and economic inequality, revenues, and spending on enrollment, and finds that only spending has an effect. Strikingly, the model is much more poorly fitted than any of the others, which suggests the presence of an omitted variable in explaining state-level school enrollment. Adding the level of enrollment in 1875 drastically alters the results: it is significant at the 99 percent level, and sharply increases the R-squared. This suggests that there is something "sticky" about school enrollment: something structural that shapes its level that is not included in the models.[22]

Model 6 is perhaps the most direct test of the structural inequality-elite preferences argument, since it examines education spending levels in 1907. The analysis shows that state and municipal revenues and the indigenous proportion of the population have a negative effect on primary school spending, the latter of which is significant at the 95 percent level. But a 1 percent increase in the proportion of the population that speaks indigenous languages is predicted to reduce education spending by .0044 pesos per capita, and since the standard deviation of 1907 education spending levels is .28 pesos per capita, this is a negligible effect in substantive terms.

Overall, these results suggest that there is reason to doubt that social and economic inequality have a sizable linear effect on the development of primary schooling. The scatterplots in Figure 4.1 confirm this finding: with a few exceptions (Campeche and the Yucatán) the data are consonant with the possibility that a low indigeneity rate is necessary for schooling to develop. But given the wide variation among cases with similar levels of indigeneity, much of the variation across cases remains unaccounted for by the demographic factor.

---

[22] It is interesting to note that spending rates are not sticky over time in the same way that enrollment rates are: the correlation between enrollment rates in 1875 and 1907 is 0.629, while the correlations for spending in 1874 and 1907 is only 0.248. Mariscal and Sokoloff claim that social inequality matters because it shapes the institutions making spending decisions, but this evidence suggests that schooling provision is more consistent over time than is school spending.

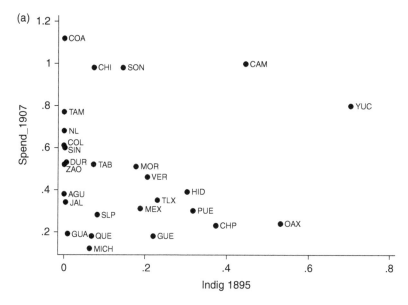
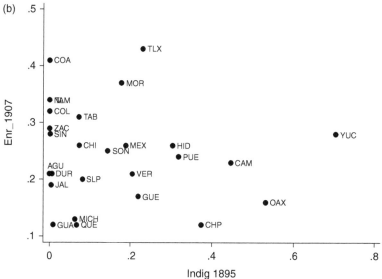

FIGURE 4.1. Indigenous population and education indicators, Mexico
Spending by state and municipal governments, 1907
Enrollment, 1907
Literacy, 1910

Educational Development

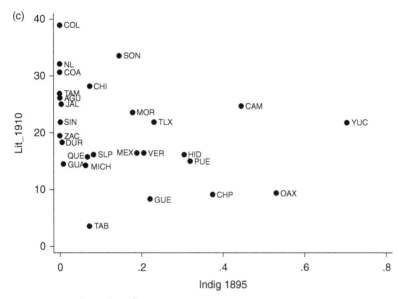

FIGURE 4.1. *(continued)*

To explore this further, we can leverage the fact that the form of administration varied across Mexican states during the Porfiriato to examine whether it affected education development. To do so, I conduct a paired comparison of the states of Sonora and Michoacán. As Figure 4.1 shows, similar proportions of the population in these two states spoke indigenous languages in 1895 – in fact, Sonora had a larger indigenous segment of its population, and was less urbanized than was Michoacán. Both of these characteristics make it an unlikely site for education development. Yet its levels of spending, enrollment, and literacy were much higher by the eve of the Revolution in Sonora than in Michoacán.[23]

The paired comparison discussed later shows that in Sonora, economic elites were excluded from administrative positions and thus unable to act on their preferences about taxation, spending, and policy.[24] By contrast, elites in Michoacán, although they held few political positions, did continue to control administrative positions and thus influence policy in a variety of realms. Demonstrating that the forms of rule are correlated

---

[23] I chose to compare these two states because of the availability of excellent regional histories for both cases: DeHart (1984) and Voss (1982) for Sonora, and Chowning (1999) for Michoacán.
[24] See García Alcaraz and Martínez Moya (2006) for a state-level education history of Jalisco that emphasizes similar factors.

with education outcomes across Mexican states, particularly in conjunction with the cross-national and cross-time findings in Chile and Peru, further buttresses the argument that they are crucial to the development of state power.

Sonora

The Restored Republic and the Porfiriato – the era of state-building efforts in Mexico – saw steady patterns of conflict between progress-seeking administrators and autonomy-craving local elites in Sonora. During the Porfiriato in particular, the governor imposed policies on the state that inflicted significant costs on elites, and effectively implemented those policies despite their opposition. Administrators were able to do so because "old landed elite families ... were for the most part deliberately excluded from the higher echelons of state power" (DeHart 1984, 183). While they maintained their social standing, the "traditional gentry" were excluded from state-level political and administrative positions. This meant that they were unable to prevent state officials from "making policy decisions without sufficient consideration for local elite interests" (ibid., 191). Thus, DeHart argues, it is no surprise that Sonora was one of the centers of elite opposition to the Díaz regime after 1910.

The exclusion of elites from crucial policy choices was a pattern during the Restored Republic. Voss (1982) describes how state officials challenged local notables as they sought to institute economic policies that transcended local concerns. To do so, Governor Pesqueira relied heavily on the power of the prefects, who he appointed, to reduce the autonomy of the municipalities, and the influence of the "prominent families that dominated them" (ibid., 208). Conflict between the prefects deployed by the governor and the municipalities dominated state politics throughout the Restored Republic. Local elites sought to reform the state constitution to make prefects accountable to elections, an effort defeated by the Governor, who sought to retain the power of appointment, and to use it to deploy loyal bureaucrats to implement his chosen policies (ibid., 251). By the time Díaz came to power, policymaking was centralized in the hands of the governor and implemented largely by deployed bureaucrats – most notably the prefects, who acted as "underlings" and "henchmen" of the governor (ibid., 279).

Tensions between Sonoran elites and state officials were particularly acute in regard to the Yaqui indigenous community. While both groups saw the need to develop the Yaqui River valley for agriculture, administrators' preference for indiscriminate deportation of the Yaqui conflicted with local elites, who valued the Yaqui as "diligent, skilled, and cheap workers in a sparsely populated region" (DeHart 1984, 180). In implementing their policies of pacification by force after 1902, the state administration (controlled by Luis Torres, an "outsider imported into the state") failed to consider "the opinions or interests of local hacendados and other Yaqui employers" (ibid., 183).

This reliance on deployed rule affected educational development. Whereas local notables were reluctant to fund primary education by approving new taxes, the state government "had ambitious plans" to spread education to rural areas (Voss 1982, 201 and 238). Because policy was implemented largely by the prefects, to the exclusion of local elites, educational spending and educational development were fairly high in Sonora.

Michoacán

In Michoacán, on the other hand, power at the state level remained in the hands of "entrenched oligarchs" (Knight 1986, 38). Although Chowning (1999, 10) describes less overlap between political and economic elites than we might anticipate, the extent of elite influence over policy in Michoacán was much higher than in Sonora. As a result, despite the fact that local elites held few elected positions during the Restored Republic or the Porfiriato, they continued to exercise influence over the policies of the state and local governments – although in "more oblique ways" (ibid., 261) than before the Liberal era.

Thus, while Sonora was characterized by deployed rule, Michoacán saw much more significant delegation of administration to local elites by the Liberal and Porfirian administrations. It is not surprising, then, that educational development lagged in Michoacán – despite the fact that the state had a smaller indigenous population, a more urban population, and fewer fiscal constraints than did Sonora. "Despite many years of state budget surpluses" (ibid., 333), educational development lagged throughout the Porfiriato, and by 1910 the state was one of the laggards in the country as a whole in the number of schools, the number of trained teachers, and the development of pedagogical training – although it had many private schools (Vaughan 1982, 55 and 61). Governors and administrators in Michoacán placated the state's elites by appointing them to "plummy offices" such as prefectures (Chowning 1999, 261). From those positions, they would have been able to disrupt policies aimed at primary school expansion, as well as other aspects of state building.

Educational development in Sonora outpaced that of Michoacán not because Sonoran elites were more amenable to it. Instead, the difference was that Sonoran elites had been more broadly pushed out of the administration by Liberal and Porfirian politicians, leaving them with less influence over policy implementation. While economic elites in Michoacán retained a degree of influence over policymaking in the state government, Sonoran elites saw even their hold over municipal administration challenged, as prefects deployed by the governor cut into the autonomy of *ayuntamientos* and implemented policies (including school-building) that impinged on the economic interests of the state's elites. This finding confirms the overall results of this chapter: against explanations that emphasize structural conditions in explaining patterns of educational development in Latin America, evidence from Chile, Peru, and Mexico supports the importance of the form of rule in determining the outcomes of efforts at school-building.

CONCLUSION

Only in Colombia was the absence of educational development the result of a failure to undertake efforts to build this aspect of state power.[25] Here, national leaders never sought to build a primary school system – nor, as we will see in the succeeding chapters, did they try to build other aspects of state power. But in Peru before 1895, and in some parts of Mexico, educational development efforts failed because their implementation was delegated to local elites. The Sokoloff hypothesis is correct to argue that economic elites were reluctant to fund educational development, which imposed taxation on them in the service of a goal they questioned. Where they could dilute the grand plans of state-builders – as in Michoacán and in Peru before 1895 – they did so. But where state builders bypassed local elites and deployed bureaucrats to implement this aspect of their state-building projects, the Sokoloff hypothesis is debunked, and schooling was built and standardized even in contexts of high social inequality. The institutions of local rule were the foundation of the precocious

---

[25] Unless one can show that Colombia was marked by substantially greater social inequality than were any of the other cases, the Sokoloff hypothesis is not sufficient to explain the absence of efforts to build schools in that case. Although the large Afro-Colombian population did create a degree of social inequality, its smaller indigenous population (in comparison with the proportion of indigenous population in Peru or Mexico) casts doubt on the possibility that Colombia saw dramatic levels of inequality by regional standards.

development of education in Chile. They underlie the altered trajectory of educational development in Peru after 1895. And they also are correlated with the state-level variation observed in Mexico. All this evidence, combined with that presented about the development of taxation and military development in Chapters 5 and 6, suggests strongly that the public administration of state building was crucial for the fate of state-building efforts.

5

Political Costs, Infrastructural Obstacles, and Tax State Development

This chapter compares the development of the tax states in the four cases. It finds that the Chilean and Mexican states established much greater extractive capacity than did their Peruvian and Colombian counterparts, as reflected in the greater impositions they could place on the population, and in the wider range of types of taxes they could collect. The chapter shows that the ideational and institutional arguments outlined in Chapters 1 and 2 account for this variation in state development. Ideas about the role of the state in development shaped tax policy choices, underlying the striking dismantling of the Colombian fiscal states and efforts to build extractive capacity in the other three cases. Institutions of local administration determined the effectiveness of tax assessment and collection where it was implemented.

As in all of the empirical chapters, the ideational and institutional account I develop is counterposed here against a set of alternative explanations that are particularly relevant for this aspect of state development. This chapter addresses two such alternatives – commodity booms and federalism – and shows that neither can account for the full pattern of variation in tax state development. I argue that the key gap in both alternative explanations is similar – they both focus on *political* obstacles, which relate to formal political institutions, and ignore the *infrastructural* challenges of taxation, which relate to state capacity.

Perhaps the most important alternative explanation for variation in tax state development is that the presence of easily tapped revenue from commodity booms accounts for the absence of extractive capacity. Later, I show that booms and busts in nitrates and guano can provide at best a partial explanation for the divergent trajectories of the two countries in which these were important historically: Chile and Peru. The presence of resource booms explains the absence of taxation: I show that both states dismantled their tax apparati as resources flowed in. But resource-based explanations tell us little about what happens when resource rents dry up. Thus, the puzzle of why Chile recovered fiscally from the end of the nitrate boom within a decade (despite significant political upheaval) while Peru's fiscal crisis lasted half a century remains. A paired comparison of the post-boom efforts to tax in the two countries shows that as opposed to the *political* costs of taxation that form the core of resource-based explanations, the greater ability of the Chilean state to overcome the *infrastructural* obstacles to taxation explains its quicker recovery. The Chilean state's ability to tax derived from the fact that it relied on deployed bureaucrats, while by contrast, the Peruvian state's post-guano efforts to tax were undermined by the unwillingness of local elites serving as state agents to overcome analogous obstacles to taxation.

A second explanation for variation in tax state development is the role of federalism. Mexico and Colombia provide a propitious context for examining this issue, since federal systems in both countries gave subnational interests a platform to restrict taxation by the national government. Yet while federalism explains the origins of a distinct political dynamic of taxation that was absent in Peru and Chile, it cannot explain the much greater tax state development in Mexico than in Colombia. Here, again, we must turn to the role of ideas. Central governments in Colombia chose to pursue development through limited state intervention, and to finance this small government with import duties, which remained until the late 1920s the dominant source of revenue. In Mexico, by contrast, state leaders drew on a more interventionist version of liberalism, and sought the power to collect a wide range of other taxes. By negotiation and innovation, they steadily expanded the range of taxes collected by the federal government at the expense of the states. Thus while federalism established similar challenges in Mexico and Colombia, it cannot explain the divergent outcomes. Additionally, the Mexican case, like that of Chile, shows the crucial role of deployed rule, which ensured the effective collection of taxes. Even more than in the realm of education (discussed in Chapter 4), the Porfirian state aggressively centralized control over tax administration, and removed it from the hands of subnational government and local elites. The result, like in Chile, was significant development of a tax state; something that Colombian leaders did not seek, and Peruvian leaders could not accomplish.

Thus, the ideational and institutional arguments advanced in Chapters 1 and 2 can better account for variation in tax state development than either of these two alternative explanations. To develop this argument, I begin by discussing how we should measure the state's extractive capacity. The second part of the chapter describes the trajectories of tax state development in the four cases. I then engage in two paired comparisons of the cases, each of which is designed to evaluate the power of my argument against one of the alternative explanations. As discussed earlier, Peru and Chile are paired to evaluate the commodity boom explanation, and the limits of federalism as an explanation for variation in tax state development are explored in the narratives on Colombia and Mexico.

OPERATIONALIZING TAX STATE DEVELOPMENT

Taxation is central to the study of state power and state-society relations. But as Lieberman (2002) shows, different aspects of taxation shed light on different aspects of the state. Care is therefore needed in extrapolating from evidence about taxation to conclusions about the state. To assess the state's infrastructural power, we must design measures that capture its ability to extract taxes from its population, and how that ability varies across society and territory. To do so, this study explores two dimensions of taxation: the *types of revenue* collected by the state and the *tax burden per capita* imposed on the population. Because the commonly used tax ratio conflates the state's capacity to tax with the regime's willingness to do so, I set it aside and opt for these more fine-grained assessments of the extractive capacity of the state.

Tax Types

Scholars often draw conclusions about state power from information on the types of taxes collected by the national government (Chaudhry 1999). The requirements for collection vary across tax types in two ways relevant to infrastructural power. First, taxes vary in their *spatial distribution of incidence*. Those taxes that can be collected in a small number of central locations require a more skeletal administrative apparatus than do those that require the presence of agents throughout the territory.[1] Thus,

---

[1] In addition to the implications of a tax type for the spatial reach of the state, I also discuss the available evidence about spatially uneven imposition and collection of taxes.

TABLE 5.1. *Revenue sources ranked by implications for state power*

Tax type	Nature of assessment needed	Intensity of penetration required	Territorial reach required
Import duties	Customs inspection at port(s) of entry	Low	Low
Export taxes	Inspection at production site or port of exit	Low	Low
Monopoly production	Control of distribution	Low	Medium
Consumption taxes	Control of distribution	Low	Medium
Tolls, internal duties, and fees for service	Inspection on roads/rivers at certain points	Low	Medium
Professional license fees	Audit of services	Low	Medium
Sales taxes	Audit of bills of sale	Medium*	Medium
Head taxes	Census of population	Medium	High
Land area taxes	Land survey or cadastral maps	Medium	High
Income taxes	Income data	High	High
Land value taxes	Detailed land census	High	High
Taxes on non-land wealth	Detailed property census	High	High

* This assessment is based on the limited set of transactions that were subject to sales taxes in the cases under investigation. As this set of transactions expands, this tax would move higher in the rankings of intensity.

a state that relies heavily on customs duties – collected only at major ports of entry and exit – requires little in terms of extractive capacity throughout the vast remainder of its national territory, while the taxation of domestic commerce, wealth, or income likely requires the state to have a much greater reach. Second, taxes vary in the *difficulty of assessment and collection* required to extract revenue. For example, it is easier (although less precise) to impose a tax based on the area of land owned than a tax on the value of land, or to impose customs duties by weight rather than by value (Scott 1998).

By combining these two dimensions, as shown in Table 5.1, we can array the range of state revenue sources by the extent of infrastructural power required for their collection.[2] Each row of the table represents a significant source of state revenue in the countries investigated in this study. They are listed in increasing order of infrastructural power: those at the top of the chart require only minimal levels, while those at the bottom imply a truly capable state. The second column briefly describes typical collection procedures as they are reflected in records examined for the four cases; the rightmost two columns assess the two dimensions of collection challenges for that tax type. In the remainder of this chapter, I use the distribution of state revenues according to this ranking to assess its ability to penetrate society for extractive purposes. While there may be some debate over the scoring of particular tax types, the overall pattern for any case should be robust to any disputes about where an individual tax type should be placed in this table.

Tax Burden

I also use the *tax burden*: the amount of taxation imposed by the state directly on its citizens as a second measure of the extractive dimension of state power.[3] I exclude duties on the exports of raw materials, monopoly profits, and customs duties because they are not imposed directly on the population. Thus, the tax burden is calculated by summing taxes on income, property, and wealth, sales taxes, inheritance taxes, and various fees for service and permits, and dividing this quantity by the size of the population. This provides a measure of the average amount of revenue extracted by the state per capita directly from its citizens. This amount can be calculated at the national level, and compared across time or across countries with appropriate adjustments for inflation and purchasing power where possible. By combining information on the tax burden with information on the broader set of revenue sources of the state, we can get a nuanced picture of its power to tax.

COMPARATIVE DEVELOPMENT

I begin with a summary of the comparative development of taxation in the four cases so that the variation to be explained is clearly shown. The discussion that follows reveals striking variation across cases. I periodize

[2] Lieberman (2002, table 3) produces a similar list, but Table 5.1 arrays the actual revenue sources that were used by states in the four cases.
[3] A helpful discussion of how to choose among the myriad options for operationalizing this concept appears in Lieberman (2002).

the discussion of Chile and Peru to parse out the effects of the commodity booms in those cases. I also highlight how the federal institutions in Colombia and Mexico posed obstacles to tax collection by the national state. Yet once these factors are accounted for, we will see that the cases follow patterns similar to those seen in our investigations of education and coercion: the absence of a state-building project in Colombia, state-building efforts in Peru stymied by reliance on delegation to local elites, which allowed those actors to block fiscal imposition, and concerted, successful state building in Mexico and Chile that depended centrally on the implementation efforts of deployed local officials.

Tax Types

Chile

Extractive capacity grew sharply in Chile in the first century after independence, as reflected in the growth of direct taxation, and in the rise of internal taxation as a complement to customs revenues, which nevertheless remained the most important source of state revenues throughout the period. Although direct taxation declined with the nitrate boom after 1880, gains in the state's extractive capacity were not lost. The changing composition of the Chilean tax structure is summarized in the series of snapshots in Table 5.2.

Pre-nitrate tax state development: After independence, the Chilean state relied heavily on foreign debt and asset confiscation, reflecting its weakness[4] (MHAC 1834, 3ff). Limited revenues came mainly from customs takings and monopolies: the state lacked the capacity to assess and collect taxes directly from the population. In 1840, only about 2 percent of government revenue came from internal taxation. But internal taxation increased almost forty-fold between 1840 and 1875, rising to 20% of total revenue by 1845 and remaining steadily above 10 percent until 1885. Thus, between about 1840 and the War of the Pacific (1879–1883), the Chilean state developed extensive tax capacity.

This period also saw a change in the *types* of internal taxes collected. In 1840, internal tax revenue came entirely from monopoly rents on tobacco, playing cards, and salt. A tithe collected from the heads of households rose in prominence, and made up the majority of tax collection in Chile in both 1845 and 1850. In 1853, the *contribución territorial*

---

[4] Data in this discussion draws on the MHAC for various years and the statistical series in Mamalakis (1976) and Wagner et al. (2000).

TABLE 5.2. *Chilean revenue sources, selected years*

Tax type	1841	1860	1875	1895	1927
Customs duties	59.0%	59.1%	57.3%	31.6%	28.2%
Resource rents		7.3%		62.3%	28.3%
Monopoly production	21.2%	14.5%	13.1%		
Consumption taxes					
Tolls, internal duties, and fees for service				3.9%	
Professional license fees					
Sales taxes	3.5%				
Head taxes	11.6%				
Land area taxes				0.0%	
Income taxes					9.7%
Land value taxes		7.1%	7.9%		
Taxes on non-land wealth					7.9%

Source: Wagner et al. (2000).

(a 7.11 percent tax on the value of landholdings) was introduced, which by 1855 made up the largest portion of internal taxation, about 37.5 percent of the total internal tax collected. This tax represented a significant leap in the state's infrastructural power, since it inaugurated the assessment of property holdings by the state – some 31,000 properties, for instance, in 1861. In the 1870s, as the country was gripped by economic crisis, taxes on inheritance, property, and income were introduced (Sater 1976, 326ff). By 1882, these taxes were the third most important source of revenue. While this trajectory of increasing capacity was cut short by the onset of the nitrate boom after 1885, it is clear that extractive capacity had grown sharply since 1840.

The nitrate boom and national government taxation: With victory in the War of the Pacific, Chile seized massive nitrate fields from Peru and Bolivia. Nitrate proceeds drove a near-doubling in government revenues between 1886 and 1890, and dominated them until the end of World War I. In response, the national government eliminated nearly all other forms of taxation (Mamalakis 1976, 213). Internal taxes declined to a tenth of their 1885 level by 1895, and by 1900, the only one remaining was the *papel sellado*.

Reliance on nitrate duties left state revenues vulnerable to fluctuations in the nitrate market, and this concern drove state leaders to begin to reintroduce taxation even at the height of the boom. To supplement nitrate revenue, in 1902 a tax on alcohol was introduced, followed by a tax on insurance companies in 1905, on tobacco, playing cards, and inheritances in 1910, and on banks in 1912 (Bowman and Wallerstein 1982, 451). The introduction of these taxes, however, does not undo the overall trend of heavy dependence on nitrate revenues during the early twentieth century.

Nitrate exports began to falter during World War I before collapsing in 1920, and government revenues plummeted. In response, the state turned back to internal taxation, which tripled between 1913 and 1920, at which point it was fifty times the 1900 level. By 1920, the Chilean state was generating over 25 percent of its income from internal taxation, relying heavily on a property tax introduced in 1915 that generated over 5 million pesos annually. By the mid-1920s, the Chilean state had not just returned to its pre-nitrate levels of extractive capacity, but was actually stronger than it had been prior to the nitrate boom. Although the capacity-intensive taxes introduced between 1840 and the onset of the nitrate boom disappeared during the boom, they quickly reemerged thereafter. Rather than being replaced by customs revenues, the lost resource rents were replaced with increases in domestic taxation. In Chile, the nitrate boom had limited long-term effects on the fiscal state. It is this strikingly fast recovery from the collapse of the nitrate boom that sets Chile apart from the Peruvian experience.

Peru

As discussed in Chapter 3, the Peruvian state was unique in that domestic taxation actually made up a significant share of its revenue in the initial decades after independence. The head tax on the indigenous population represented the second largest share of tax revenue in 1846, suggesting a state that could impose extraction on its population. Head tax collection was actually rather effective in the 1840s as the government was able to collect more revenues than it had projected.[5] With the onset of the guano boom in the 1840s, internal taxation was eliminated. The state's extractive capacity would remain vestigial long after the boom ended in the 1870s. The trends are summarized in the snapshots in Table 5.3.

Guano and the decay of the Peruvian tax state, 1845–1875: As guano revenues flowed after the mid-1840s, the state began a "step-by-step dismantling of surviving direct taxes" (Gootenberg 1989, 122). The most dramatic step was the 1854 elimination of the head tax. This shift

---

[5] Data in Tantaleán Arbulú (1983), Appendix, Table Four, my calculations.

TABLE 5.3. *Peruvian revenue sources, selected years*

Tax type	1846	1865	1890	1923–1924
Customs duties	26.3%	22.0%	48.2%	42.5%
Resource rents	8.4%	75.2%		
Monopoly production				
Consumption taxes			15.3%	24.4%
Tolls, internal duties, and fees for service				
Professional license fees				
Sales taxes				
Head taxes	21.5%			
Land area taxes				
Income taxes				
Land value taxes				
Taxes on non-land wealth				

Sources: Tantaleán Arbulú (1983, Appendix), Extracto Estadístico del Perú 1929–1930, and Contreras and Cueto (1999, 218).

"significantly lessened the presence of the guano-era state in the highlands" where the indigenous population was concentrated (Klarén 2000, 163). As the state came to rely more heavily on guano revenue, its ability to penetrate the national periphery disappeared, and its extractive capacity sharply eroded. Dependence on guano even replaced customs as a source of income. Guano revenues became a form of emergency finance, as state dependence on loans rose. To maximize up-front revenue, the state auctioned off gross export rights to whoever could provide the largest up-front loan most quickly, rather than collect even per-ton taxes on the guano (Gootenberg 1993). There was, in short, no fiscal state in Peru by the end of the guano era.

Post-guano crisis, 1875–1895: In the aftermath of the guano collapse, Peru entered a major crisis of state that incorporated defeat in the War of the Pacific, the resulting loss of its nitrate fields, several years of Chilean occupation, and a decade of internal conflict. Given this litany of disasters, it is no surprise that the state found taxation difficult. Postwar governments sought revenue by reintroducing a head tax and by fiscal decentralization that made departments responsible for their own expenses. The head tax made up about 50 percent of budget projections, but collection fell far short of this amount (Thurner 1997, 105). While generating little revenue, the introduction of the head tax, as discussed further later, triggered the largest uprising since independence (Thurner

1997). Postwar governments also introduced consumption taxes on alcohol, tobacco, opium, matches, and salt. None of these required significant intensity of penetration, since they were assessed on distributors rather than on sellers and consumers. The costs these taxes imposed on the population also prompted major revolts, and collection also suffered from smuggling and evasion. Thus, after guano collapsed, the state remained strikingly weak, a sharp contrast to the recovery of extractive capacity seen in Chile.

The civilista tax state and its limits, 1895–1919: The recovery of extractive capacity was strikingly slow by comparison to Chile. One set of obstacles was political. In an attempt to generate revenue, state officials confronted political opposition as they sought to tax recovering commodity exports: mine owners gained a fifteen-year exemption in 1890, and sugar producers blocked any export tax on agricultural products (Thorp and Bertram 1978, 30). But the most important obstacle was the simple inability to effectively extract revenue from the population. This forced the state to continue to fill its coffers mainly from consumption taxes, import duties, and foreign loans.

The state did generate significant revenue from what its records call "direct taxes" in the early twentieth century: these generated 14.6 percent of annual government revenue between 1899 and 1939 – about half the level of consumption taxes (28.8 percent) and customs revenues (32.8 percent).[6] While this appears to reflect a state with significant infrastructural power, a more detailed look undercuts that view.[7] The label "direct tax" was deeply misleading: revenue in this category included fees on mining and agricultural exports, charges for professional and industrial licenses (collected only in Lima and Callao), and a tax on industrial company revenue. Thus although "direct taxes" contributed to the recovery of the Peruvian tax state after about 1915, this does not reflect increased infrastructural power. Instead, the Peruvian tax state remained vestigial, depending for the vast majority of its revenues on customs, tobacco and salt monopolies, and consumption taxes on alcohol and other commodities. The contrasting post-boom trajectories of Chile and Peru are explored in detail later.

---

[6] These figures are based on my calculations from data in various years of the *Extracto Estadístico*.
[7] Unfortunately, little data about the composition of the category labeled "direct taxes" is available before 1925. The discussion here is based on data from 1925–1931, and its utility depends on the assumption that infrastructural power was not lower in 1925 than in preceding decades – a reasonable claim given a holistic view of Peruvian history.

Commodity booms did not sharply distort fiscal development in our other two cases, so the presentation of their fiscal evolution does not require the same periodization. It does, however, require addressing the role of federalism, which affected tax policy in both countries.

Colombia

The limited development of Colombia's tax state can clearly be seen in Table 5.4. In the first quarter century after independence, the Colombian state generated most of its revenue from three sources: customs revenue (31.3 percent), the tobacco monopoly (24.5 percent), and the salt monopoly (12.3 percent).[8] As of 1850, the Colombian state collected no direct taxes. This pattern continued throughout the first century after independence: the state continued to rely heavily on customs revenue and monopoly production. This failure to develop any tax capacity left the state vulnerable to fluctuations in world trade, and unable to impose any taxes on its population.

The Liberal Reforms after 1849 involved two significant changes to taxation. Both reflect the disdain for the state held by Colombia's Liberals in their development vision. First, a wide range of taxes (most importantly the tax on alcohol) were devolved to subnational authorities, who would thereafter retain a great degree of fiscal autonomy. Despite sporadic policy initiatives and the nominally centralist character of the 1886 constitution, taxation thereafter remained largely in the hands of subnational units (Cruz Santos 1966, 40–41). Second, the tobacco monopoly and many other taxes were eliminated in 1850, resulting in a 47 percent decline in national government revenues between 1849 and 1851[9] (McGreevey 1971, 86). Reformers hoped that eliminating the tobacco monopoly would spur economic growth via tobacco export, allowing the national government to draw revenue from duties on increased imports. Absent other sources of revenue, dependence on customs increased after 1850. These generated 63 percent of national government revenues from 1850 to 1900 (Rosenthal 2001, 33–34). Import duty collection was limited by the rampant smuggling in Caribbean ports (Posada-Carbó 1996, 228).

Salt taxes also remained significant, making up 16 percent of national revenues between 1850 and 1900, and reaching as high as 29 percent

[8] These figures are drawn from Rosenthal (2001) and are based on annual data for twenty-one years between 1824 and 1850.
[9] Park (1985, 54) cites an 1870 calculation claiming that the reforms cost the government half its potential income between 1850 and 1870.

TABLE 5.4. *Colombian revenue sources*

Tax type	1835–1836	1870	1911	1927
Customs duties	36.4%	54.6%	65.3%	62%
Resource rents				
Monopoly production	53.1%	26.3%	7.8%	5.5%
Consumption taxes				
Tolls, Internal duties, and fees for service		8.8%		11.5%
Professional license fees				
Sales taxes	0.4%		4.8%	2.4%
Head taxes				
Land area taxes				
Income taxes				
Land value taxes				
Taxes on non-land wealth				

Sources: Deas (1982, 326 fn100), McGreevey (1971, 40), Park (1985, 56), Cruz Santos (1966, 141). Sales taxes were primarily generated from *papel sellado*, and fees for service are overwhelmingly from railroads.

in 1865 (Park 1985, 57–58). Although the salt monopoly violated the Liberal edict of minimal government, and was highly unpopular, it was retained because it was "simply too important to be eliminated" once other revenue sources were gone (Rosenthal 2001, 28). Another significant source of revenue was the *degüello* tax on cattle slaughter. Deas describes this tax as both progressive (since the poor did not eat beef) and fairly easy to collect since it was rare for cows to be slaughtered exclusively for personal consumption, meaning that they had to be brought to market.[10] In 1874, it was the main revenue source for the country's subnational entities (Deas 1982, 305–307). When the national government claimed jurisdiction over it in the 1886 constitution, it quickly became the third largest source of revenue in the budget (Cruz Santos 1966, 38–41).

Although the economy was transformed by the boom in coffee production after 1887, no direct revenue for the state resulted. An 1895 proposal to tax coffee exports was met with major opposition not only from coffee producers but from those who saw the tax as a violation of laissez-faire principles (Bergquist 1986, 52). With the trade crisis of World War I, an income tax was introduced in 1918, but it generated 1.7 percent of government revenues in 1919 and remained marginal

[10] Posada-Carbó (1996, 217) disagrees.

well into the 1930s. Even in the late 1920s, customs represented 62 percent of government revenue, and railroad fees 11.5 percent. Salt sales remained significant at 5.5 percent of revenues, while *papel sellado* and the income tax remained of minimal importance, at 2.4 percent and 1.5 percent, respectively (Deas 1982, 325). The composition of tax types continued to reflect a strikingly weak state. Although this was in part a function of the devolution of taxes to the subnational level, it also reflected the belief of Colombian political elites that increasing state fiscal capacity would not promote the development they sought.

Mexico

Mexico's federal constitution, like Colombia's, limited the taxes available to the national government. Yet its trajectory of tax state development was distinct, as Liberal and Porfirian officials made aggressive efforts to reduce their reliance on customs revenues by developing the capacity of the national state to tap many revenue streams. The evolution of tax types in Mexico reveals two broad trends (see Table 5.5). First, it reveals a steady increase in reliance on internal taxation. Second, this internal taxation is increasingly composed of revenue sources that require significant infrastructural power. Together, these changes show that the Mexican state increased its capacity to extract from its population during the Liberal and (especially) the Porfirian eras. This increase was also reflected in the penetration of land surveys, census administration, and state regulation of property rights even into remote regions like Chiapas (Bobrow-Strain 2007, 52ff).

In the post-independence era (1821–1867) 62.3 percent of state revenues came from customs duties (Pérez Siller 2004, 50). Endemic internal conflict often prevented customs revenues from reaching federal coffers, and allowed challengers to national power to use customs revenue to fund insurrection (Ludlow 2002, Vol. 1, p. 336). Beginning with the first Liberal governments, leaders sought to reduce dependence on customs, driven by these concerns, but also by a belief that export taxes were an obstacle to economic development. Early efforts fell victim to political instability, and internal taxation by the federal government largely remained limited to duties on the transit of goods into the Federal District and the territories of Baja California and Tepic (the *alcábala*). But after 1867 political stability allowed state leaders to begin the building of extractive capacity.

TABLE 5.5. *Mexican revenue sources, selected years*

Tax type	1856	1873	1895	1910
Customs duties	67.4%	68.5%	44.9%	44.4%
Resource rents				
Monopoly production				
Consumption taxes				
Tolls, internal duties, and fees for service		7.0%	3.3%	6.3%
Professional license fees				
Sales taxes		12.8%	35.7%	29.6%
Head taxes				
Land area taxes				
Income taxes				
Land value taxes		3.2%	3.2%	5.7%
Taxes on non-land wealth				

Source: Carmagnani (1994, Appendix 3), Tenenbaum (1986, Appendix, Tables A and C). Despite its changing composition over time, I coded the *timbre* as a sales tax for all years. This coding decision is chosen in order to understate the capacity of the Mexican state, since over time, the *timbre* came to encompass a range of tax types. The land value tax, the *contribución predial*, was collected only in Mexico City and the federal territories.

The centerpiece of reform was the introduction of the *timbre* in 1871. Generating at least 29 percent of revenue every year between 1890 and the revolution, the *timbre* became the most important internal tax collected by the federal government. The *timbre* contained multiple components, which came over time to include more infrastructurally demanding tax types. In its original form, it was comprised of the *contribución federal*, a surcharge on all state and local taxes, and a stamp tax levied on official documents and the consumption of certain luxury goods. An important institutional innovation in the *contribución federal* was a shift in the burden of this surcharge from state governments to taxpayers, which ended conflict between levels of government over tax revenues (Castañeda Zavala 2001; Uhthoff 2004). Between 1867 and 1910, it represented 7 to 13 percent of total federal revenue. In nominal terms, *contribución federal* revenues grew fivefold between 1867 and 1906, declining slightly on the eve of the revolution. This tax appears consonant with a weak state, since it required little penetration of the economy by the federal government. But Uhthoff (2004) shows that the *contribución federal* led to the construction of a direct relationship between the central state and its citizens because it relied on federal tax collectors to inspect the state and local tax bills of citizens throughout the national territory. This process of revenue centralization shows how the Mexican state steadily worked to overcome the obstacles of federalism to fiscal capacity.

Over time, the set of revenue sources included in the *timbre* increased, revealing a state inserting itself into an increasingly wide range of economic activity. Taxes on tobacco, alcohol, and perfume were added in 1881 (Carmagnani 1989, 478). State officials responded to complaints from producers of these goods about the unfair burden imposed on their sectors by this new tax: rather than exempting the complaining industries, they increased the scope of the tax to also include soaps, pharmaceuticals, playing cards, textiles, and some foods. The *renta interior*, a tax on the consumption of all domestic manufactured goods beyond basic needs, was introduced in 1887 (Carmagnani 1989, 483). As discussed later, this tax was eliminated in 1893 in negotiations between federal and state governments over the balance of fiscal federalism. Yet its introduction and the collections that resulted reflect a sharply more powerful central state than existed several decades earlier.

Thus, the increasing revenues generated from internal taxes and the broader range of economic activity and wealth on which they fell reflect significant growth in the state's extractive capacity. Whereas at the beginning of the Liberal period, the state generated no revenues from internal taxation outside the Federal District, it generated more than 40 percent of its revenues from domestic taxation in 1910. This trajectory is a sharp contrast from what was observed in Colombia, where federalism also created political obstacles to the extractive power of the national government.

Tax Burden

In addition to the types of taxes a state collects, we can also assess its capacity to extract by examining the tax burden it imposes on its population. As explained earlier, this tax burden is measured by per capita internal taxation. A comparison of the four countries (to the extent allowed by data limitations) reveals striking divergence, even after the effects of the resource booms in Chile and Peru are taken into account. The tax burdens in Chile and Mexico far outstripped those in Peru and Colombia.

Chile

The inflation-adjusted trajectory of the Chilean tax burden is shown in Figure 5.1. Over the course of the pre-1885 era, the state steadily

Tax State Development

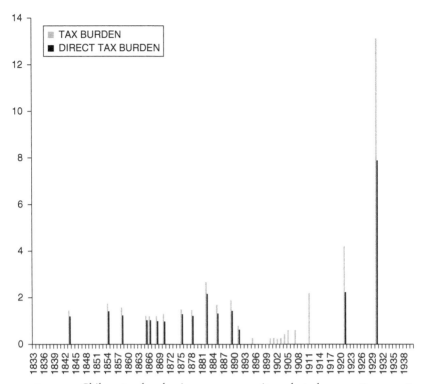

FIGURE 5.1. Chilean tax burden in pesos per capita, selected years, 1833–1938. Data from Wagner et al. (2000).

built the ability to impose taxes on its population. The onset of the nitrate boom led the tax burden to disappear as internal taxation was essentially eliminated, although it slowly crept up as the instability of nitrate revenues spurred diversification of revenue streams. With the nitrate collapse, the tax burden leaped back up. By 1920, real internal taxation per capita was already 50 percent higher than its pre-nitrate level, and by 1930, the Chilean state's extraction from its population had tripled once again. Thus we see a state that developed the power to tax before the nitrate boom, stopped taxing as resource rents flowed in, but quickly and aggressively reasserted its power to tax once the nitrate boom ended.

Municipal taxation in Chile: In addition to national government taxation, Chileans were subject to municipal taxes. Municipalities could get national government permission to impose certain taxes, most of which were earmarked for a particular purpose such as the operation of butcheries, street lighting, and street cleaning. From the mid-1850s through

1881, these taxes grew steadily.[11] The average municipal tax burden per capita (nominal data, based on a population-weighted average of sixty-two municipalities) rose from slightly over 0.5 pesos per capita in 1869 to over 2 pesos per capita during the War of the Pacific. As explored in more detail later, municipal taxation rose after the 1891 decentralization and continued to do so throughout the nitrate boom. In 1903, municipal taxes were two pesos per capita, rising to 4.2 pesos per capita in 1911, and 9.9 in 1920.[12]

Municipal taxes were one way in which revenue was extracted from the Chilean population even during the resource boom. The revenues generated by municipal taxation flowed into the coffers of local administration, not those of the central state. Thus, at first glance it appears that this taxation is irrelevant to an analysis of national state development. Yet there are two reasons to temper this view. First, this taxation was under the authority of the national state: it had to be explicitly authorized by the national government. Municipal authorities had to explain the type of tax they wanted to collect, and the purpose for which it would be earmarked, in order to be authorized to impose it.[13] Second, as explored in more detail later, this municipal taxation was pivotal in the rapid reassertion of national taxation when the nitrate trade collapsed. Because municipalities continued to collect taxes and maintain the relevant infrastructure, the challenges to reimposing taxation that national authorities faced were greatly reduced.

Peru

The evolution of the tax burden over time shows very clearly the weakness of the Peruvian state. The contrast with Chile during and after the commodity booms in both countries is especially striking, and will be explored in detail later. The data in Figure 5.2, calculated from the sum of all direct internal taxes for the years available during the guano boom, show that the elimination of the *contribución indígena* reduced internal taxes per capita by nearly 90 percent. Thereafter, the state imposed a minimal burden on its population.

The territorial unevenness of tax collection also reveals the tax state's weakness. Taxation during the guano era was almost nonexistent, outside

---

[11] Based on twenty-one years of municipal tax data, 1856–1891, collected from various government sources.
[12] Calculated from nominal municipal tax data from Mamalakis (1976). The value for 1920 is calculated using 1921 population data.
[13] This was true even after the 1891 decentralization law.

Tax State Development

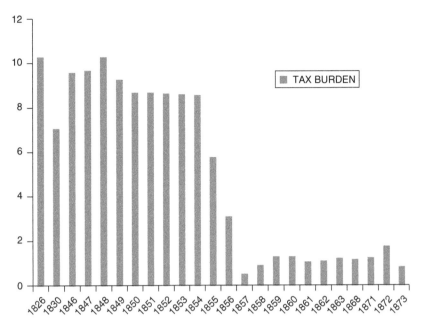

FIGURE 5.2. Peruvian tax burden, soles per capita, selected years, 1849–1873.
Sources: *Memorias* of Ministerio de Hacienda, various years and Tantaleán Arbulú (1983).

a few cities. During the guano era, the provinces were abandoned as sites of revenue collection even though *de jure* their population was subject to the few taxes that remained on the books. This absence of the state from the interior can be seen in various kinds of tax collections. Table 5.6 shows no collection of license fees for businesses and industries in ten of the nineteen departments, and no taxation at all in some Amazonian departments. The overwhelming majority of collections were from just five departments: Lima and its port of Callao, and Arequipa, Junín, and Cuzco, which contained the largest secondary cities in the country. The tax state simply did not exist outside a few large cities.

After the end of the guano boom, as discussed earlier, the Peruvian state struggled to re-impose taxes. Before 1900 it was unable to generate any revenue at all from impositions on its population. The tax burden rose tenfold between 1899 and 1920 – and although this data (in Figure 5.3) are not corrected for inflation, this does represent a real increase.[14] This reveals a state that gradually gained the ability to impose taxes on its

---

[14] The price index needed in order to correct for inflation during this period does not exist.

TABLE 5.6. *Tax collection by department, Peru, selected years*

Depts.	Urban property tax			Rural property tax			Industrial tax			License fees		
	1855	1863	1869	1855	1863	1869	1855	1863	1869	1855	1863	1869
Ancash	385	564	34	12,834	7,636	1,484		1,833	955			
<u>Arequipa</u>	<u>3,224</u>	<u>1,612</u>		<u>25,663</u>	<u>15,015</u>	<u>435</u>		<u>452</u>		<u>3,541</u>	<u>2,136</u>	<u>343</u>
Ayacucho	1,349	496	248	10,050	4,220	865		26				
Amazonas				502	121			32				
Cajamarca		150	295		2,674	2,744		2,002	512			
<u>Callao</u>		<u>11,491</u>	<u>5,000</u>		<u>448</u>	<u>224</u>				<u>7,013</u>	<u>10,670</u>	<u>14,088</u>
<u>Cuzco</u>	<u>1,420</u>	<u>1,304</u>	<u>652</u>	<u>14,692</u>	<u>10,741</u>	<u>12,272</u>		<u>1,106</u>	<u>3,140</u>	<u>3,108</u>		
Huancavelica	266	532	343	3,121	3,648	1,067		1,137	54			
Huánuco			355			5,128			30			
Ica		364			2,929						1,964	63
<u>Junín</u>	<u>5,043</u>	<u>5,274</u>	<u>3,169</u>	<u>20,161</u>	<u>8,202</u>	<u>18,977</u>			<u>4,679</u>		<u>3,802</u>	<u>4,320</u>
La Libertad	2,539	1,118	548	17,161	6,206	5,508		3,488	787	1,360	917	178
<u>Lima</u>	<u>32,917</u>	<u>45,520</u>	<u>58,694</u>	<u>34,126</u>	<u>4,089</u>	<u>10,442</u>		<u>21,919</u>	<u>10,672</u>	<u>56,549</u>	<u>72,686</u>	<u>76,063</u>
Loreto												
Moquegua	608	2,549		7,303	9,306	749		2,304	750	2,648	3,838	4,519
Piura	638	660	118	2,997	1,315	752		1,315	1,124			552
Puno	94	68		6,713	13,305	5,684		2,540	99			
Tarapacá												
Total	50338	73565	71325	157178	91718	68200		40017	24671	76074	97876	101995
Share from underlined depts.	84.64%	88.63%	94.66%	60.21%	41.97%	62.10%		58.67%	74.95%	92.29%	91.23%	92.96%

Source: Tantaleán Arbulú (1983, Appendix, Table 17) Underlined cells are data for the departments from which the vast majority of revenue was generated.

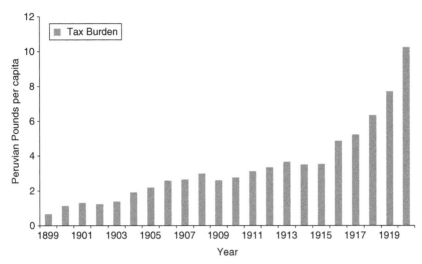

FIGURE 5.3. Peruvian tax burden in Peruvian pounds per capita, 1899–1920.
Sources: *Memorias* of Ministerio de Hacienda, various years.

population, overcoming significant obstacles, both political and infrastructural. Yet this finding must be tempered, as discussed earlier, by a realization that most of these taxes were far from capacity-intensive: the Peruvian state did increase its ability to extract during the Civilista era, but could only rely on certain kinds of revenue. Thus its capacity remained far lower than that of its southern neighbor.

Colombia

Because it relied primarily on import duties, the Colombian state never imposed a significant burden in direct taxes on its population. Indeed, even including indirect taxes and all other sources of revenue, the "weight" of the state was quite limited. An 1871 estimate, quoted by Malcolm Deas (1982, 310) was that government revenues, at less than one peso per capita, were one-third the level of Mexico's, one-fifth those of Chile, and one-twelfth those of guano-flush Peru. Revenues only declined from this level: an 1898 estimate pegged the per capita tax income of the national government, including both internal and customs revenues, at 80 centavos, a decline in real terms of 20 percent over the previous twenty years (ibid., 313).

Additionally, as in Peru, many parts of Colombian society and territory remained exempt from even this limited tax burden. The state never developed any tax capacity in the Llanos federal territories, which were under national government control. Property rights

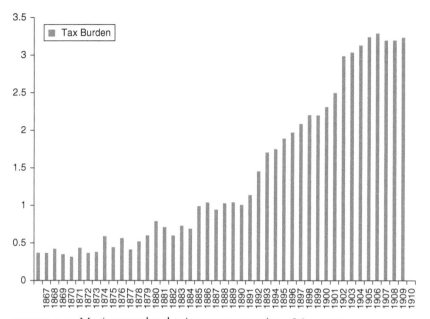

FIGURE 5.4. Mexican tax burden in pesos per capita, 1867–1910.
Sources: Internal taxation is calculated from data in Carmagnani (1994, Appendix 3). Population data are taken from Meyer and Sherman (1995, 466).

were completely absent from the region of Casanare, and a land transfer tax could not be collected because no titles were on file with the government (Rausch 1993, 174, 306). The limited spatial reach of the state was also reflected in customs collections: over 90 percent of customs revenues came from only four ports: Santa Marta, Sabanilla-Barranquilla, Cartagena, and Buenaventura (Park 1985, 56). Little tax was collected from the steady flow of cattle and other goods across the Venezuelan border. Sixty-two and a half percent of salt revenue between 1855 and 1897 was generated from a single salt mine complex, Zipaquirá (Rosenthal 2001, 34). In all, the state generated much of its revenue from a few isolated locations where it enjoyed some degree of control; much of the rest of the country remained outside the reach of its fiscal bureaucracy.

Mexico

Calculating the tax burden in Mexico is difficult because only nominal data are available. Nevertheless, its growth over the course of the Porfiriato is striking. In 1874, internal taxes per capita were 0.37 pesos, while by 1910 they had grown to 3.23 pesos, as seen in Figure 5.4. This increase of nearly 800 percent must far exceed the inflation rate. Thus the trend of increasing the tax burden is still quite clear, and is consonant with the overall pattern of increasing fiscal capacity in Mexico described earlier.

EXPLAINING VARIATION IN TAX CAPACITY

Because taxation lies at the core of the state's capacity, scholars have focused on its development in studying state building and state-society relations. Two robust currents of literature – one on the effects of commodity booms and the other on federal institutions as an obstacle to tax state development – have received much attention in recent years. In the following paired comparisons, I show the limitations of each of these explanations in accounting for variation across our four cases.

I begin with the comparison of Chile and Peru, both of which saw their fiscal development distorted by massive commodity booms. The paired analytic narrative that follows reveals the limits of "resource curse" explanations in their inability to account for variation in tax state development outside these exceptional periods. To account for the rapid recovery of Chile from commodity collapse, and the absence of a similar trend in Peru, I show that we must shift from the politics of taxation to its administration, and highlight the role of local state agents in determining the state's capacity to tax.

Deciding to Tax: Resource Rents and Political Costs

Resource endowments are perhaps the factor most commonly cited to explain the state's extractive capacity.[15] As Dunning (2008, 46) writes, a broad consensus holds that "resource booms lead to a decline in taxation and a decimation of extractive efforts on the part of the state."[16] The logic is that because taxation is more politically costly than the

---

[15] Most scholars use resource dependence (share of government revenue generated from resource rents) rather than resource abundance (share of GDP generated from resource rents) to identify cases where commodity booms affect state development. But there is, of course, a problem with endogeneity here – a state dependent on resources *by definition* has low infrastructural power because it generates little revenue from other sources (Kurtz 2009).

[16] Chaudhry (1997) makes a similar argument. Notice that resource booms need not have a similar effect on other elements of state capacity – see Saylor (2014) for an account of how commodity booms can, under certain conditions, lead to the development of other elements of the state.

alternative of relying on resource rents to fund public good provision, when leaders have an alternative source of revenue, they will substitute away from taxation. Indeed, this may be sufficient to explain the elimination of national taxation during certain periods in both Peru and Chile.[17]

But as the description earlier of the dismantling of taxation during the booms in Peru and Chile suggests, this argument is convincing in accounting for state weakness *while resources provide revenues*. We should be cautious, however, about applying this argument to explain overall variation in tax state development. While resource dependence is sufficient to explain the lack of taxation, its absence tells us nothing about levels of taxation. We can draw no conclusions about why post-boom recovery took so much longer in Peru than in Chile despite booms that were equivalent in length and in their distortionary effects on the economy.[18] The political costs underpinning the resource-dependence argument cannot account for variation in taxation in non-boom conditions.

In addition to the political costs, I argue that a complete theory of tax state development must also take into account another kind of cost of taxation: the *infrastructural* or administrative obstacles that must be overcome for taxes, once legislated, to be collected.[19] These administrative challenges – the existence of tax records and accounting infrastructure, the presence of police able and willing to enforce the rulings of tax collectors, and the like – explain the implementation of tax policy, and thus the relationship between tax policy and tax outcomes. This shift of the focus to the *capacity to tax*, to administration rather than politics, can account for variation in tax state development outside boom times.

---

[17] Notably, resource dependence is not the only explanation for the decision not to tax: as shown later, the laissez-faire ideology of Liberal leaders in Colombia explains the failure to introduce taxation in that country.

[18] Paredes (2013) disputes ths comparability of these two booms, arguing that their differential timing led them to have different effects on tax state development. This argument depends on the counterfactual claim that, had the guano boom in Peru arrived later, it would have had a different effect because the Peruvian state would have developed greater capacity. The development of education and coercion (discussed in Chapters 4 and 6), which were less distorted by the guano boom than was taxation, cast doubt on this claim.

[19] Although her focus is on what I have called the "political costs" argument, Karl (1997, 61) hints at the importance of the administrative costs of taxation in explaining the weakness of petro-states.

Implementing Taxation: Forms of Rule and Effective Administration

When states do try to tax – whether after resource booms or more broadly – their ability to do so depends on the extent of the infrastructural or administrative challenges posed by taxation. Here, again, we see the importance of delegated and deployed rule. Where states administer their periphery through delegated rule, as in Peru, the argument of this book predicts that efforts to tax will founder because of the disinclination of local officials to implement tax policy. But under deployed rule, I expect that local officials will have incentives to maintain a level of state power in their communities, which induces them to play an active part in tax state development.

The decision to tax, and the ability to implement tax policy, then, are each partial explanations for tax state development in Chile and Peru. The former is sufficient to explain the elimination of taxes, and explains why commodity booms distort the tax state. But when resource rents disappear, local administration matters. During and after the nitrate boom in Chile, the actions of local state agents were central to overcoming the infrastructural obstacles to taxation. In post-guano Peru, by contrast, local elites serving as state agents in fact created many of these roadblocks to tax administration. Even when the state sought to cut local elites out of tax administration, their central role in other aspects of local governance allowed them to undermine taxation. As a result, whereas Chile recovered its ability to tax its population within a decade after nitrates ran out, Peru took fifty years to undergo an analogous transition and was left with a much weaker tax state.

Peru: Local State Agents and the Failure to Tax after the Guano Boom

The absence of taxation in Peru after the guano ran out demands explanation. An examination of this period reveals the important role of infrastructural obstacles to taxation in addition to the political costs highlighted by existing scholarship. It highlights how administration through delegation to local elites diluted collection efforts, meaning that those internal taxes that made it through the political process were ineffectively implemented and failed to generate projected revenue.

Political Costs
Much analysis of Peru's post-guano fiscal failures has focused on the political obstacles to taxation. Scholars point to one notable instance in

particular: the refusal of Congress to approve taxes to fund the defense of Lima during the Chilean invasion of 1879 (Kurtz 2009, 496). Political opposition also explains the failure to tax primary product exports after these sectors recovered in the 1890s. The mining lobby managed to gain a fifteen-year exemption in 1890, and sugar producers were able to block any export tax on agricultural products (Thorp and Bertram 1978, 30). No export taxes were introduced until 1916, preventing the state from generating revenue from this source.

But political opposition to taxation only goes so far in explaining the failure of the state to tax. For during the years after the collapse of the guano trade – and after 1895 in particular – a range of taxes *was* instituted in Peru. Yet the Peruvian state was unable to generate any revenue from the taxes on its books. This failure revealed sizable gaps in the state's infrastructural power: its absence of records and administration, and the absence of effective policing to enforce taxation. In the discussion that follows, I highlight how the reliance on local elites to administer the national periphery shaped these failings. Because of the failure of local state agents to effectively impose taxation, the state struggled to generate revenue from a head tax, consumption taxes and monopolies, and other direct and indirect taxes. Although revenue did grow (in nominal terms) over the first two decades of the twentieth century, the painful process of tax collection further reflected the weakness of the Peruvian state.

Failure of the Head Tax
As described earlier, the first efforts to restore taxation after the War of the Pacific centered on the reintroduction of a head tax – which now, unlike in previous iterations, would fall on the entire population rather than just the indigenous segment. But collections fell far short of assessments. The failure to generate revenue cannot be blamed on decentralization: in Chile, as shown earlier, local governments continued to generate taxes even during decentralization. Nor were the fiscal shortfalls driven by political costs. The Cáceres government, ruling in a context of abject crisis and allowing little voice to the population, had no trouble imposing this tax. The problems came in its collection. Important to this failure was the lack of policing power, another aspect of the infrastructural weakness of the state. Collection was also hampered by the absence of reliable population statistics (Thorp and Bertram 1978, 121). But even more central was the fact that the state was unable to penetrate indigenous society to organize collection. Forced instead to rely on local elites, its ability to induce them to impose a new tax on their communities was limited.

This can be seen most clearly in the 1885–1886 Atusparia uprising in Ancash, the largest revolt in nineteenth-century Peru.[20] The central actors in this revolt were indigenous authorities, who were responsible for collecting from their jurisdictions. The state, in other words, did not penetrate these communities, relying instead on the mediation of community leaders.[21] Unrest was triggered when these local officials publicly petitioned the government for relief from the burden of tax collection, asking for reduced payments (Thorp and Bertram 1978, 55). When this protest was met with repression, a massive insurgency broke out. A central part of ensuring regional peace in Ancash was the negotiation of tax payments over the subsequent decade. In other words, the government largely conceded in its attempts to tax; this reflects the weakness of the Peruvian state. Each year, local officials refused the taxation schedules sent from Lima, and forced the national government to bargain with the threat of further uprising. As a result of this annual bargaining, taxes fell far short of expectations, with collections averaging about 15 percent of assessed levels between 1886 and 1895 in Huaraz, and reaching a low of 1 percent in 1887 (Thorp and Bertram 1978, 104ff). Thus the first major attempt to reimpose taxation, after the War of the Pacific and Chilean occupation, ended in abject failure because of the inability of the state to force its local representatives to make the population pay.[22]

We might think that since revolts reflect opposition to taxation, they should be seen as a political rather than infrastructural obstacle. Yet there are two reasons to see these as an indicator of the state's inability to implement tax policy effectively. First, they arose at the time of imposition rather than as policy is being made – thus, in Michael Mann's terms, they are related to the infrastructural rather than the despotic power of the state. Thus, they contrast with instances of political obstacles to taxation, such as the refusal of Congress to pass a tax bill for the defense of Lima in 1879 cited earlier. Second, a state with greater coercive capacity would have been able to overcome this opposition, highlighting once again the interconnected nature of the various aspects of infrastructural

---

[20] Thurner (1997) offers a definitive account, on which this discussion is based. He argues that this revolt was not motivated purely by fiscal causes; nonetheless, the attempt to impose a tax seen as illegitimate and overly burdensome did play a pivotal role.
[21] In this instance, the delegation of authority to local elites resembles what is elsewhere described as indirect rule, since these local elites – indigenous leaders – administered the communities using customary law. As discussed in Chapter 2, however, most local administration in Peru did not take this form.
[22] Although Thurner's evidence about the absence of collections comes from Huaraz, a more general pattern of illusory budgets can be seen in the national-level data as well.

power. The enforcement of taxation depends on the ability to effectively deploy policing power – and because the Peruvian state could not do the latter, it could not do the former. Thus, it is appropriate to see this generalized pattern of uprising against taxation as an infrastructural obstacle to tax collection. The absence of effective coercion, discussed in Chapter 6 and traced to the role of local elites in security administration, undermined the state's efforts to tax.

Resort to Consumption Taxes

The failure of the head tax became complete with its abolition by the Piérola government shortly after its ascension to power in 1896. With the failure of the head tax, and export taxation precluded due to the political power of producers, the government turned to a series of consumption taxes. Here, too, the fundamental obstacles to taxation were infrastructural: the inability to induce compliance with taxes legislated in Lima. While these consumption taxes were fairly easy to assess, they prompted major revolts, the most important of which are listed in Table 5.7.

Notably, these revolts took place in significant regional centers, reflecting the inability of the state to impose taxes even in large and important cities such as Cuzco, Chiclayo, and Puno. Most galling for the population was the imposition of the salt monopoly by Piérola in 1896, as can be seen from the large number of revolts that year. The monopoly increased salt prices by as much as 400 percent. As a result, despite appeals to national pride in promises that its revenue would allow the rescue of Tacna and Arica from the Chileans, the salt tax led to a wave of unrest. It was only with a massive show of force that the state generated revenue from these taxes, although they remained a significant stream of revenue through much of the twentieth century. Thus, we see nothing in Peru like "quasi-voluntary compliance" with taxation (Levi 1988).

Another, not unrelated, factor undermining the collection of consumption taxes was the willingness of local administrators to grant tax relief for political gain. Nugent (1997) shows that local state agents in Chachapoyas used their control over taxation to win the support of local lower classes. As elites competed for access to administrative positions, one strategy of coalition building was granting tax relief. Nugent (1997, 69) argues that "tax relief was a favor that could be withdrawn at any time, and thus was an effective way of disciplining peasants and artisans." Relief from consumption taxes on staples like salt, tobacco, and matches represented a significant economic boon, and the dilution of tax administration for political gain sharply reduced the funds entering state coffers.

TABLE 5.7. *Anti-fiscal revolts in Peru, 1885–1896*

Location	Year	Location	Year
Ancash	1885	Cuzco	1894
Puno	1886–1887	La Mar	1895
Huánuco	1886	Cerro de Pasco	1896
Castrovirreyna	1887	Ilave	1896
Chiclayo	1887	Huanta	1896
Andahuaylas	1892	Cuzco	1896
Cerro de Pasco	1893	Juli	1896

Source: Kapsoli (1977).

Despite the fact that these taxes were on the books, they generated little in the way of revenue due to the reluctance of local elites charged with tax collection to impose on their coalition of local allies and clients. Delegated rule facilitated these practices by peopling the administration with bureaucrats who had deep local ties, and by reducing the salience of sanctions from the national government. Thus it in several ways reduced the effectiveness of tax administration.

Tax Reform Efforts

To remedy these faults, as they did with education, the Civilistas sought to remove tax administration from the hands of local elites. In 1902, tax collection was contracted to a private firm, the *Compañia Nacional de Recaudación* (CNR).[23] Officials hoped that privatization would eliminate the obstacle that local elites posed to tax administration. Indeed, it should have done so, since the firm tended to appoint nonlocal department heads to administer tax collection (Nugent 1997, 51). At the provincial level, however, the CNR relied on locally chosen officials, which tended to undermine tax collection. Moreover, these company agents were chosen in consultation with the subprefect, who was deeply rooted in the local community. Additionally, the officials had to be escorted by police to protect them and the funds they collected, and the police were under the aegis of the subprefect. Nugent finds evidence that the subprefect "could withhold protection for tax collections" or "instruct his governors not to cooperate with the tax collection process" (51). Despite the privatization

---

[23] In 1912, the CNR was replaced by another private firm, the *Compañía Recaudadora de Impuestos*, and taxation remained in the hands of private firms well into the twentieth century. To my knowledge, no systematic study of this company has been written.

of tax administration, it remained firmly in the control of delegated state agents and therefore suffered in terms of implementation.

Conclusion

By the end of the Civilista era, the Peruvian state had regained some ability to tax. Internal taxation recovered to its pre-boom levels by 1920, marking the end of the post-guano crisis. But efforts to build the tax state had foundered. The CNR, established in an effort to remove local elites from tax administration, had failed to do so. Proposals to develop more infrastructurally complex taxes on income and wealth failed to generate any revenue, and state coffers continued to depend on customs and consumption taxes. Although (nominal levels of) taxation rose, the state's infrastructural power – as reflected in the ability to extract revenue from its population – saw little development. That Civilista taxation was limited to infrastructurally "easy" taxes reflected the continuing weakness of the Peruvian tax state, leaving it largely dependent on trade taxes and foreign loans for subsequent decades.

Chile: Deployed Rule and the Recovery of Taxation after the Nitrate Boom

In striking contrast to Peru, the Chilean state recovered fairly quickly from the dramatic collapse of nitrate revenues, overcoming the infrastructural obstacles to taxation when it needed to do so. This strikingly rapid recovery poses a puzzle for scholars of state development. The roots of this outcome – which diverged sharply from the Peruvian experience – can be found at the local level. I argue that even as resource booms filled national state coffers, and local elites who dominated municipal governments displayed unwillingness to tax themselves, local state agents sought continued taxation because they depended on the reach of the state for legitimacy and power vis-à-vis the communities in which they served. In this section, I show that pressures from deployed bureaucrats both pushed the national government to devolve taxes to the local level rather than eliminating them, and pressed municipal authorities (who were elected from their communities after 1891) to enforce the laws on the books and collect the taxes devolved to them. Thus, Chile's reliance on deployed administration limited the distortionary effects of the resource boom and decentralization on its fiscal state. Because of the pressures of local state agents throughout the boom, municipal governments continued to tax, and this sharply reduced the infrastructural obstacles to the post-nitrate reassertion of Chile's tax state.

Tax State Development

Decentralization and Municipal Taxation

The beginning of the nitrate boom coincided with a decentralization reform that devolved many powers to local governments[24] (Eaton 2004, 93ff). Scholars have focused on its political manifestation: not only the election of local authorities but the end to presidential interference in elections (Valenzuela 1977, 193ff). But its administrative dimension was also crucial. The 1891 Municipal Autonomy Law (*Ley de Comuna Autónoma*) transferred many taxes to municipal governments, including all major non-customs sources of government revenue. Eaton (2004, 95) claims that rather than taxing, local authorities used their leverage over the election of national legislators to demand the delivery of revenue for local projects. Thus, he argues that the decentralization led to significant state weakening.

Yet there are two reasons to believe that municipal taxation was crucial for state extractive capacity. First, tax collection, independent of revenue generated, implied a continuity in record-keeping and administration that would later reduce the infrastructural costs of restoring national taxation. Second, the historical record shows, in contrast to Eaton's claims, that municipal taxation was quite significant. As Table 5.8 shows, municipal taxation reached between 5 and 10 percent of customs revenues for the period 1903–1911, climbing to one-quarter of customs revenues by 1920. Until 1915, municipal taxes were higher than was the internal taxation of the national government.[25]

With decentralization, municipalities assessed property values, monitored the sale of alcoholic beverages, and regulated the exercise of professions and activities.[26] Property records included lists of each property owner with the values of his lands and structures.[27] Municipal review commissions responded to citizen complaints about the valuations, and revised the rolls on a regular basis.[28] Although the schedule for revision

---

[24] In terms of the typology of decentralization developed in Falleti (2010), this was a political and fiscal decentralization, with only a limited administrative component.

[25] Although data limitations prevent a systematic analysis, evidence suggests that the federal subsidy to municipalities as a share of municipal revenues *declined* during the nitrate years.

[26] On the introduction of municipal fees for the sale of alcoholic beverages, see, for example, MINT 1891, 146ff for decrees instituting alcohol taxes in the municipalities of Pisagua, Iquique, Tacna, Arica, Copiapó, Antofagasta, Chañaral, and Caracoles.

[27] For a detailed account of the kinds of property subject to and exempt from this tax, see the Ley de Comuna Autónoma, Articles 36–39. For administrative procedures of this and other taxes, see Articles 44ff.

[28] For a list of municipal taxes authorized as of 1892, see Fondo Ministerio de Hacienda vol. 2173 for text of January 29, 1892 law. On property value rolls, see Fondo Ministerio de Hacienda vol. 2009 for partial records of the 1889 Aváluo de propiedades urbanos, MINT 1892, 9 for complaints by the Intendente of Tacna about the need for a new

TABLE 5.8. *National and municipal taxation, Chile, 1903–1920*

Year	Customs revenues	Internal taxation	Municipal taxation
1903	69,587,478	1,907,763	6,234,120
1904	82,373,479	1,870,277	6,405,915
1905	90,804,726	2,473,901	6,214,258
1906	103,275,273	3,230,042	6,775,820
1907	111,970,973	4,338,287	8,686,735
1908	107,929,384	3,992,589	10,702,546
1909	113,281,315	3,206,771	9,376,322
1910	129,185,901	9,270,906	7,159,567
1911	136,356,438	12,145,679	14,331,709
1912	148,719,355	13,211,788	16,468,138
1913	158,483,825	17,635,439	19,782,838
1914	107,879,784	15,236,512	21,074,442
1915	90,558,998	33,250,023	21,977,145
1916	139,052,723	30,149,294	24,480,935
1917	163,358,723	34,267,559	27,643,229
1918	185,877,910	40,555,981	32,897,564
1919	74,528,194	45,660,075	34,120,351
1920	149,212,638	50,430,507	37,097,779

Data is in current year (nominal) pesos. According to Remmer (1984, 154), inflation ran between 5 and 9 percent per year between 1891 and 1924.
Source: *Anuario Estadístico de Chile*, various years.

was not systematic, municipal documents in the national archives show that individual municipalities did issue new tax rolls.[29] Another municipal tax, the *impuesto de mercados*, required daily collection of fees from market stall occupants (MINT 1887, 60). Thus the infrastructural capacity required for intensive taxation continued to exist at the municipal level during the nitrate era.

Deployed Rule and the Continuity of State Extractive Capacity

Municipal authorities were composed of wealthy members of their communities, and were often unwilling to impose taxes on themselves.[30] Yet

---

provincial tax roll, and MINT 1894: II, 408 for mention of a new survey in Vichuquén, among many other examples.

[29] For example, a new *rol de avaluos* was issued in 1912 in Malloa (Fondo Municipalidad de Malloa, vol. 1, p. 183). Wright (1973, 244) notes the existence of rolls of the value of agricultural properties for 1874, 1888, and 1908.

[30] See, for example, the refusal of Coquimbo landowners in 1892 to pay taxes that funded the rural police (MINT 1892, 314).

data for 1908 and 1909 (AE 1909: III, 14ff) show that some 30 percent of municipal revenue came from the *impuesto de haberes* that was levied on wealth, the second largest revenue source after the many permits issued. This tax only applied to holdings over 2,000 pesos – in other words, it only fell on the most wealthy segment of local society. This suggests that something made municipal governments willing to impose taxes on the wealthy and locally powerful.

The pressure this required came from local agents of the central state. In this newly decentralized context, the incentives of local state agents became crucial. The historical reliance on deployed rule had created a class of local state agents who gained power vis-à-vis the communities in which they served as the state's presence in their communities increased. Thus, whereas resource dependence could have turned the state's presence in the interior into a "fiction" as it did in Peru, local state agents prevented this outcome. First, they pressed national authorities with their concerns about the post-decentralization decay of state development in their communities and demanded intervention. Second, they pressed municipal authorities to continue taxation in order to fund those services, and intervened (where the constitution allowed them to do so) to ensure that taxes were collected and services delivered.

Pressure on the National Government

In the pre-nitrate era, local state agents had drawn on earmarked portions of the taxes they collected to pursue their local priorities. They feared that the elimination of national taxation would force them to depend on nitrate revenues from Santiago to fund the increased policing, primary education, and transportation improvements that increased the reach of the central state into their jurisdictions. Thus as momentum gathered for decentralization, governors and intendentes pushed for new tax responsibilities for local government (see, for example, MINT 1887, 255). Concern also manifested itself in consistent outcry against decentralized administration in their reports to the Ministry of the Interior, before and after its 1891 implementation. Governors and other local officials used the platform of their reports to authorities in Santiago to highlight the failures of municipal administration and call for a degree of recentralization. Because national officials saw decentralization as an unquestioned good, local officials chose not to tilt at windmills by calling for its abolition. Instead they pressed for piecemeal reform, often pointing to specific measures where centralized authority was particularly necessary. One example was the poor quality of the 1895 census, in which data collection at the local level was carried out by municipal authorities rather than by central state agents as in past iterations (MINT 1897, 41–42).

Governors also offered criticism of decentralization. They claimed to be unable to comment on many aspects of governance in their departments because it was in the hands of local authorities (see, for example, MINT 1894: II, 266). Governors and other officials complained that local administration was "disorganized" (MINT 1895, 314), that it had no benefits for citizens (458), and that "it is impossible to know on what its revenues are spent because nobody has been able to observe what services it fulfills" (MINT 1910, 1029). Municipal authorities were criticized for being disinterested in effective governance: the governor of Petorca, for example, complained that his department had no rural police "through the fault of the *mayores contribuyentes*, who considered them unnecessary" (MINT 1893–1894, 218). This concern about the "lack of public spirit" of municipal authorities (MINT 1899, 6) was a trope of the *Memorias* of Governors during the years after decentralization. Another trope was a critique of partisan and patronage politics in municipal administration, which was cited as a font of poor public good provision (see, for example, MINT 1894, II: 378, on the partisan nature of rural police, and MINT 1895, 625, on the use of public funds for patronage rather than for public good provision). Another axis of criticism was the misallocation of funds: governors and other local officials reported that municipal authorities failed to spend revenues on the services for which they were earmarked (MINT 1910, 943ff). This complaint often centered on road building, which had become a municipal responsibility after 1893. By their constant reminder of the failures of decentralization, local state agents kept the national government aware of administration throughout the country even as state coffers filled with nitrate rents.

Intervention at the Municipal Level

Chile's *intendentes* and *governors*, and their representatives at the municipal level also spurred the collection of municipal taxes. These interventions to continue collection prevented the erosion of extractive capacity that often accompanies both resource booms and fiscal decentralization in a context of high social inequality. This influence operated through several channels.

Perhaps most important was the formal power that the central state's local agents retained after decentralization. Although decentralization limited their formal participation in municipal decision making, central state agents still presided over all municipal government sessions, and had veto power over any municipal legislation they judged as "harmful to public order" (Ley de Comuna Autónoma, Article 104). Although municipal officials could appeal vetoes to the Supreme Court, this still gave national government officials significant leverage. Using this power, governors resolved conflict and deadlock over municipal budgets. In Búlnes in 1893, for example, the municipality's failure to agree on a budget led to the elimination of a police force that could not be funded. The governor intervened to decree that the previous year's budget would apply, reinstated taxation, and restored the police force (MINT 1894: II, 529–530).

Additionally, local state agents used their platform to press municipal authorities to increase taxation. This pressure most commonly revolved around the *impuesto de haberes*, because municipal authorities (Ley de Comuna Autónoma, Article 35) could choose the rate at which this tax was assessed, between 0.1 percent and 0.3 percent of wealth. State agents often complained about the failure of municipal authorities to raise the rate, and raised this issue in municipal council meetings (see MINT 1910, 45 for one example from the department of Achao). A parallel dynamic emerged in the funding of education. Although municipal authorities were responsible for funding primary schools, the national government continued to oversee and inspect education. As a result, when taxes were insufficiently collected for schooling, complaints trickled up through the education bureaucracy as described in Chapter 4 (see, for example, MIP 1894, xxi).

Third, national government inspectors reviewed municipal accounts to ensure that taxes were collected without irregularities, and *intendentes* provided more general oversight and pressure for policy implementation with their regular visits through their provinces, on which they were required to report to the Minister of the Interior.[31] This meant that although municipal authorities made tax policy, they were accountable to the national government. The quality of reports by local state agents during this period (as compiled in the various ministerial *Memorias* and intendants' reports) remained high, as municipal governments were held to a high standard of public service provision.

The End of the Nitrate Boom and the Leap in Internal Taxation
When the nitrate boom collapsed during World War I with the invention of a chemical process for producing artificial fertilizers, the Chilean

---

[31] For one example of this oversight, see Fondo Municipalidad de Malloa, vol. 1, p. 331.

state entered into a deep fiscal crisis that also fostered political instability. Without any major export commodity that could generate customs duties, the state had to rely on internal taxes – the same kinds of taxes that had resulted in widespread riots and ineffective collection for decades after the end of the guano boom in Peru.

By contrast to Peru, the Chilean state quickly and effectively restored the collection of internal taxation. Some of this effort was carried out by placing new fiscal levers in the hands of municipal governments. A tax on the value of household possessions was added in 1919, which generated over 3 million pesos in its first year and 5 million in the second. By increasing the rate of collection of taxes already on the books, and by adding new taxes that were easy to collect based on information already collected, the municipalities were able to generate significant additional revenue to make up for the shortfall in customs revenues.

The state also began to re-nationalize the taxes that municipalities had collected throughout the nitrate era, increased the rates, and relied for collection on the state infrastructure that had survived the fiscal distortions of the nitrate boom (Eaton 2004, 23). A national tax on property was introduced in 1915 and generated over fifteen million pesos for each of the next five years. By 1919, with the nationalization of the tax on household possessions, internal taxation reached more than half the level of customs revenue (which included nitrate exports).

These taxes were able to generate significant revenues very quickly because the state was able to rely on the property records and land surveys that had already been carried out when these taxes were collected at the municipal level during the nitrate boom. Even as taxes were eliminated at the national level, more than 200 municipalities had continued to gather data about the economic activity, wealth, and occupation of their residents, and to collect significant quantities of tax throughout the twentieth century. As the external sources of revenue collapsed, the Chilean state had detailed information at its fingertips on land values and even the furniture and other property of residents throughout the country. Municipal governments had kept these records largely because of the pressures and interventions of the deployed agents of the central state. The continued infrastructural power of the state during the nitrate era – and not only its ability to overcome the political costs of imposing taxes on its citizens – underlay its quick recovery.

Federalism and Tax State Development in Colombia and Mexico

The comparison of Colombia and Mexico, both federal systems with much tax authority initially assigned to the states rather than to the national government, reveals the limits of that institutional factor in accounting for trajectories over time. In both cases, the federalist constitutions restricted the range of taxes that the federal government could institute, and allowed subnational authorities to use their influence over the national legislature to undermine efforts to tax. In both cases, federalism acted as a political obstacle to fiscal policymaking (Rodden and Wibbels 2002).

Yet the difference between Mexico and Colombia is striking. While Colombian national leaders regularly introduced policies reinforcing the fiscal autonomy of their states, Mexican leaders, committed to a project of concerted state building, sought to undermine those limits by pushing for changes in the balance of fiscal federalism. By contrast, as in the development of coercive power and primary education, the disinclination of state leaders to expand the powers of the state is sufficient to explain the absence of effective taxation in Colombia. This can be seen both in the dismantling of national taxation in the initial Liberal Reform period and in the limited efforts to centralize the country's fiscal federalism by more moderate governments thereafter. The laissez-faire vision of development, not federalism, accounts for Colombia's failure to develop tax capacity.

In Mexico, state leaders faced perhaps the biggest set of obstacles to taxation, as they confronted the legacy of decades of post-independence chaos and a federal system that sharply limited the taxes they could institute. Yet a concerted state-building project used creative legislation, negotiation, and the full range of its constitutional powers to expand its ability to tax at the expense of the states. The expansion in the extractive capacity of the central state, as the evidence that follows shows in detail, derived from the increasing bureaucratization of tax administration, and from the placement of this developing bureaucracy in the hands of deployed state agents rather than those of local elites.

Laissez-Faire Liberalism and Reluctance to Tax in Colombia

Perhaps nowhere was the commitment to laissez-faire liberalism among Colombian elites more apparent than in the realm of taxation. Although the Hilario López tax reforms that began in 1850 were the most dramatic instance in this pattern, there was never a sustained effort to build a tax state in Colombia before the López Pumarejo government of the 1930s. As a result of this disinclination toward state building, central authority never developed in Colombia.

The Hilario López government that came to power in 1849 believed that "individuals left alone to pursue their intellectual and material interests would contribute to the progress of civilization and the well-being of society in general" (Rausch 1993, 62). In the realm of taxation, this view underlay the belief that taxes were "detrimental to national growth" (ibid., 68). The result, as discussed earlier, was the elimination of the tobacco monopoly and several other revenue sources, and the cession of others – most notably the alcohol tax – to the provinces, "with the expectation that many provinces would abolish them altogether and that those which were retained would provide on the regional level the few services that Liberals were willing to admit were indeed the responsibility of the government" (ibid., 68). As a result of these changes, historians find that the state ceded half of its revenue in pursuit of its liberal principles. In 1870, state and local governments took in more revenue than did the national government (McGreevey 1971, 88).

The "Regeneration" of 1886 saw centralization of political authority in the national government. But even during this period, tax administration remained decentralized (Santos 1966, 40–41). Only sporadic crises drove attempts to raise taxes: the Civil War of 1895, the collapse of international trade after 1917, and the Great Depression and war with Peru in 1932. The first of these saw a proposal to tax coffee exports defeated by growers. The second saw the establishment of an income tax (which generated negligible revenue), as well as imposts on medicine, matches, carbonated beverages, and beer (Junguito and Rincón 2007, 246). Yet direct taxes only became a significant source of revenue after further reforms under López Pumarejo in the 1930s.

Before that period, a laissez-faire approach to taxation marked Liberals and Conservatives both. This can be seen in their proposals to reform revenue generation. No influential proposal broached the possibility of building a powerful tax state. Instead, they proposed alterations of import duties, taxes on vices like alcohol and tobacco, and the nationalization of revenue sources (cattle slaughter tax, alcohol tax, and the like) that had been devolved to subnational authorities.[32] When ordinary

---

[32] See Deas (1982, 310ff) for several nineteenth-century proposals, and Junguito and Rincón (2007, 241–249) for details of proposed and implemented reforms during the first thirty years of the twentieth century.

Tax State Development   195

revenues fell particularly far short of expenditures, the state regularly turned to the expedients of domestic and foreign loans, forced loans, and the sale of vacant lands to fill its coffers with extraordinary revenues rather than ever try to develop tax administration.

Deas (1982) argues that, due to the poverty of its residents and the country's limited domestic and international trade, Colombian governments faced an uphill battle in trying to tax. Yet the record of the period between 1850 and 1930 reveals a striking disinclination by the national government to insert itself into the economic lives of its citizens. As in the other aspects of the state, no effort was made to develop taxation in Colombia before the Great Depression. Once again, Colombia is a case where no state-building project emerged; its state weakness can be traced to the uniquely anti-statist worldview of its political elites.

Mexico: Deployed Rule and the Expansion of Federal Taxation

Mexico and Colombia faced similar challenges to tax state development in the form of federal institutions. But Mexican state leaders, who did not share the laissez-faire bent of their Colombian counterparts, pursued the centralization of fiscal authority. And as in Chile, taxation was implemented by deployed state agents, who could be pressured to comply with the state-building initiatives of the national government. The result was that as the federal government asserted its authority to collect taxes, its local representatives carried this authority into their jurisdictions and generated revenue.[33] Over time, the increased professionalization and centralization of tax collection reinforced this pattern, giving the central state greater power to collect the taxes it chose. While in Chile the mechanism linking deployed rule to tax state development was the initiative of local agents, the more important mechanism in Mexico was that deployed rule facilitated the state's ability to ensure that tax collectors fulfilled their duties.

This section explores various pieces of evidence that show the increasingly effective implementation of taxation by the central state's officials. Additionally, it explores the evolving nature of Mexican fiscal federalism: over time, the federal government's penetration of local society grew at the expense of that of its component states. The increased centralization of tax administration, and its increasing reliance on deployed

---

[33] By contrast, in places where tax administration remained in the hands of local elites, it foundered. For clear evidence of this in the case of Porfirian Chiapas, see Bobrow-Strain (2007, 78–79).

rule, turned tax policy into reality. As the state relied increasingly on its bureaucracy deployed throughout the national territory, its capacity to tax increased. Yet this upward trend in infrastructural power left Mexico behind its Chilean counterpart for three reasons: first, the state chose not to tax wealth, exports, or domestic commerce, believing that to do so would impinge on domestic economic growth. Second, the abject failure of the state to tax before 1857 left its fiscal power at strikingly low levels when the Liberals took power. And third, the central government faced significant political obstacles to taxation from its constituent states, which could use their power in Congress to protect their autonomy from the central state's reach.

Thus, this section highlights both the role of central state bureaucrats in increasing the state's tax capacity, and the limits of those gains in comparative perspective. Drawing on detailed studies by historians of the administration of particular revenue sources, I trace the increased reliance on deployed bureaucrats and the consequences for extractive capacity in two specific arenas of taxation: the *timbre*, and the assessment and sale of vacant land by the state. I conclude by exploring the unique political challenges of federalism for extractive capacity in Mexico, showing how central state extractive capacity increased despite the political obstacles of federalism.

Beyond these two specific administrative histories, a broader examination of tax state development shows a series of Liberal and Porfirian reforms that gave federal state agents increasing power over taxation. By the late Porfiriato, tax administration was firmly in the hands of federal bureaucrats. In 1906, two corps of oversight were created: *inspectores*, who supervised tax collection, and *visitadores*, who oversaw the inspectors and other tax officials (Carmagnani 1989, 489). Tax administration overall was overseen by federal agents stationed in "nearly every" state capital, who operated alongside officers responsible for each tax type (Ludlow 2002: II, 208). Alongside these improvements to internal taxation, a parallel series of customs reforms improved the efficiency of collection in that arena as well (ibid., II, 158ff). Overall, the Mexican state sharply increased its extractive capacity during the Liberal and Porfirian eras. This stemmed from the placement of taxation in the hands of the federal bureaucracy, which extended its reach through the national territory. The reliance on deployed rule meant that, as Pérez Siller (2004) concludes, the state was able to effectively generate revenue from the taxes on its books by the end of the nineteenth century.

Administrative Reforms of the Timbre

As the most important component of internal taxation, the *timbre* is particularly fertile ground for the study of extractive capacity.[34] Before 1893, the *timbre* was collected by state and local officials, who remitted funds to the finance ministry. The result was significant irregularity in its collection, and the failure of the tax to translate into "a real, daily presence of the federal state" (Carmagnani 1989, 486). After 1893, a series of reforms would begin to insert the central state directly into the full range of transactions to which it applied. A first measure imposed a layer of federal *timbre* inspectors, who oversaw its administration by local and state officials. This was followed, in 1900, by the establishment of a corps of federal contractors to carry out collection in place of the local authorities. In 1906, a further reform created a tax inspection system that divided the country into six regions, appointing two layers of inspectors to oversee tax administration throughout the country. Thus by the end of the Porfiriato, the *timbre* was collected by the federal government rather than states, in a system that (although reliant on contractors) was overseen by federal inspectors. Along with the increasingly wide range of tax streams included in the *timbre* that was described earlier, this greater systematization and centralization of taxation represented the increased infrastructural power of the federal state, as it removed both subnational authorities and local elites from the extractive apparatus.

Surveying Vacant Land

As political stability became cemented, rural land in many parts of Mexico rose in value, which led to state intervention in the land market. In 1855, the Liberal government made the alienation of public lands – their identification, mapping, and sale – a federal responsibility, nullifying local and state power to intervene in their allocation. Unclaimed land was assigned to the federal government, which had the power to distribute it as it saw fit. Most importantly for the state, this land could be sold to generate revenue. The survey of land was also a pre-requisite for the construction of a system of land taxation, which had been stymied by "the cloudy and disordered state of property relations in rural areas" (Holden 1994, 11). But the conversion of vacant land into a source of revenue required a land survey to identify its extent. The process of surveying reflects the broader trend in state finance: its progressive centralization in

---

[34] This discussion is based on Carmagnani (1989, 486ff).

the hands of the federal government, the exclusion of local elites from its administration, and the growing effectiveness of central state oversight.[35]

The survey of vacant land in Mexico began in earnest in the 1870s and peaked between 1883 and 1893. The scale of the endeavor can be seen in the fact that the sale of vacant land generated an average of 5.9 percent of all federal revenue between 1867 and 1910, and 23.5 percent of revenue between 1883 and 1890.[36] Surveys were conducted by private firms, compensated for their services with one-third of the vacant land they mapped.[37] This model of administration, analogous to tax farming, was chosen because it kept both local interests and the national government out of the potentially explosive demarcation of private property. Accepting private contracting of the survey implied accepting the most common mode of surveying private firms used. This was the "deductive method," in which companies surveyed an area, subtracted private holdings (based on the information on the titles of landowners) and arrived at a number of vacant hectares. This method was inaccurate, but politically and infrastructurally less costly since it did not involve measuring the bounds of private property (49ff). Survey firms tended to be disinterested in surveying locations with small or complicated vacant lands, which were not worth the cost, meaning that many regions remained unmapped. In other words, this was far from a "real cadastral survey" (56), a reality that the Porifirian regime was willing to accept. So long as the survey process generated vacant land that could be sold by the federal government to generate revenue, and generated little unrest, the government accepted its limitations.

Yet despite the limits of the survey process – most importantly the reliance on private firms and the limited accuracy – it did represent a dramatic insertion of the federal government into rural Mexico, part of the Porfirian project of broadening the reach of "civilization" and state authority across the national territory (Meyer 1986, 187). Approximately 30 percent of Mexico's land was surveyed between 1883 and 1893, including large proportions of the more remote, thinly populated states of Campeche, Chiapas, Chihuahua, Sonora, Sinaloa and Tabasco, and the territories of Baja California and Tepic (Holden 1994, 17). Surveying was further centralized in 1902, when a decree banned private companies

---

[35] This discussion is based on Holden (1994).
[36] My calculations from Carmagnani (1994), Appendix III, using his data on "ventas y arriendos."
[37] Notably, these private firms were rarely local elites: see Holden (1994, Appendix) for details on the composition of survey firms.

Tax State Development

from the practice, reserving it (and all of the vacant land identified) for the national government (Holden 1994, 108). This growing assertion of federal government intervention in the land market reflects the broader trends of state centralization of finance through the Porfiriato, a reflection of its commitment to building its infrastructural power.

The Federal Government and Mexico's States

As it sought to expand its extractive capacity, the central state confronted institutional obstacles to taxation posed by federalism. Reflecting the autonomy of the states, the 1857 constitution restricted the federal government to certain taxes, and allowed the states to generate any other form of revenue they chose. Because of its desire to promote trade and thus its revenues, the federal government long sought to abolish states' rights to tax the domestic commerce that crossed their borders: the *alcábala*.[38] State elites resisted repeated federal efforts to do so, using their influence in Congress to thwart bills proposing bans on this important source of their revenue, which in 1890 represented more than half the revenue of many states (Ludlow 2002, vol. 2, p. 195). This was the most salient instance of the political difficulties of taxation under Mexico's federal system.

Yet as federal taxation grew, an opportunity to settle this conflict appeared. States protested increased federal taxation – and in particular the *renta interior* introduced in 1887 that applied to the consumption of domestic manufactures – as double taxation on their citizens. In response to the outcry by state governors and their congressional representatives, the federal government offered to eliminate the *renta interior* if states would drop the *alcábala*. To assure states of its good intentions, the federal government moved first, dropping one of its new revenue streams. In turn, the states allowed the *alcábala* to be banned in 1896. Once internal commerce duties were eliminated, the federal government immediately raised import duties accordingly, and this revenue went directly into federal coffers.

There is significant debate among historians about the implications of this agreement. On the one hand, Carmagnani (1989, 486) sees it as a "significant retreat of fiscal modernization" because the consumption tax on manufactured goods was abolished. In his view, the early

---

[38] Pérez Siller (2004, 149–150) suggests that the timing of efforts to eliminate the *alcábala* relates to federal fiscal crises, hinting that the federal government was interested in expropriating this revenue stream rather than receiving the benefit of domestic commerce from its elimination.

1890s saw a shift from fiscal modernization to revenue maximization, as the state gave up efforts to develop new tax streams and focused on improved administration of existing sources (principally the *timbre*) and the promotion of increased economic activity to increase its revenue. By contrast, Uhthoff (2004) argues that the central state was strengthened by the elimination of the *alcábalas* because the central state raised its revenues at the expense of the states, while eliminating what was (in both ideological and pragmatical terms) a less than optimal source of revenue. In either case, this active pursuit of central tax authority on the part of the Mexican state is in sharp contrast to its counterpart in Colombia.

Although Mexico's states retained significant fiscal autonomy throughout the pre-Revolutionary period, we can conclude that this did not prevent the increased strengthening of the central state. The federal government claimed the right to a wide range of tax streams, expanded that claim at the expense of the states, and collected those taxes directly and in an increasingly effective manner. The federal system posed an obstacle to taxation by the central government, largely because the legislature created a forum in which state governments could veto policy initiatives designed to increase the power of the federal state while claiming certain taxes for themselves. But through negotiation, compromise, and institutional reform, the Liberal and (particularly) the Porfirian federal state was able to wear away this opposition, setting the stage for even greater centralization of fiscal authority in the post-revolutionary era. The gains of the pre-revolutionary era, which would become consolidated after 1920, were the result of a concerted effort to build a tax state, which was implemented by deployed bureaucrats who put legislation into practice in a concerted manner throughout the national territory.

CONCLUSION

While resource booms and federalism shape the challenges faced by tax state builders, this chapter shows that they are insufficient to account for variation in tax state development. Instead, we must look to the role of ideas to explain why Colombian leaders were content to continue to rely on customs revenues, and why they were unwilling to impose a wider range of taxes even in times of fiscal crisis. Additionally, we must look to institutions of local rule to explain why some efforts to tax succeed while others fail. The foundering of Peruvian efforts to tax when guano revenues ran out can be traced to the fact that administration was dependent on local elites. On the other hand, the striking fiscal recovery after the nitrate boom in Chile resulted from the roles of local state agents in pressing for increased taxation in the communities in their jurisdiction. The Porfirian state in Mexico understood this, as can be seen from its aggressive efforts to place fiscal administration in the hands of deployed bureaucrats.

The evidence presented here becomes more compelling in conjunction with the evidence for a similar argument in explaining the variation in education development. A similar set of factors can account for variation in these two distinct aspects of state development, and can do so better than can the prominent alternative explanations developed by scholars who treat each dimension independently. This suggests that rather than treating the evolution of taxation and education separately, scholars should pursue unified explanations for why states expand their capacity in some contexts but not others. I continue the effort to do so in the next chapter, which considers the development of the coercive dimension of state power.

6

Local Administration, Varieties of Conscription, and the Development of Coercive Capacity

In parallel to Chapters 4 and 5, this chapter explores the development of coercive capacity, which I define as the ability to mobilize force and exercise it effectively. All four countries had strikingly small armies across the period under investigation, and their mobilization for war had no lasting effect on military development, as armies were disbanded and soldiers released in the immediate aftermath of combat. However, coercive capacity diverged in two important ways. Cases varied sharply in their ability to mobilize fighting forces *when needed*, and in the existence of a truly *national* army rather than the forces of a particular region or *caudillo*. While over time the Chilean and Mexican states came to be able to summon an increasingly effective and *national* army, the Peruvian and Colombian states could not.

This chapter shows that the ideational and institutional explanation I advance can account for patterns of variation across the four cases. It begins by addressing an important alternative explanation common in accounts of state building – the claim that war makes states. I show that participation in war cannot explain the divergent paths of military development, since all four states were embroiled in similar levels of international and domestic conflict and faced similar challenges to their authority. War did not make states in Latin America. The effects of war on coercive capacity are a more direct test of this relationship than is the more indirect effect of war on extraction, which can be mediated by a set of alternative means of war finance (Downing 1992; Centeno 2002). The finding later in this discussion that war had no effect on army size casts doubt on the presence of a causal link between war-making and state-making in Latin America.

The second part of the chapter explores how each of the four states mobilized in response to international and domestic crises. The difference between cases in state capacity begins to emerge: at moments of crisis, variation among the cases is revealed in the state's ability to mobilize troops in response to a threat. The case studies show, for example, that in the War of the Pacific Chile was able to deliver twice as many troops to Peruvian territory than Peru could muster in defense of its own capital. The Colombian and Peruvian states struggled (and sometimes failed) to defend themselves against threats, yet by comparison the Chilean state shone in response to challenges and the Mexican state performed increasingly effectively, although in the end it fell at the hands of a 1910 uprising.

Having shown the limits of a key alternative explanation and described the extent of variation in state capacity, the third part of the chapter moves to explain this variation. To do so, I focus on the *means* of military recruitment as a place to isolate the effects of ideas and institutions on state capacity. The means of recruitment varied across cases, and had implications for the efficiency of mobilization. Where conscription was systematic and routine, populations accepted the burden of military participation to a greater extent. But where it was ad hoc and coercive, military service remained conflictual rather than being marked by what Levi famously described as "quasi-voluntary compliance" (Levi 1997).

Systematic, routine, legalized conscription emerged in Chile. As I show, this derived directly from its administration by deployed bureaucrats, who had an interest in military effectiveness and were willing to overcome the unpopularity of conscription. The result was an army that (in comparative perspective) could mobilize large numbers of troops, saw low desertion rates, and integrated Chileans from nationwide into a single fighting force. These are three characteristics of an effective army. By contrast, conscription in Colombia and Peru was forcible and ad hoc, and tended to be carried out by military units on an as-needed basis. The result in both cases was that mobilization was difficult, desertion and resistance to conscription were commonplace, and troops tended to be unmotivated in combat outside their home region. Because units were populated with troops from particular locations, nothing like a national army emerged; instead the national military was little more than a series of regional militias. In Peru, this outcome resulted from the unwillingness of local elites serving as administrators under delegated rule to comply with conscription edicts from the capital, leaving military units with no choice but to fill their ranks by forcible recruitment. In Colombia, this outcome derived from the disinclination of the national government to increase its coercive capacity; military recruitment was first systematized only in 1911, and even then only to a minimal extent.

Mexico represents an intermediate case, where state builders inherited a war-torn polity with fragmented armed forces that had local and regional loyalties. Here, in other words, the preexisting weakness of the state in coercive terms (described in Chapter 3) played a role. The competition among military forces for recruits led to less forcible conscription practices; but among these were often guarantees that service could be locally based and under locally selected officers, a practice that would need to be changed for military development to be complete. Porfirio Díaz was able to undermine these locally focused forces and begin a transition to a national army even under these difficult circumstances, largely because of his alliance with the *jefes políticos*, who tended to be deployed from the capital and therefore cooperative in military modernization efforts. Thus, Mexican state building, facilitated by deployed rule, allowed it to partially overcome the legacies of its particularly severe post-independence state crisis.

WAR AND THE STATE: LIMITS OF THE "BELLIC" APPROACH

Perhaps the most commonly cited explanation for state building is war. Most accounts of state formation in early modern Europe assert that (to use one-half of Tilly's felicitous phrase) "war made the state" (Tilly 1975, 42). Because the prosecution of war required the construction of a bureaucracy that could extract resources and manpower from society, and because weak states were wiped off the map, war is said to have created strong states in the European context. But Centeno (2002) has shown that this argument does not apply to Latin America. The region has never seen total war (with the exception of Paraguay's effort in the War of the Triple Alliance), and therefore states have not had to develop the mobilizational and extractive capacity that characterizes the European states. Latin America's wars could more aptly be described as skirmishes than as major conflicts. They required few soldiers, and were funded by international and domestic debt rather than by the development of taxation. Thus, Centeno concludes that the absence of total war in Latin America explains why its states are universally weaker than are their European counterparts.

But we might suppose that conflict can still help to explain why some states *within* the region have more infrastructural power than do

TABLE 6.1. *War (various specifications) and army size, country-decades*

DV	Model 1 Army size		Model 2 Army size		Model 3 Army size		Model 4 Army size		Model 5 Army size		Model 6 Army size	
Constant	0.556	0.889	0.495	0.062	2.111***	0.450	0.725***	0.162	0.685***	0.107	2.166***	0.471
War	−0.039	0.160	0.059	0.114	0.034	0.152	0.045	0.111	−0.058	0.161	0.079	0.156
WarYears	0.026	0.035			−0.031	0.036			0.017	0.038	−0.044	0.039
CumWarYears	−0.006	0.005			−0.053***	0.016			−0.005	0.005	−0.059***	0.018
CivilWar			−0.055	0.105			0.044	0.112	−0.143	0.150	−0.174	0.147
CivilYears									0.025	0.027	0.032	0.025
CumCivilYears									−0.007**	0.003	0.005	0.007
Country Dummies	NO		NO		YES		YES		NO		YES	
# obs	113		113		113		113		113		113	
F	0.61		0.24		3.17		2.26		1.30		2.68	
Prob>F	0.6120		0.7906		0.0007		0.0168		0.2620		0.0019	
R-squared	0.0164		0.0043		0.2758		0.1973		0.0687		0.2930	
Adj R squared	−0.0106		−0.0138		0.1889		0.1099		0.0160		0.1837	

* Significant at 90%.
** Significant at 95%.
*** Significant at 99%.

All data from Centeno (2002); all models OLS.
War = current war; Waryears = years of war in last decade; Cumulative War = years of war since independence.
Model 1: just the three war variables.
Model 2: just current war and civil war.
Model 3: same as model 1, but with country dummies, many of which are significant at 99% level and negatively signed.
Model 4: same as model 2, but with country dummies: Colombia, Mexico, and Brazil are significant and negatively signed.
Model 5: all 3 measures of each kind of war.
Model 6: Model 5 with country dummies: cumulative war significant and negative; six country dummies significant and negative.
[A model with current war, recent war, current civil war, recent civil war, country dummies is not shown because none of the variables were significant].

205

others. To examine this possibility, I conduct a simple region-wide statistical test. Using data in Centeno (2002), I compile a dataset of wars in Latin America since independence, and the size of the army at the end of each decade since 1850 as a proportion of the population.[1] Under various model specifications, international war has very little effect on army size – there is no effect for current war, nor for years of war in the previous decade, and this holds when dummy variables for individual countries are included. Civil war, under either specification (and specified as total years of civil war since independence) has no effect on army size[2] (see Table 6.1). War, then, did not even lead to increased army size in the region.[3]

THE CAPACITY TO MOBILIZE

Moving beyond army size to more nuanced assessments of state capacity involves reconsidering the relationship between war and the state. A measure of the state's *capacity* to mobilize is the ability to move from a peacetime equilibrium of relatively little force to a wartime state of intense mobilization when necessary. The increase in army size at moments when war looms reflects the state's ability to penetrate society and effectively implement policy. To score the cases on this dimension of state capacity, I examine the military conflicts in which each was embroiled during the long nineteenth century, and consider how the capacity to mobilize and deploy forces changed over time. Where mobilization took place quickly and systematically, this indicates that the state was powerful. Where

---

[1] Data come from Centeno (2002). Army size data is in Table 5.1; data on wars is in Table 2.1. I focus only on the army, leaving out the navy, both because the army was the largest branch of the military and due to data availability. National Guard units and other "men in arms" are discussed later.

[2] The only specification of war that does have an effect on army size is the cumulative number of years of international war since independence, which has a statistically significant but *negative* effect on the proportion of the population enrolled in the army. For every year of war since independence, the current size of the army is reduced by nearly 0.06% of the population. This result is statistically significant at the 99% confidence level in a linear regression model (n=113 country-decades). This is a sizable effect, since most data points for the army size fall between 0 and 1% of the population. Since several countries in the sample had nearly thirty years of war in the period, this suggests that the size of the army in these countries was cut by more than 50% due to a history of war. Certainly this pattern is in tension with the claim that war makes states.

[3] Nor did external rivalry, as Thies (2005) suggests. Rivalry was ubiquitous in all four cases, and yet most are not marked by the slow accretion of state power that Thies finds for the twentieth century. For a case-based reevaluation of the relation Thies claims to find between international rivalry and state building, see Saylor and Soifer (2008).

states could only deploy smaller forces and mobilize troops in a scatter-shot fashion, we can conclude that they were weak. The evidence from threats in the four cases can be compared synchronically and diachronically. Within-case comparison highlights the evolution of state power in a given case over time, and the material that follows is presented in that manner. Cross-case comparison reveals variation in the power of the four states at any given moment.

Chile

Figure 6.1 shows the size of the Chilean army from 1827 (shortly after independence) through 1912. A first glance at the figure highlights the fact that the army was usually very small. Over time, the army grew from levels below 3,000 for the 1840s (notably, this is *after* the first War of the Pacific) to levels around 7,000 by 1910, a rate of growth that did not even keep pace with population. More important, however, as an indicator of the state's capacity to mobilize its population when necessary are the several huge spikes in Figure 6.1. The two largest spikes respond to the War of the Pacific and the 1891 Civil War, but the Chilean army also increased rapidly in size in response to a series of threats to the state, both internal and external: the war against the Peru-Bolivian Confederation (1836–1839), the 1859 Revolution (but not the 1851 Revolution), the war with Spain in 1865–1866, the War of the Pacific that began in 1879, the 1891 Civil War, and border tensions with Argentina in the late 1890s. As the nineteenth century wore on, and the state's power increased, it became increasingly effective at mobilizing military power when it saw fit.

In the 1836–1839 war with Bolivia and Peru, it took Chile nine months to dispatch its first force of 2,200 officers and men to the battlefront.[4] After this force was defeated, it took eight months to organize the second force of 5,400. Not long theraftr, by the time of the 1851 and 1859 Civil Wars, the state's capacity had already increased: it could mobilize an equivalent number of troops much more quickly.

By the time of the War of the Pacific, the mobilizational capacity of the Chilean state had grown dramatically. Officially, Chile began the war in April 1879 with 3,500 officers and men under arms, although the fiscal

---

[4] These assessments of mobilization are largely based on the descriptions of military campaigns in various volumes of the *Historia del Ejército Chileno* (HEC). Although this source is an official military history, and therefore potentially subject to bias, its descriptions are echoed by independent investigations of particular conflicts, such as Sater (2007), and it is commonly cited by historians.

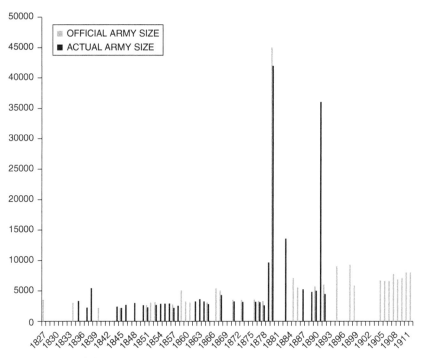

FIGURE 6.1. Chilean army size, 1827–1912.
Sources: Data from various volumes of the HEC, and various *Memorias* of the War Ministry, and Hernandez Ponce (1984). Official figures represent the size of the army as set by the executive branch, while actual figures represent actual force sizes.

crisis of the late 1870s likely reduced the number below this level. By October 1879, nearly 10,000 men were under arms: the size of the army had tripled in six months. It doubled again by the middle of 1880, and doubled again to reach nearly 42,000 by the end of that year when the campaign of Lima was launched. In other words, during the War of the Pacific, the army ranks grew tenfold; more than 36,000 officers and men were mobilized and dispatched to the battlefield.

This notable increase in the capacity of the state to mobilize forces to defend itself can also be seen in the 1891 Civil War. Faced with a battle against the forces supporting the Congress, President Balmaceda raised the size of the army from about 5,000 to more than 36,000 in six months. In addition, the Congressional forces (not included in Figure 6.1) numbered nearly 10,000 officers and men (HEC 7, 132ff). Thus, the Chilean state, by century's end, was able to mobilize tens of thousands of men for combat within a matter of months, a vast improvement over its ability in the 1830s.

With the end of each of these threats, the army was decreased in size quite rapidly, as seen most dramatically in the demobilization of thousands of troops within two months after the occupation of Lima in January 1881 (HEC 6, 226–227), and the reduction in unit size and dissolution of multiple infantry units (HEC 4, 167) in the immediate aftermath of the departure of the Spanish navy from the Chilean coast in 1867. Even at the turn of the twentieth century, tensions with Argentina highlight the same pattern: significant forces were mobilized rapidly in the late 1890s as tensions rose, but Sater and Herwig (1999, 72) claim that army size was cut in half almost immediately after a treaty resolved the dispute in October 1904.

The Chilean state also mobilized the country's National Guard when it needed to respond to both internal and external challenges, making its coercive capacity even more impressive. The first war with Peru and Bolivia saw National Guard units mobilized to a limited extent as reserve units used for domestic policing (Hernandez Ponce 1984, 95ff). Guard units were also mobilized to respond to military revolts in 1850–1851 (HEC 4, 70ff) and to a greater extent in the more protracted fighting of the 1851 Civil War, where Guard units were mobilized in both the southern and central campaigns (HEC vol. 4, pp. 88, 94, 96, 98). The 1859 Civil War saw a similar pattern of National Guard mobilization[5] (HEC 4, 145–149). More significant mobilization of the National Guard occurred during the War of the Pacific: more than 200 guard units were mobilized, reorganized, or activated in 1879 and 1880 (HEC 10, Appendix 1). In mid-1883, more than 13,000 guard members were serving active duty in the war against Peru and on the southern frontier when the army units were mobilized against Peru (HEC 6, 438). Thus, the Chilean state's increasing capacity to summon forces for its defense grew even larger when we consider the National Guard alongside the Army.

Peru

Data is too fragmentary to compile a time series of army size for Peru like the one shown for Chile earlier. But it does permit the examination of mobilization in response to the six[6] international wars that Peru fought between independence and 1870, as well as the subsequent War of the Pacific. The six wars listed in Table 6.2 involved significant army campaigns, and Peru won three of them, defeating Bolivian forces in 1828,

---

[5] Both civil wars of the 1850s also saw some National Guard units join rebel forces.
[6] I exclude the war with Spain 1865–1866, since it was conducted entirely as a naval battle.

TABLE 6.2. *Peruvian nineteenth-century wars and army mobilization*

Years	Opponent	Maximum peruvian mobilization
1827–1828	Bolivia	5,000
1828–1829	Gran Colombia	7,500*
1835–1836	Bolivia	10,000**
1836–1839	Chile	6,000***
1841	Bolivia	5,377
1859–1860	Ecuador	8,000
1866	Spain	Army not significantly mobilized
1879–1883	Chile	7,246**** 19,000

* This figure does not include the 4,500 troops that Gamarra and La Fuente mobilized in the southern highlands that never reached the battlefront, or the Peruvian reserve army of 8,000.
** This figure represents Gamarra's army of "4,000 troops and 6,000 indios" in this conflict. (Citation from Dellepiane 1943, 333).
*** This figure represents the size of the army of the Peru-Bolivian Confederation, and not exclusively Peruvian forces.
**** The first figure derives from HEC 5, 108, and reflects the mobilization of Peruvian forces in October 1879: six months after war was declared and when the first confrontations of the war began. The second figure represents the size of the force mobilized to defend Lima from Chilean attack in early 1881.

Source: Dellepiane (1943) vol. 1.

Gran Colombian forces in present-day Ecuador in 1829, and Ecuadorian forces in 1860. Yet in each case, fewer than 10,000 troops were mobilized for combat.[7] This low level of mobilization is consonant with Centeno's argument about limited war in Latin America, and casts doubt on the notion that war made the Peruvian state.

The 1879–1883 War of the Pacific revealed Peru's limited coercive capacity, especially in comparison to Chile's. Six months after war was declared, Peru could mobilize only 7,246 officers and men on the battlefront; the smallest army at this time of the three combatants. After the defeat of this force, Peru struggled to organize an army to defend Lima from Chilean attack (Kurtz 2009, 496). Edicts ordered the mobilization of all males aged sixteen to sixty, and yet Lima was defended by a "poorly equipped and led 19,000 man improvised militia" substantially smaller than the attacking Chilean force (Klarén 2000, 189). The key implication

[7] Data about military mobilization in this section is based largely on Dellepiane (1943).

for our purposes is this level of mobilization compared to those in the earlier conflicts described earlier: Peru was barely able to mobilize more troops in the 1880s than in the early post-independence decades. In this sense, there was no increase in coercive capacity.

Coercive capacity did improve in one sense: the army came firmly under the aegis of the national government by mid-century. In the 1820s and 1830s various military *caudillos* each had their own armies, and chose to cooperate or to withhold their forces from unified combat against enemies for their own purposes. Gamarra, a military caudillo from Cuzco, was notorious for this practice throughout the first two decades after independence.[8] Castilla was able to put an end to this practice, and create the Peruvian national army. Yet the army failed to become a *unified* national force; as late as the War of the Pacific, Peruvian forces were often divided into "troops" and "indios" (Méndez 2005). Thus, the size of the Peruvian forces in these campaigns overstates the number of troops that were trained and organized as part of the Peruvian national army. Even with that overestimate, we can see that the Peruvian state saw much smaller gains in coercive capacity over the state-building period than did its Chilean counterpart.

Colombia

Even in comparison to Peru, the coercive capacity of the Colombian state was quite limited. The strikingly anti-statist attitudes of mid-century Colombian liberals, highlighted in the previous chapters on taxation and education, can be seen in the military realm as well. The army remained vestigial at best, and the national government went so far as to grant legal status to other armed forces even as they challenged the central state. This was a state that had no particular commitment to developing any coercive capacity, and no concern about retaining a monopoly of legitimate force.

The army numbered about 3,000 during the 1830s in the aftermath of the conflicts that tore apart the Gran Colombian confederation, and did not grow much from that level for the remainder of the century (see Figure 6.2). Liberals, who took power in 1849, strongly considered eliminating the standing army altogether (Bushnell 1993, 112). Its size was slashed, falling as low as 400 men for much of the 1850s, and to 109

---

[8] Dellepiane (1943, vol. 1, 299–344) makes this practice clear. See also Walker (1999, chapter 5).

(officers *and* troops) in 1856. Scheina (2003, I, 496) cites an average size of 1,200 between 1855 and 1874. When Nuñez took power in 1880, he made some efforts to increase the role of the army in the service of national stability and unity (Park 1985, 210). Only in the 1880s did the size of the standing army return to the levels of the 1830s and surpass 3,000. After this point, the army ranks consistently numbered more than 5,000, and often more than 6,000. But between 1890 and 1921, while the country's population rose by more than 50 percent, the army did not increase in size. Colombia, in other words, saw little or no growth of coercive capacity by this crude measure.

Yet a better measure of coercive capacity than the size of the standing army is the ability of the state to mobilize troops for war when needed. Since Colombia was not embroiled in any international war between 1830 and 1930, we must look to mobilization for internal security. Examining the Colombian state's response to internal threats reveals that it remained strikingly lacking in its ability to mobilize in response to a threat. The severity of internal threat can be approximated with data from McGreevey (1971, 88) on deaths in combat per decade and months of conflict per decade. Neither of these measures of severity of internal threat is systematically associated with army size.[9] Only in the 1890s, which was marked by the most severe civil war since independence, do we see significant mobilization.[10] Otherwise, domestic conflict appears not to have spurred significant military development.

A second manifestation of the state's weakness is the ability of challengers to mobilize forces equal to or larger than those of the national government (Cardona 2008, 94). Valencia Tovar (1993, Vol. 2) cites several examples of opponents to national authority mobilizing forces equivalent to those of the national army. And even when single opposition armies did not match those of the national government in size, Bogotá was still vulnerable to defeat: the modal pattern for civil wars in Colombia was multiple concurrent uprisings by regional leaders, which the central state was unable to address simultaneously (Earle 2000). Indeed the success of

---

[9] The overall correlation between months of conflict per decade and maximum army size per decade is actually negative. While the causal relationship here cannot be identified, we can conclude that protracted internal conflict was not associated with increased military mobilization.

[10] The correlation between combat deaths and army size is 0.77; removing the decade of the 1900s reduces it to 0.19. This suggests that there was little relationship between the severity of conflict and army size before 1900.

Conscription and Coercive Capacity 213

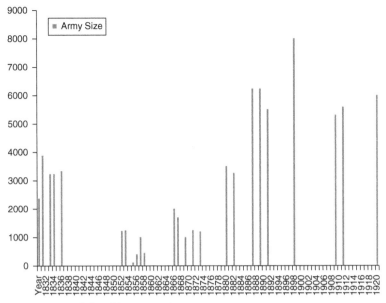

FIGURE 6.2. Colombian army size, 1830–1930.
Source: Cardona (2008, 93).

several armed movements in seizing the state during the nineteenth century reveals its limited coercive capacity most clearly.

Figure 6.2 shows that the army grew sharply under Nuñez in the 1880s. But this increase overstates the gains in coercive capacity. The limits of Nuñez's efforts to ensure a domestic monopoly of force can clearly be seen in several aspects of his policies. First, his public order law of 1880 restricted the rights of the national government to intervene in state-level politics without the invitation of the relevant individual state governments. National leaders, in other words, accepted the possibility of overthrow of state governments and ceded the right to intervene to prevent such instability. Even more dramatically, Nuñez-era law allowed state governments to import weapons for their own purposes; affirming in an 1881 law that "under the federal constitution the states have the right to buy, import, and possess arms and war materials" (Park 1985, 209). The federal government, in other words, enjoyed nothing resembling a monopoly of force in Colombia, and was willing to tolerate this situation. Nuñez was no different from his predecessors in this sense: national leaders had since 1863 been regularly notified about state imports of weapons and never acted to block these actions.

The War of 1,000 Days was a unique instance of mass military mobilization. The war began with fairly small armies, akin to those mobilized for earlier internal conflicts, but mobilization escalated in preparation for the May 1900 battle of Palonegro, which was the largest military engagement on Colombian soil to date, pitting more than 10,000 troops on each side (Bergquist 1986, 149). After the Liberal defeat, the war devolved into guerrilla violence, which spurred further recruitment of forces on both sides; McGreevey (1971, 88) estimates the maximum army size at 29,000. Although the size of force mobilized was great, a closer examination of this episode reveals the limited coercive capacity of the state. Military commanders had massive difficulties compelling troops to do anything more than defend "their own homes" (Bergquist 1986, 164–165). The national army of the War of 1,000 Days was, in other words, more like a series of local militias pressed into service that "refused to pursue guerrillas outside their own districts" (ibid., 165). And although the state was able to increase the size of the army, it was unable to command compliance even over officers who regularly "neglected their duties" (165) and betrayed the government cause, or to prevent massive desertion by soldiers.

For this and other reasons, the government found itself strikingly unable to combat the Liberal guerrillas effectively. As guerrilla violence dragged on for more than two years, elites of all political stripes began to feel threatened, leading them to "minimize their long-standing differences and [act] to bring the conflict to a close" (ibid., 157). Additionally, the specter of United States meddling in Panama and the loss of that province motivated peace efforts. This led to the settlement of the conflict. With peace, the standing army was cut sharply, falling back to 5,300 by 1910. The army would remain at this small size until the 1930s.

Mexico

The challenge of military development in Mexico was different than in the other cases. Rather than difficulties in mobilizing troops to meet threats to the state, the state confronted tens of thousands of men in arms who were neither unified nor loyal to the national government. Gains in the state's coercive capacity in Mexico, then, are reflected not only in the number of troops that could be summoned, but also in the increased centralization of military force. To capture this process, this section largely explores the complex evolution of the military over time that increased central control.

It also parallels the discussions of the other countries by comparing the state's military response to threat over time during the Porfiriato.

War against the United States (1845–1848) and resistance to the French Intervention (1862–1867), along with conflict between Liberals and Conservatives in the mid-1850s, had resulted in the mobilization of thousands of armed men (Santoni 1996). These forces, commanded by local and regional strongmen, served as the foundation for the massive decentralization of political power in mid-century Mexico. Cross-national statistical comparisons, which show that Mexico had about as many men in arms as did other Latin American countries, conceal the vast fragmentation of coercive capacity in Mexico. Instead of a national army, the country had dozens of forces, each drawn from a particular region and with a particular set of loyalties and allegiances, that came together only against foreign foe and fragmented when conflict ended. This can be seen, for example, in the fact that the early Porfirian national army numbered between 24,000 and 30,000, while various "irregular and auxiliary state forces" numbered about 70,000 (Hernández Chávez 1989, 262).

In terms of pure numbers, the historical record shows a *decline* in troop sizes over the Liberal and Porfirian eras. Upon taking power with the defeat of the French in 1867, one of the first orders of business for the Liberals was an effort, driven by both fiscal constraints and fear of armed opponents, to demobilize as many troops as possible. Hernández Chávez (1989, 267) estimates a reduction from about 80,000 to about 20,000; Fuentes (1983, 59) estimates an immediate 60 percent reduction from 70,000. Reduction in army size continued under Porfirio Díaz: Table 6.3 shows a steady but slow decline in the number of troops, and a more rapid cashiering of officers. Given the absence of external threat throughout this period, this trend is not terribly surprising.[11]

But the declining raw figures of the number of troops conceal the sizable gains that state leaders achieved in two aspects of coercive capacity. First, even as the army shrank, it came more firmly under the control of state leaders. Multiple armed forces with limited loyalty to the national government were eliminated and replaced with a professional military, loyal to national leaders, rather than to local and regional elites.

---

[11] While the United States continued to loom to the north, there was a broad consensus among policymakers that military development would not suffice to respond to an American invasion; thus scholars agree the development of Mexican coercive capacity did not respond to international threat (Hernández Chávez 1989).

TABLE 6.3. *Army size in Mexico, selected years, 1884–1910*

Year	Officers	Troops
1884	3,684	30,366
1896	3,288	
1899	3,501	26,131
1905	3,396	24,758
1907	2,855	24,841
1910	2,365	22,980

Source: Hernández Chávez 1989, 286.

Second, the ability of the state to respond to security threats increased, even as the brute size of the army declined.

Both Liberals and Porfirians sought to boost military centralization and effectiveness. But they were hampered by the fact that they had come to power with the support of local forces (chiefly National Guard units) seeking greater autonomy. Both by design and because of the centrifugal nature of the fighting that brought the Liberals to power in 1857, the National Guard could not be a reliable arm of the central state because it represented fundamentally local and state-level Liberal interests (Hamnett 1996, 666). Even when the new constitution placed the National Guard under the control of Congress, the centralization Mexico City sought was hampered by a law that held that Congress could only order units outside their local community with the consent of local officials. And because Congress itself feared many of the Liberal centralizing measures, which were associated with the empowering of the presidency at Congress's expense, it proved reluctant to change this legal obstacle to centralization (Hamnett 1996, 680–681).

Liberals made fairly little progress on this front. Deep distrust of the army left them reluctant to rebuild it, and therefore they were reliant on the National Guard. Local Guard units could neither be molded into a national force nor disbanded (which would cost thousands of jobs) as Liberals sought to centralize and increase coercive power. The balancing act of "the subordination of regionalism to nationalism without destroying federalism with centralism" was a very difficult one (Perry 1978, 5). Rather than addressing this issue head on, Liberals opted for incremental measures to weaken their reliance on the Guard. Juárez created a series of military colonies to garrison hostile and remote areas, and increased the size of the military reserve as a way to avoid the political challenges of decommissioning thousands of officers and soldiers (Neufeld 2009, 17 and 46). He also began to use the army rather than the National Guard, at least in some cases, to put down revolts. But this represented only limited progress in military development, leaving the same challenge to confront Díaz when he took power in 1876.

Like the Liberals, Díaz rode localized military force to national power, leading a successful revolt in 1876 that was heavily supported by National Guard units (Neufeld 2009, 17). Upon taking power, he found other localized forces with similar ambitions. Like his Liberal predecessors, he would find it politically difficult to centralize military force, and even harder to disband localized forces. Yet significant progress was made during the Porfiriato. Two policies were the cornerstones of his efforts to build effective centralized coercion.

One was the 1888 elimination of the National Guard, which did not fit into plans for a centralized military in Mexico. Recognizing the danger posed by units that had fundamentally local loyalties, especially after units joined local uprisings in several cases in the 1880s, Díaz sought to demobilize the National Guard entirely (Thomson with LaFrance 1999, 250). This process faced resistance, at times violent, both from soldiers concerned about losing salary and from regional commanders concerned about losing armed loyalists (ibid., 260). But Díaz pushed through with eliminating the Guard, and replaced its internal security role with army units.

Second, Díaz made fundamental changes to the army. Most centrally, he divided it between permanent and auxiliary forces, relying on the former and keeping the second in reserve in their home regions for deployment as needed. Graduates of the reorganized officer training schools (opened in 1869 and 1879) populated the permanent army; the old guard were relegated to the auxiliary forces. While they thus remained a burden on the state's coffers, Díaz was able to layer a new professional officer corps over the old regional caudillos (Hernández Chávez 1989, 264). Boundaries between the two forces were hard to cross; the new permanent force developed a professional officer corps without directly challenging the auxiliary forces that were threatened by the Díaz reforms.

At first, Díaz relied on auxiliary units of the army to replace the National Guard in its policing capacity. This was both cheaper and less overtly centralist than deploying the permanent units without local ties into a state. But a series of local uprisings in the early 1890s revealed the problems with this strategy, as auxiliary units refused to fight against their fellow residents[12] (Hernández Chávez 1989, 277). This confirmed the distrust Díaz had of the auxiliary corps, and the 1896 military reforms involved massive cuts of the auxiliary forces. Díaz retired six of seven generals, more than three-quarters of colonels, and similarly high proportions of high-ranking officers (ibid., Table 2).

Over the course of the Porfiriato, the territorial reach of the state's coercive power spread quite widely and centralized coercive power increased. Table 6.4 shows that troops in significant numbers were present in every one of Mexico's states after 1895. Díaz divided the country into eleven military zones, whose boundaries did not overlap with state borders. Regular rotation of officers and units also contributed to increased central government control over the army (Lieuwen 1968, 2). Detachments were deployed far and wide, reaching far beyond state capitals and economic centers to "communities, towns, neighborhoods, and countryside – often to places that had scarcely seen the federal presence previously" (Neufeld 2009, 178). The entry of small corps of troops to small towns in remote areas, as Neufeld describes, served a dual role of enhancing security and undermining localism. Combined with the extension of railroad and telegraph networks that could summon and deliver reinforcements, small detachments could more effectively respond to threats.

The relatively high level of coercive capacity can also be seen in the state's responses to two prominent outbreaks of regional unrest (the Yaqui rebellions and the aftermath of the Yucatán Caste War), and even in the performance of the Porfirian army in the 1910 revolution. The state responded to rebellion by entering the Sonoran heartland of the Yaqui, an indigenous community, with a massive military intervention (along with some development initiatives) (Hu-DeHart 1988, 161). Yaqui insurgents were "crushed" in 1887 by the "larger and better equipped federal army" (ibid., 162), and the federal government took charge of developing a long-term pacification program to prevent further irruption of violence. With the failure of initial efforts, and further uprising, the Díaz government turned to the wholesale deportation of the Yaqui. Beginning in 1902, thousands were shipped to the south of Mexico, in a policy of "genocide through deportation" (Neufeld 2009, 184). Others were forcibly conscripted into military units sent to the Yucatán. This brutal policy extirpated the Yaqui guerrillas by draining their sea of community

---

[12] On earlier similar incidents, see Reina (1980, 30–31).

TABLE 6.4. *Troops stationed by state, Mexico, 1895–1910*

	1895	1900	1910
TOTAL	33,226	38,588	36,720
Aguascalientes	233	265	377
Baja	289	244	377
Campeche	1,530	214	45
Chiapas	232	358	223
Chihuahua	622	1,241	1,268
Coahuila	656	392	1,211
Colima	272	84	102
Distrito Federal	6,753	8,543	9,175
Durango	571	680	292
Guanajuato	1,936	1,686	1,230
Guerrero	946	900	470
Hidalgo	607	827	689
Jalisco	1,729	3,488	951
México	498	931	1,558
Michoacán	331	1,404	1,323
Morelos	1,818	197	549
Nuevo León	1,773	1,614	976
Oaxaca	2,219	2,421	1,760
Puebla	1,189	2,591	1,855
Querétaro	416	413	669
Quintana Roo	0	0	1,239
San Luís Potosí	529	416	1,143
Sinaloa	634	646	234
Sonora	1,029	4,638	2,918
Tabasco	152	170	66
Tamaulipas	1,405	1,008	808
Tepic	385	625	1,387
Tlaxcala	347	346	390
Veracruz	1,845	1,260	1,694
Yucatán	1,619	236	876
Zacatecas	661	750	865

Source: *Estadísticas Económicas del Porfiriato: Fuerza de Trabajo y Actividad Económica por Sectores* (Mexico: El Colegio de México) 1960, p. 56.

support, and brought an end to the conflict (Hu-DeHart 1988, 166). Once the region was depopulated, the Yaqui River valley was resettled under military control, with modernization projects and infrastructural development undertaken to draw investors. This "taming" of the Yaqui regions reflected the coercive capacity of the Porfirian state, as well as its modernizing ambitions.

Increasingly effective coercive intervention also brought an end to longstanding conflict in the Yucatán that persisted for decades after the Caste War, festering largely because insurgent Mayan forces could arm themselves and evade the military by crossing the international border into British Honduras.[13] A holistic strategy, devised in the 1890s, attempted nothing less than the full incorporation of the region. This included military intervention, the settlement of colonists from elsewhere in the country, and infrastructure development. Federal efforts were explicitly designed to exclude local elites, both because their cooperation was in question, and due to fear that the Maya would not accept rule by the Yucatecan elites they had been fighting for decades. The military component of the intervention included thousands of troops, with particularly high numbers in the final offensive of the conflict in early 1901. Both of these initiatives involved extensive campaigns and thousands of troops, a reflection of the state's ability to mobilize overwhelming force and impose regional stability.

The rapid fall of the Porfirian state at the start of the Mexican Revolution seems to call into question the scoring of the Mexican state as relatively strong, since theorists beginning with Skocpol (1979) have emphasized state weakness as crucial in revolutions. Yet an examination of the military's performance in the war demonstrates its coercive capacity: as Vanderwood (1976, 579) puts it, the Porfirian counterinsurgency was "unsuccessful, but not necessarily inept." The state fell for reasons largely independent of its coercive capacity. Hampered by problems of personalism that disrupted military coordination, by difficulties with supply chains and communication, and (most of all) by the ability of rebels to seek sanctuary north of the U.S. border, Díaz found himself unable to defeat the Maderista insurgency centered in Chihuahua. As the guerrilla war dragged on, perceptions of the regime's stability shifted sharply, and this triggered cascading defections by elites from the Díaz coalition. Although the state faced an uphill battle it would eventually lose, the army remained well organized; defeat came in spite of, and not because of, its performance.

LOCAL OFFICIALS AND MILITARY RECRUITMENT

The earlier discussion demonstrates that a gulf in mobilizational capacity emerged over the nineteenth century among our four cases. Chile

---

[13] This paragraph draws heavily on Macías Richard (1999).

developed a well-oiled mobilizational apparatus for military deployment; and Mexico was also relatively capable of effective military mobilization by the late Porfiriato and had gone a long way toward unifying the armed forces in the country under the control of the national government. By contrast, Peru saw no such gains in coercive capacity. To explain variation among these three cases, I turn once again to the form of local administration, and argue that deployed rule (as in Chile and Mexico) facilitated state development while delegated rule (as in Peru) tended to undermine it.

The logic linking the incentives of local officials to military mobilization feeds through conscription. The ability of the central state to mobilize troops depended on its ability to generate compliance from its local agents. But conscription was costly for local officials: as Deas (2002, 86) writes, "Like taxation, it was rarely popular. Public order being often precarious, governments were reluctant to spread alarm and perturbation. Resistance to recruiting and conscription through riot, *bochinche*, was commonplace." Where local officials regularly complied with conscription edicts, it became systematized and routine, and populations accepted the burden of military participation to a greater extent. The result was less desertion and an easier time mobilizing men in arms when necessary. Conscription by civilian officials also contributed to the emergence of a national military identity, since it tended to result in units that mixed recruits from various regions. Thus deployed bureaucrats contributed to the development of coercive capacity, as shown in the cases of Chile and Mexico that follow.

But under delegated rule, local state agents were less likely to comply with conscription edicts. Mobilization took place in an ad hoc manner, carried out as necessary by the military and often by force. The result was that conscription remained conflictual. Recruitment in Peru was never marked by the quasi-voluntary compliance that routinization brought, and desertion was higher. Because military units conscripted en masse, the composition was more regionally homogeneous, and the army never served as a "school for the nation." Delegated rule was key in undermining the implementation of mobilization policies in Peru. The evidence shows that in these three cases, local administrative institutions shaped coercive practices, and thus the coercive facet of state capacity.

Understanding the Colombian state's lack of coercive capacity requires us to turn to the ideational component of my argument: I show that state weakness can result from the failure of national officials to ever develop systematic policy. In the coercive realm, this left local officials and military units to their own devices in the area of conscription even during wartime. The result was that conscription remained ad hoc and conflictual, frustrating mobilization efforts when the state needed them most. Once again, we see that state weakness in Colombia and Peru derives from distinct causal pathways; I address this issue in detail in the Conclusion.

Deployed Rule, Legal-Formal Conscription, and Chilean Military Effectiveness

By the 1840s, military ranks in Chile were filled with a combination of volunteers and those sentenced to military service by local judicial officials (Resende Santos 2007, 135). Volunteers were often motivated by enlistment bonuses, which were particularly high for those with previous army experience who were willing to reenlist (Sater and Herwig 1999, 67). Because local state agents were responsible for conscription in Chile, and because forcible enlistment was largely eliminated, conscription took place with a veneer of legality that legitimized and routinized military service. This quasi-voluntary, rather than coerced, compliance with military service both reflected the greater ability of the Chilean state to penetrate local society and improved its military effectiveness. Both of the mechanisms linking deployed rule to increased state capacity were at work in this context. Although conscription was not popular, and the court sentences of military service engendered significant resistance, the central state could and did sanction local officials who did not meet recruitment quotas. Beyond the threat of sanctions, local agents were also willing to bear the costs of enforcing conscription because they lacked private sources of coercion and therefore needed an effective military to help maintain order in their jurisdictions (HEC vol. 4, 16).

The effects of compliance with conscription policies on coercive capacity were manifold. First, the greater cohesion of the Chilean military can be seen in the low levels of desertion from its army. For example, during the second War of the Pacific, a force of nearly 4,000 soldiers involved in a year-long campaign in the Peruvian highlands suffered only 103 desertions (HEC vol. 6, pp. 295–296). Second, systematic conscription mixed troops from across the country within each unit rather than leading to individual units recruiting exclusively from the zones in which they were stationed. This helped to create a sense of an army fighting for the Chilean nation. Beginning in 1862, the army began the practice of rotating units through the country, which severed any remaining connection between a particular unit and a "home region." Third, lacking local ties, troops could effectively complement police forces in maintaining social order. Thus the capacity to compel Chileans to enlist in the army also contributed to the capacity to maintain an internal monopoly of force. Because they knew that the army served as a guarantor of regional security, and because of the ability of the central state to sanction them, local authorities were willing to designate young (predominantly poor) men for service, and the army no longer had to fill its ranks by forcible conscription.

The only sizable deviation from this model of systematic conscription was undertaken by President Balmaceda during the 1891 civil war. With much of the military siding with his congressional opponents, Balmaceda built a new fighting force largely through press-gangs. By contrast to the motivated and disciplined forces built by his opponents, this practice of Balmaceda produced a force of "hesitant if not indifferent soldiers" that refused to fight and deserted *en masse*, leading directly to his defeat (Sater and Herwig 1999, 47). By contrast, his opponents engaged in more systematic recruitment to fill military ranks, promising civilian back pay to enlistees and spreading recruitment widely to limit its effects on the local economy (ibid., 49). This army, which looked more like Chilean armies of previous decades, triumphed easily, reinforcing the link between conscription practices and coercive capacity.

Conscription became more systematized when Chile undertook a massive military modernization project at century's end (Resende Santos 2007). Driven both by response to foreign threats (largely from Argentina) and by the vision of Prussian advisers, systematic conscription underwent a series of reforms between 1893 and 1900 (Sater and Herwig 1999, 81–83). A draft lottery held in each municipality included all males aged twenty to forty-five, although exemptions tended to favor the upper classes and the politically connected (ibid., 102–103). Sater and Herwig term conscription a "failure" (95) based on its unequal incidence. But a glance elsewhere in the region calls that judgement into question: as they themselves demonstrate, the Chilean state was able by 1898 to activate 60,000 reserve troops when war with Argentina loomed. The focus on the limitations of this mobilization – equipment, training, and leadership – makes too little of the degree of coercive capacity demonstrated in mobilizing so many Chileans to military bases in preparation for combat. After the 1900 conscription reform, the state's capacity to mobilize escalated even further: one military attaché cited in Sater and Herwig (1999, 109) estimated that 200,000 reservists (out of a population of 3.1 million) could be mobilized within six months.

Chile's elites were not well disposed to the military.[14] Sater and Herwig (1999, 97) highlight the interventions of landed elites to limit military use of railroads during harvest time, and refer to the "hatred" of employers and wealthy farmers for conscription (105). But elite interference with conscription was absent not because they approved of it, but because they were *excluded from local administration by the deployment of bureaucrats*. Where they were able to interfere with military policies costly to them, such as the use of railroads during harvest time, elites did so. Conscription, however, like taxation and education development, was out of their control because it was administered by bureaucrats *deployed* to the localities where they implemented policies emanating from state-builders in Santiago. The form of administration was crucial in the successful development of coercive capacity, as it was for the other elements of Chilean state strength.

Mexico: Voluntary Enlistment and Legalistic Recruitment

The *leva* or forced enlistment is commonly cited in accounts of the conditions of the nineteenth-century Mexican army. Neufeld (2009), for example, refers to conscripts as "cannon meat" (43) and claims that conscripts were taken "from their communities by force of arms and law" (39). Yet forcible impressment was in fact fairly rare in Mexico by regional standards. Most conscription in late nineteenth-century Mexico seems to have operated in a much more legal and formal manner, as suggested by Neufeld's own use of the term "force of law" in the citation just mentioned. The Mexican armed forces could fill their ranks in this manner thanks to their reliance on deployed rule. And the legal nature of most military recruitment facilitated mobilization both in the regionally controlled National Guard and, over time, in the centralizing Porfirian army.

The first glimmers of systematic conscription emerged during the war with the United States. Obligatory universal service was considered for the first time by Mexican politicians, who were driven to "ignore the spectre of an armed and angry *pueblo*" and mobilize the masses (Thomson 1990, 35). Wartime governments created the National Guard, for which registration was obligatory and nearly universal; no purchasing of substitutes was allowed. This compulsory registration stayed on the books for more than a decade.

---

[14] Kurtz (2009, 507) disagrees, claiming that Chilean elites were willing to tolerate it, but offers no explicit evidence for this claim.

As both sides competed to mobilize troops in the 1857 civil war, conditions of recruitment notably improved, shifting from legal enforcement to inducements. Liberals recruited on the grounds of ideological sympathy, by highlighting the tax exemptions awarded to guardsmen, and by promising that Guard units would serve close to home and remain under local, and often indigenous, control. The result was that voluntary enrollment dominated. As Thomson writes in his study of communities in Puebla, "People chose to join the Guard. Even if driven to serve by poverty or landlessness, few were forced to serve against their will" (ibid., 37). A crucial shift in 1858 instituted a tax, the *contribución de rebajadas*, imposed on all who chose not to serve in the National Guard. Payment of the tax, or Guard service, was a guarantee against military recruitment (Thomson 1990, 38). This generated a consistent pattern of voluntary enrollment in the National Guard; Thomson (1990, 42) even highlights some communities that had an "enthusiastic response" to mobilization. This tax thus created a legal framework of eligibility for conscription into both the military and the National Guard.

With the escalation of conflict during the French Intervention, recruitment became more routinized. Thomson (1993, 213ff) describes three models of recruitment by the various forces in addition to the model described previously of voluntary recruitment based on ideological appeals and tax exemptions. First and most commonly, local officials were charged with sentencing deserters, vagrants, and other "undesirables" to military service. This option, in somewhat modified terms, would dominate recruitment until the revolution. A second model, operative only when local states of emergency were declared, placed the recruitment and equipment of troops under the control of local commanders, who could impose these burdens on the communities where they were stationed and require a certain number of "volunteers" for service. This practice was common in the early stages of the war of the French Intervention (1861–1862). Forcible impressment by military units was the third option; in this model a unit occupied a town on a Sunday or market day, and rounded up victims to escort them to the battlefield. This option, both "ineffective and politically counterproductive," was only used in times of desperation during the French intervention and thereafter (Thomson 1993, 219). The most common model of conscription during the Liberal era, assignment by legal sentence, thus placed the responsibility for filling military ranks in the hands of local officials. The active participation of local officials with this mode of military mobilization allowed the Mexican state to mobilize troops largely by means other than forcible impressment.

Under Porfirio Díaz, military recruitment continued to operate largely via legal sentencing. These practices, although somewhat coercive, were more routinized than the forcible impressment by army units described later in Peru and Colombia. National officials (the Secretary of War and the *Jefes de Reemplazo* he appointed for each state) and state governors set quotas for each *jefe político* to meet, and these officials "delegated it to municipal officials or personally worked to gather the needed men" (Neufeld 2009, 51). The *jefe político* was free to fill his assigned quota as he chose, with the restriction that recruitment could *not* take place by force – indeed the *jefe* himself was charged with preventing forcible recruitment by other actors, a power that apparently sought to prevent military units from filling their ranks extralegally.

The practice of military recruitment was incredibly unpopular: Neufeld, for example, claims that it was "one of the most despised institutions of the Porfirian era" (ibid., 50–51). Recruitment generated resistance, especially from peasants and the urban poor, whether overt protest or evasion. Military law banned forcible recruitment, requiring that all soldiers be volunteers or selected by lottery. This formed the basis for legal challenges to recruitment, which were successful enough to cause concern among high ranking military officers (Neufeld 2009, 63ff). The legalistic veneer of conscription practices increased their legitimacy in the eyes of the population, even if legality did not necessarily make them popular. Yet *jefes* seemingly complied quite regularly with the order to impose military quotas on their populations. Indeed, Neufeld (52) claims that they often went above and beyond the call of duty in sending recruits. We must acknowledge that in part this was because the power to assign local male residents to military service strengthened the hold of local officials over the communities where they ruled; it also provided opportunities for profit and the removal of enemies. And *jefes políticos* could force prisoners, the poor, and local "troublemakers" to bear the costs of service, allowing them to conscript without affecting the locally prominent and powerful.

But the central factor in explaining the compliance of local agents was the incentives of deployed rule. As Neufeld (2009, 51) writes, local officials faced "pressure from above" to fill army ranks, and were induced to comply. Given that they came from outside the communities they ruled, were more loyal to Porfirio Díaz than to local interests, and had no ties to local National Guard units or alternative options for local security provision, *jefes* also stood to benefit from military development for protection against local contention. These two factors, consistent with the broader argument about deployed rule, explain why they complied with orders to send conscripts to military training.

The compliance of local officials with recruitment edicts allowed them to take place through legal means. Legal conscription contributed to military effectiveness in several ways. First, desertion rates, although significant, appear to have been lower than the rates seen in Peru or Colombia. Second, army units (although not the National Guard) mixed residents of many regions. For example, troublesome conscripts and deserters from various parts of the country were often sent far from home to the Yucatán, where units mingled soldiers from nationwide (Macías Richard 1999). Combined with significant military education and the fact that many units served in the Yaqui and Yucatán campaigns, the Mexican army did become a school for inculcating nationalism among the Mexican population.

At the end of the Porfiriato, conscription had become largely formal, relying primarily on local authorities such as *jefes políticos* and local judges, rather than taking the form of coercive impressment by military units. These practices survived even during the early years of the revolution: as the Madero revolt grew, and recruitment became both more difficult (due to the defections of local officials) and more urgent, forcible impressment still remained on the margins of state practice. Instead, monetary bonuses were used to increase the appeal of military service. The result was a loyal army rank and file through the early phases of conflict, which only fell apart with the more fractal post-1913 phase of the Revolution. Systematic legal conscription practices eroded as multiple armed actors turned to force to fill their ranks; desertion, which had become relatively rare in the Porfiriato, rose sharply in Huerta's army (Vanderwood 1976, 555). Yet this sharp decline should not conceal the serious increase in the coercive capacity of the Mexican state in the five decades before the Revolution.

Delegated Rule and Peruvian Military Weakness

For most of the nineteenth century, conscription in Peru was the responsibility of subprefects, who were overwhelmingly selected from among local elites. Local notables had little interest in conscription because it created a national army that threatened their established local power, and because it removed Indian laborers who were economically vital to their estates (Kurtz 2013). Since they were able to draw on their connections and local power to raise private security forces, local officials in Peru did not rely exclusively on the national army to protect them against threats to their power. Additionally, conscription was unpopular and therefore generated the risk of reprisals. In one instance, "following the recruitment of nearly ten soldiers in Cuzco, an anonymous group raided and laid waste to the house of the subprefect responsible for the measure" (Muecke 2004, 175).

As a result of these incentives characteristic of delegated rule, local officials in Peru often shirked and avoided the conscription duties assigned to them by presidential order, and ignored regulations governing military recruitment. For example, although the 1872 military service law set population-based recruitment quotas for each province, not a single province saw full compliance.

Because local officials were so reluctant to participate in conscription, military units had to fill their own ranks from the populations of the regions in which they were located (MGUERRA 1845, 4). Conscription by military units operated by force and extralegally, and thus it lacked any legitimacy. It also led to a concentration of recruiting in the heavily indigenous southern highlands region of Peru, where "the army scoured the countryside of the *altiplano* from one end to another" when troops were needed (Jacobsen 1993, 132–133). Due to their recruitment by force and by "notoriously cruel methods," Peruvian conscripts were not loyal to their army (Méndez 2005, 243). Desertion by these impressed soldiers was consistently high, even during the transport of troops to the front in 1879 (Contreras and Cueto 1999, 137). Officers were occupied just as much with policing new recruits for desertion as with battlefield training.

The failure of local officials to collaborate with conscription also had an effect on the army's role in nation building. Unlike the regional heterogeneity of Chilean and Mexican army units, the Peruvian army was not a place where recruits came into contact with a cross section of the nation. Instead they encountered their fellow poor from the province where the unit was most recently based. For example, the Dos de Mayo regiment in 1878 recruited 343 soldiers from the department of Ayacucho, where it was deployed to put down a revolt, in a single month (MGOB 1878, 77). Impressed troops were more likely to desert, more poorly trained, and less nationally representative. The Peruvian army was much further from the ideal of a "nation under arms," had many more discipline problems, and was less effective on the battlefield. The inability of the guano-era

Peruvian state to mobilize a sizable, unified, reliable army caused its defeat by Chile in the second War of the Pacific.

Just as in education and taxation, the Aristocratic Republic saw a program of military development that sought to increase the state's reach. Rather than addressing the problems of conscription, however, the reforms mostly focused on professionalizing the military and preparing it for more success in international warfare – a priority for the government, given smoldering tensions with Chile and tense relations with its other neighbors. Particular attention was paid to officer training corps and tactics, which were acquired from the French military training mission that arrived in 1896. Yet little changed below the officer corps; conscription still centered on coerced impressment, and the ranks remained far from a unified, disciplined, national army. This highlights the uneven nature of state building during the Aristocratic Republic, as Peru saw much less progress in coercive capacity than in the realm of education. Indeed, González-Cueva (2000) cites evidence of forcible conscription as recently as the 1995 conflict with Ecuador.

The Absence of Systematic Recruitment Efforts in Colombia

Just as in the realms of taxation and education, the development of conscription shows that Colombia's state leaders made very limited efforts to increase the state's power. Indeed, no effort was made to systematize conscription at all and no national policy governing military recruitment was ever enacted. This left the task of conscription in the hands of individual military unit commanders, who had to fill their ranks when needed by any means available. Whereas the Peruvian army filled its ranks in a similar manner because local officials did not cooperate with edicts from Lima, no such edicts were even issued in Colombia.[15] The absence of systematic conscription procedures hampered the performance of the army in ways similar to those seen earlier in the Peruvian case, weakening it in the face of domestic challengers. Indeed, because conscription was often carried out by violent means, recruitment drives *contributed* to opposition support (Deas 2002).

Systematic historical study of Colombian conscription is limited.[16] Accounts of mid-nineteenth-century civil wars show that both Liberals

---

[15] Delpar (1981, 87) cites a requirement that each state (during the 1880s) contribute to the army in proportion to its population, but this contained no edicts on the *form* of recruitment, and was never implemented.

[16] Deas (2002) sketches the terrain to be explored and the limits of previous scholarship.

and Conservatives relied on "both volunteers and unwilling recruits" (Sanders 2010, 29). Military units appealed for volunteers, but filled much of their ranks by conscription, including forcible impressment. The army filled its ranks through "time-tested methods of forced recruitment of lower-class men" (Bergquist 1986, 133). The army vastly over-represented "Indians from Boyacá and Cundinamarca" rather than from the country as a whole (Delpar 1981, 87). Soldiers were recruited as needed by military units in or near the locations where fighters were needed, and often marched straight into battle. The result was an untrained army full of soldiers with questionable loyalty and quality, which was strikingly ineffective on the battlefield.

This pattern is not dissimilar from that seen in the other cases in the first decades after independence, but military recruitment policies in those countries emerged as part of state-building efforts. What sets Colombia apart from the other cases is the absence of efforts to change this policy and systematize military recruitment in any manner. As late as the War of 1,000 Days, most recruitment continued to take place by ad hoc forcible recruitment. Bergquist (1986, 135–136) describes conscription by "groups of armed men" targeting poor people without any legal procedure. The result was that desertion and military discipline were a major problem for unit commanders, and resistance to conscription was widespread, and at times violent.

The violence of impressment by all sides in the War of 1,000 Days, and the resulting failures of the army, did place the issue of recruitment squarely at the center of the postwar Reyes reform efforts. Yet his response failed to address the core issue. Although forced recruitment was formally abolished in 1907, no system of filling army ranks was put in place. The only new legislation governed the terms of volunteer enrollment; no other means of recruitment was enacted. The disinclination of political elites to increase state capacity thus continued to account for the weakness of the Colombian state.[17]

CONCLUSION

This chapter began by showing that differential participation in conflict does not explain the variation in state coercive power across the

---

[17] The fact that Colombia did not develop systematic conscription until well into the twentieth century may indeed be one factor underlying the pattern of elite conflict spiraling into generalized violence at various points in Colombian history.

four cases. Instead, war (whether international or internal) posed challenges to state leaders that *revealed* the extent of their ability to mobilize compliance. War, in other words, did not make states; it tested them. Over the nineteenth century, state leaders in Chile developed increasingly effective means of mobilizing an army, and security from both domestic and international threats increased as a result. This derived from the role of deployed bureaucrats in the task of conscription. These officials systematized it and made recruitment routine and relatively consensual and efficient; the army that resulted saw more homogenization and less desertion. In Mexico, too, *jefes políticos* complied with conscription edicts, leading to the development of a national army for the first time during the Porfiriato. Progress here was slower, largely because state leaders had to tread carefully to avoid conflict with the multiple armed groups that existed when state building began. But particularly during the Porfiriato, significant steps were taken toward the emergence of a powerful national army.

By contrast, Peruvian and Colombian state leaders continued to struggle to fill military ranks. In Peru, this derived from a continued reliance on local elites for recruitment; delegation to these disinterested officials made the policies ineffective. In Colombia, no efforts were made to systematize the military's recruitment. In both cases, the absence of systematic conscription and the reliance on forcible recruitment hampered military mobilization, poisoned state-society relations, and weakened the homogenizing effect of a national army. By examining conscription, then, we see how delegated rule (in Peru) and the absence of a state-building project (in Colombia) each led to a striking absence of coercive capacity.

Conclusion

This book has explored the origins of state strength and weakness in Latin America. Unlike most extant scholarship on state development, I have sought to explain two distinct types of variation in state building. The framework I have developed seeks to account for the decision to build the state, and for the fate of state-building efforts. Thus it explains why state-building efforts succeed, founder, or fail to emerge. Although it increases the number of "moving pieces" involved, the construction of a unified framework to account for the full range of state capacity trajectories has some important payoffs. After pulling together the account developed in the preceding chapters in the first section of the Conclusion, I address the extent to which it can be applied more generally across South America. I then turn to highlighting some of the implications of the argument developed in this book and the analytical choices that underpin it. I discuss the importance of long-term historical processes in accounting for contemporary state weakness in the region, the place of ideas in accounts of state building the central role of equifinality in explanations of state development, and the relative importance of the two causal factors – ideational and administrative – for the outcomes observed across the region. I close with some implications of my argument for contemporary nation-building projects in post-conflict settings.

THE EMERGENCE AND OUTCOMES OF STATE-BUILDING EFFORTS

I have argued that it is crucial to understand why sometimes political elites unite around state building as an important means to development, while at other times they do not. In a context where war and other threats to the survival of the state were not present, factors identified by existing scholarship under-determine variation in state capacity. This is because the political decision to pursue state building has not been theorized, and state building has been reduced to a reaction to structural conditions rather than a political choice. In developing an explanation for why state-building efforts emerge, I have focused on a combination of ideational and material factors, and argued that state-building initiatives were more likely to be undertaken in countries characterized by a unified political economy with a central capital city at its core. Under these circumstances, leaders tended to share a more developmentalist liberal vision and to believe that the promotion of "order" and "progress" entailed the development of state institutional capacity and its extension across the national territory. Where leaders instead confronted a polycentric network of urban centers with fragmented regional political economies, they did not see state building as a viable means for pursuing development, and were more likely to endorse a laissez-faire stance toward the national state and to pursue economic and political development at the regional level. The former pattern, of a single national center, a developmentalist version of liberalism, and concerted state-building efforts, described Mexico in the Liberal and Porfirian eras, Chile, and Peru. The latter pattern of multiple salient and self-sufficient regions, conflict over the role of the national state, and the absence of a state-building projects accounted for Colombia's strikingly weak state.

Unlike most scholarship on state building, my account also investigates why, once state-building projects are undertaken, they tend to succeed or fail. This question is simply neglected by the existing scholarship, which overlooks the fact that state-building efforts do not always succeed and thus risks falling into the fallacy of assuming that where a weak state is found, a state-building effort must not have been pursued. A more persuasive approach to variation in state capacity is to develop a theoretical account of state-building failure. I argue that the institutional choices made by leaders in populating the bureaucracy shape the fate of state-building efforts. In particular, I focus on the differential effects of deployed and delegated rule. Where leaders relied on *deployed rule*, sending outsiders into communities to serve as administrators and implementers of state policies, state-building efforts were more successful, but under *delegated rule*, where local elites were appointed to bureaucratic posts, state-building efforts foundered.[1] Two mechanisms underlie this divergence: first, deployed bureaucrats could more easily be held accountable by the central state, since a larger share of their income depended on their position. Second, because deployed bureaucrats possessed less local authority independent of the presence of the central state, they had an independent interest in increasing its presence in the communities where they serve. It was this factor, and not the failure of a state-building project to emerge, that accounted for state weakness in guano-era Peru.

Alternative Explanations

In developing this account, I have also considered and shown the limits of a range of alternative explanations. Chapter 1 showed that geography did not shape state-building outcomes by affecting the cost-benefit calculations of state leaders. Indeed, mountainous or rugged terrain, size, and other geographic factors are weakly associated with state development outcomes. Chapter 3 addressed the possibility that other historical moments might hold the key to the divergence among cases: there I showed that neither differences in colonial rule, nor the nature of the independence period and its immediate aftermath, determined state-building trajectories in the four cases. Chapter 4 showed that ethnic diversity, commonly said to account for variation in public good provision more generally and education in particular, cannot account for variation in efforts by national state leaders to promote education development. The significant gains in education development in Peru during the Aristocratic Republic (1895–1919) highlight the limits of this argument most clearly, since the change from earlier periods in Peruvian history was not that social inequality declined (in fact, most scholars see this as a period where elite dominance increased) but that a shift to increase reliance on deployed rule prevented elite preferences about education from affecting its implementation. Chapter 5, which explored the development of extractive

---

[1] Chapter 3 provides an account of the choice of delegated or deployed rule in the cases of Chile, Peru, and Mexico, showing that it was not a result of preexisting variation in state capacity but instead the product of a complex, historically specific set of factors. There I show that only where state leaders faced a perceived threat of subaltern revolt to systemic stability, where they did not see traditional local elites as an obstacle to development, and where the currency of patronage by which alliances between central and local elites were cemented was political rather than administrative were the ranks of state administration populated with local elites. It was the combination of these three factors that distinguished guano-era Peru from the other state-building moments under study, produced delegated rule, and thus underpinned failed state building in that case.

Conclusion

capacity, confronted two more alternative explanations. There, I showed that resource dependence can only be a partial explanation for variation in state capacity, since it is overly focused on the political costs of taxation. Resource dependence can account for why governments *choose* not to tax; it cannot account for variation in the *capacity* to tax where commodity booms are absent. Comparing Peru and Chile after the end of their commodity booms, and tracing the different difficulties which the two states faced in recovering lost revenues, Chapter 5 made the limits of the resource dependence explanation clear. Nor does federalism account for variation in extractive capacity; the comparison of Mexico and Colombia showed that the distinct obstacles this set of institutions placed on the extractive capacity of the central state were overcome in the former case but not in the latter. Finally, Chapter 6 addressed the role of war in the development of the state's coercive capacity and showed that the nature of war in Latin America is better seen as a crucible that *tests* the state rather than as a forge that *makes* the state. Against arguments about the "bellic" roots of state development, I found that in Latin America the capacity to mobilize, train, and deploy troops was not associated with the onset of war, its duration, or its severity.

A BROADER PERSPECTIVE ON LATIN AMERICAN STATE BUILDING

This book has made two claims about the causes of state capacity drawing on the detailed study of four country cases. One of these can be easily evaluated in a broader set of cases; the other requires more intensive data collection and remains to be verified in future research. I first explore the relationship between urban primacy and the emergence of a state-building consensus, generalizing the framework developed in Chapter 1 to the ten major countries of Spanish America. The claim that the delegation of administrative posts to local elites undermined state-building efforts is more difficult to test due to data limitations; I provide some evidence from Argentina to supplement the detailed discussion of this issue in Chapter 2.

Urban Primacy and the Origins of State-Building Projects

I argued in Chapter 1 that the absence of salient regionalism was necessary for state-building efforts to emerge because it would lead to fairly muted regionalist conflicts over public good provision, and a fairly unified

TABLE 7.1. *Urban primacy and the emergence of state building*

Country	Primacy score	State-building project predicted?	Actual state-building project?	Predicted correctly?
Uruguay	0.84	YES	YES	YES
Argentina	0.66	YES	YES	YES
Peru	0.6	YES	YES	YES
Mexico	0.55	YES	YES	YES
Chile	0.53	YES	YES	YES
Ecuador	0.47	NO	NO	YES
Bolivia	0.46	NO	NO	YES
Colombia	0.44	NO	NO	YES
Paraguay	0.39	NO	PARTIAL	NO (international threat)
Venezuela	0.39	NO	PARTIAL	NO (primacy changes)

The urban primacy score used for Mexico here is from 1867 and is higher than the 1850 score used in Chapter 1; as discussed there, this later score more accurately captures the dominance of Mexico City during the state-building era. All other scores come from Table 1.1.

national economy. This facilitates the emergence of an elite consensus around the idea that increased state authority was central to development, rather than a more laissez-faire vision of how development might be pursued. I showed in the three empirical chapters that this difference in ideas about development accounted for Colombia's distinct trajectory, in which no salient and sustained state-building project emerged.

But to what extent does this variation in regionalism and ideas about development account for variation across a broader set of cases? In exploring this set of issues, I focus on the ten countries of Spanish South America, excluding Brazil because its nineteenth-century history was so distinct in the extent of administrative and political continuity from colonialism to independence. The leftmost column of Table 7.1 shows the urban primacy score for each country, using the same data and methods used in Chapter 1. Urbanists generally consider an urban primacy score of more than 0.5 – meaning that the largest city in a country has the same population as the next three cities combined – to be characterized by a primate urban distribution. Based on this, I describe the cases that fit this pattern as "high primacy" cases and expect them to be dominated by a single national center, to have a relatively consistent elite consensus

Conclusion   237

around state capacity as a means to development, and to pursue state building during the Liberal era. Cases that score below 0.5 on urban primacy are ones where multiple large cities exist, and where regional tensions and self-sufficient regions are likely to undermine the emergence of a developmentalist vision in which state building is central to economic development and political stability.

Based on this, the second column of Table 7.1 codes whether a state-building project should be expected to emerge in a given country during the Liberal era, given the score for urban primacy. The third column summarizes the brief case studies that follow, showing whether developmentalist or laissez-faire liberalism took hold, and whether a state-building project emerges. The rightmost column simply shows whether the prediction of the urban primacy–state building argument holds in each case. As the table prefaces, and the discussions that follow confirm, all but two cases are predicted correctly. For the two cases that are mis-predicted, a brief discussion of Paraguay helps to shed light on the limits of the argument I have developed, and suggests the limits of using urban primacy as a measure of the absence of salient regionalism. The case of Venezuela shows that change over time in urban primacy is associated with the timing of state building.

High Primacy, Concerted State-Building Efforts Emerge

ARGENTINA. The dominance of Buenos Aires reflected in the high urban primacy score for Buenos Aires actually understates the power of the capital. Many of the other large cities listed in the 1869 census were located in the littoral provinces near the capital, and deeply tied into its economic orbit. Indeed, Buenos Aires held sway over the entire country, since it was the only major point of export for agricultural production from the interior. Although the early decades after independence saw massive center-periphery conflict in Argentina, the country never had the self-contained regional economies that marked cases like Colombia. This lack of salient regionalism, as discussed later, underpinned a robust developmentalist liberal consensus. Buenos Aires and the provinces had a shared economic interest in export promotion, and a shared commitment to developing links between zones of export production and the port of Buenos Aires (Richmond 1989, 1).

Underneath the struggle between Buenos Aires and the provinces was a consensus on the model of state-led export-based development. By the 1850s, the provinces "now openly espoused ideas earlier identified with the Unitarists" (Rock 1987, 120). The weakening of regionalist divisions accelerated with economic development. In part, this was driven by the rapid demographic and economic growth of Buenos Aires, which became ever more dominant relative to the rest of the country. But economic development in the interior also underpinned the robustness of the consensus around national unification.

Although it had precursors under Rosas, the first true manifestation of the statist developmental project in Argentina can be seen in the 1853 constitution, which called for a state project of education, immigration and colonization, railroad development, and the promotion of domestic production (Rock 1987, 124). Alberdi and other mid-century liberals "regarded economic growth as the potential consequence, rather than the cause of state building" and believed that what they called "national organization" would promote rapid economic growth (Rock 2000, 179). An elite consensus "inherited a positive view of state power" rather than a laissez-faire view (Rock 2002, 4). After an imposed settlement between Buenos Aires and the provinces, the Mitre government that came to power in 1862 sought to put these ideals into practice. His administration created a bureaucratic apparatus, a tax system, and a national postal system, seeking explicitly to extend the reach of the state into the national interior. Importantly, all this institutional development was undertaken *before* the 1865–1870 war with Paraguay.[2] Sarmiento, returning to power in 1868, expanded the ambit of the central state by undertaking a major education development project (Rock 1987, 130). "Deliberate government programs" also sought to promote immigration, and the development of small and medium-scale agricultural production (Rock 1987, 141). A further agreement to protect flour, sugar, and wine production underpinned a consensus around the extension of infrastructure development – railroads – to Mendoza and Tucumán. Succeeding governments continued these efforts, which included the 1880s "Conquest of the Desert" extermination campaign aimed at the indigenous population as part of its project of national "civilization" as well as more benign initiatives of railroad building and education development. Rock (1987, 184) describes the Roca government as Porfirian (not surprising given its slogan of "Peace and Administration"), undertaking a positivist project of peace and administration that was designed to attract the

---

[2] The war did allow the central state to "strike new blows against caudillismo in the interior" resulting in "a much stronger central authority in the north and west" (Rock 1987, 128).

investment and immigration seen as the "keys to progress." Throughout the second half of the nineteenth century, then, the developmentalist consensus in Argentina, which at times was explicitly positivist, underpinned a sustained state-building effort (Richmond 1989, 20).

URUGUAY. Uruguay was torn by civil war for the first fifty years after its independence, leaving it with a strikingly weak state as of about 1870 (López-Alves 2000, chapter 2). But this conflict had no salient regional cleavage. Instead, Blancos and Colorados differed on how the country should respond to political tensions in Brazil and Argentina (Kurtz 2013, 126). In short, reflecting its strikingly high urban primacy score (and likely its small size), Uruguay had no salient regionalism, or any sense of self-contained regional economies. Liberals had "aspirations" of state building as a way to enrich Montevideo and attract foreign investment (Rock 2000, 182). Here, too, the Liberal project that emerged placed the extension of state authority at the center of the agenda for development, and this effort was sustained for the last quarter of the nineteenth century.

LaTorre, who came to power in the 1870s, sought to extend the state's reach into the interior as a way to stimulate economic development through policing, communication and transport infrastructure, a judicial system, education, and bureaucratic development (López-Alves 2000, 92). The core element of this effort, as Kurtz (2013, 117) points out, was the creation and enforcement of property rights – the state's intervention in the rural economy, in other words, was seen as a central element of development. In short, the Uruguayan consensus held that the extension of state authority into the interior was central to achieving economic development and political stability, and helping the country to overcome the dark decades of poverty and conflict it had endured after its independence. The same era also saw a massive expansion of public schooling with the 1877 Law of Common Education.

State building was a central element of the Liberal project of the late nineteenth century, culminating with the massive initiatives of the two Batlle administrations after 1903. As Kurtz (2013, 211) writes, a "political consensus about the expansion and strengthening of state institutions" emerged during this time. The Batlle reforms were nothing less than a radical transformation of the Uruguayan state, expanding both its strength and its scope in arenas such as economic management, social programs, labor regulation, and taxation, especially of the agricultural sector. This was the last step in the emergence of the region's most effective state during the initial state-building era.

Low Primacy, No State-Building Efforts Emerge

BOLIVIA. With an urban primacy score of 0.46, Bolivia fell toward the more fragmented end of the continuum of Latin American states. And as expected, the country saw high regional tensions, conflicts between regions over public good provision, and an elite consensus that, when it did emerge, made little effort to extend state authority through the national territory. As in Uruguay, political stability emerged late, coming only after Bolivia's 1880 defeat in the War of the Pacific, in which the country suffered fairly little in military terms but lost its coastal provinces, which contained not only access to the sea but the massive nitrate producing regions that would lay the foundation for Chile's economic boom described in Chapter 5. The war defeat firmly convinced elites that stable government was sorely needed. And the rise of silver mining, which had begun in the 1860s and 1870s, provided a fiscal foundation for its emergence (Klein 1969, 13–15). "Classic 19th century civilian rule" – a broadly liberal, civilian government, emerged in 1880 (Klein 2003, 143).

But while this elite consensus would hold for the next fifty years, little in the way of a state-building project emerged. Elites agreed on an export-based economic model, but they agreed on little else (Klein 2003, 143). There was no broad support for national unification or the centralization of political authority. Mine owners' interests in the state essentially began and ended with transportation development, and their preferences here (for a railroad linking the mines to the coast) diverged from those of other regional and sectoral actors. Conflict between the mining territory of Potosí and Sucre and the growing city of La Paz erupted in full-fledged civil war in 1899, which was resolved by making La Paz the center of government.[3]

The rise of tin mining after 1900 shifted elite dynamics once again. The remainder of the domestic economy "remained rural, commercially disconnected, and primarily oriented to local and fragile markets" (ibid., 249). Because traditional agriculture (with the exception of production in the Cochabamba region) largely and increasingly served local markets, rural elites had no interest in forging the political consensus needed to extend state authority. Nor did tin mining elites, who were famously uninterested in national politics; they funded a railroad linking their mines to the (now) Chilean port of Antofagasta with private funds, choosing not to seek state support. With the construction of the railroad, intra-regional

---

[3] Many historians see a broader trend of regionalist tensions that endured long thereafter (Paredes 2013, 245–246; Vergara 2012).

trade in the south collapsed, and the balkanization of Bolivia deepened (Paredes 2013, 116–117).

Elites, centered in the country's various regions, looked to the state increasingly as its coffers swelled with tin export revenue. But each region's politicians brought distinct visions of development to the table. The city of Santa Cruz, for example, "clamored" for a railroad line connecting it to the capital, with the slogan of *Ferrocarril o nada* (Paredes 2013, 261). As Paredes describes, "the increasing wealth of the state, the conviction of [President] Montes that railways were the true carriers of progress, and the increasing and sometimes conflicting demands of the regional landed elites led the government to initiate a big railway crusade. ... The program consisted of eleven lines, all to be started at the same time" (ibid., 262). This was the climax of the Bolivian state's attempt to satisfy the distinct preferences of elites in the country's many salient regions. It did so with an immense foreign borrowing program, leading to debt. And when the railroad efforts failed, this log-rolling model was replaced with an explicit decision not to centralize political authority. Lacking a single national center, or any national market, Bolivia was an archipelago of fragmented economic regions only loosely connected to the tin mining boom that filled government coffers. Under these conditions, even political stability brought no concerted state-building project; Bolivia closely resembled Colombia not only in its level of urban primacy but in the trajectory of absent state development it followed.

ECUADOR. Ecuador was a particularly striking instance in which regionalist tensions undermined any potential unified state-building project. The result was a state so weak that the country did not even conduct a full national census until 1950, more than a century after independence. The country's political economy was polarized between Quito, the capital located in the highlands, and the coastal seaport of Guayaquil, which was at least as powerful in political and economic terms. Because of the power of Guayaquil, state building could not unfold as the extension of Quito's influence over the national territory. This was not a case of self-sufficient regional economies as in Colombia or Bolivia. Instead, the more important mechanism undermining state building was tensions between regions with distinct public good preferences. These manifested in disputes over tariffs, education, water management, public works, sanitation, and transportation, and were especially intense around the construction of railroads linking Quito to the coast. Coastal planters had no need for this major undertaking, and did their best to thwart it (Henderson 1997, 172). Because there was little money economy elsewhere in the country, the flow of trade through Guayaquil "provided the state with opportunities to impose a variety of direct and indirect taxes," which were seen as unjust and fed regionalist rhetoric and conflict (Rodríguez 1985, 53). This led to pressures for the decentralization of tax revenue, which the national government was forced to grant. Regionalist tensions drove five major domestic conflicts in the nineteenth century, and "intermittent civil war" from 1895 to 1916 (ibid., 37). As the price for domestic peace, regionalist leaders "insisted that all areas simultaneously receive a share of public projects" (ibid., 92). Congress, desperate to maintain political stability, simply approved every public works project proposed by any of its members; this obviated any sort of national decision making and concerted development effort. Regionalism directly underpinned the absence of state building in Ecuador during the first century after independence; despite ample revenues from cacao exports, a state-building project never emerged due to tensions between Quito and Guayaquil over development priorities.

Mis-Predicted Cases

PARAGUAY. Paraguay also scored very low on urban primacy, meaning that we should expect to find no state-building project in that case. But despite the fact that the population was spread across various towns (Paraguay remained a highly rural country long after urbanization began in most of Latin America) it had no salient economic regions. With a small domestic market, economic activity centered on export agriculture (Abente 1989, 77). All of the country's production traveled downriver to the Atlantic, as did all imports. This meant that despite the low urban primacy, Paraguay had neither the self-sufficient regions nor the divergent public good preferences that I have argued tended to prevent the emergence of state-building projects. Indeed, Pastore (1994) argues that the 1850s and 1860s saw state building, as the national government sought to intervene in the economy to promote export production. This state-building project shared a similar emphasis on the development of transportation and communications infrastructure – railroads and telegraphs. But in two fundamental ways, it took a very different form than was seen in the other cases. First, it centered on land expropriation and labor coercion, as an 1846 decree made yerba mate (the country's main export) a state monopoly. Plantations were either harvested by the army directly or by "state-sponsored slavery" (López-Alves 2000, 208). Second, there was an overwhelming emphasis on the military, which (given fiscal constraints) crowded out spending on any other aspects of state-building (Pastore 1994, 322). Although explaining the first difference is beyond the scope of my argument – for my purposes all that matters is that Paraguay saw a concerted state-building effort in the 1850s and 1860s – the second difference reveals an important scope condition of the theoretical framework developed in this book. The geopolitical position of Paraguay, as a buffer between Argentina and Brazil, meant that state leaders saw military defense as a crucial aspect of export promotion – productive regions had to be defended from the "competition of predatory neighboring states" (Pastore 1994, 297). State building as a means to economic development in pre-1870 Paraguay centered less on making markets, citizens, and political stability, and more on international defense.

This unique geo-political position led Paraguay into a uniquely disastrous war with Brazil, Argentina, and Uruguay from 1865 to 1870. Conflict killed a large share of the population, and also brought increased foreign domination of the economy, and of Paraguayan politics. The result, Abente (1989, 83) argues, was that from 1870 through the 1920s the Paraguayan state, re-born "weak by design" after the war, took a strikingly laissez-faire approach to development. The state's behavior during this period cannot be easily linked to the economic regionalism argument I have developed, or at least none of the historiography makes the connection – one should note, however, the increased regional economic diversification in this period with the rise of cattle, timber, and cotton exports in distinct parts of the country. Abente traces the content of Paraguayan liberalism largely to the influence of foreign economic actors, and to defeat in war. These factors, both resulting from Paraguay's unique position between Argentina and Brazil, make its trajectory in the Liberal era (1870–1936) an outlier in terms of my predictions. In the earlier period, Paraguay had a unified economy and state building despite a low score for urban primacy – its experience matched the predictions of my theory but the case was coded wrong on regionalism by the urban primacy indicator. In the later period, it had no state building, but because this unfolded for reasons other than those I theorized, I cannot claim that my argument explains the Liberal era.

VENEZUELA. Despite its low urban primacy score, as reported in Table 7.1, Venezuela did see some state building beginning in the 1890s. Yet as discussed later, it is no coincidence that this initiative began only after the massive growth of Caracas and its rise as a national center. Thus, the over-time shift in Venezuela explains why the prediction of disinclination toward state building turns out not to hold in that case, and provides further evidence in support of the regionalism argument I have developed.

More than any other country except Colombia, Venezuela's division into multiple salient economic regions was reflected in its political development. This division was reinforced by fragmentation during the independence conflict, which led to the emergence of local militias rather than a single national army (López-Alves 2000, 201). But regionalism was also shaped by the form of the political economy – each of the ports along the Atlantic, for example, had "close links to its own hinterland," creating salient regional economies (Ewell 1984, 14).

Regionalism directly prevented the emergence of state building. Maracaibo and the Guayana region "openly challenged the authority of Caracas on several occasions" and actively resisted the extension of central political authority (Tarvear and Frederick 2006, 69). The 1864 Constitution, coming in the aftermath of the Federal Wars (1858–1863) empowered local political actors and fundamentally weakened the *de jure* powers of the national state. Like the 1849 Constitution in Colombia discussed in Chapter 1, this was a direct reflection of the salience of regionalism. The subsequent attempt to reverse this devolution, the centralization project of the Guzmanato (1870–1888), reveals the absence of state building in post-independence Venezuela: although it was an attempt to bring political order, it was limited to "empowering caudillos, who in turn refrained from waging war on the central state" (López-Alves 2000, 198). There was no attempt to extend central authority or the institutions of the central state through the national territory, and the vision of development through immigration and transportation development was expected to unfold through private initiative (Ewell 1984, 21). Yet even this effort met sizable resistance, especially from the gold-producing region of Guayana, which saw little to be gained from immigration or railroad development.

If the account so far suggests that Venezuela's absence of state building is well predicted by regionalism, Venezuela's over-time trajectory reinforces the power of the regionalist argument. After 1870, the country saw a slow concentration of population and power in Caracas and the north coast, with a concomitant decline in the salience of regional divisions, and a rise in economic ties between the capital and many formerly self-sufficient regions (Ewell 1984, 9). Not coincidentally, by the end of the 1890s, a slow shift toward a more developmentalist liberalism began to emerge; the country saw, under Cipriano Castro (president 1899–1908) the "timid beginnings of the state commitment to a responsibility for economic development" and a slow shift away from "classical laissez-faire" (ibid., 29). The first two decades of the twentieth century saw the creation of order, the nationalization and professionalization of the army, massive road-building, and an end to tax farming, which sharply increased national government revenue. In short, the rise of Caracas after 1870 prefigured the state building that unfolded between 1900 and 1920. Shortly thereafter, of course, massive oil revenues began to flow into state coffers, transforming the state in fundamental ways that set Venezuela apart from other countries in the region (Tinker Salas 2009). But both the absence of a state-building project in the nineteenth century, and the emergence of a limited effort after 1900 match the proposed link between regionalism and the content of liberalism.

CENTRAL AMERICA. The claim that the absence of regionalism was associated with the emergence of state-building efforts also finds support in the political development of Central America during the nineteenth century, where all five of the independent countries also saw significant state-building efforts.[4] This, too, is consistent with the prediction that the absence of salient regionalism would be associated with statist visions of liberal development. The absence of salient regionalism in Central America, and the orientation of politics around single national centers in each country, was to some extent determined by the small size of the national territory. But where it did exist in the early decades after independence, its erosion set the stage for subsequent state-building efforts. In Nicaragua, the 1850s establishment of Managua as a compromise capital between the dominant cities of León and Granada resolved the regional cleavage and allowed a state-building consensus to emerge and endure during the "Thirty Years" and the Zelaya administration, which made significant gains before being cut off with U.S. intervention after 1909 (Mahoney 2001, 100–101). And despite the fact that its urban population was distributed across several large towns in the central and western highlands, Guatemala was unified in economic terms around coffee production, lacking both challengers to the center and sizable, politically powerful self-sufficient regions.

State building efforts in Guatemala, El Salvador, and Costa Rica were associated with the rise of the coffee economy and a clear vision of the state's role in pursuing development via coffee exports. The emergence of the banana trade after 1900 in certain parts of the territories of Guatemala

---

[4] Panama only gained independence from Colombia in 1904, and Belize remained a British colony until the late twentieth century.

and Costa Rica did not create regionalist tensions over public good provision, since private companies controlled those fairly unpopulated regions and provided the infrastructure necessary for export rather than placing demands on the state. State-building efforts were most limited in Honduras; it is no coincidence that this country, among those in Central America, most closely resembled cases like Colombia in the lack of economic connections among its regions, as it was divided into what one historian (cited in Mahoney 2001, 104) described as multiple "hermit societies." This lack of a national market that generated an imperative for national unification led Honduran state-building efforts to emerge relatively late and to be relatively muted in character; Mahoney shows that the liberal reform agenda in Honduras was born weak and then undermined by international economic intervention. Thus the overall pattern of concerted state-building efforts by Liberals, as well as temporal variation in its emergence in Nicaragua and the partial exception of Honduras are all consonant with the argument I have advanced about regionalism and the origins of state-building efforts.

Forms of Rule and the Outcomes of State-Building Efforts

Chapter 2 developed an account of the success and failure of state-building efforts. The claim that the success of state building depended on administration through deployed rule should only be tested in cases where state-building projects emerged; thus, Colombia, Ecuador, Bolivia, pre-1899 Venezuela, and Paraguay after 1870 can be set aside.[5] The universe of cases, beyond those discussed in Chapter 2, includes Argentina, Uruguay, Venezuela 1899–1920s, and Paraguay 1852–1870. Unfortunately, evidence on the use of deployed or delegated rule in the administrations of additional cases is scarce. The limited available evidence, however, supports the claim that deployed rule fed increased state capacity. I draw here on secondary source accounts of Argentine political development, and find that (consistent with the prediction of my argument) deployed rule characterized the administration in this case of successful state building.

Argentina 1862–1916

If my argument holds, as a case of successful state building, Argentina should be characterized by significant reliance on deployed rule. Some

---

[5] The analytical distinction between emergence and success has implications for theory testing. Explanations for the success of state-building projects should not be tested in cases where state building did not occur. It would be incorrect, in other words, to test my theory by examining the correlation between patterns of administration or political stability and

evidence suggests this was the case. The early state-building era in Argentina saw the defeat of the caudillos that had militarily dominated the country in early years, and the "consolidation of the national state in the provinces" (Rock 2002, 56–57). Over the course of the 1860s and 1870s, the federal government established control. It did so largely by building alliances with governors, who were allowed to use provincial administration as a means of building "their own networks of authority" through appointments (Rock 2002, 71). A consensus not only among scholars but among contemporary observers was that patronage was a central element of the logic of Argentinean administration, beginning in the 1860s and continuing long thereafter (Salvatore 2013).

Alongside this increasingly tightly woven patronage network, we see some hints that this was not a case of delegation to local elites. As my argument predicts we should find in a case that saw significant state building, offices in the rank and file of the Argentinean administration tended not to be held by local elites. Governors were an exception: they did tend to be local elites, especially in the early state-building era when these positions still were used to co-opt regional caudillos. At this time, we can still talk about certain states, like Tucumán, being controlled by single families (Richmond 1989, 31). But the central government began under Mitre in 1862 to slowly oust provincial governors, replacing them (in at least some cases) with outsiders, such as the governor of San Juan installed in 1859 (Rock 2002, 17.) Military commanders, appointed and rotated by the central government, also brought the central state's authority in and weakened local power monopolies. By the time Roca came to power in 1880, a local observer described governors nationwide as "accessible to the suasion of the Chief of the Executive" (quoted in Rock 2002, 107).

Below the rank of governor, the Argentinean administration diverged from delegation to local elites in two key ways. One important difference, although it still indicates the presence of some degree of delegation to locals in Argentinean administration, was that when positions went

---

state capacity, since I have claimed that these factors only underlie the success of those state-building efforts that emerge. In those countries where state-building efforts never emerge, my theory makes no prediction at all about their effects on levels of state capacity. Instead, the onset of state-building efforts acts as a scope condition on these proposed relationships. The explicit definition of these scope conditions will prevent scholars from inappropriately testing explanations for successful and failed state building outside them. On the issue of scope conditions on theoretical claims in multi-causal arguments, see Soifer (2012a).

to locals, they tended not to be the most powerful members of the local community. Instead, as Rock (2002, 79) notes for the province of Buenos Aires, there was an "absence of strong links between the justices [of the peace] and the rural gentry." While this shows that at least a share of Argentinean administrative appointments cut out lower *power holders*, these appointments did go to *locals*.

More supportive of my account is that "expert bureaucracies" played a central role in the extension of state authority during this period (Salvatore 2013). These experts, who were not governors or justices of the peace (territorial officials) but school directors, teachers, and other functional administrators, "acquired an important degree of power and respect in local communities" (ibid., 226). An "army of teachers" spread through the country, trained in normal schools, to bring education to fruition, and a corps of professional school inspectors emerged to replace local councils of parents in overseeing education programming, in a pattern that closely mirrored the institutionalization of Chilean education. A similar development and deployment of a professional bureaucracy characterized the field of public health (ibid., 227). Salvatore's crucial claim is that this spread of technical expertise could coexist, although not without some tension, with a patronage-based system of appointment. Argentina appears to have seen a more gradual version of what unfolded in Mexico during the Porfiriato: the establishment of parallel networks of administration that excluded local elites alongside the longstanding means of patronage used to bind center to locality and incorporate local caudillos into the ruling coalition. Over time, the increasing reliance on outsider experts seems to have allowed state building to succeed.

This cursory examination of other cases in the region provides evidence that largely supports the two key arguments advanced in this book. First, urban primacy and the absence of salient regionalism shaped the nature of political projects pursued by mid-century political elites, influencing whether these took the form of state building, or of more laissez-faire strategies of development. Second, reliance on deployed rule was necessary for the success of these efforts not only in Mexico, Chile, and post-1895 Peru (as shown in the preceding chapters) but also in Argentina. Ideas and local administration combined to shape the emergence and outcomes of state-development efforts during the Liberal era, and thus underlie the variation that emerged in state capacity across Latin American countries during the first century after independence.

Conclusion

THE END OF THE LIBERAL ERA

The relative political calm of the Liberal era that has been the context of this book came to an end early in the twentieth century as the viability of that economic model began to be called into question. With the emergence of new social actors, political instability reappeared at levels not seen since the early post-independence decades. A major economic crisis, which was closely associated with (although not entirely reducible to) the Great Depression, also played a crucial role in destabilizing the Liberal-era dominance of elites. The collapse of the Liberal coalitions of the long nineteenth century and the emergence of new social actors into the political arena beginning in the early twentieth century drove an upsurge in political instability across the region.

This instability can be seen in all four of the cases under study in the preceding chapters. In Colombia, debates over how to respond to the "social question" split the Liberal Party beginning in the 1930s and fueled the decade-long horror of *La Violencia* that began after the 1948 assassination of Liberal Party leader and presidential candidate Jorge Eliecer Gaitán. In Mexico, of course, the Revolution that began in 1910 lasted for a decade, and was followed by another major conflict in the late 1920s, the Cristero War. In Chile, the 1925 overthrow of Alessandri capped a period of coalitional instability and set off seven years of frequent regime change, and in Peru major unrest in the southern highlands in the 1920s presaged conflict between APRA and other political actors that erupted after 1930. Instability was not unique to these four cases; it erupted in the form of major strikes, coups, and civil wars across South America. This instability marked the end of the elite-dominated political coalitions that oversaw the divergent state-building trajectories discussed in this book. These elites were driven out of their dominance of the political arena, as politics and public policy were transformed in lasting ways after about 1920 across Latin America. As a result, the elite coalitions and ideational consensus behind Liberal development projects collapsed.

State building, of course, continued into the twentieth century. The emergence of new actors, and a shift in the challenges to development perceived by state elites, prompted a renewed emphasis on state building. The Depression, and the broader collapse of export-led growth as an economic model, drove state leaders to pursue heavier state intervention in the economy and a shift away from the promotion of primary product exports. New social actors placed pressures on the state that led to efforts at labor market regulation and a degree of welfare provision. In many ways, then, state building was a central feature of political projects that emerged in the Depression and its aftermath. This especially characterized those populist projects that built a multi-class coalition centered on organized labor movements (Collier and Collier 1991). State building was also a focus of the middle-class reformist coalitions that emerged later in the century in places like Chile, Peru, and Brazil (Belaúnde 1965; Davis 2004).

But even as state building unfolded during the post-Liberal era, the differences in state capacity that were inherited from the Liberal era – especially in the territorial reach of the state's capacity to perform basic functions – remained visible. The cross-national differences in state strength in 1920 were not superseded by the later expansion of state welfare and social service bureaucracies. Instead, these initial differences in the state's territorial reach persisted, as weak states continued to lag in their ability to extend basic services to the entire population and were even, at times, limited in their ability to monopolize force. Throughout the subsequent decades, and even as state-building efforts proceeded, those states that lacked an effective reach into the national periphery by 1920 continued to lag in extension into those outlying regions, and in their ability to carry out basic state functions across the national territory.

This can be seen most clearly in terms of the provision of basic services, one of the core dimensions of state capacity considered in the previous chapters. Primary school enrollment, for example, grew steadily across all countries in the region, especially after 1950. But those states with lower illiteracy rates in 1920s remain at the top of regional rankings seventy years later. The key difference between high and low performing countries is revealed in their ability to extend their reach throughout the national territory, in the state's ability to penetrate populations not only in important regions and sectors, but nationwide. As Table 7.2 shows, national average data make literacy rates in our four cases seem indistinguishable – all four countries had national literacy rates of between 86 and 89 percent. But wide differences appear at the subnational level: for example, in Colombia, ten departments containing nearly 13 percent of the population had literacy rates below 80 percent in 2005, while none of Chile's regions had a literacy rate below 81 percent according to the 2002 census. Similar patterns can also be seen in the provision of other basic services, like vaccination, and in the administration of the national census and other sorts of core government functions; in all of these areas, the reach of the state in Mexico and Chile continues to outpace that of Peru or Colombia.

TABLE 7.2. *Beyond national averages in literacy, four cases*

	Chile	Colombia	Mexico	Peru
Year of census	2002	2005	2005	2007
Unit (N)	Province (51)	Dept (33)	State (32)	Department (25)
National avg	87.53%	85.88%	89.05%	87.73%
St dev	2.58%	5.83%	4.54%	5.09%
% of pop in units with <70% lit	0	1.51%	0	0
Units with <70% lit	0	1 (La Guajira)	0	0
% of pop in units with <80% lit	0	7.90%	10.44%	13.12%
Units with <80% lit	0	6 (Sucre, Cordoba, Guaiana, Choco, Vichada, La Guajira)	3 (Chiapas, Guerrero, Oaxaca)	5 (Cajamarca, Ayacucho, Huanuco, Huancavelica, Apurimac)

The persistence over time of divergent trajectories of state capacity strongly implies that the roots of contemporary state strength and weakness are deeply historical. Given that most explanations of state development, including the one advanced in this book, take the form of historical causation, this is not surprising. But state capacity is, of course, not simply a historical curiosity: contemporary stateness is at the center of social science scholarship and policy discourse about Latin America.[6] That rankings on state capacity today are, as the Introduction showed, so well predicted by those a century in the past has important implications for considering contemporary stateness.

Given the deep continuities demonstrated in this book, and the fact that the contemporary divergence between strong and weak states in Latin America is so well explained by the divergence a century ago, understanding state strength and weakness in the region requires taking the weight of history seriously. First, it suggests a need to rethink the state crises of the 1980s and 1990s in places like Colombia and Peru, and to see their deep historical roots rather than leaping to the conclusion

---

[6] See, for example, the special issue of *Revista de Ciencia Política* (2012) for a broad range of perspectives on the importance of stateness in Latin America.

that contemporary factors account for state weakness. To fail to consider the weight of history in studying state weakness, in other words, risks misidentifying its causes. Second, taking a presentist perspective risks over-predicting the possibility of change: failing to recognize the long-term historical continuities of stateness in Latin America can lead to an overestimation of the prospects for gains in state capacity under single administrations or as the result of temporally truncated initiatives. Third, ignoring the weight of history leads to overstated claims of "state crisis" or "state collapse" in places like contemporary Mexico that ignore the long history of effective stateness as countries confront challenges to political order. Ignoring historical continuity grants too much causal weight to short-term causes, and neglects the importance of the full set of conditions that this book has shown must be present for state-building efforts to emerge in a sustained way, and to succeed.

THEORIZING STATE BUILDING

The argument and findings of the preceding chapters also have important theoretical implications. This book breaks new theoretical ground in the study of state building in two related but analytically distinct ways. First, it integrates ideational factors into the account of state building, and second, it develops an account for both the *emergence* and the *success* or *failure* of state-building efforts. Both of these analytical moves have implications for the broader state-building literature.

Bringing Ideas into State Development

By contrast to the existing scholarship on state development, I highlight that ideational factors play a part in accounting for the divergent trajectories traced by my cases. Rather than directly connecting characteristics of the political or economic environment to incentives for state building, I argue that the relationship between structure and choice is mediated by leaders' perceptions and beliefs. In particular, I focus on the ways in which ideas shape how rational incentives are perceived, and determine which strategies resonate with political leaders as an appropriate response to their objective material situation. Rather than taking a deductive approach in deciding how state leaders *should* have responded to the incentives they faced, I investigate the content of their ideas, and account for how they actually *did* respond.

The independent force of ideational factors can be found in both parts of the argument developed in this book. First, and most prominently, the broader ideological vision of state leaders affected whether they pursued "order and progress" through a state-building project or through a coherent set of laissez-faire policies. It was the distinctly anti-statist ideological vision of Colombian leaders that underpinned the absence of state building in that case, and set that country on its distinct trajectory. I argued in Chapter 1 that the anti-statist vision resonated with Colombia's uniquely polycentric political and economic geography, but this does not imply that they were reducible to geography. Indeed, I argued against most existing geographic explanations for state building that connect the two through a cost mechanism, and emphasized that ideas explain how geography influences the decision of state leaders whether or not to increase the capacity of the national state in pursuit of development.

Second, ideas played an important role in the choice of delegated and deployed rule. Where there was a substantial threat of indigenous or subaltern revolt, the willingness of state leaders to risk upsetting local hierarchy and damaging their relations with local elites by establishing deployed rule depended in large part on their ideological vision for state development. Where they had come to believe that traditional elites were an obstacle to development – as in Liberal Mexico and post-1895 Peru – state leaders were willing to undermine the power of traditional elites through deployed rule even at the risk of revolt. But where they did not believe that development required the elimination of tradition, they were willing to respond to the threat of revolt by cementing ties to local elites. Here too, then, the choices made by state leaders cannot be explained by incentives alone. We must also understand the ideas they had in mind as they pursued development.

In both of these components of the argument, we can see that a focus on purely material factors cannot account for the variation we observe in outcomes. Had we only focused on material factors in accounting for the onset of state-building efforts, the common challenges to political stability, economic development, and social peace would make the choice of different means of pursuing those goals quite surprising. And had we only focused on material factors in accounting for the choice between delegated and deployed rule, we would not understand the choices of state leaders to opt for deployed rule despite the threat of indigenous revolt during Peru's Aristocratic Republic, or during the Liberal era in Mexico. Material factors, in other words, underpredict the variation we observe. State leaders respond in different ways to the incentives created by very similar material incentives. This does not mean, of course, that they are not strategic. But it does imply that the effects of rational incentives are mediated by broader political ideologies that unite a spectrum of political interests and affect which of the set of plausible responses to a particular situation "resonate" or "fit." In my account, then, ideas play a role very close to Weber's famous "switchmen" that "determined the tracks along which action has been pushed by the dynamic of interest." Weber claims that "from what and for what one wished to be redeemed and, let us not forget, could be redeemed, depended upon one's image of the world" (Weber 1958, 280). In my account, state leaders arrived at very different diagnoses of the means by which they should respond to very similar crises; these different diagnoses depended on their broader ideological visions – their images of the world.

Integrating the ideas of state leaders into accounts of state development beyond Latin America would allow scholars to ask similar questions about where and why state-building efforts emerged, and why they took particular forms. Ideas have been understudied in the historical European cases in part because considerations of survival narrowed the options available to state leaders. Yet rather than assuming that state leaders had such a limited set of choices as they responded to international threats, an examination of the range of responses is in order. Uncovering the history of the losers in early modern Europe – what Davies (2011) calls its "vanished kingdoms" might reveal distinct ideational visions underlying their erasure from the map.[7]

Ideas have been understudied as a causal factor in contemporary state building as well. Those scholars of post-colonial cases who downplay the role of ideas tend to either see leaders' actions as determined directly by the threats they face (Slater 2010) or, more commonly, by calculations of the costs incurred and revenues to be gained from state expansion (Herbst 2000; Bates 2008). On the other hand, James Scott (1998, 2009) places ideas front and center, arguing that state leaders motivated by a "high modernist" vision seek to reshape society in fundamental ways through making it legible, standardized, and homogeneous. These two views of the contemporary state are in striking contrast to one another, and scholars on both sides of the debate point to the experiences of particular cases in support of their overarching claim about the nature of state motivations.

---

[7] This issue is taken up later from a different angle when I explore what the scholarship on European state building has to say about the emergence of state-building efforts.

The way in which ideas are given causal power in my argument is more subtle than in either of these two existing positions. Unlike Herbst, Bates, and Slater, I see state leaders as more than profit maximizers (for the former two) or Slater's threat minimizers. Instead I argue that the strategies chosen in response to opportunities and threats – their choice of how to try to seize opportunities or whether and how to minimize threats – are shaped by their ideological visions. But unlike Scott, I find a range of ideological visions among state leaders. Not all state leaders are in the grip of what he described in *Seeing Like a State* as a "high modernist" vision that calls for the reordering of society, but neither are all state leaders best seen as motivated only by revenue-based considerations.[8] Against Herbst, then, I argue that state inaction can be seen as motivated by ideology and not just by the sorts of cost-benefit calculations he emphasizes. And against Scott, I allow for the possibility that state leaders choose not to pursue state building; laissez-faire models of development can, once again, be grounded in ideology. Rather than assuming that all state leaders are pursuing the same goal, or that when they are they will choose the same means under the same set of material incentives, we should instead consider the possibility that state leaders' decision making about how to pursue development is shaped by their ideological visions.

Separating Emergence and Success

In a second departure from the status quo in the state-building literature, I separately theorize the emergence of state-building efforts and their success. I have argued in this book that analytically distinct sets of factors explain the emergence of state-building efforts, and the success of only some of those efforts. The causal factors I have emphasized, a developmentalist (as opposed to laissez-faire) elite consensus and deployed (as opposed to delegated) rule, are not analytically equivalent independent variables. Instead, the first is a necessary and sufficient condition for state-building efforts to emerge, while the latter is necessary for those efforts that do emerge to succeed. Making explicit this distinction

---

[8] In Scott's more recent work (2009) the pursuit of legibility has come to be seen as a constant ideological vision underpinning state actions across a wide range of cases. My position falls closer to his earlier (1998) view that acknowledged that not all state leaders held a high modernist vision and pursued wholesale social transformation. For a fuller elaboration of the argument that state leaders face a range of options for ruling in any given situation, which includes both Scott's forcible legibilization and much less intrusive possibilities, see Slater and Kim (forthcoming).

between explanations of the emergence and success of state-building efforts highlights the place of equifinality in accounts of state weakness.

The discussion in the previous chapters traces two distinct logical paths leading to state weakness. A first is the absence of a state-building project; among our core cases, this was the path traced by Colombia, and several of the shadow cases discussed earlier also followed this path. A second is marked by the failure of concerted state building; this was the case in Peru before 1895. A complete account of the causes of state capacity must explore both pathways, by asking both what prompts state-building efforts, and what conditions are necessary for those efforts to succeed, but few studies do so. Thus they fall short of being logically complete accounts of variation in state capacity.

Scholars of European cases have generally failed to problematize the origins of state-building efforts, since most see military competition as a constant and powerful pressure forcing states to respond or get wiped off the map.[9] Because scholars only study the survivors of European wars, we simply do not know why those cases that were wiped off the map did not survive.[10] There are several logical possibilities. First, but least theoretically interesting for scholars of state building, is the possibility that the losers built effective states but were defeated nevertheless because of size, wealth, geographic location, or other factors that determined their military fate. Two alternatives are the absence of state-building efforts, and the failure of state-building efforts. We simply do not know which of what Tilly estimates as 500 political units in early modern Europe followed each of these paths, and therefore we lack a complete theory of European state development.[11]

In the face of this dilemma, most scholars simply assume that the onset of military competition created a constant state-building imperative across Europe at some point in the early modern era. This lets them set aside explanations for the choice to increase state capacity to focus on the success and failure of state-building efforts. Ertman (1997) is a partial exception; he argues that the *timing* of military competition varied over cases, explaining (in his study of a set of survivors) the forms of

---

[9] A few scholars, such as Deborah Boucoyannis (n.d.) and Spruyt (1994), argue that war did not drive state building in early modern Europe, but the consensus sees geopolitical competition as crucial to forming European states.

[10] This, of course, is a commonly noted problem in the literature; Tilly (1975, 14–15) describes the tradeoffs between prospective and retrospective studies of state formation.

[11] Davies (2011) provides a series of case studies of these "vanished kingdoms" but fails to develop a systematic theory of state weakness in Europe.

Conclusion

administration constructed and thus long-term trajectories of state capacity. But he, too, fails to consider cases in which state-building efforts did not emerge at all. For Ertman and most other scholars of European state building, the decision to undertake state building is not a choice: there is no other alternative. Even Tilly (1992), in distinguishing between coercion-centered and capital-centered paths to European state development, focuses on the range of ways in which states respond to the threat of war, and fails to problematize the emergence of state-building projects.

The most important exception to this failure to explain the emergence of state-building efforts is Downing's (1992) study of the survival of medieval constitutionalism. He argues that where military competition was financed through intensified domestic taxation, constitutionalist institutions were dismantled in favor of absolutism – this explains the paths traced by France and Prussia. But where other conditions prevailed, constitutionalism could survive. States that could, as Sweden did, rely on foreign resource mobilization avoided absolutism. So did the Dutch Republic, which drew on allies for defense, on capital markets as an alternative to taxation, and on geography as a substitute for military modernization. In both of these cases, despite war, major state-building efforts were avoided. But Downing also argues that England before 1688 avoided absolutism because it was not embroiled in major conflict. He thus avoids both of the standard truisms in the European state-building literature: the first sees war as an omnipresent threat, and the second assumes that the onset of war automatically triggers state building. The English case debunks the first truism; the Dutch and Swedish cases debunk the second. With these two analytical moves, Downing explains why state-building efforts emerged in some cases but not others in early modern Europe rather than just assuming either (to quote Tilly 1975) that war made states or that states made war.

If most scholarship on European cases takes the emergence of state-building efforts for granted, most scholarship on the developing world elides the explanation of the success and failure of those efforts. When we move away from early modern Europe to a context where interstate competition is less intense, the weak are not erased from the map. This is particularly true, as Jackson and Rosberg (1982) and Herbst (2000) show, for post-1945 states, for whom international norms of territorial integrity and nonintervention have been particularly strong. But in Latin America, too, over a longer time span, state weakness has not led to the elimination of countries from the map: although significant territory has changed hands (usually in the aftermath of warfare) and early post-independence confederations in Central America and the northern Andes fell apart, there have been no instances in which a country was wholly incorporated into another. If in Europe, historical accuracy demands that we more carefully theorize the (non)emergence of state-building efforts, scholarship of the developing world needs to more carefully account for state-building failure.

To fail to account for the conditions that determine the success and failure of state-building efforts is to risk what Slater (2010, 13) calls "crude and discredited modes of functionalist reasoning." Yet even Slater himself does not fully theorize the success and failure of elite responses to systemic threats; he limits himself to arguing what he calls "inverted functionalism": "if no threat, no response" (ibid., 13). Other scholars do no better. Herbst (2000), for example, simply ignores the possibility that state-building efforts might emerge and fail in colonial or post-independence Africa. Instead, he argues that state leaders choose the optimal level of state capacity based on the costs of administrative extension and the benefits of tax revenue. The result is that many states in sub-Saharan Africa were born, and remain, strikingly weak. An alternative, of course, is that state leaders tried and failed to build states, but Herbst fails to discuss this logically possible path to state weakness.

We can only develop, for example, a full theory of the effects of war on state capacity if we specify factors that determine success and failure of state-building efforts once war had spurred them. Barnett (1992) makes such an argument, claiming that the outcome of an increase or decrease in state power is shaped by the strategy chosen by the government in response to the threat. When adopted in the context that spurs state building, they produce variation in the outcome of interest. It is the strategy chosen in response to an external threat, not the threat itself, that shapes the state power outcomes caused by war. This theoretical insight points the way to sharper analyses of the relationship between war and the state by pointing our attention to *variation in response to international threat* as our focus of interest. State power may grow, and state-society relations may be altered, by war. But whereas Tilly's famous "states made war and war made states" only identified a relationship, Barnett develops a set of predictions about when this relationship will and will not hold. This set of predictions depends on the causal mechanism he has elaborated (strategy of resource mobilization), which can only be identified by distinguishing between the conditions that drive emergence and success, and seeing the international threat of war as the former rather than the latter.

Causal Importance

When confronted with a causally complex account like the one developed in this book, a natural question relates to the relative importance of each of its components. In particular, we can ask how to evaluate the relative importance of state-building absence and state-building failure in explaining state weakness. Given the equifinality of negative outcomes I have theorized and demonstrated, which of the two steps in the causal chain to state strength trips up more Latin American cases? Table 7.3 provides some evidence we can use to answer this question. It shows the presence or absence of state building in each case arrayed on the vertical axis, and the level of urban primacy and salient regionalism, based on data from Table 1.1 and discussions earlier in this chapter, on the horizontal axis. Where necessary, I have placed a single country in multiple cells to reflect periods that marked qualitative shifts in the trajectory of state capacity.

What can we conclude from this table? First, because there are only two cases in violation of this logical relationship, we can conclude that urban primacy is, as predicted, probabilistically necessary for state capacity. As described earlier, one of these cases, Paraguay 1852–1870, is mis-predicted because of the anomalous geopolitical threats it faced, which were unique in regional perspective. The second, Venezuela, is likely mis-coded, since it saw (as discussed previously) a shift toward increased urban primacy precisely during the period indicated.

Second, and more relevant, we can conclude that many cases fall along with Colombia in the "salient regionalism, no state building" cell. This suggests that rather than defining a scope condition that is rarely violated, explaining the non-emergence of state building in Latin America accounts for a lot of the variation in state capacity. In formal terms, urban primacy and the ideological visions with which it is associated are of high causal relevance, since only one case where it exists did not see state building. To understand state weakness in Latin America, this suggests, we must understand why political elites did not see state building as a means to development. By contrast, the path of state-building failure, traced only by the case of Peru, seems to be a regional outlier, the only country with a high score on urban primacy but no state-building success. In explaining the initial variation in state strength and weakness in Latin America, the ideational and geographic factors that prompted the emergence of state-building efforts appear to be more important than those determining why some succeeded while others failed.

TABLE 7.3. *Urban primacy and state building*

Successful state building	Urban primacy	
	Low	High
No	Bolivia Colombia Ecuador Paraguay (1870–1936) Venezuela (1864–1899)	Peru (1845–1895)
Yes	Paraguay (1852–1870) Venezuela (1899–1920s)	Argentina Chile Mexico Peru (1895–1919) Uruguay

HISTORICAL STATE BUILDING AND CONTEMPORARY "NATION BUILDING"

The recent upsurge of concern about state weakness in many contexts of political instability has prompted a call for lessons from historical cases for contemporary efforts. The findings of this book about the comparative experiences of Liberal-era Latin America generate several such implications. A first such insight relates, once again, to the important distinction between the factors underlying the emergence of state-building projects, and the factors underlying their success. State-building projects have, in recent years, emerged in many places, introduced not by a domestic political coalition but by the international community. Yet few of these efforts at nation-building have succeeded. This suggests that policy recommendations must focus attention on why these efforts have not borne fruit: if the roots of state weakness in Latin America are largely found in the *absence* of state-building efforts in many countries, the problem of state-building *failure* looms large in many contemporary cases. Yet as Brownlee (2007, 315) shows, the policy literature on contemporary state building has tended to take a "volitional" approach to state building, in which commitment, duration, and resources are seen as the keys to the construction of an effective state. The belief is that devoting enough resources to the effort over a sufficient period of time will suffice. But resources, even when spent over several decades, are not sufficient, as we saw in the case of guano-era Peru, to ensure the increased ability of the state to effectively penetrate society and implement policy. Here,

Conclusion 261

the lessons of cases where state-building efforts fail must be examined so that we can generate systematic knowledge about where, when, and why state-building efforts have failed to produce significant gains in state capacity.[12]

In that sense, this book's examination of historical cases of state-building failure in places like guano-era Peru has important implications. The finding that reliance on local elites as administrators in the national periphery fundamentally undermined state-building efforts in guano-era Peru suggests that delegating power to local strongmen, while possibly generating stability by cementing their alliances with the central government, will cripple state-building efforts. There may, of course, be reasons to cement these sorts of alliances anyway; state capacity is not a goal pursued in a vacuum, but in relation to other desiderata such as political stability or an end to violence. Hutchcroft (2000), for example, shows how state building and the promotion of civil society institutions were in tension during American colonial rule in the Philippines. But the clear and consistent relationship between reliance on local elites and the failure of state building in Peru points to the importance of taking the design of local administrative institutions seriously.

In many contexts, local elites are not only a potential ally for the state but a potential challenger (Luna and Feldmann 2012). State-builders confront elites that possess not only power at the local and regional level but the potential to spoil state-building efforts. The construction of alliances with these actors is often necessary for state building to even be pursued in a consistent and coherent manner. Here, the argument of this book generates another important policy implication about *how* these alliances are constructed.[13] Chapter 3 argued that in terms of effects on state capacity, the type of patronage used in creating coalitions with these local strongmen can have an important effect. Alliances built through political patronage – access to elected office – may be less damaging than those built on access to appointments in the administration of local communities. Peruvian state building during the guano era failed because state leaders built coalitions with local elites, and because they did so through administrative appointments rather than via an electoral coalition. Should designers of a state-building project face this sort of choice,

---

[12] As Brownlee (2007) traces, policymakers have drawn nearly all of their conclusions about how to state-build from the rare (and overdetermined) success stories of postwar Germany and Japan.
[13] For another account that explores the range of strategies available to state leaders in confronting challengers to their rule, see Slater and Kim (forthcoming).

the findings of this book suggest that they should consider building those alliances through elected positions rather than through administrative appointments. Only by distinguishing failed state building in guano-era Peru from the absent state building in Colombia could we identify these possible institutional prescriptions. Historical cases of state-building success and failure, in short, are not only of interest to scholars of history. Instead, understanding the paths traced by the countries examined in this book, and by historical cases more generally, is necessary to help identify policy recommendations for successful state building.

Works Cited

Abbott, Jared A, Matthias vom Hau, and Hillel David Soifer (2013) 'Transforming the Nation? The Bolivarian Education Reform in Context' (Paper presented at LASA 2013, Washington, DC).
Abente, Diego (1989) 'Foreign Capital, Economic Elites, and the State in Paraguay during the Liberal Republic (1870–1936)' *Journal of Latin American Studies* vol. 21 #1 (February) pp. 61–88.
Aboites Aguilar, Luis (2003) *Excepciones y Privilegios: Modernización Tributaria y Centralización Política en México, 1922–1972* (El Colegio de México).
Aboites Aguilar, Luis, and Luis Jáuregui, eds. (2005) *Penuria sin Fin: Historia de los Impuestos en México Siglos XVIII-XX* (Mexico, DF: Instituto Mora).
Acemoglu, Daron, Simon Johnson, and James A. Robinson (2001) 'Colonial Origins of Comparative Development' *American Economic Review* vol. 91 pp. 1369–1401.
   (2002) 'Reversal of Fortune: Geography and Institutions in the Making of the Modern World Income Distribution' *Quarterly Journal of Economics* vol. 118 pp. 1231–1294.
Acemoglu, Daron and James A. Robinson (2012) *Why Nations Fail: The Origins of Power, Prosperity, and Poverty* (Crown Books).
Adelman, Jeremy (2006) *Sovereignty and Revolution in the Iberian Atlantic* (Princeton, NJ: Princeton University Press).
Ades, Alberto F. and Edward L. Glaeser (1995) 'Trade and Circuses: Explaining Urban Giants' *The Quarterly Journal of Economics* vol. 110 #1 pp. 195–228.
Albertus, Michael, and Oliver Kaplan (2013) 'Land Reform as a Counterinsurgency Policy: Evidence from Colombia' *Journal of Conflict Resolution* vol. 57 #2 pp. 198–231.
Alesina, Alberto and Enrico Spolaore (2005) *The Size of Nations* (Cambridge, MA: MIT Press).
Alexander, Robert J. (2007) *A History of Organized Labor in Peru and Ecuador* (Westport, CT: Praeger).

Allina-Pisano, Jessica (2004) 'Sub Rosa Resistance and the Politics of Economic Reform: Land Redistribution in Post-Soviet Ukraine' *World Politics* vol. 56 (July) pp. 554–581.

Anderson, Benedict (1983) *Imagined Communities: Reflections on the Origin and Spread of Nationalism* (London: Verso).

Anderson, Perry (1974) *Lineages of the Absolutist State* (New York: New Left Books).

Angell, Alan (1972) *Politics and the Labor Movement in Chile* (Oxford: Oxford University Press).

Ansell, Ben W. (2010) *From the Ballot to the Blackboard: The Redistributive Political Economy of Education* (New York: Cambridge University Press).

Auyero, Javier (2007) *Routine Politics and Violence in Argentina: The Gray Zone of State Power* (Cambridge: Cambridge University Press).

Báez Osorio, Miryam (2006) *La Educación en los Orígenes Republicanos de Colombia* (Tunja: Universidad Pedagógica y Tecnológica de Colombia).

Baland, Jean-Marie, and James A. Robinson (2008) 'Land and Power: Theory and Evidence from Chile' *American Economic Review* vol. 98 #5 pp. 1737–1765.

Barbier, Jacques A. (1980) *Reform and Politics in Bourbon Chile 1755–1796* (Ottawa: University of Ottawa Press).

Barnett, Michael (1992) *Confronting the Costs of War* (Princeton, NJ: Princeton University Press).

Barrantes, Emilio (1989) *Historia de la Educación en el Perú* (Lima: Mosca Azul).

Barzel, Yoram (2002) *A Theory of the State: Economic Rights, Legal Rights, and the Scope of the State* (Cambridge: Cambridge University Press).

Bates, Robert H. (2008) *When Things Fell Apart: State Failure in Late-Century Africa* (New York: Cambridge University Press).

Bauer, Arnold (1975) *Chilean Rural Society from the Spanish Conquest to 1930* (Cambridge: Cambridge University Press).

Bazant, Jean (1991) 'From Independence to the Liberal Republic 1821–1867' in Leslie Bethell, ed. *Mexico since Independence* (Cambridge: Cambridge University Press) pp. 1–48.

Bazant, Mílada (1993) *Historia de la Educación durante el Porfiriato* (México DF: El Colegio de México).

Bazant, Mílada (1998) 'Los Inspectores y los Vecinos de los Pueblos Determinan la Suerte de los Maestros Mexiquenses: 1874–1910' in Pilar Gonzalbo Aizpurú, ed. *Historia de la Educación y la Enseñanza de la Historia* (Mexico, DF: El Colegio de México) pp. 63–88.

Beatty, Edward (2001) *Institutions and Investment: The Political Basis of Industrialization in Mexico before 1911* (Stanford, CA: Stanford University Press).

Belaúnde, Fernando (1965) *Peru's Own Conquest* (Lima: Latin American Studies Press).

Bello, Andrés (1997) *Selected Writings*, edited and translated by Iván Jaksic (Oxford: Oxford University Press).

Bengoa, José (1985) *Historia del Pueblo Mapuche* (Santiago: Ediciones Sur).

Bengoa, José (1999) *Historia de un Conflicto: el Estado y los Mapuches en el Siglo XX* (Santiago: Planeta).

Bensel, Richard (1984) *Sectionalism and American Political Development, 1880–1980* (Madison: University of Wisconsin Press).
  (1990) *Yankee Leviathan* (Cambridge: Cambridge University Press).
Bergman, Marcelo (2009) *Tax Evasion and the Rule of Law in Latin America* (University Park: Penn State University Press).
Bergquist, Charles W. (1986) *Coffee and Conflict in Colombia 1886–1910* (Durham, NC: Duke University Press).
Bergquist, Charles W., Ricardo Peñaranda, and Gonzalo Sánchez C., eds. (2001) *Violence in Colombia 1990–2000: Waging War and Negotiating Peace* (Wilmington, DE: Scholarly Resources).
Berman, Sheri (1998) *The Social Democratic Moment: Ideas and Politics in the Making of Interwar Europe* (Cambridge, MA: Harvard University Press).
  (2001) 'Ideas, Norms, and Culture in Political Analysis' *Comparative Politics* vol. 33 #2 (January) pp. 231–250.
  (2006) *The Primacy of Politics: Social Democracy and the Making of Europe's Twentieth Century* (Cambridge: Cambridge University Press).
Bethell, Leslie, ed. (1993) *Chile Since Independence* (New York: Cambridge University Press).
Blanchard, Peter (1982) *The Origins of the Peruvian Labor Movement 1883–1919* (Pittsburgh, PA: University of Pittsburgh Press).
Blyth, Mark M. (1997) 'Any More Bright Ideas? The Ideational Turn of Comparative Political Economy' *Comparative Politics* vol. 29 #2 (January) pp. 229–250.
Bobrow-Strain, Aaron (2007) *Intimate Enemies: Landowners, Power, and Violence in Chiapas* (Durham, NC: Duke University Press).
Bonilla, Heraclio (1989) *Estado y Tributo Campesino: La Experiencia de Ayacucho* (Lima: IEP) Documento de Trabajo #3.
  (2001) *Metáfora y Realidad de la Independencia en el Perú* (Lima: IEP).
Bonilla, Heraclio, and Karen Spalding (1981) 'La Independencia en el Perú: Las Palabras y los Hechos' in Heraclio Bonilla et al., *La Independencia en el Perú* (Lima: IEP).
Boone, Catherine (2003) *Political Topographies of the African State* (Cambridge: Cambridge University Press).
Bowman, John, and Michael Wallerstein (1982) 'The Fall of Balmaceda and Public Finance in Chile: New Data for an Old Debate' *Journal of InterAmerican Studies and World Affairs* 24 no. 4 pp. 421–460.
Bowman, Kirk S. (2002) *Militarization, Democracy, and Development: The Perils of Praetorianism in Latin America* (University Park: Penn State University Press).
Brewer, John (1990) *The Sinews of Power: War, Money, and the English State, 1688–1783* (Cambridge, MA: Harvard University Press).
Brinks, Daniel (2008) *The Judicial Response to Police Killings in Latin America: Inequality and the Rule of Law* (Cambridge: Cambridge University Press).
Britton, John A., ed. (1994) *Molding the Hearts and Minds: Education, Communications, and Social Change in Latin America*. (Wilmington, DE: SR Books).

Brooks, Sarah (2009) *Social Protection and the Market in Latin America* (Cambridge: Cambridge University Press).
Brownlee, Jason A. (2007) 'Can America Nation Build?' *World Politics* vol. 59 #2 (January) pp. 314–340.
Burr, Robert N. (1965) *By Reason or Force: Chile and the Balancing of Power in South America, 1830–1905* (Berkeley: University of California Press).
Bushnell, David (1954) *The Santander Regime in Gran Colombia* (Newark: University of Delaware Press).
  (1993) *The Making of Modern Colombia: A Nation in Spite of Itself* (Berkeley: University of California Press).
Bushnell, David, and Neill Macaulay (1994) *The Emergence of Latin America in the Nineteenth Century*, 2nd ed. (Oxford: Oxford University Press).
Callaghy, Thomas M. (1984) *The State-Society Struggle: Zaire in Comparative Perspective* (New York: Columbia University Press).
Cammett, Melani, and Lauren Morris MacLean (2011) 'Introduction: The Political Consequences of Non-state Social Welfare in the Global South' *Studies in Comparative International Development* vol. 46 #1 (Spring) pp. 1–21.
Camp, Roderic Ai (1991) *Mexican Political Biographies, 1884–1934* (Austin: University of Texas Press).
  (1995) *Political Recruitment across Two Centuries: Mexico, 1884–1991* (Austin: University of Texas Press).
Campbell, John L. (1993) 'The State and Fiscal Sociology' *Annual Review of Sociology* 19, pp. 163–185.
Campbell, Margaret V. (1959) 'Education in Chile, 1810–1842' *Journal of Inter-American Studies* vol. 1 #3 pp. 353–375.
Campos Harriet, Fernando (1960) *Desarrollo Educacional, 1810–1960* (Santiago: Editorial Andres Bello).
Cardona, Christopher M. (2008) 'Politicians, Soldiers, and Cops: Colombia's *La Violencia* in Comparative Perspective' (PhD Dissertation, Department of Political Science, University of California Berkeley).
Carmagnani, Marcello (1989) 'El Liberalismo, los Impuestos Internos y el Estado Federal Mexicano, 1857–1911' *Historia Mexicana* vol. 38 #3 pp. 471–496.
  (1994) *Mercado y Estado, Historia de la Hacienda Publica en Mexico, 1857–1910* (Mexico, DF: El Colegio de México).
Carpenter, Daniel P. (2001) *The Forging of Bureaucratic Autonomy* (Princeton, NJ: Princeton University Press).
Castañeda Zavala, Jorge (2001) 'El Contingente Fiscal en la nueva nación mexicana, 1824–1861' in Marichal, Carlos and Daniela Marino, eds., *De Colonia a Nación: Impuestos y política en México, 1750–1860* (Mexico, DF: El Colegio de México) pp. 135–187.
Centeno, Miguel Ángel (1994) *Democracy within Reason: Technocratic Revolution in Mexico* (University Park: Penn State University Press).
  (2002) *Blood and Debt: War and the Nation State in Latin America* (University Park: Penn State University Press).
  (2007) *Warfare in Latin America* (2 volumes) (Hampshire: Ashgate).
Chanda, Areendam, and Louis Putterman (2005) 'State Effectiveness, Economic Growth, and the Age of States' in Lange, Matthew, and Dietrich Rueschemeyer,

eds., *States and Development: Historical Antecedents of Stagnation and Advance* (Basingstoke: Palgrave MacMillan), pp. 69–91.
Chaudhry, Kiren Aziz (1999) *The Price of Wealth* (Ithaca, NY: Cornell University Press).
Cheibub, José Antonio (1998) 'Political Regimes and the Extractive Capacity of Governments: Taxation in Democracies and Dictatorships' *World Politics* 50 no. 3, pp. 349–376.
Chowning, Margaret (1999) *Wealth and Power in Provincial Mexico: Michoacán from the Late Colony to the Revolution* (Stanford, CA: Stanford University Press).
Christie, Keith H. (1979) 'Gamonalismo in Colombia: an Historical Overview' *North-South: Canadian Journal of Latin American Studies* vol. 4 pp. 42–59.
CIESIN (Center for International Earth Science Information Network), Columbia University (2007) *National Aggregates of Geospatial Data: Population, Landscape, and Climate Estimates, v.2 (PLACE II)* (Palisades, NY: CIESIN, Columbia University) Available at: sedac.ciesin.columbia.edu/place/
Coatsworth, John H. (1978) 'Obstacles to Economic Growth in Nineteenth Century Mexico' *The American Historical Review* vol. 83 #1 (February) pp. 80–100.
  (1981) *Growth against Development: The Economic Impact of Railroads in Porfirian Mexico* (DeKalb: Northern Illinois University Press).
  (1988) 'Patterns of Rural Rebellion in Latin America: Mexico in Comparative Perspective' in Friedrich Katz, ed. *Riot, Rebellion, and Revolution: Rural Social Conflict in Mexico* (Princeton, NJ: Princeton University Press) pp. 21–62.
  (1998) 'Economic and Institutional Trajectories in Nineteenth-Century Latin America' in Coatsworth, John, and Alan M. Taylor, eds. *Latin America and the World Economy since 1800* (Cambridge, MA: Harvard University Press) pp. 23–54.
  (2008) 'Inequality, Institutions, and Economic Growth in Latin America' *Journal of Latin American Studies* vol. 40 #3 pp. 545–569.
Collier, David (1976) *Squatters and Oligarchs* (Baltimore, MD: Johns Hopkins University Press).
Collier, David, and Ruth Berins Collier (1991) *Shaping the Political Arena* (Princeton, NJ: Princeton University Press).
Collier, Simon (2003) *Chile: The Making of a Republic, 1830–1865* (New York: Cambridge University Press).
Collier, Simon and William F. Sater (1996) *A History of Chile 1808–1994* (Cambridge: Cambridge University Press).
Compendio Estadístico del Perú (2001) (Lima: Instituto Nacional de Estadística e Informática).
Contreras, Carlos (1996) *Maestros, Mistis y Campesinos en el Perú Rural del Siglo XX* (Lima: IEP) Documento de Trabajo #80.
  (2001) *Ideales Democráticos, Realidades Autoritarias: Autoridades políticas locales y descentralización en el Perú a finales del siglo XIX* (Lima: IEP) Documento de Trabajo #113.
  (2004) *El Aprendizaje del Capitalismo: Estudios de Historia Económica y Social del Perú Republicano* (Lima: IEP).

(2005) 'The Tax Man Cometh: Local Authorities and the Battle over Taxes in Peru, 1885–1906' in Jacobsen, Nils, and Cristóbal Aljovín de Losada, eds. *Political Cultures in the Andes, 1750–1950* (Durham, NC: Duke University Press) pp. 116–135.

Contreras, Carlos, and Marcos Cueto (1999) *Historia del Perú Contemporaneo* (Lima: IEP).

Coronil, Fernando (1997) *The Magical State: Nature, Money, and Modernity in Venezuela* (Chicago: University of Chicago Press).

Cosio Villegas, Daniel (1956) *Historia Moderna de México* (México DF: Editorial Hermes).

Covarrubias, José Díaz (1993) *La Instrucción Pública en México* (originally published in 1875 by Imprenta del Gobierno) (México: Colección Tlahuicole).

Crabtree, John (2008) 'Introduction: A Story of Unresolved Tensions' in Crabtree, John, and Laurence Whitehead, eds. *Unresolved Tensions: Bolivia Past and Present* (Pittsburgh, PA: University of Pittsburgh Press) pp. 1–7.

Cruz, Nicolás (2002) *El Surgimiento de la Educación Secundaria Pública en Chile, 1843–1876 (El Plan de Estudios Humanista)* (Santiago: DIBAM).

Cruz Santos, Abel (1966) 'Economía y Hacienda Pública de le República Unitaria a la Economía del Medio Siglo' in *Historia Extensa de Colombia* vol. 15, part II (Bogotá: Ediciones Lerner).

Cuadro Sinóptico Histórico (1910) (Mexico City: Secretaría de Fomento, Colonización e Industria).

Cuadro Sinóptico y Estadístico de la República Mexicana (1900) (Mexico City: Dirección General de Estadística).

Dargent, Eduardo (2011) 'Agents or Actors? Assessing the Autonomy of Economic Technocrats in Colombia and Peru' *Comparative Politics* vol. 43 #3 (April) pp. 313–332.

(2015) *Technocracy and Democracy in Latin America: Experts Running the Government* (Cambridge: Cambridge University Press).

Davies, Norman (2005) *God's Playground: A History of Poland Vol. I: The Origins to 1795* (New York: Columbia University Press).

(2011) *Vanished Kingdoms: The Rise and Fall of States and Nations* (New York: Viking Press).

Davies, Thomas (1970) *Indian Integration in Peru: A Half Century of Experience, 1900–1948* (Lincoln: University of Nebraska Press).

Davis, Diane E. (2004) *Discipline and Development: Middle Classes and Prosperity in East Asia and Latin America* (Cambridge: Cambridge University Press).

Deas, Malcolm (1982) 'The Fiscal Problems of Nineteenth Century Colombia' *Journal of Latin American Studies* vol. 14 #2 (November) pp. 287–328.

(1993) *Del Poder y la Gramática y Otros Ensayos sobre Historia, Política y Literatura Colombianas* (Bogotá: Tercer Mundo Editores).

(2002) 'The Man on Foot: Conscription and the Nation-State in Nineteenth Century Latin America' in James Dunkerly, ed. *Studies in the Formation of the Nation-State in Latin America* (London: ILAS) pp. 77–93.

(2010) 'Inseguridad y Desarrollo Económico en Colombia en el Primer Siglo de Vida Republicana Independiente: Unas Consideraciones Preliminares' in

Meisel Roca, Adolfo, and María Teresa Ramírez, eds. *Economía Colombiana del Siglo XIX* (Bogotá: Fondo de Cultura Económica) pp. 674–705.
DeHart, Evelyn Hu (1984) 'Sonora: Indians and Immigrants on a Developing Frontier' in Benajamin, Thomas, and William McNellie, eds. *Other Mexicos: Essays on Regional Mexican History, 1876–1911* (Albuquerque: University of New Mexico Press) pp. 177–211.
Dellepiane, Carlos (1943) *Historia Militar del Perú* 2 vols. (Lima: Imprenta del Ministerio de Guerra).
Delpar, Helen (1981) *Red against Blue: The Liberal Party in Colombian Politics, 1863–1899* (Tuscaloosa: University of Alabama Press).
Departamento Administrativo Nacional de Estadística (1985) *50 Años de Estadísticas Educativas* (Bogotá: DANE).
de Ramón, Armando (1999) *Biografías de Chilenos: Miembros de los Poderes Ejecutivo, Legislativo y Judicial* (Santiago Editores Universidad Católica de Chile) 4 volumes.
Desch, Michael C. (1996) 'War and Strong States, Peace and Weak States?' *International Organization* vol. 50 #2 (Spring) pp. 237–268.
DeShazo, Peter (1979) 'The Valparaíso Maritime Strike of 1903 and the Development of a Revolutionary Labor Movement in Chile' *Journal of Latin American Studies* vol. 2 #1 (May) pp. 145–168.
de Soto, Hernando (1989) *The Other Path* (New York: Harper and Row).
Díaz Zermeño, Héctor (1979) 'La Escuela Nacional Primaria en la Ciudad de México' *Historia Mexicana* vol. 29 pp. 59–90.
Dix, Robert (1987) *The Politics of Colombia* (London: Praeger).
Domínguez, Jorge I. (1980) *Insurrection or Loyalty: The Breakdown of the Spanish American Empire* (Cambridge, MA: Harvard University Press).
Downing, Brian (1992) *The Military Revolution and Political Change* (Princeton, NJ: Princeton University Press).
Drinot, Paulo (2011) *The Allure of Labor: Workers, Race, and the Making of the Peruvian State* (Durham, NC: Duke University Press).
Dunning, Thad (2008) *Crude Democracy: Natural Resource Wealth and Political Regimes* (Cambridge: Cambridge University Press).
Earle, Rebecca (2000) 'The War of the Supremes: Border Conflict, Religious Crusade, or Simply Politics by Other Means?' in Rebecca Earle, ed. *Rumours of Wars: Civil Conflict in Nineteenth Century Latin America* (London: ILAS) pp. 119–134.
Eaton, Kent (2004) *Politics beyond the Capital: The Design of Subnational Institutions in Latin America* (Stanford, CA: Stanford University Press).
Echeverry S., Alberto (1989) *Santander y la Instrucción Pública* (Bogotá: Foro Nacional por Colombia).
Edwards, Sebastian (2010) *Left Behind: Latin America and the False Promise of Populism* (Chicago: University of Chicago Press).
Egaña Baraona, Maria Loreto (2000) *La Educación Primaria Popular en el Siglo XIX en Chile: Una Práctica de Política Estatal* (Santiago: DIBAM).
Elliott, John H. (2006) *Empires of the Altlantic World: Britain and Spain in America, 1492–1830* (New Haven, CT: Yale University Press).

Encina, Francisco A. (1982) *Resumen de la Historia de Chile*, edited and summarized by Leopoldo Castedo (Santiago: Zig Zag) volumes II, III, IV.
Engerman, Stanley L., and Kenneth L. Sokoloff (1997) 'Factor Endowments, Institutions, and Differential Patterns of Growth among New World Economies: A View from Economic Historians of the United States' in, Stephen Haber, ed. *How Latin America Fell Behind* (Stanford, CA: Stanford University Press) pp. 260–304.
  (2002) 'Factor Endowments, Inequality, and Paths of Development among New World Economies.' Working paper No. 9259, National Bureau of Economic Research.
Ertman, Thomas (1997) *Birth of the Leviathan* (Cambridge: Cambridge University Press).
Estadísticas Históricas (1975) (Bogotá: DANE).
Estadísticas Sociales del Porfiriato (1956) (Mexico City: Secretaría de Economía, Dirección General de Estadística).
Estado Mayor General del Ejército (various years) *Historia del Ejército de Chile* (10 volumes) (Santiago: Colección Biblioteca Militar).
Estefane Jaramillo, Andrés (2004) 'Un Alto en el Camino para Saber Cuántos Somos: Los Censos de Población y la Construcción de Lealtades Nacionales, Chile Siglo XIX' *Historia (Santiago)* vol. 37 #1 (June) pp. 33–59.
Evans, Peter (1995) *Embedded Autonomy: States and Industrial Transformation* (Princeton, NJ: Princeton University Press).
Ewell, Judith (1984) *Venezuela: A Century of Change* (Stanford, CA: Stanford University Press).
Falcon, Ramona (1988) 'Charisma, Tradition, and Caciquismo: Revolution in San Luís Potosí' in Friedrich Katz, ed. *Riot, Rebellion, and Revolution: Rural Social Conflict in Mexico* (Princeton, NJ: Princeton University Press) pp. 417–447.
Falleti, Tulia G. (2010) *Decentralization and Subnational Politics in Latin America* (New York: Cambridge University Press).
Fearon, James, and David Laitin (2003) 'Ethnicity, Insurgency, and Civil War' *American Political Science Review* vol. 97 #1 pp. 75–90.
Fisher, John (1998) 'Commerce and Imperial Decline: Spanish Trade with the Americas, 1797–1820' *Journal of Latin American Studies* vol. 30 #3 (October) pp. 459–479.
Flórez, Carmen Elisa, and Olga Lucía Romero (2010) 'La Demografía de Colombia en el Siglo XIX' in Meisel Roca, Adolfo, and María Teresa Ramírez, eds. *Economía Colombiana del Siglo XIX* (Bogotá: Fondo de Cultura Económica) pp. 375–418.
Fowler, Will (2000) 'Civil Conflict in Independent Mexico, 1821–57: An Overview' in Rebecca Earle, ed. *Rumours of Wars: Civil Conflict in Nineteenth Century Latin America* (London: ILAS) pp. 49–86.
Frazier, Leslie Jo (2007) *Salt in the Sand: Memory, Violence, and the Nation-State in Chile, 1890 to the Present* (Durham, NC: Duke University Press).
Fukuyama, Francis (2004) *State Building: Governance and World Order in the 21st Century* (Ithaca, NY: Cornell University Press).
  (2013) 'What Is Governance?' *Governance* vol. 26 #3 pp. 347–368.

Gade, Daniel W. (1994) 'Regional Isolation in the High Provinces of Cusco and Apurímac' in Deborah Poole, ed. *Unruly Order: Violence, Power, and Cultural Identity in the High Provinces of Southern Peru* (Boulder, CO: Westview Press) pp. 31–62.

Gallo, Carmenza (1991) *Taxes and State Power: Political Instability in Bolivia, 1900–1950* (Philadelphia: Temple University Press).

Gallup, John Luke, Alejandro Gaviria, and Eduardo Lora (2003) *Is Geography Destiny? Lessons from Latin America* (New York: Inter-American Development Bank).

Galván de Terrazas, Luz Elena (1985) *Los Maestros y la Educación Pública en México* (Hidalgo y Matamoros, Tlalpan: Centro de Investigaciones y Estudios Superiores en Antropología Social).

García Alcaraz, María Guadalupe, and Armando Martínez Moya (2006) 'Poder, Educación y Region: Un Ejercicio de Reflecxión para el Estudio de las Escuelas Primarias de Guadalajara en la Segunda Mitad del Siglo XIX' in Martínez Moctezuma, Lucía, and Antonio Padilla Arroyo, eds. *Miradas a la Historia Regional de la Educación* (Mexico, DF: Universidad Autónoma del Estado de Morelos).

García Villegas, Mauricio, et al. (2011) *Los Estados del País: Instituciones Municipales y Realidades Locales* (Bogotá: Colección DeJusticia).

George, Alexander L., and Andrew A. Bennett (2005) *Case Studies and Theory Development in the Social Sciences* (Cambridge, MA: MIT Press).

Gerschenkron, Alexander (1962) *Economic Backwardness in Historical Perspective* (Cambridge, MA: Belknap Press).

Gilbert, Dennis L. (1977) *The Oligarchy and the Old Regime in Peru* (Ithaca, NY: Cornell University Press).

Gill, Anthony (1998) *Rendering unto Caesar* (Chicago: University of Chicago Press).

Gingerich, Daniel W. (2013) 'Governance Indicators and the Level of Analysis Problem: Empirical Findings from South America' *British Journal of Political Science* vol. 2 pp. 1–38.

Glave, Luís Miguel (1999) 'The Republic of Indians in Revolt' in Salomon, Frank, and Stuart B. Schwartz, eds. *The Cambridge History of the Native Peoples of the Americas* vol.III, Part 2, pp. 502–587.

Goldstein, Judith, and Robert Keohane, eds. (1993) *Ideas and Foreign Policy: Beliefs, Institutions, and Political Change* (Ithaca, NY: Cornell University Press).

Gonzales, Michael J. (1985) *Plantation Agriculture and Social Control in Northern Peru, 1875–1933* (Austin: University of Texas Press).

González-Cueva, Eduardo (2000) 'Conscription and Violence in Peru' *Latin American Perspectives* vol. 27 #3 (May) pp. 88–102.

Gootenberg, Paul (1988) 'Beleaguered Liberals: The Failed First Generation of Free Traders in Peru' in Love, Joseph L., and Nils Jacobsen, eds. *Guiding the Invisible Hand: Economic Liberalism and the State in Latin American History* (New York: Praeger) pp. 63–97.

   (1989) *Between Silver and Guano: Commercial Policy and the State in Post-Independence Peru* (Princeton, NJ: Princeton University Press).

(1990) 'Carneros y Chuño: Price Levels in Nineteenth Century Peru' *Hispanic American Historical Review* vol. 70 #1 pp. 1–56.

(1993) *Imagining Development: Economic Ideas in Peru's 'Fictitious Prosperity' of Guano, 1840–1880* (Berkeley: University of California Press).

(1995) *Población y Etnicidad en el Perú Republicano (Siglo XIX): Algunas Revisiones* (IEP Documento de Trabajo No. 71, Lima).

Gorski, Philip S. (2003) *The Disciplinary Revolution: Calvinism and the Rise of the State in Early Modern Europe* (Chicago: University of Chicago Press).

Gose, Peter (1994) 'Embodied Violence: Racial Identity and the Semiotics of Property in Huaquirca, Antabamba (Apurímac)' in Deborah Poole, ed. *Unruly Order: Violence, Power, and Cultural Identity in the High Provinces of Southern Peru* (Boulder, CO: Westview Press) pp. 165–198.

Goyer, Doreen, and Elaine Domschke (1983) *The Handbook of National Population Censuses: Latin America and the Caribbean, North America, and Oceania* (Wesport, CT: Greenwood Press).

Grez Toso, Sergio (1997) *De La 'Regeneración del Pueblo' a la Huelga General: Génesis y Evolución Histórica del Movimiento Popular en Chile (1810–1890)* (Santiago: DIBAM).

Grindle, Merilee S. (2003) '1952 and All That: The Bolivian Revolution in Comparative Perspective' in Grindle, Merilee S. and Pilar Domingo, eds. *Proclaiming Revolution: Bolivia in Comparative Perspective* (DRCLAS, Harvard University and ILAS, University of London) pp 1–21.

Haber, Stephen (1989) *Industry and Underdevelopment: The Industrialization of Mexico, 1890–1940* (Stanford, CA: Stanford University Press).

Haber, Stephen, Noel Maurer, and Armando Razo (2003) *The Politics of Property Rights* (Cambridge: Cambridge University Press).

Haggard, Stephan, and Robert R. Kaufman (2008) *Development, Democracy, and Welfare States: Latin America, East Asia, and Eastern Europe* (Princeton, NJ: Princeton University Press).

Hale, Charles A. (1968). *Mexican Liberalism in the Age of Mora, 1821–1853* (New Haven, CT: Yale University Press).

(1989) *The Transformation of Liberalism in Late Nineteenth Century Mexico* (Princeton, NJ: Princeton University Press).

Hall, Peter A. (1993) 'Policy Paradigms, Social Learning, and the State: The Case of Economic Policymaking in Britain' *Comparative Politics* vol.25 #3 (April) pp. 275–296.

Halperín Donghi, Tulio (1973) *The Aftermath of Revolution in Latin America* (New York: Harper Torchbooks).

(1988) 'Argentina: Liberalism in a Country Born Liberal' in Love, Joseph L. and Nils Jacobsen, eds. *Guiding the Invisible Hand: Economic Liberalism and the State in Latin American History* (New York: Praeger) pp. 99–116.

Hamilton, Nora (1975) 'Mexico: The Limits of State Autonomy' *Latin American Perspectives* vol. 2 #2 pp. 75–108.

Hamnett, Brian R. (1977) 'Process and Pattern: A Re-examination of the Ibero-American Independence Movements, 1808–1826' *Journal of Latin American Studies* vol. 29 pp. 279–328.

(1996) 'Liberalism Divided: Regional Politics and the National Project during the Mexican Restored Republic, 1867–1876' *Hispanic American Historical Review* vol. 76 #4 pp. 659–689.

Hanson, E. Mark (1986) *Educational Reform and Administrative Development: The Cases of Colombia and Venezuela* (Stanford, CA: Hoover Institution Press, Stanford University).

Hanson, Jonathan and Rachel Sigman (2011) *Measuring State Capacity: Assessing and Testing the Options* (paper presented at the annual meetings of the American Political Science Association).

Hanson, Stephen E. (2003) 'From Culture to Ideology in Comparative Politics' *Comparative Politics* vol. 35 #3 (April) pp. 355–376.

Hardoy, Jorge (1968) *Urban Planning in Pre-Columbian America* (New York: Braziller).

Hart, John M. (1988) 'The Southwestern Mexico Peasants' War: Conflict in a Transitional Society' in Friedrich Katz, ed. *Riot, Rebellion, and Revolution: Rural Social Conflict in Mexico* (Princeton, NJ: Princeton University Press) pp. 249–268.

Hartlyn, Jonathan (1988) *The Politics of Coalition Rule in Colombia* (Cambridge: Cambridge University Press).

Hazen, Dan C. (1978) 'The Politics of Schooling in the Nonliterate Third World: The Case of Highland Peru' *History of Education Quarterly* vol.18 #4 (Winter) pp. 419–443.

Hechter, Michael (2000) *Containing Nationalism* (Oxford: Oxford University Press).

Heise González, Julio (1974) *Historia de Chile: El Período Parlamentario* (Santiago: Editorial Andrés Bello).

Helg, Aline (1987) *La Educación en Colombia, 1918–1957* (Bogotá: Editorial CEREC).

Henderson, Paul (1997) 'Cocoa, Finance, and the State in Ecuador, 1885–1925' *Bulletin of Latin American Research* vol.16 #2 pp. 169–186.

Heraclio, Bonilla and Karen Spalding (2001) *La Independencia del Perú, las palabras y los hechos* (Lima: IEP) (Initial publication 1972).

Herbst, Jeffrey (2000) *States and Power in Africa* (Princeton, NJ: Princeton University Press).

Hernández Chavez, Alicia (1989) 'Orígen y ocaso del ejército porfiriano' *Historia Mexicana* vol. 39 #1 pp. 257–296.

(2006) *Mexico: A Brief History* (Berkeley: University of California Press).

Hernández Ponce, Roberto (1984) 'La Guardia Nacional de Chile: Apuntes sobre su Orígen y Organización, 1808–1848' *Historia* vol. 19 pp. 53–114.

Herr, Pilar M. (2001) 'Indians, Bandits, and the State: Chile's Path toward National Identity, 1819–1833' (PhD Dissertation, Department of History, Indiana University).

Herrera, Martha Cecilia (1999) *Modernización y Escuela Nueva en Colombia* (Bogotá: Plaza y Janés Editores).

Hirschman, Albert (1970) *Exit, Voice, and Loyalty* (Cambridge, MA: Harvard University Press).

Holden, Robert H. (1994) *Mexico and the Survey of Public Lands: the Management of Modernization* (DeKalb: Northern Illinois University Press).

Hu-DeHart, Evelyn (1988) 'Peasant Rebellion in the Northwest: The Yaqui Indians of Sonora, 1740-1976' in Friedrich Katz, ed. *Riot, Rebellion, and Revolution: Rural Social Conflict in Mexico* (Princeton, NJ: Princeton University Press) pp. 141-175.

Humphreys, Macartan, Jeffrey D. Sachs, and Joseph E. Stiglitz, eds. (2007) *Escaping the Resource Curse* (New York: Columbia University Press).

Hünefeldt, Christine (1989) 'Poder y Contribuciones: Puno 1825-1845' *Revista Andina* 7 no. 2, 367-407.

Hunt, Shane J. (1973) 'Growth and Guano in Nineteenth Century Peru' Discussion Paper 34, RPED (Woodrow Wilson School, Princeton).

(1985) 'Growth and Guano in Nineteenth Century Peru' in Conde, Roberto Cortés, and Shane J. Hunt, eds. *The Latin American Economies: Growth and the Export Sector, 1880-1930* (New York: Holmes and Meier) pp. 255-319.

Hutchcroft, Paul D. (2000) 'Colonial Masters, National Politicos, and Provincial Lords: Central Authority and Local Autonomy in the American Philippines, 1900-1913' *The Journal of Asian Studies* vol. 59 #2 (May) pp. 277-306.

Jackson, Robert H., and Carl G. Rosberg (1982) 'Why Africa's Weak States Persist: the Empirical and the Juridical in Statehood' *World Politics* 35 no. 1, pp. 1-24.

Jacobsen, Nils (1988) 'Free Trade, Regional Elites, and the Internal Market in Southern Peru, 1895-1932' in Love, Joseph L., and Nils Jacobsen, eds. *Guiding the Invisible Hand: Economic Liberalism and the State in Latin American History* (New York: Praeger) pp. 145-176.

(1993) *Mirages of Transition: The Peruvian Altiplano, 1780-1940* (Berkeley: University of California Press).

Jaramillo Uribe, Jaime (1964) *El Pensamiento Colombiano en el Siglo XIX* (Bogotá: Editorial Temis).

Jáuregui, Luis (2005) 'Los Orígenes de un Malestar Crónico: Los Ingresos y los Gastos Públicos de México, 1821-1855' in Aguilar, Aboites Luis, and Luis Jáuregui, eds. (2005) *Penuria sin Fin: Historia de los Impuestos en México Siglos XVIII-XX* (Mexico, DF: Instituto Mora), pp. 79-114.

Jimeno, Camilo García, and James A. Robinson (2010) 'Élites, Prosperidad y Desigualdad: Los Determinantes de la Detentación de Cargos Públicos en Antioquia durante el Siglo XIX' in Meisel Roca, Adolfo, and María Teresa Ramírez, eds. *Economía Colombiana del Siglo XIX* (Bogotá: Fondo de Cultura Económica) pp. 617-673.

Jones, Kristine L. (1999) 'Warfare, Reorganization, and Readaptation at the Margins of Spanish Rule: The Southern Margin (1573-1882)' in Salomon, Frank, and Stuart B. Schwartz, eds. *The Cambridge History of the Native Peoples of the Americas* vol.III, Part 2, pp. 138-187.

Joseph, Gilbert, and Daniel Nugent (1994) *Everyday Forms of State Formation: Revolution and the Negotiation of Rule in Modern Mexico* (Durham, NC: Duke University Press).

Junguito, Roberto (2010) 'Las Finanzas Públicas en el Siglo XIX' in Meisel Roca, Adolfo, and María Teresa Ramírez, eds. *Economía Colombiana del Siglo XIX* (Bogotá: Fondo de Cultura Económica) pp. 41-137.

Works Cited

Junguito, Roberto, and Hernán Rincón (2007) 'La Política Fiscal en el Siglo XX en Colombia' in Robinson, James, and Miguel Urrutia, eds. *Economía Colombiana del Siglo XX: un Análisis Cuantitativo* (Bogotá: Fondo de Cultura Económica) pp. 239–312.

Karl, Terry Lynn (1997) *The Paradox of Plenty: Oil Booms and Petro-States* (Berkeley: University of California Press).

Katz, Friedrich (1988a) 'Introduction: Rural Revolts in Mexico' in Friedrich Katz, ed. *Riot, Rebellion, and Revolution: Rural Social Conflict in Mexico* (Princeton, NJ: Princeton University Press) pp. 3–17.

(1988b) 'Rural Rebellions after 1810' in Friedrich Katz, ed. *Riot, Rebellion, and Revolution: Rural Social Conflict in Mexico* (Princeton, NJ: University Press) pp. 521–560.

(1991) 'The Liberal Republic and the Porfiriato, 1867–1910' in Leslie Bethell, ed., *Mexico Since Independence* (New York: Cambridge University Press) pp. 49–124.

Kaufman, Herbert (1967) *The Forest Ranger: A Study in Administrative Behavior* (Washington, DC: Resources for the Future).

Kaufman, Robert, and Joan Nelson, eds. (2004) *Crucial Needs, Weak Incentives* (Princeton, NJ: Woodrow Wilson Center Press).

Klarén, Peter (2000) *Peru: Society and Nationhood in the Andes* (New York: Oxford University Press).

Klein, Herbert S. (1969) *Parties and Political Change in Bolivia, 1880–1952* (Cambridge: Cambridge University Press).

(1991) *Bolivia: The Evolution of a Multi-Ethnic Society* (Oxford: Oxford University Press) Second Edition.

(2003) *A Concise History of Bolivia* (Cambridge: Cambridge University Press).

Knight, Alan (1986) *The Mexican Revolution* (2 volumes) (Lincoln: University of Nebraska Press).

(1990) 'Mexico c.1930–46' in Leslie Bethell, ed. *The Cambridge History of Latin America, vol. 7: Latin America since 1930, Mexico, Central America, and the Caribbean* (New York: Cambridge University Press) pp. 3–82.

(1992) 'The Peculiarities of Mexican History: Mexico Compared to Latin America, 1821–1992' *Journal of Latin American Studies* vol. 24 (Quincentenary Supplement) pp. 99–144.

(2002) *Mexico: The Colonial Era* (Cambridge: Cambridge University Press).

(2013) 'The Mexican State, Porfirian and Revolutionary, 1876–1930' in Centeno, Miguel, and Agustín Ferraro, eds. *State and Nation Making in Latin America and Spain: Republics of the Possible* (Cambridge: Cambridge University Press) pp. 116–138.

Kohli, Atul (1994) 'Where Do High Growth Political Economies Come From? The Japanese Lineage of Korea's Developmental State' *World Development* vol. 22 #9 pp. 1269–1293.

(2004) *State Directed Development: Political Power and Industrialization in the Global Periphery* (Cambridge: Cambridge University Press).

Kristal, Efraín (1987) *The Andes Viewed from the City: Literary and Political Discourse on the Indian in Peru, 1848–1930* (New York: Peter Lang).

Kurtz, Marcus J. (2009) 'The Social Foundations of Institutional Order: Reconsidering War and the Resource Curse in Third World State Building' *Politics and Society* vol. 37 #4 pp. 479–520.

(2013) *Latin American State Building in Comparative Perspective: The Social Origins of Institutional Order* (New York: Cambridge University Press).

Kurtz, Marcus J. and Andrew Schrank (2007) 'Growth and Governance: Models, Measures, and Mechanisms' *Journal of Politics* vol. 69 #2 (May) pp. 538–554.

La Porta, Rafael, Florencio López de Silanes, Andrei Shleifer, and Robert W. Vishny (1998) 'Law and Finance' *Journal of Political Economy* v.106 #6 pp. 1113–1155.

Lange, Matthew (2004) 'British Colonial Legacies and Political Development' *World Development* vol. 32 #6 pp. 905–922.

(2009) *Lineages of Despotism and Development: British Colonialism and State Power* (Chicago: University of Chicago Press).

Lange, Matthew, and Hrag Balian (2008) 'Containing Conflict or Instigating Unrest? A Test of the Effects of State Infrastructural Power on Civil Violence' *Studies in Comparative International Development* vol. 43 #3–4 pp. 314–333.

Larson, Brooke (1999) 'Andean Highland Peasants and the Trials of Nation-Making during the Nineteenth Century' in Salomon, Frank, and Stuart B. Schwartz, eds. *The Cambridge History of the Native Peoples of the Americas* vol. III, Part 2, pp. 558–703.

(2004) *Trials of Nation-Making: Liberalism, Race, and Ethnicity in the Andes, 1810–1910* (New York: Cambridge University Press).

Leal Buitrago, Francisco, Ladrón de Guevara, and Andrés Dávila (1990) *Clientelismo: El Sistema Político y Su Expresión Regional* (Bogotá: Tercer Mundo Editores).

Lebot, Ivon (1978) *Elementos para la Historia de la Educación en Colombia en el Siglo XX* (Bogotá: DANE).

LeGrand, Catherine (1986) *Frontier Expansion and Peasant Protest in Colombia, 1830–1936* (Albuquerque: University of New Mexico Press)

Levi, Margaret (1988) *Of Rule and Revenue* (Berkeley: University of California Press).

(1997) *Consent, Dissent, and Patriotism* (New York: Cambridge University Press).

Levitsky, Steven and Maria Murillo (2009) 'Variation in Institutional Strength' *Annual Review of Political Science* vol. 12 pp. 115–133.

Levitsky, Steven, and Lucan A. Way (2010) *Competitive Authoritarianism: Hybrid Regimes after the Cold War* (Cambridge: Cambridge University Press).

Lieberman, Evan S. (2002) 'Taxation Data as Indicators of State-Society Relations: Possibilities and Pitfalls in Cross-National Research' *Studies in Comparative International Development* 36 no. 4, (Winter) pp. 89–115.

(2003) *Race and Regionalism in the Politics of Taxation in Brazil and South Africa* (Cambridge: Cambridge University Press).

Lieuwen, Edwin (1968) *Mexican Militarism: The Political Rise and Fall of the Revolutionary Army* (Albuquerque: University of New Mexico Press).

Lipset, Seymour M., and Stein Rokkan (1967) 'Cleavage Structures, Party Systems, and Voter Alignments: An Introduction' in Lipset and Rokkan, eds. *Party Systems and Voter Alignments: Cross-National Perspectives* (New York: Free Press).

Lipsky, Michael (1980) *Street-Level Bureaucracy: Dilemmas of the Individual in Public Services* (New York: Russell Sage Foundation).

Llinás Álvarez, Édgar (1978) *Revolución, Educación, y Mexicanidad* (México, DF: UNAM).

López-Alves, Fernando (2000) *State Formation and Democracy in Latin America, 1810–1900* (Durham, NC: Duke University Press).

Love, Joseph L. (1988) 'Structural Change and Conceptual Response in Latin America and Romania, 1860–1950' in Love, Joseph L., and Nils Jacobsen, eds. *Guiding the Invisible Hand: Economic Liberalism and the State in Latin American History* (New York: Praeger) pp. 1–33.

Loveman, Brian (1993) *The Constitution of Tyranny: Regimes of Exception in Spanish America* (Pittsburgh, PA: University of Pittsburgh Press).

(2001) *Chile: The Legacy of Hispanic Capitalism* 3rd ed. (New York: Oxford University Press).

Loveman, Mara (2005) 'The Modern State and the Primitive Accumulation of Symbolic Power' *American Journal of Sociology* vol. 110 #6 (May) pp. 1651–1683.

Loy, Jane Meyer (1971) 'Primary Education during the Colombian Federation: The School Reform of 1870' *Hispanic American Historical Review* vol. 51 #2 (May) pp. 275–294.

Ludlow, Leonor, ed. (2002) *Los Secretarios de Hacienda y Sus Proyectos* (Mexico, DF: UNAM) 2 volumes.

Luna, Juan Pablo, and Andreas Feldmann (2012) 'States and Challengers: A Conceptual Typology' (unpublished paper, Pontificia Universidad Católica de Chile).

Lustick, Ian S. (1993) *Unsettled States, Disputed Lands* (Ithaca, NY: Cornell University Press).

Lynch, John (1986) *The Spanish American Revolutions, 1808–1826* (New York: Norton).

Macías Richard, Carlos (1999) 'El Territorio de Quintana Roo: Tentativas de Colonización y Control Militar en la Selva Maya, 1888–1902' *Historia Mexicana* vol. 49 #1 (July–September) pp. 5–54.

Mahoney, James (2000) 'Path Dependence in Historical Sociology' *Theory and Society* vol. 29 #1 pp. 507–548.

(2001) *The Legacies of Liberalism: Path Dependence and Political Regimes in Central America* (Baltimore, MD: Johns Hopkins University Press).

(2010) *Colonialism and Post-Colonial Development: Spanish America in Comparative Perspective* (New York: Cambridge University Press).

Mahoney, James, and Matthias vom Hau (2005) 'Colonial States and Economic Development in Spanish America' in Lange, Matthew, and Dietrich Rueschemeyer, eds. *States and Development: Historical Antecedents of Stagnation and Advance* (New York: Palgrave Macmillan) pp. 92–116.

Mainwaring, Scott, and Timothy R. Scully, eds. (2010) *Democratic Governance in Latin America* (Stanford, CA: Stanford University Press).
Mallon, Florencia E. (1983) *The Defense of Community in Peru's Central Highlands* (Princeton, NJ: Princeton University Press).
  (1995) *Peasant and Nation: the Making of Post-Colonial Mexico and Peru* (Berkeley: University of California Press).
  (2005) *Courage Tastes of Blood: The Mapuche Community of Nicolás Ailío and the Chilean State* (Durham, NC: Duke University Press).
Mamalakis, Markos J. (1976) *The Growth and Structure of the Chilean Economy: From Independence to Allende* (New Haven, CT: Yale University Press).
Mamdani, Mahmood (1996) *Citizen and Subject: Contemporary Africa and the Legacy of Colonialism* (Princeton, NJ: Princeton University Press).
Mann, Michael (1984) 'The Autonomous Power of the State: Its Origins, Mechanisms, and Results' *European Journal of Sociology* vol. 25 #2 pp. 185–213.
Mariscal, Elisa and Kenneth L. Sokoloff (2000) 'Schooling, Suffrage, and the Persistence of Inequality in the Americas, 1800–1945' in Stephen Haber, ed. *Political Institutions and Economic Growth in Latin America* (Stanford CA: Hoover Institution Press) pp. 159–218.
Márquez, Graciela (2005) 'Aranceles a la Importación y Finanzas Públicas: Del Porfiriato a la Crisis de 1929' in Aguilar, Aboites Luis, and Luis Jáuregui, eds. (2005) *Penuria sin Fin: Historia de los Impuestos en México Siglos XVIII-XX* (Mexico, DF: Instituto Mora) pp. 141–160.
Martínez Jiménez, Alejandro (1973) 'La Educación Elemental en el Porfiriato' *Historia Mexicana* v. 32#4 (April–June) pp. 514–552.
Mata, Javier F. and Sebastian Ziata (2009) *User's Guide on Measuring Fragility* (Bonn and Oslo: German Development Institute and United Nations Development Programme).
McCaleb, Walter (1921) *The Public Finances of Mexico* (New York: Harper and Brothers).
McEvoy, Carmen (1994) *Un Proyecto Nacional en el Siglo XIX: Manuel Pardo y Su Visión del Perú* (Lima: PUCP).
McFarlane, Anthony (1984) 'Civil Disorders and Popular Protests in Late Colonial New Granada' *Hispanic American Historical Review* vol. 64 #1 (February) pp. 17–54.
  (1993) *Colombia before Independence: Economy, Society, and Politics under Bourbon Rule* (New York: Cambridge University Press).
McGreevey, William P. (1971) *An Economic History of Colombia, 1845–1930* (Cambridge: Cambridge University Press).
Meisel Roca, Adolfo, and María Teresa Ramírez, eds. (2010) *Economía Colombiana del Siglo XIX* (Bogotá: Fondo de Cultura Económica).
Meltzer, Allan H., and F. Scott Richard (1981) 'A Rational Theory of the Size of Government' *Journal of Political Economy* 89: pp. 914–927.
Méndez, Cecilia (2005) *The Plebeian Republic: The Huanta Rebellion and the Making of the Peruvian State, 1820–1850* (Durham, NC: Duke University Press).

Meyer, Jean (1986) 'Mexico: Revolution and Reconstruction in the 1920s' in Leslie Bethell, ed. *The Cambridge History of Latin America, Vol. V, c.1870–1930* (Cambridge: Cambridge University Press) pp. 155–194.
Meyer, Michael C., and William L. Sherman (1995) *The Course of Mexican History*, 5th ed. (Oxford: Oxford University Press).
Middlebrook, Kevin (1995) *The Paradox of Revolution: Labor, the State, and Authoritarianism in Mexico* (Baltimore, MD: Johns Hopkins University Press).
Migdal, Joel S. (1988) *Strong Societies and Weak States: State-Society Relations and State Capabilities in the Third World* (New York: Cambridge University Press).
  (2001) *State in Society: Studying How States and Societies Transform and Constitute One Another* (New York: Cambridge University Press).
Milla Batres, Carlos, ed. (1994) *Enciclopedia Biográfica e Histórica del Perú Siglos XIX-XX* (ten volumes) (Lima: Editorial Milla Batres).
Molina, Iván, and Steven Palmer (2004) 'Popular Literacy in a Tropical Democracy: Costa Rica, 1850–1950.' *Past and Present* 184: 169–208.
Monteón, Michael (1982) *Chile in the Nitrate Era: The Evolution of Economic Dependence, 1880–1930* (Madison: University of Wisconsin Press).
  (1998) *Chile and the Great Depression: The Politics of Underdevelopment, 1927–1948* (Tempe: Arizona State University Press).
Montero, Cármen, ed. (1990) *La Escuela Rural: Variaciones sobre un Tema* (Lima: FAO).
Monteverde, Alessandro (1999) 'La Delincuencia en Aconcagua entre 1850 y 1900 a través de Documentos y Periódicos' *Revista de Estudios Histórico-Jurídicos* #21, pp. 159–169.
Muecke, Ulrich (2004) *Political Culture in Nineteenth Century Peru: The Rise of the Partido Civil* (Pittsburgh, PA: University of Pittsburgh Press).
Needell, Jeff (2013) 'The State and Development under the Brazilian Monarchy' in Centeno, Miguel Ángel, and Agustin Ferraro, eds. *State and Nation Making in Latin America: Republics of the Possible* (Cambridge: Cambridge University Press) pp. 79–99.
Neufeld, Stephen (2009) 'Servants of the Nation: The Military in the Making of Modern Mexico, 1876–1911' (PhD Dissertation, History Department, University of Arizona).
Newland, Carlos (1994) 'The Estado Docente and Its Expansion: Spanish American Elementary Education, 1900–1950' *Journal of Latin American Studies* 26 no.2 pp. 449–467.
North, Douglass C. (1981) *Structure and Change in Economic History* (New York: Norton).
  (1990) *Institutions, Institutional Change, and Economic Performance* (Cambridge: Cambridge University Press).
Nugent, David (1997) *Modernity at the Edge of Empire: State, Individual, and Nation in the Northern Peruvian Andes, 1885–1935* (Stanford, CA: Stanford University Press).
Nuñez, Javier (2005) 'Signed with an X: Methodology and Data Sources for Analyzing the Evolution of Literacy in Latin America and the Caribbean, 1900–1950' *Latin American Research Review* 40 no.2, pp. 117–135.

Nunn, Frederick (1970) *Chilean Politics 1920–1931: The Honorable Mission of the Armed Forces* (Albuquerque: University of New Mexico Press).
Nunn, Nathan, and Diego Puga (2012) 'Ruggedness: The Blessing of Bad Geography in Africa' *Review of Economics and Statistics* vol. 94 #1 (February) pp. 20–36.
Obregón, Javier Sáenz, Óscar Saldarriaga, and Armando Espina (1999) *Mirar la Infancia: Pedagogía, Moral, y Moderndidad en Colombia, 1903–1946* (Bogotá: Ediciones Foro Nacional por Colombia) 2 volumes.
O'Donnell, Guillermo (1973) *Modernization and Bureaucratic Authoritarianism* (Berkeley: University of California Press).
  (1993) 'On the State, Democratization and Some Conceptual Problems: A Latin American View with some Glances at Post-Communist Countries' *World Development* 21 no. 8, pp. 1355–1369.
Olson, Mancur (1993) 'Dictatorship, Democracy, and Development' *American Political Science Review* vol.87 #3 pp. 567–576.
Orlove, Benjamin (1994) 'The Dead Policemen Speak: Power, Fear, and Narrative in the 1931 Molloccahua Killings (Cusco)' in Deborah Poole, ed. *Unruly Order: Violence, Power, and Cultural Identity in the High Provinces of Southern Peru* (Boulder, CO: Westview Press) pp. 63–96.
Ortega, Luis (1984) 'Nitrates, Chilean Entrepreneurs, and the Origins of the War of the Pacific' *Journal of Latin American Studies* vol. 16 pp. 337-380.
Padgen, Anthony (1987) 'Identity Formation in Spanish America' in Canny, Nicholas, and Anthony Padgen, eds. *Colonial Identity in the Atlantic World, 1500–1800* (Princeton, NJ: Princeton University Press) pp. 51–94.
Palacios, Marco (1980) *Coffee in Colombia: An Economic, Social, and Political History* (New York: Cambridge University Press).
  (2006) *Between Legitimacy and Violence: A History of Colombia, 1875–2002* (Durham, NC: Duke University Press).
Palmer, David Scott (1977) 'The Politics of Authoritarianism in Spanish America' in James M. Malloy, ed. *Authoritarianism and Corporatism in Latin America* (Pittsburgh, PA: University of Pittsburgh Press) pp. 377–412.
Papponet-Cantat, Christiane (1994) '*Gamonalismo* after the Challenge of Agrarian Reform: The Case of Capacmarca, Chumbivilcas (Cusco)' in Deborah Poole, ed. *Unruly Order: Violence, Power, and Cultural Identity in the High Provinces of Southern Peru* (Boulder, CO: Westview Press) pp. 199–222.
Paredes, Maritza (2013) 'Shaping State Capacity: A Comparative Historical Analysis of Mining Dependence in the Andes, 1840s-1920s' (PhD Dissertation, Department of International Development, Oxford University).
Park, James William (1985) *Rafael Nuñez and the Politics of Colombian Regionalism, 1863–1886* (Baton Rouge: Louisiana State University Press).
Pastore, Mario (1994) 'State-Led Industrialization: The Evidence on Paraguay, 1852–1870' *Journal of Latin American Studies* vol. 26 #2 (May) pp. 295–324.
Peloso, Vincent (1999) *Peasants on Plantations: Subaltern Strategies of Labor and Resistance in the Pisco Valley, Peru* (Durham, NC: Duke University Press).

Perry, Laurens Ballard (1978) *Juárez and Díaz: Machine Politics in Mexico* (DeKalb: Northern Illinois University Press).
Pierson, Paul (1994) *Dismantling the Welfare State: Reagan, Thatcher, and the Politics of Retrenchment* (Cambridge: Cambridge University Press).
  (2000a) 'Increasing Returns, Path Dependence, and the Study of Politics' *American Political Science Review* vol. 94 #2 pp. 251–268.
  (2000b) 'The Limits of Design: Explaining Institutional Origins and Change' *Governance* vol. 13 #4 (October) pp. 475–499.
  (2004) *Politics in Time: History, Institutions, and Political Analysis* (Princeton, NJ: Princeton University Press).
Pike, Frederick B. (1967) *The Modern History of Peru* (Westport, CT: Praeger Press).
Pinto Rodríguez, Jorge (2003) *La Formación del Estado y la Nación, y el Pueblo Mapuche: de la Inclusión a la Exclusión* (Santiago: DIBAM).
Pittman, Dewitt Kenneth (1989) *Hacendados, campesinos y políticos: las clases agrarias y la instalación del Estado oligárquico en México, 1869–1876* (Mexico, DF: Fondo De Cultura Economica USA).
Poole, Deborah (1994a) 'Introduction: Anthropological Perspectives on Violence and Culture – a View from the Peruvian High Provinces' in Deborah Poole, ed. *Unruly Order: Violence, Power, and Cultural Identity in the High Provinces of Southern Peru* (Boulder, CO: Westview Press) pp. 1–30.
  (1994b) 'Performance, Domination, and Identity in the *Tierras Bravas* of Chumbivilcas (Cusco)' pp. 97–132 in Deborah Poole, ed. *Unruly Order: Violence, Power, and Cultural Identity in the High Provinces of Southern Peru* (Boulder, CO: Westview Press).
Posada-Carbó, Eduardo (1996) *The Colombian Caribbean: A Regional History, 1870–1950* (Oxford: Clarendon Press).
Powell, Walter W., and Paul J. Dimaggio, eds. (1991) *The New Institutionalism in Organizational Analysis* (Chicago: University of Chicago Press).
Przeworski, Adam, and Fernando Limongi (1997) 'Modernization: Theories and Facts' *World Politics* vol. 49 #2 (January) pp. 155–183.
Putnam, Robert (1993) *Making Democracy Work* (Princeton, NJ: Princeton University Press).
Quiroz, Alfonso W. (1988) 'Financial Leadership and the Formation of Peruvian Elite Groups, 1884–1930' *Journal of Latin American Studies* vol. 20 #1 (May) pp. 49–81.
Rámirez, María Teresa, and Irene Salazar (2010) 'El Surgimiento de la Educación en Colombia: En qué Fallamos?' in Meisel Roca, Adolfo, and María Teresa Ramírez, eds. *Economía Colombiana del Siglo XIX* (Bogotá: Fondo de Cultura Económica) pp. 419–482.
Ramírez, María Teresa, and Juana Patricia Téllez (2007) 'La Educación Primaria y Secundaria en Colombia en el Siglo XX' in Robinson, James, and Miguel Urrutia, eds. *Economía Colombiana del Siglo XX: Un Análisis Cuantitativo* (Bogotá: Fondo de Cultura Económica) pp. 459–517.
Rausch, Jane M. (1993) *The Llanos Frontier in Colombian History, 1830–1930* (Albuquerque: University of New Mexico Press).

(1999) *Colombia: Territorial Rule and the Llanos Frontier* (Gainesvile: University Press of Florida).
Reed, Nelson (1964) *The Caste War of Yucatan* (Stanford, CA: Stanford University Press).
Reina, Leticia (1980) *Las Rebeliones Campesinas en México, 1819–1906* (Mexico, DF: Siglo XXI).
Remmer, Karen L. (1984) *Party Competition in Argentina and Chile: Political Recruitment and Public Policy, 1890–1930* (Lincoln: University of Nebraska Press).
Rénique, José Luis (1994) 'Political Violence, the State, and the Peasant Struggle for Land (Puno)' in Deborah Poole, ed. *Unruly Order: Violence, Power, and Cultural Identity in the High Provinces of Southern Peru* (Boulder, CO: Westview Press) pp. 223–246.
  (2004) *La Batalla por Puno: Conflicto Agrario y Nacion en los Andes Peruanos* (Lima: IEP).
República de Colombia, Departamento de Contraloría *Anuario de Estadística General* (Bogotá: Imprenta Nacional) (Various years).
Resende Santos, João (2007) *Neorealism, States, and the Modern Mass Army* (Cambridge: Cambridge University Press).
Richmond, Douglas W. (1989) *Carlos Pellegrini and the Crisis of the Argentine Elites, 1880–1916* (Westport, CT: Praeger Press).
Riedl, Rachel Beatty (2009) 'Institutions in New Democracies: Variation in African Party Systems' (PhD Dissertation, Department of Politics, Princeton University).
Rock, David (1987) *Argentina 1516–1987: From Spanish Colonization to Alfonsín* (Berkeley: University of California Press).
  (2000) 'State-Building and Political Systems in Nineteenth Century Argentina and Uruguay' *Past and Present* #167 pp. 176–202.
  (2002) *State Building and Political Movements in Argentina, 1860–1916* (Stanford, CA: Stanford University Press).
Rodden, Jonathan, and Erik Wibbels (2002) 'Beyond the Fiction of Federalism: Macroeconomic Management in Multitiered Systems' *World Politics* vol. 54 (July) pp. 494–531.
Rodríguez, Linda A. (1985) *The Search for Public Policy: Regional Politics and Government Finances in Ecuador, 1830–1940* (Berkeley: University of California Press).
Rojas, Cristina (2002) *Civilization and Violence: Regimes of Representation in Nineteenth Century Colombia* (Minneapolis: University of Minnesota Press).
Romero, Matías (1898) *Geographical and Statistical Notes on Mexico* (New York: Knickerbocker Press).
Rosenthal, Joshua M. (2001) 'La Salina de Chita: Fiscal Policy and Local Power in Provincial Colombia' (PhD Dissertation, Department of History, Columbia University).
  (2012) *Salt and the Colombian State: Local Society and Regional Monopoly in Boyacá, 1821–1900* (Pittsburgh, PA: University of Pittsburgh Press)
Ross, Michael L. (2001) *Timber Booms and Institutional Breakdown in Southeast Asia* (New York: Cambridge University Press).

Ruiz-Esquide, Andrea (2000) 'Migration, Colonization, and Land Policy in the Former Mapuche Frontier: Malleco, 1850–1900' (Dissertation presented to the Department of History, Columbia University).

Safford, Frank (1976) *The Ideal of the Practical: Colombia's Struggle to Form a Technical Elite* (Austin: University of Texas Press).

(1988) 'The Emergence of Economic Liberalism in Colombia' in Love, Joseph, and Nils Jacobsen, eds. *Guiding the Invisible Hand: Economic Liberalism and the State in Latin American History* (New York: Praeger) pp. 35–62.

(1991) 'Race, Integration, and Progress: Elite Attitudes and the Indian in Colombia, 1750–1870' *Hispanic American Historical Review* vol. 71 #1 pp. 1–33.

(2010) 'El Problema de Los Transportes en Colombia en el Siglo XIX' in Meisel Roca, Adolfo, and María Teresa Ramírez, eds. *Economía Colombiana del Siglo XIX* (Bogotá: Fondo de Cultura Económica) pp. 523–574.

Safford, Frank, and Marco Palacios (2002) *Colombia: Fragmented Land, Divided Society* (New York: Oxford University Press).

Salvatore, Ricardo D. (2013) 'Between Empleomanía and the Common Good: Expert Bureaucracies in Argentina, 1870–1930' in Centeno, Miguel, and Agustín Ferraro, eds. *State and Nation Making in Latin America and Spain: Republics of the Possible* (Cambridge: Cambridge University Press) pp. 225–246).

Sanders, James E. (2010) 'Subaltern Strategies of Citizenship and Soldiering in Colombia's Civil Wars: Afro- and Indigenous Colombians' Experiences in the Cauca, 1851–1877' in Foote, Nicola, and René D. Harder Horst, eds. *Military Struggle and Identity Formation in Latin America: Race, Nation, and Community during the Liberal Period* (Gainesville: University of Florida Press) pp. 25–41.

Santos Granero, Fernando, and Frederica Barclay (2002) *La Frontera Domesticada: Historia Económica y Social de Loreto, 1850–2000* (Lima: PUCP).

Sater, William F. (1973) 'Chile during the First Months of the War of the Pacific' *Journal of Latin American Studies* vol. 5 #1 (May) pp. 133–158.

(1976) 'Economic Nationalism and Tax Reform in Late Nineteenth-Century Chile' *The Americas* pp. 311–335.

(2007) *Andean Tragedy: Fighting the War of the Pacific, 1879–1884* (Lincoln: University of Nebraska Press).

Sater, William F., and Holder H. Herwig (1999) *The Grand Illusion: The Prussianization of the Chilean Army* (Lincoln: University of Nebraska Press).

Sausi Garavito, María José Rhi (2001) 'El Deber Fiscal durante la Regencia y el Segundo Imperio: Contribuciones y Contribuyentes de la Ciudad de México' in Marichal, Carlos, and Daniela Marino, eds. *De Colonia a Nación: Impuestos y Política en México, 1750–1860* (Mexico City: El Colegio de México) pp. 247–275.

(2005) '¿Cómo Aventurarse a Perder lo Que Existe? Una Reflexión sobre el Voluntarismo Fiscal Mexicano del Siglo XIX' in Aguilar, Aboites Luis, and Luis Jáuregui, eds. (2005) *Penuria sin Fin: Historia de los Impuestos en México Siglos XVIII-XX* (Mexico, DF: Instituto Mora), pp. 115–140.

Saylor, Ryan R. (2008) 'Commodity Booms, Political Coalitions, and State Building in Latin America and Africa' (PhD Dissertation, Department of Politics, University of Virginia).

(2012) 'Sources of State Capacity in Latin America: Commodity Booms and State Building Motives in Chile' *Theory and Society* vol. 41 #3 pp. 301–324.

(2014) *State Building in Boom Times: Commodities and Coalitions in Latin America and Africa* (Oxford: Oxford University Press).

Saylor, Ryan R., and Hillel David Soifer (2008) 'Rivalry and State Building in Latin America: Tracing and Adjudicating Competing Causal Mechanisms' (unpublished paper, University of Tulsa and Temple University).

Scarritt, Arthur (2005) 'The Battle of Burnt Bread: Indigenous Mobilization and Land Loss in the Peruvian Highlands, 1982–2003' (Ph.D. Dissertation, Department of Sociology, University of Wisconsin).

Scheina, Robert L. (2003) *Latin America's Wars* (two volumes) (Washington, DC: Brassey's).

Scott, James C. (1976) *The Moral Economy of the Peasant: Rebellion and Subsistence in Southeast Asia* (New Haven, CT: Yale University Press).

(1998) *Seeing Like a State: How Various Schemes to Improve the Human Condition Have Failed* (New Haven, CT: Yale University Press).

(2009) *The Art of Not Being Governed* (New Haven, CT: Yale University Press).

Scully, Timothy (1992) *Rethinking the Center: Party Politics in Nineteenth and Twentieth Century Chile* (Stanford, CA: Stanford University Press).

Serrano, Sol (1995–1996) 'De Escuelas Indígenas sin Pueblos a Pueblos sin Escuelas Indígenas: la Educación en la Araucanía en el Siglo XIX' *Historia* 29, pp. 423–474.

Shafer, D. Michael (1994) *Winners and Losers: How Sectors Shape the Developmental Prospects of States* (Ithaca, NY: Cornell University Press).

Sikkink, Kathryn (1991) *Ideas and Institutions: Developmentalism in Brazil and Argentina* (Ithaca, NY: Cornell University Press).

Siller, Javier Pérez (2004) *Los Ingresos Federales del Porfirismo* (Puebla, Mexico: Universidad Autónoma de Puebla).

Silva, Patricio (2008) *In the Name of Reason: Technocrats and Politics in Chile* (University Park: Penn State University Press).

Silva Olarte, Renán (1989) 'La Educación en Colombia, 1880–1930' in Alvaro Tirado Mejía, ed. *Nueva Historia de Colombia* (Bogotá: Editorial Planeta) vol. IV, pp. 61–86.

Sinkin, Richard (1979) *The Mexican Reform, 1855–1876: A Study in Liberal Nation-Building* (Austin: University of Texas Press).

Skuban, William E. (2007) *Lines in the Sand: Nationalism and Identity on the Peruvian-Chilean Frontier* (Albuquerque: University of New Mexico Press).

Slater, Dan (2008) 'Can Leviathan Be Democratic? Competitive Elections, Robust Mass Politics, and State Infrastructural Power' *Studies in Comparative International Development* vol. 43 #3–4 pp. 252–272.

(2010) *Ordering Power: Contentious Politics and Authoritarian Leviathans in Southeast Asia* (Cambridge: Cambridge University Press).
Slater, Dan, and Sofia Fenner (2011). State Power and Staying Power: Infrastructural Mechanisms and Authoritarian Durability *Journal of International Affairs* vol. 65 #1 pp. 15–29.
Slater, Dan, and Diana Kim (2015) 'Standoffish States: Nonliterate Leviathans in Southeast Asia' *TRaNS* vol.3 #1.
Slater, Dan, and Erica Simmons (2010) 'Informative Regress: Critical Antecedents in Comparative Politics' *Comparative Political Studies* vol. 43 #7 (July) pp. 886–917.
Slater, Dan, and Daniel Ziblatt (2013) 'The Enduring Indispensability of the Controlled Comparison' *Comparative Political Studies* vol. 46 #10 (October) pp. 1301–1327.
Smith, Gavin (1989) *Livelihood and Resistance: Peasants and the Politics of Land in Peru* (Berkeley: University of California Press).
Snyder, Richard (2001) *Politics after Neoliberalism: Reregulation in Mexico* (Cambridge: Cambridge University Press).
 (2001b) 'Scaling Down: The Subnational Comparative Method' *Studies in Comparative International Development* vol. 36 #1 pp. 93–110.
Snyder, Richard, and Angelica Durán-Martínez (2009) 'Does Illegality Breed Violence? Drug Trafficking and State-Sponsored Protection Rackets' *Crime, Law, and Social Change* vol. 52 pp. 253–273.
Soifer, Hillel David (2008) 'State Infrastructural Power: Conceptualization and Measurement in Empirical Analysis' *Studies in Comparative International Development* vol. 43 #3–4 (November) pp. 231–251.
 (2009) 'The Sources of Infrastructural Power: Evidence from Nineteenth Century Chilean Education' *Latin American Research Review* vol. 44 #2 pp. 158–180.
 (2012a) 'The Causal Logic of Critical Junctures' *Comparative Political Studies* vol. 45 #12 (December), pp. 1572–1597.
 (2012b) 'Measuring State Capacity in Contemporary Latin America' *Revista de Ciencia Política*, special issue on 'States and Challengers in Contemporary Latin America' vol. 32 #3 (November–December) pp. 585–598.
 (2013a) 'State Power and the Redistributive Threat' *Studies in Comparative International Development* vol. 48 #1 (March) pp. 1–22.
 (2013b) 'Elite Preferences, Administrative Institutions, and Educational Development during Peru's Aristocratic Republic (1895–1919)' Chapter in Centeno and Ferraro, eds. *Paper Leviathans* (Gainesville: University Press of Florida).
Soifer, Hillel David and Matthias vom Hau (2008) 'Unpacking the "Strength" of the State: The Utility of State Infrastructural Power' *Studies in Comparative International Development* vol. 43 #3–4 (November) pp. 219–230.
Spruyt, Hendrik (1994) *The Sovereign State and Its Competitors* (Princeton, NJ: Princeton University Press).
Staples, Anne (1979) 'Alfabeto y Catecismo: Salvación del Nuevo País' *Historia Mexicana* vol. 29 #1 (July–September) pp. 35–58.

(1992) 'Alfabeto y Catecismo, Salvación del Nuevo País' in Josefina Zoraida Vásquez, ed. *La Educación en la Historia de México* (México, DF: El Colegio de México) pp. 69–92.
(1998) 'Los Poderes Locales y las Primeras Letras' in Pilar Gonzalbo Aizpurú, ed. *Historia de la Educación y la Enseñanza de la Historia* (Mexico, DF: El Colegio de México) pp. 47–62.
Stasavage, David (2011) *States of Credit: Size, Power, and the Development of European Polities* (Princeton: Princeton University Press).
Stein, Stanley (1981) 'Bureaucracy and Business in the Spanish Empire, 1759–1804: Failure of a Bourbon Reform in Mexico and Peru' *Hispanic American Historical Review* vol. 61 #1 (February) pp. 2–28.
Steinmo, Sven (1993) *Taxation and Democracy* (New Haven, CT: Yale University Press).
Stevens, Donald F. (1991) *Origins of Instability in Early Republican Mexico* (Durham, NC: Duke University Press).
Stinchcombe, Arthur L. (1968) *Constructing Social Theories* (Chicago: University of Chicago Press).
Subercaseaux, Benjamin (1944) *Chile, o una Loca Geografía* (Santiago: Ediciones Ercilla).
Szuchman, Mark D. (1990) 'Childhood Education and Politics in 19th Century Argentina: The Case of Buenos Aires' *Hispanic American Historical Review* vol. 70 #1 pp. 109–138.
Tanck de Estrada, Dorothy (1973) 'Las Escuelas Lancasterianas en la Ciudad de México 1822–42' *Historia Mexicana* vol. 22 #4 (April–June) pp. 494–513.
(1977) *La Educación Ilustrada 1786–1836: Educación Primaria en la Ciudad de México* (Mexico, DF: El Colegio de México).
Tantaleán Arbulú, Javier (1983) *Politica Económico-Financiera y la Formación del Estado: Siglo XIX* (Lima: CEDEP).
Tarrow, Sid (1998) *Power in Movement: Social Movements and Contentious Politics* (New York: Cambridge University Press).
Tarvear, H. Michael, and Julia C. Frederick (2006) *The History of Venezuela* (London: Palgrave).
Taylor, Lewis (2006) *Shining Path: Guerrilla War in Peru's Northern Highlands, 1980–1997* (Liverpool: Liverpool University Press).
Tenenbaum, Barbara (1986) *The Politics of Penury: Debts and Taxes in Mexico, 1821–1856* (Albuquerque: University of New Mexico Press).
'The Growing Power of the Republic of Chile' (1884) *Atlantic Monthly* (July) pp. 110–117.
Thelen, Kathleen, and Sven Steinmo (1992) 'Historical Institutionalism in Comparative Politics' in Steinmo, Sven, Kathleen Thelen, and Frank Longstreth, eds. *Structuring Politics: Historical Institutionalism in Comparative Politics* (Cambridge: Cambridge University Press) pp. 1–33.
Thies, Cameron G. (2004) 'State Building, Interstate and Intrastate Rivalry: A Study of Post Colonial Developing Country Extractive Efforts, 1975–2000' *International Studies Quarterly* vol. 48 #1 pp. 53–72.
(2005) 'War, Rivalry, and State-Building in Latin America' *American Journal of Political Science* vol. 49 #3 (July) pp. 451–465.

(2006) 'Public Violence and State Building in Central America' *Comparative Political Studies* vol. 39 #10 pp. 1263–1282.

(2007) 'The Political Economy of State Building in Sub-Saharan Africa' *The Journal of Politics* vol. 69 #3 pp. 716–731.

Thomson, Guy P. C. (1990) 'Bulwarks of Patriotic Liberalism: The National Guard, Philharmonic Corps, and Patriotic Juntas in Mexico, 1847–1888' *Journal of Latin American Studies* vol. 22 #1 pp. 31–68.

(1993) 'Los Indios y el Servicio Militar en el México Decimonónico. Leva o Cuidadanía?' in Antonio Escobar Ohmsted, ed. *Indio, Nación, y Comunidad en el México del Siglo XIX* (Mexico, DF: Centro de Estudios Mexicanos y Centroamericanos) pp. 207–251.

with David G. LaFrance (1999) *Patriotism, Politics and Popular Liberalism in 19th Century Mexico* (Wilmington, DE: Scholarly Resources).

Thomson, Ian and Dietrich Angerstein (2000) *Historia del Ferrocarril en Chile* (Santiago: DIBAM).

Thorp, Rosemary, and Geoffrey Bertram (1978) *Peru 1890–1977: Growth and Policy in an Open Economy* (New York: Columbia University Press).

Thurner, Mark (1997) *From Two Republics to One Divided: Contradictions of Postcolonial Nationmaking in Andean Peru* (Durham, NC: Duke University Press).

Tilly, Charles (1975) 'Reflections on the History of European State-Making' in Charles Tilly, ed. *The Formation of National States in Western Europe* (Princeton, NJ: Princeton University Press) pp. 3–83.

(1985) 'State Making as Organized Crime' in Evans, Peter, Dietrich Rueschemeyer, and Theda Skocpol, eds. *Bringing the State Back In* (New York: Cambridge University Press) pp. 169–191.

(1992) *Coercion, Capital, and European States, AD 990–1992* (Cambridge, MA: Blackwell).

Tinker Salas, Miguel (2009) *The Enduring Legacy: Oil, Culture, and Society in Venezuela* (Durham, NC: Duke University Press).

Topik, Steven (1988) 'The Economic Role of the State in Liberal Regimes: Brazil and Mexico Compared, 1888–1910' in Love, Joseph L., and Nils Jacobsen, eds. *Guiding the Invisible Hand: Economic Liberalism and the State in Latin American History* (New York: Praeger) pp. 117–144.

Tutino, John (1986) *From Insurrection to Revolution in Mexico: Social Bases of Agrarian Violence, 1750–1940* (Princeton, NJ: Princeton University Press).

Uhthoff López, Luz María (2004) 'La Difícil Concurrencia Fiscal y la Contribución Federal, 1861–1924: Notas Preliminares' *Historia Mexicana* vol. 54 #1 pp. 129–178.

(2005) 'La Fiscalidad y la Revolución Constitucionalista' in Aguilar, Aboites Luis, and Luis Jáuregui, eds. (2005) *Penuria sin Fin: Historia de los Impuestos en México Siglos XVIII-XX* (Mexico, DF: Instituto Mora), pp. 161–188.

(2003) 'Hacía la Institucionalización de la Hacienda Pública: la Participación de Guillermo Prieto' in Brian F. Connaughton, ed. *Poder y Legitimidad en México en el Siglo XIX: Instituciones y Cultura Política* (Mexico: UNAM) pp. 431–450.

UNDP (2009) *Por una densidad del estado al servicio de la gente.*
Urzúa Valenzuela, German (1970) *Evolución de la Adminstración Pública Chilena, 1818–1968* (Santiago: Editorial Jurídica de Chile).
Valencia Tovar, Álvaro (1993) *Historia de las Fuerzas Militares de Colombia* (Bogotá: Planeta).
Valenzuela, Arturo (n.d.) 'Political Elites in the Chilean Parliamentary Republic' (unpublished manuscript).
 (1977) *Political Brokers in Chile: Local Government in a Centralized Polity* (Durham, NC: Duke University Press).
Vanderwood, Paul J. (1970) 'Genesis of the Rurales: Mexico's Early Struggle for Public Security' *Hispanic American Historical Review* vol. 50 #2, pp. 323–344.
 (1976) 'Response to Revolt: The Counter-Guerrilla Strategy of Porfirio Díaz' *Hispanic American Historical Review* pp. 551–579.
 (1990) 'Explaining the Mexican Revolution' in Jaime Rodriguez O., ed. *The Revolutionary Process in Mexico* (UCLA Latin American Studies Volume 72) pp. 97–114.
 (1998) *The Power of God against the Guns of Government: Religious Upheaval in Mexico at the Turn of the Nineteenth Century* (Stanford, CA: Stanford University Press).
 (1992) *Disorder and Progress: Bandits, Police, and Mexican Development* (Wilmington, DE: SR Books).
Vaughan, Mary Kay (1982) *The State, Education, and Social Class in Mexico, 1880–1928* (DeKalb: Northern Illinois University Press).
 (1987) 'Primary Schooling in the City of Puebla, 1821–1860' *The Hispanic American Historical Review* vol. 67 #1 (February) pp. 39–62.
 (1997) *Cultural Politics in Revolution: Teachers, Peasants, and Schools in Mexico, 1930–1940* (Tempe: University of Arizona Press).
Vázquez, Josefina Zoraida (1967) 'La República Restaurada y la Educación: Un Intento de Victoria Definitiva' *Historia Mexicana* vol. 17 #2 (October–December) pp. 200–211.
Vázquez de Knauth, Josefina ed. (1970) *Nacionalismo y Educación en México* (México, DF: El Colegio de México).
Veliz, Claudio (1980) *The Centralist Tradition in Latin America* (Princeton, NJ: Princeton University Press).
Ventresca, Marc (1995) 'When States Count: Institutional and Political Dynamics in Modern Census Establishment, 1800–1993' (PhD Dissertation, Stanford University).
Vera, Robustiano (1886) *Lei de Régimen Interior de la República de Chile* (Valparaíso, Chile: Imprenta y Librería Americana).
Vergara, Alberto (2012) 'Conflicto regional, estado central, y sociedad periférica en Bolivia y Perú: un análisis histórico comparado' (Ph.D. Dissertation, Université de Montréal Political Science Department).
vom Hau, Matthias (2008) 'State Infrastructural Power and Nationalism: Comparative Lessons from Mexico and Argentina' *Studies in Comparative International Development* vol. 43 #3-4 pp. 334–354.

(2009) 'Unpacking the School: Textbooks, Teachers, and the Construction of Nationhood in Mexico, Argentina, and Peru' *Latin American Research Review* 44: 127–154.

Voss, Stuart F. (1982) *On the Periphery of Nineteenth Century Mexico: Sonora and Sinaloa, 1810–1877* (Tucson: University of Arizona Press).

Vu, Tuong (2010) 'Studying the State through State Formation' *World Politics* vol. 62 #1 pp. 148–175.

Wagner, Gert, José Jofré, and Rolf Lüders (2000) 'Economía Chilena 1810–1995: Cuentas Fiscales' Documento de Trabajo #188, Instituto de Economía, Universidad Católica (Santiago, Chile).

Waldner, David (1999) *State Building and Late Development* (Ithaca, NY: Cornell University Press).

Walker, Charles F. (1999) *Smoldering Ashes: Cuzco and the Creation of Republican Peru, 1780–1840* (Durham, NC: Duke University Press).

Weber, Eugen (1976) *Peasants into Frenchmen: The Modernization of Rural France, 1870–1914* (Stanford, CA: Stanford University Press).

Weber, Max (1958) 'Politics as a Vocation' in Gerth, H. H. and C. Wright Mills, eds. *From Max Weber: Essays in Sociology* (New York: Oxford University Press) pp. 77–128.

Winters, Jeffrey A. (2011) *Oligarchy* (New York: Cambridge University Press).

Woll, Allen A. (1975) 'For God or Country: Historical Textbooks and the Secularization of Chilean Society, 1840–1890' *Journal of Latin American Studies* 7 pp. 23–43.

Womack, John Jr. (1986) 'The Mexican Revolution, 1910–1920' in Leslie Bethell, ed. *The Cambridge History of Latin America, Vol. V, c.1870–1930* (New York: Cambridge University Press) pp. 79–154.

Woods, Ngaire (1995) 'Economic Ideas and International Relations: Beyond Rational Neglect' *International Studies Quarterly* vol. 39 #2 (June) pp. 161–180.

Wright, Thomas C. (1973) 'Origins of the Politics of Inflation in Chile, 1888–1918' *The Hispanic American Historical Review* vol. 53 #2 (May) pp. 239–259.

Yashar, Deborah (2005) *Contesting Citizenship in Latin America: The Rise of Indigenous Movements and the Post-Liberal Challenge* (Princeton, NJ: Princeton University Press).

Yeager, Gertrude M. (1983) 'Women's Roles in Nineteenth Century Chile: Public Education Records, 1843–1883' *Latin American Research Review* vol. 18 #3 pp. 149–156.

(2005) 'Religion, Gender Ideology, and the Training of Female Public Elementary School Teachers in 19th Century Chile.' *The Americas* vol. 62 #2 pp. 209–243.

Young, Crawford (1994) *The African Colonial State in Comparative Perspective* (New Haven, CT: Yale University Press).

Zeitlin, Maurice (1984) *The Civil Wars in Chile (Or the Bourgeois Revolutions That Never Were)* (Princeton, NJ: Princeton University Press).

Ziblatt, Daniel (2006) *Structuring the State: The Formation of Italy and Germany and the Puzzle of Federalism* (Princeton, NJ: Princeton University Press).

Zipf, George K. (1941) *National Unity and Disunity* (Bloomington, IN: Principia Press).

Zuleta, María Cecilia (2003) 'De Viejos y Nuevos Impuestos: El Estado y Los Contribuyentes Frente a la Abolición de las Alcábalas en México a Finales del Siglo XIX' in Brian F. Connaughton, ed. *Poder y Legitimidad en México en el Siglo XIX: Instituciones y Cultura Política* (Mexico: UNAM) pp. 451–496.

Zuleta, María Cecilia (2004) 'Hacienda Pública y Exportación Henequenera en Yucatán, 1880–1910' *Historia Mexicana* vol. 54 #1 pp. 179–247.

Index

Abente, Diego, 243
accommodationist ideology, in guano era, 118–19
Adelman, Jeremy, 95n8
administration, 82–6, 180, 180n19, 181. *See also* delegated rule; deployed rule; tax administration; territorial administration
administrative appointments. *See* appointments
administrative institutions, 61–82, 62–5
administrative patronage. *See* patronage
administrative reforms, of *timbre*, 197
administrative slippage, 64n6
administrators, 154–5, 184–5
Africa, 85, 258
African states, 7, 21
agents, 61n2, 62. *See also* state agents
agiotistas (loan providers), 102
agricultural properties, rolls of, 188n29
agriculture, of Chile, 111–12
Alberdi, Juan Bautista, 238
Albertus, Michael, 27n2
alcábala (excise tax), 100, 100n9, 101, 199–200, 199n38
Alesina, Alberto, 33n9
Alessandri, Jorge, 249

Amazon, 30, 31–2, 32n7
American Civil War, 33
Ancash, Peru, 183
Antioquia, Colombia, 44
anti-statist consensus, 52–5, 253
anti-statist vision of development. *See* laissez-faire vision of development
anti-traditional ideology, 116–18, 119–20
Antofagasta, Chile, 240–1
Anuarios Estadísticos, 48
appointment decrees, 66–70, 66n8, 77–8
appointments, 60–1. *See also* deployed appointments
  central government controlling, 74
  in Chile, 71n10, 71n13, 74–5, 109–13
  decree analysis, 66–70, 66n8
  as delegated, 71n12
  in Mexico, 71n10, 113–14
  national projects influencing, 116–20
  of outsiders, 81
  overview of, 107–23
  patronage influencing, 120–3
  perceived threats influencing, 107, 108–16
  in Peru, 71n10, 71n13, 114–16

291

appointments (*cont.*)
  in political biographies, 71–4
  practices, 107–23
  qualitative evidence shedding light on, 74–82
  refusals of, 76–7
  traditional authority influencing, 116–20
Araucana, 48–9
Araucanía, 48–9, 111
El Araucano, 66, 66n8
Arequipa, Peru, 40, 78
Argentina, 37, 110, 209, 223, 237–9, 246–8
  central state authority in, 238n2
Aristocratic Republic (Peru), 3n5, 17, 52, 79–80, 144–7
  deployed rule in, 68, 86
  military in, 229
  schools in, 130
armies. *See also* mobilization capacity; recruitment
  of Chile, 111, 112, 222–3
  of Colombia, 211–14
  independence, 95
  of Mexico, 227
  of Peru, 106, 227–9
  war influencing size of, 206, 206n1, 206n2
assimilation, 48–9, 51, 111n20
Atlantic coast, 42
Atsuparia uprising, 183, 183n20
authority, 64–5. *See also* traditional authority
Ayacucho, Peru, 228

Baja California, Mexico, 130
Balmaceda (president), 208, 223
banditry, in Chile, 103, 109–10, 111n21
Barnett, Michael, 258
Barranquilla, Colombia, 42
Basadre, Jorge, 99
Bates, Robert H., 255
Batlle administrations, Uruguay, 239
Battle of Ayacucho, 95
Battle of Boyacá, 95
Battle of Lircay, 103
Bauer, Arnold, 39, 74, 113n24
Bazant, Mílada, 132
Belize, 245n4
bellic approach, 27, 204–6
Bengoa, José, 109
Bergquist, Charles W., 230
Berman, Sheri, 56
Bertram, Geoffrey, 76n16
Blancos, Uruguay, 239
Bobrow-Strain, Aaron, 81–2, 195n33
Bogotá, Colombia, 41, 43, 91
Bolívar, Simón, 95
Bolivia, 1, 2, 71n13, 145, 240–1. *See also* War of the Pacific
  capital city of, 33n9
  Chile's war with, 207, 209
Boucoyannis, Deborah, 256n9
Bourbon Reforms, 82, 89–94, 89n2
Boyacá, Colombia, 42
Brazil, 239
British Empire, 85, 88
British Honduras, 220
Britton, John A., 140n15
Brownlee, Jason A., 260, 261n12
Buenaventura, Colombia, 42
Buenos Aires, Argentina, 37, 237–8, 248
Búlnes, Chile, 191
bureaucracies, 61n2, 80–2, 83, 248
bureaucratic appointments. *See* appointments
bureaucratic networks, 83–4
bureaucratic professionalism, 2n4
bureaucratic quality, 60
bureaucrats, 60–1, 141, 196. *See also* appointments; authority; deployed bureaucrats; officials; state agents
Bushnell, David, 53, 55

cacao, 42n16
Cáceres, Andrés Avelino, 144
Cáceres government, Peru, 78, 119–20, 182
Callao, Peru, 35, 37, 40, 106
Camp, Roderic Ai, 71–2, 71n9

Index

capital city, 33n9
Caracas, Venezuela, 243, 244–5
career politicians, 78–9
Carmagnani, Marcello, 199–200
Cartagena, Colombia, 42
Casanare, Colombia, 98, 177–8
case studies, 15–17
Caste War, 105
Castilla, Ramón, 51, 211
Castro, Cipriano, 244–5
catastro (real estate tax), 100
Catholic Church, 130–1, 135–6
cattle slaughter tax. *See degüello* (cattle slaughter) tax
Cauca, 42, 43, 53
caudillismo, 238n2
caudillos, 117–18, 211
Caupolicán, Chile, 141
causal mechanisms, 62–5
censuses, 1–2, 13–14, 14n16, 80, 148. *See also* education census of 1902, in Peru
  in Chile, 98
  of Peru, 40, 145–6
  of schools, 98
Centeno, Miguel, 6–7, 18, 204, 206, 206n1
Central America, 245–6
central state
  authority, 25, 238n2
  oversight capacity of, 63n3
Chachapoyas, Peru, 76n16
Chaudhry, Kiren Aziz, 179n16
Chiapas, Mexico, 81–2, 195n33
Chihuahua, Mexico, 220
Chile. *See also* Mapuche; National Guard; nitrates; War of the Pacific
  agriculture of, 111–12
  appointment decrees, 66–70, 66n8, 77–8
  appointments in, 71n10, 71n13, 74–5, 109–13
  army of, 111, 112, 222–3
  assimilation in, 111n20
  banditry in, 103, 109–10, 111n21
  Bolivia's war with, 207, 209
  Bourbon Reforms influencing, 90–1
  bureaucratic networks in, 83–4
  bureaucrats in, 141, 189, 190–1, 222
  Catholic Church in, 136
  census in, 98
  civil war in, 111, 111n21, 111n22, 208–9, 223
  clearly deployed appointments in, 68, 69, 70
  commodity booms influencing, 158–9
  commodity busts influencing, 158–9
  conscription in, 203, 222–4
  constitution of, 98
  curriculum in, 132
  decentralization in, 187–8, 187n24
  deployed bureaucrats in, 124–5
  deployed rule in, 73–4, 73n14, 77–8, 86, 113, 186–92, 195, 222–4
  education in, 98, 124–5, 138–40, 156–7
  elites in, 75, 103–4, 110, 112–13, 224, 224n14
  extractive capacity of, 158, 163–4, 188–9
  governors in, 189, 190, 191
  guerrilla warfare in, 96, 103, 109–10, 111–13
  independence of, 94–5
  inequality in, 140n14
  infrastructure development of, 31
  insurrection in, 111
  intendants in, 84
  internal taxation in, 165, 191–2
  literacy in, 250–1
  military of, 222–4
  mobilization capacity of, 207–9, 220–1
  monopoly of force in, 103–4, 223
  municipal taxation in, 173–4, 187–8
  nitrates influencing, 164–5, 172–3, 191–2
  perceived threats to, 109–13
  Peru invaded by, 181–2
  Peru's war with, 207, 209

Chile (*cont.*)
  political biographies of, 72–3
  in post-independence crisis, 98, 100, 103–4
  primary schools in, 127, 128–9
  school inspection in, 133, 140–3
  school materials in, 131–2
  schools in, 124–5, 129n4, 129n5
  state leaders in, 6, 124–5, 139–40
  state strength of, 111n20
  systemic stability in, 109–13
  tax burden in, 172–4
  tax state development in, 181, 195
  tax types in, 163–5
  taxation in, 100, 180, 186–92
  teachers in, 130, 141
  terrain of, 31
  territorial administration in, 63n5, 84
  textbooks in, 131, 131n7
  threat defense of, 203
  uprising in, 111
  urban primacy in, 38–9
  violence in, 109–13
  war and, 18, 52
Chiloé, Chile, 98, 141
Chowning, Margaret, 118, 153n23, 155
Christie, Keith H., 41
Chuquisaca, Bolivia, 2
church-state relations, 47, 48
Cisneros, Pedro, 146n20
civil service reform, 84
civil wars, 33, 38, 74. *See also* mobilization capacity
  in Chile, 111, 111n21, 111n22, 208–9, 223
  in Colombia, 43, 53–4, 94–5, 212–13
  in Uruguay, 239
Civilista era, Peru, 52, 116, 119
Civilista governments, Peru, 146–7
Civilistas, Peru, 78–80, 119–20, 120n29, 122–3, 167–8
civilization, 46–8, 52–5
CNR. *See* Compañía Nacional de Recaudación (CNR)

Coatsworth, John, 50, 105n14, 138n12
coercive capacity, 202–4, 214–20, 215n11, 221–2, 230–1. *See also* conscription; mobilization capacity
coffee, 42n16, 44
Colombia. *See also* liberal reforms; War of 1000 Days
  anti-statist consensus of, 52–5, 253
  army of, 211–14
  Bourbon Reforms influencing, 91–2
  Catholic Church in, 130–1, 135–6
  civil war in, 43, 53–4, 94–5, 212–13
  civilization in, 52–5
  coercive capacity of, 221–2
  coffee in, 44
  commodity booms in, 44–5
  conflict in, 104
  conscription in, 203–4
  Conservatives in, 52–3, 55
  constitution of, 53–5
  curriculum in, 132
  development in, 44–5, 52–5, 137
  direct taxes in, 194
  divergent preferences in, 42–4
  education in, 98, 124, 134–7, 156, 156n25
  elites in, 52–3, 104, 137, 229–30
  extractive capacity of, 158
  federalism in, 193
  guerrilla warfare in, 96, 214
  independence of, 94–5
  laissez-faire in, 53–5, 135n10, 180n17, 193–5
  Liberals in, 52–3, 55, 211–12
  literacy in, 250–1
  mandatory schooling in, 134–7
  mobilization capacity of, 211–14, 212n9, 212n10
  monopoly of force in, 104
  national government of, 53–5
  in post-independence crisis, 98, 100–1, 104
  public works in, 43–4
  railroads in, 43–4, 45
  rebellion in, 53–4

Index

recruitment in, 229–30, 229n15
regions of, 42–5, 42n14
revenue reforms in, 194–5, 194n32
revolts in, 91
school inspection in, 133
school materials in, 132
schools in, 98, 127–30
self-sufficient regions in, 44–5
state leaders in, 124
state weakness of, 124, 221–2
tax burden in, 177–8
tax state development in, 159–60, 193
tax types in, 168–70
taxation in, 100–1, 180n17, 193–5
teachers in, 130–1
textbooks in, 132
threat defense of, 203, 212
transport in, 55
uprisings in, 212–13
urban primacy in, 41–6, 41n12
war in, 52–3, 55
weapons in, 213
colonial impact, mechanisms of, 88–9
colonial legacies, 88–94. *See also* Bourbon Reforms
colonial political institutions, 91n3
colonial rule, 65n7, 89–94, 261. *See also* Japanese colonial rule
Colorados, Uruguay, 239
commodity booms, 44–5, 158–9, 179n15. *See also* nitrates
commodity busts, 158–9
Compañia Lancasteriana, 99
Compañia Nacional de Recaudación (CNR), 79–80, 185–6, 185n23
Comunero Rebellion, Colombia, 91
Concepción, Chile, 38, 71n12
Concordato, 136
conscription, 11, 79, 203–4, 221, 222–4, 227–9. *See also* mobilization
conscription exemption tax. *See contribución de rebajadas* (conscription exemption tax)
conservatives, 49, 52–3, 55, 114
constitution, 53–5, 98, 99, 117, 244

Constitutional Congress, 117
Constitutional Convention, 41
consumption taxes, 184–5
Contreras, Carlos, 75, 79n19, 83, 83n20, 146n20
contribución de rebajadas (conscription exemption tax), 225
contribución federal, 171–2
contribución indígena (head tax), 85n21, 100, 101, 102–3, 103n13, 165
collections, 183n22
failure of, 182–4
Copiapó, Chile, 38
Coquimbo, Chile, 188n30
Córdoba, Colombia, 2
cost structure, state leaders influenced by, 21
Costa Rica, 245–6
costs of state building, 25–7, 254, 255
Cristero War, Mexico, 249
Cundinamarca, Colombia, 41, 42
currency of patronage, 107–8, 120–3
curriculum, 132, 146
customary law, 60, 85–6, 85n22
customs duties, 102, 170–2
Cuzco, Peru, 115, 228

Dargent, Eduardo, 2n4
Davies, Thomas, 254, 256n11
de Ramón, Armando, 71n9, 72–3
Deas, Malcolm, 41n12, 169, 177, 194n32, 195, 221, 229n16
decentralization, 187–8, 187n24, 189, 190–1
decentralization law, 174n13
degüello (cattle slaughter) tax, 169
DeHart, Evelyn Hu, 153n23, 154
delegated appointments, 71n12
delegated rule, 62–82, 107–8, 121, 221
administrative slippage under, 64n6
deployed rule compared with, 62–82
in Peru, 116, 227–9
state leaders choosing, 87–8, 108

Index

Dellepiane, Carlos, 210n7, 211n8
Delpar, Helen, 229n15
department heads. *See jefes de departamento* (department heads)
deployed appointments, 67–70, 78
deployed bureaucrats, 22, 63–4, 124–5
deployed rule, 107–8, 107n17
   administrative slippage under, 64n6
   in Argentina, 246–8
   in Aristocratic Republic (Peru), 68, 79–80, 86, 144–7
   in Chile, 73–4, 73n14, 77–8, 86, 113, 186–92, 195, 222–4
   definition of, 62
   delegated rule compared with, 62–82
   educational development influenced by, 155
   extractive capacity and, 188–9
   in Liberal Mexico, 120
   in Mexico, 73–4, 73n14, 80–2, 86, 115–16, 118, 195–200, 226–7
   in Peru, 73–4, 73n14, 75–80, 86, 116, 120, 125
   in Porfirian Mexico, 120, 121–2
   state agents influenced by, 142
   state leaders choosing, 87–8, 108–9
   state-development efforts influenced by, 124–5
deputy governor, in Peru, 83–4
Desaguadero, Peru, 145
desertions, 222, 227
Deustua, Alejandro, 144–5
development, in Colombia, 44–5, 52–5, 137
Diario Oficial, 66n8
Díaz, Porfirio, 81, 118, 121, 204, 217–18
Díaz regime, 154, 218–19. *See also* Porfiriato
diezmo (tithe), 100
direct rule, in British Empire, 88
direct taxes, 167–8, 167n7, 194
domestic manufactured goods tax. *See renta interior* (domestic manufactured goods tax)

domestic threats, 18
Domínguez, Jorge I., 93
Domschke, Elaine, 13–14
Downing, Brian, 7, 21, 257
Dunning, Thad, 179–80
Dutch Republic, 21–2, 257

Eastern Cordillera, Colombia, 42
Eaton, Kent, 187
Ecuador, 1, 33, 229, 241–2
education, 10, 71n12. *See also* primary schooling; primary schools; public primary schooling; schools; textbooks
   in Chile, 98, 124–5, 138–40, 156–7
   in Colombia, 98, 124, 134–7, 156, 156n25
   in Mexico, 99, 124, 125–6, 138–40, 147–56, 157
   in Peru, 99, 124, 125, 138–40, 143–7
education census of 1902, in Peru, 145–6
education development. *See also* school inspection
   in Chile, 156–7
   in Colombia, 156, 156n25
   deployed rule influencing, 155
   dimensions, 126–7
   indicators, 126–7
   inequality and, 138–40
   in Mexico, 147–56, 157
   overview of, 156–7
   in Peru, 157
   during post-independence crisis, 97–103
   social conditions influencing, 125–6
   state agents and, 142–3
Education Ministry, 140–1, 143
Egaña Baraona, Maria Loreto, 130n6, 142
El Salvador, 245
elected offices, 121
elite preferences, in Mexico, 151
elites, 4–5, 65n7, 232–3, 234n1. *See also* landowners, in Mexico; patronage

Index

administrators' conflict with, 154–5
appointments influenced by, 75
in Argentina, 247–8
in Aristocratic Republic, 144–5
in Bolivia, 240–1
in Chile, 75, 103–4, 110, 112–13, 224, 224n14
in Colombia, 52–3, 104, 137, 229–30
in guano era, 118–19
ideas influencing, 24–5
in Mexico, 49–50, 81, 114, 116–18, 153–6, 195n33
in Peru, 51–2, 75–80, 76n16, 78–80, 119–20, 122–3, 146–7, 183n21, 227–8
state leaders' coalitions with, 261–2
state leaders excluding, 22
tax administration in hands of, 195n33
Encina, Francisco A., 98
Engerman, Stanley, 138n12, 140n15
England, 21–2, 257
enlistment, 224–7
Ertman, Thomas, 7, 256–7
Europe, 6–7, 18, 34n10, 48, 254, 258
excise tax. *See* alcábala (excise tax)
expert bureaucracies, 248
extractive capacity of states, 158, 163–4, 188–9

Falleti, Tulia G., 187n24
Fearon, James, 27n2
Federal District, Mexico, 131, 134, 147
federal government, of Mexico, 199–200, 199n38
federal taxation, Mexico, 195–200
Federal Wars, 244
federalism, 159, 193
finance, 96, 102
flour exports, 39
forced enlistment. *See* leva (forced enlistment)
forced loans, 102n11
forcible impressment, 225–6
foundational wars, 94–6
Fowler, Will, 104–5

France, 257
French Intervention, 49, 225
Fukuyama, Francis, 10n10
functionalism, 21, 258

Gaitán, Jorge Eliecer, 249
geography, 4–5, 17, 20, 25–45. *See also* urban primacy
Germany, 261n12
Gingerich, Daniel W., 2n4
Goldstein, Judith, 46n18
González-Cueva, Eduardo, 229
Gootenberg, Paul, 40, 51n21, 102n12, 115n26, 119
Gorski, Philip S., 7
Government Effectiveness, 13n15
governors
 in Argentina, 247
 in Chile, 189, 190, 191
 decentralization criticized by, 190
 in Mexico, 80–2, 121–2, 154, 155, 156
 in Peru, 75, 83–4
Goyer, Doreen, 13–14
Granada, Nicaragua, 245
Great Depression, 249–50
Guanajuato, Mexico, 93
guano, 5, 78, 86, 115n26, 158–9, 180n18
 Peru influenced by, 165–7
 taxation after boom of, 181–6
guano era, 51n21, 116, 118–19, 120, 121, 174–5
Guatemala, 245–6
Guayana, Venezuela, 244
Guayaquil, Ecuador, 33, 241–2
Guerra a Muerte (War to the Death), 96, 109
guerrilla warfare, 96, 103, 109–10, 111–13, 214, 218–20. *See also* Sendero Luminoso

Haber, Stephen, 118
haciendas, 116–17
Hale, Charles A., 117
Hall, Peter A., 46n18
Hamnett, Brian R., 95n8

Hanson, Jonathan, 10n9
head tax. *See contribución indígena* (head tax)
health, 77
HEC. *See Historia del Ejército Chileno* (HEC)
Hechter, Michael, 62
Helg, Aline, 130, 133, 135
Herbst, Jeffrey, 7, 21, 27, 32n6, 32n8, 85, 255, 257, 258
Hernández Chávez, Alicia, 215
Herr, Pilar M., 110n18
Herwig, Holder H., 209, 223–4
Hidalgo revolt, Mexico, 94
high modernist vision, 254–5
highlands, 43n17
Hilario López, José, 135, 193–4
Historia del Ejército Chileno (HEC), 207n4
Holden, Robert H., 198n37
homicide rate, 2
Honda, Colombia, 43
Honduras, 246
Huancané revolt, Peru, 51
Huanta, Peru, 96, 106, 114n25
Huaraz, Peru, 183, 183n22
Huaylas region, Peru, 75n15
Huerta, Victoriano, 227
Hünefeldt, Christine, 103n13
Hutchcroft, Paul D., 261

Ica, Peru, 76–7
ideas, 19–20, 24–5, 46–55, 46n18, 56–8, 252–5
ideology, in Porfirian Mexico, 118. *See also* accommodationist ideology, in guano era; anti-traditional ideology
illiteracy, 1
immunizations, 2n3
impuesto de haberes, 188–9, 191
impuesto de mercados, 188
independence, 94–6, 105. *See also* post-independence crisis
indigenous authorities, 85
indigenous population, 51, 114–15, 115n26, 144–5. *See also* Araucana

indirect rule, 85–6, 85n21, 183n21
inequality, 138–40, 140n14, 151
infrastructural power, of states, 204–6. *See also* Mann, Michael; state capacity; state power; state strength
inspection. *See* school inspection
inspectors (*inspectores*), 83–4, 141–3, 145, 196
institutional capacity, 2n4
institutional change, in Peru, 143–7
insurgency, 30, 218–20
insurrection, in Chile, 111
insurrectionary leaders, 74
intendancy, 90
intendants, 84
internal taxation, 165, 170–2, 191–2
International Road Federation World Road Statistics, 11n14
international threats, 18
intra-regional variation, 6–9
Iquitos, Peru, 31
Iturbide, Agustín, 95–6

Jackson, Robert H., 257
Jacobsen, Nils, 92n4
Jalisco, Mexico, 153n24
Japan, 261n12
Japanese colonial rule, 88–9
Jauja, Peru, 40
jefes de departamento (department heads), 78–9
jefes de provincia (provincial chiefs), 78–9
jefes políticos (political leaders), 81, 204, 226
Jesuits, 89n2
Juárez, Benito, 121, 216–17
jungles, 27n2, 30, 31, 32n7
Junguito, Roberto, 194n32

Kaplan, Oliver, 27n2
Karl, Terry Lynn, 180n19
Kaufman, Herbert, 61n2
Keohane, Robert, 46n18
Kim, Diana, 255n8, 261n13
Klarén, Peter, 102n12

Index

Knight, Alan, 93, 118, 122
Kohli, Atul, 88–9
Kurtz, Marcus J., 7, 8, 8n7, 9, 13n15, 19, 224n14, 239

La Guajira, Colombia, 2
La Paz, Bolivia, 240
laissez-faire, in Colombia, 53–5, 135n10, 180n17, 193–5
laissez-faire vision of development, 26
Laitin, David, 27n2
landowners, in Mexico, 81–2, 116–17
Lange, Matthew, 85, 88
Larson, Brooke, 51
LaTorre, Lorenzo, 239
laws, 174n13, 213. *See also* customary law
legal sentence, conscription by, 225–6
legitimacy, 64–5
León, Nicaragua, 245
Letelier, Valentin, 84
leva (forced enlistment), 224
Levi, Margaret, 203
Ley de Caminos, 43
Ley de Comuna Autónoma (Municipal Autonomy Law), 187
Ley de Régimen Interior, 84
Liberal era, end of, 249–52
Liberal Mexico, 116–18, 120, 253
liberal reforms, 46n19, 49–50, 168
liberalism, 46–8
liberals, 52–3, 55, 119n27, 131, 211–12. *See also* Liberal Mexico
Liberals, 85n21, 114, 147, 214
liberum veto, Poland, 21
Lieberman, Evan S., 160, 162n2
Lima, Peru, 31, 35, 37, 40–1, 76, 80, 129, 131, 181–2, 210–11
literacy, 2, 11n13, 148, 151, 250–1
Llanos, Colombia, 95, 177
loan providers. *See agiotistas* (loan providers)
loans, 102, 102n11
local officials, military recruitment and, 220–30
logrolling, 43
López Pumarejo, Alfonso, 194

López-Alves, Fernando, 7
Los Angeles, Chile, 111
Lustick, Ian, 21n19

Macaulay, Neill, 53
Macías Richard, Carlos, 220n13
Madero revolt, 220, 227
Magdalena River, 42, 43, 43n17, 45
Mahoney, James, 8n7, 15, 88, 246
Mainwaring, Scott, 11n12
Malinowski, Ernest, 51
Malloa, Chile, 188n29
Mallon, Florencia, 92n4, 92n5, 114–15
Mamalakis, Markos J., 100n9, 163n4, 174n12
Managua, Nicaragua, 245
mandatory schooling, in Colombia, 134–7
Mann, Michael, 9, 9n8, 10, 183
Mapuche, 109, 110–13. *See also* War to the Death
Maracaibo, Venezuela, 42n16, 244
Mariscal, Elisa, 138n12, 139, 140n14, 140n15, 151n22
Martínez Moya, Armando, 153n24
McEvoy, Carmen, 51n22, 119n28
McGreevey, William P., 212, 214
medical officials. *See médicos titulares* (medical officials)
médicos titulares (medical officials), 77
Meltzer-Richard model, 138n13
Méndez, Cecilia, 106n16
Mexican Porfiriato. *See* Porfiriato
Mexican Revolution, 220
Mexican-American War, 105
Mexico. *See also* Liberal Mexico; National Guard; Porfiriato; Restored Republic
administrators in, 154–5
appointments in, 71n10, 113–14
army of, 227
Bourbon Reforms influencing, 92–4
bureaucracy of, 80–2, 83
bureaucrats in, 196
coercive capacity of, 214–20, 215n11

Mexico (*cont.*)
  conflict in, 117
  conscription in, 204
  Conservatives in, 49
  constitution of, 117
  cross-state variation in, 147–56
  customs duties in, 170–2
  deployed rule in, 73–4, 73n14, 80–2, 86, 115–16, 118, 195–200, 226–7
  education in, 99, 124, 125–6, 138–40, 147–56, 157
  elite preferences in, 151
  elites in, 49–50, 81, 114, 116–18, 153–6, 195n33
  enlistment in, 224–7
  extractive capacity of, 158
  federal government of, 199–200, 199n38
  federalism in, 193
  governors in, 80–2, 121–2, 154, 155, 156
  guerrilla warfare in, 218–20
  independence achieved in, 95–6
  intendancy in, 90
  internal taxation in, 170–2
  landowners in, 81–2, 116–17
  liberal reforms in, 49–50
  Liberals in, 131, 147
  literacy in, 148, 151
  loans of, 102
  mobilization capacity of, 214–20, 221
  monopoly of force in, 104–5
  national government of, 81
  order in, 49–50
  patronage in, 121–2
  peasants in, 105, 113–14
  perceived threats to, 113–14
  political biographies of, 71–2
  Porfirian regime in, 50
  in post-independence crisis, 99, 101–2, 104–5, 106–7
  progress in, 49–50
  railroads in, 50
  recruitment in, 224–7
  revolts in, 49, 93, 94, 94n7, 105, 105n15, 113–14, 227
  revolution in, 130, 220, 249
  school enrollment in, 148, 151, 151n22
  school inspection in, 133–4
  schools in, 99, 127, 128–9
  spending of, 151n22
  state leaders in, 6, 113, 139, 140
  states of, 199–200
  structural inequality in, 151
  systemic stability in, 113–14
  tax burden in, 178–9
  tax collectors in, 195
  tax state development in, 159–60, 193
  tax types in, 170–2
  taxation in, 100, 101–2, 193, 195–200
  teachers in, 131
  textbooks in, 132–3
  urban primacy in, 38, 39–40, 41
  urbanization in, 151
  U.S.'s war with, 215n11, 224
  wars of, 101, 105, 215n11, 224, 249
México, Mexico, 134
Mexico City, Mexico, 39–40, 50, 81, 99
Michoacán, Mexico, 148, 153–4, 155–6
mid-century liberalism, 46–8
Migdal, Joel, 60, 66
military, 222–4, 227–9, 242–3. *See also* armies; coercive capacity; conscription; enlistment; mobilization capacity; recruitment
military mobilization. *See* mobilization
military recruitment, 220–30, 221
Milla Batres, Carlos, 71n9, 72
mining, 240–1
Mitre, Bartolomé, 238
mobilization, 11n12
mobilization capacity, 206–21, 212n9, 212n10, 230–1

Index

Molina, Iván, 140n1
monopolies
　salt, 169, 184
　tobacco, 90, 93n6, 100, 101, 168
monopoly of force, 103–7, 223
Morelos, Mexico, 122
mountainous terrain, 27n2, 30–1
Muecke, Ulrich, 76, 119, 122
Municipal Autonomy Law. *See Ley de Comuna Autónoma* (Municipal Autonomy Law)
municipal taxation, in Chile, 173–4, 187–8

Napoleonic Wars, 95
nation building, 260–2
national council of nobles. *See sejm*, Poland (national council of nobles)
National Guard, 209, 209n5, 216–17, 224–5
national projects, 116–20, 119n28
nationalism, 95n8
naval vessels, 96
negotiation, 59–60
Neufeld, Stephen, 218, 224, 226
New Granada. *See* Colombia
New Spain. *See* Mexico
Newland, Carlos, 128–9
Nicaragua, 245, 246
nitrates, 158–9, 164–5, 172–3, 186–92, 191–2
Nugent, David, 76n16, 76n17, 84, 122, 184, 185
Núñez, Rafael, 54, 55, 212, 213
Nunn, Nathan, 27n2

O'Donnell, Guillermo, 9
officials, 65, 75n15. *See also* appointments; bureaucrats; delegated rule; deployed rule; local officials, military recruitment and; medical officials; state agents
O'Higgins, Bernardo, 110–11
oil boom, 32
opportunities as motive for state building, 18–20

Palacios, Marco, 41
Palmer, David Scott, 88
Palmer, Steven, 140n1
Palonegro battle, 214
Panama, 41, 53, 214, 245n4
Pando, Bolivia, 2
Paraguay, 238, 238n2, 242–3, 259
Pardo, Manuel, 51, 51n22, 119, 146
Pardo administration, Peru, 132
Paredes, Maritza, 7–8, 180n18, 241
Park, James William, 42n13, 168n9
Pasco, Peru, 76–7
passports, 115
Pasto, Colombia, 96
Pastore, Mario, 242
Patria Boba, Colombia, 95–6
patrimonialism, in administration, 82–3
patronage, 107–8, 120–3
peasants, 105, 105n15, 113–14
perceived threats, 107, 108–16
Perry, Laurens Ballard, 121
Peru. *See also* Aristocratic Republic (Peru); Civilista era, Peru; Civilistas Peru; Civilistas; guano; guano era; head tax; War of the Pacific
　anti-traditional ideology in, 119–20
　appointments in, 71n10, 71n13, 114–16
　army of, 106, 227–9
　Bourbon Reforms influencing, 92
　bureaucratic networks in, 83–4
　Catholic Church in, 136
　census of, 40, 145–6
　Chile invading, 181–2
　Chile's war with, 207, 209
　clearly deployed appointments in, 68–70, 78
　commodity booms influencing, 158–9
　commodity busts influencing, 158–9
　conscription in, 203, 227–9
　constitution of, 99
　consumption taxes in, 184–5
　curriculum in, 132, 146
　customs duties used by, 102

Peru (cont.)
  decree analysis, 66–70, 66n8
  decrees in, 77–8
  delegated rule in, 116, 227–9
  deployed rule in, 73–4, 73n14, 75–80, 86, 116, 120, 125
  deputy governor in, 83–4
  direct taxes in, 167–8, 167n7
  education development in, 157
  education in, 99, 124, 125, 138–40, 143–7
  elites in, 51–2, 75–80, 76n16, 78–80, 119–20, 122–3, 146–7, 183n21, 227–8
  extractive capacity of, 158
  finance used by, 102
  governors in, 75, 83–4
  guano influencing, 165–7
  independence of, 96
  indigenous population of, 114–15, 115n26, 144–5
  indirect rule in, 183n21
  institutional change in, 143–7
  intendancy in, 90
  liberals in, 119n27
  military of, 227–9
  military recruitment in, 221
  mobilization capacity of, 209–11, 221
  monopoly of force in, 105–7
  patronage in, 122–3
  perceived threats to, 114–16
  political biographies of, 72
  in post-independence crisis, 99, 102–3, 105–7
  primary schools in, 145–6
  progress in, 51–2, 119n27
  railroads in, 51
  rebellion in, 96, 106
  reforms in, 78–80
  refusals in, 76–7
  regions in, 40–1
  revolts in, 51, 91, 92, 92n4, 94, 114–15, 184–5
  school inspection in, 133, 145
  schools in, 99, 127–9, 130
  Spain's war with, 209n6
  state agents in, 181–6
  state in, 51–2
  state leaders in, 6, 139, 140
  state weakness of, 182, 222
  systemic stability in, 114–16
  tax burden in, 174–7
  tax reform in, 185–6
  tax state development in, 181–6
  tax types in, 165–7, 167–8
  taxation in, 100, 102–3, 180
  teachers in, 131
  territorial administration in, 63n5, 84
  textbooks in, 132, 146
  uprising in, 183, 183n20
  urban primacy in, 38, 40–1
  war and, 18, 52, 209–11
El Peruano, 66, 66n8, 75, 76n18, 77, 78
Petorca, Chile, 190
Philippines, 65n7
Piérola, Nicolás de, 120, 144, 145–6, 184
Pincheira brothers, 103, 109
Pittman, Dewitt Kenneth, 122
Poland, 21–2
policy instruments, ideas as, 46n18
political biographies, 71–4
political costs, 179–80, 181–2
political leaders. See jefes políticos (political leaders)
political patronage. See patronage
polycephalic population distribution, 35, 37
population, 34–7, 34n11. See also censuses
Porfirian Mexico, 118, 120, 121–2, 220
Porfirian regime, 50
Porfirians, 81–2
Porfiriato, 81, 116, 132–3, 154
Portales, Diego, 104
Posada-Carbó, Eduardo, 42n14, 104
positional authority, 64–5
post-independence crisis, 96–107
Potosí, Bolivia, 240
power, 64–5, 120. See also state power
prefectoralism, 62

Index 303

press-gangs, 223
primary schools, 127, 128–9, 145–6
progress, 46–50, 51–2, 119n27, 137
protector de escuela (school overseer), 141
provincial chiefs. See *jefes de provincia* (provincial chiefs)
Prussia, 257
public administration. See administration
public goods, provision of, 33–4
public primary schooling, 126–34, 137, 151, 250
public works, in Colombia, 43–4
Puebla, Mexico, 99
Puga, Diego, 27n2
Puno, Peru, 76n18, 92

quasi-voluntary compliance, 203
Quito, Ecuador, 33, 241

railroads, 39, 43–4, 43n17, 45, 50, 51, 240–1
Ramírez, María Teresa, 134
real estate tax. See *catastro* (real estate tax)
rebellion, 53–4, 96, 106
recruitment, 224–7, 229–30, 229n15
Reform War, Mexico, 49
reforms, 46n19, 78–80. See also administrative reforms, of *timbre*; Bourbon Reforms; civil service reform; liberal reforms; revenue reforms, in Colombia; tax reform, in Peru
refusals, 76–7
Regeneration, 54, 194
regional salience, 32–45
regionalism, 32n8, 33–7
regions, 5, 25, 31–2, 32n6, 40–1, 42–5, 42n14. See also urban primacy
renta interior (domestic manufactured goods tax), 172, 199–200
resource abundance, 179n15, 180
resource booms, 179n16. See also commodity booms; guano; nitrates
resource dependence, 179n15, 180

resource rents, 179–80
Restored Republic, 116–18, 121, 154
revenue, in Aristocratic Republic, 79–80
revenue reforms, in Colombia, 194–5, 194n32
revolts, 105n14
  in Colombia, 91
  consumption taxes prompting, 184
  in Mexico, 49, 93, 94, 94n7, 105, 105n15, 113–14, 227
  of peasants, 105, 105n15, 113–14
  in Peru, 51, 91, 92, 92n4, 94, 114–15, 184–5
  taxation and, 183–4, 183n20
Reyes, Rafael, 230
rivalry (interstate), 206n3
roads, 11n14, 43n17
Roca government, 238–9
Rock, David, 238, 248
Rodríguez, Linda A., 33
rol de avaluos, 188n29
Rosas, Juan Manuel de, 238
Rosberg, Carl G., 257
Rosenthal, Joshua M., 168n8
rubber boom, 32
ruggedness, 30–1
Ruiz-Esquide, Andrea, 111–12
Rule of Law, 13n15

salt, 169, 178, 184
Salvatore, Ricardo D., 248
Samper, Miguel, 54
San Martín, José de, 95
Santa Anna, Antonio López de, 49, 105
Santa Anna government, 99
Santa Cruz, Bolivia, 241
Santa Marta, Colombia, 42
Santander, Colombia, 42, 42n16, 44
Santander regime, 101
Santiago, Chile, 31, 38–9, 74, 98, 110
Sarmiento, Domingo Faustino, 238
Sater, William F., 207n4, 209, 223–4
Saylor, Ryan R., 7, 8n7, 19, 179n16, 206n3
Scheina, Robert L., 212

school director, 76n18
school enrollment, in Mexico, 148, 151, 151n22
school inspection, 133–4, 140–3, 145
school materials, 131–2. *See also* textbooks
school overseer. *See protector de escuela* (school overseer)
schooling, 79. *See also* mandatory schooling, in Colombia
schools, 98–9, 124–5, 127–30, 129n4, 129n5, 145. *See also* curriculum; enrollment; primary schooling; primary schools; public primary schooling; school materials
Schrank, Andrew, 9, 13n15
Scott, James, 60, 254, 255, 255n8
Scully, Timothy R., 11n12
secession, 33
seignorage, 101
sejm, Poland (national council of nobles), 21
self-sufficient regions, 44–5
Sendero Luminoso, 106n16
short-term finance, 102, 102n12
Sierra, Justo, 118
Sigman, Rachel, 10n9
Siller, Pérez, 196, 199n38
Sinkin, Richard, 117
sisal, 39
situado (subsidy), 90, 187n25
Skocpol, Theda, 220
Skuban, William E., 21n19
Slater, Dan, 7, 17, 18, 110n19, 255, 255n8, 258, 261n13
Snyder, Richard, 32n6
social conditions, educational development influenced by, 125–6
Sokoloff, Kenneth, 138n12, 139, 140n14, 140n15, 151, 151n22, 156, 156n25
Sonora, Mexico, 148, 153–5, 156
South Korea, 88–9
Southeast Asia, 27
Spain, 85n22, 95, 96, 109, 209n6
Spanish America, 82–3, 88. *See also* Bourbon Reforms

Spanish South America, 236–46
Spolaore, Enrico, 33n9
Spruyt, Hendrik, 34n10, 256n9
Staples, Anne, 99
state agents, 142–3, 181–6, 189, 190–1, 222. *See also* bureaucrats; delegated rule; deployed rule; officials
state building, 8, 82–6, 204–6, 232, 235–48, 252–62
state capacity, 123. *See also* education; extractive capacity of states; mobilization; mobilization capacity; state development; state power; state strength; state weakness; taxation
  definition, 9–11
  historical trends, 11–15
  measures, 9–11
  resource booms influencing, 179n16
  variation in, 1–9, 17–23, 87, 203, 251
state capture, reforms as, 46n19
state collapse, 252
state development, 2–3
  in Argentina, 237–9
  commodity booms influencing, 179n15
  deployed rule influencing, 124–5
  geography and, 27–45
  ideas brought into, 252–5
  size facilitating, 29
  in Uruguay, 239
state extractive capacity. *See* extractive capacity of states
state failure, 21n20
state leaders, 234n1, 252–5, 255n8, 261n13
  in Chile, 6, 124–5, 139–40
  in Colombia, 124
  cost structure influencing, 21
  delegated rule chosen by, 87–8, 108
  deployed rule chosen by, 87–8, 108–9
  elites' coalitions with, 261–2
  elites excluded by, 22
  geography influencing, 25–7

Index

ideas influencing, 19–20
  in Mexico, 6, 113, 139, 140
  in Peru, 6, 139, 140
state power, 89–94, 126–7
state strength, 107n17, 111n20, 142, 251–2
state weakness, 22–3, 221–2, 251–2, 257–8. *See also* post-independence crisis
  causal importance, 259
  of Colombia, 124, 221–2
  overview of, 87
  of Peru, 182, 222
  regionalism's relationship with, 33–7
state-building efforts
  alternative explanations, 234–5
  failure of, 3, 20–3, 21n20, 45, 59–86, 233–4
  ideational foundations of, 46–55
  outcomes of, 61–82, 232–5, 246–8
  as proactive, 4n6
  success of, 3, 5–6, 59–86, 233–4, 246n5, 255–8
  urban primacy influencing, 20, 235–46
state-building efforts emergence, 3–5, 17–20, 232–5, 246n5, 255–8
  overview of, 24–58
  urban primacy influencing, 25, 32–45, 235–46
state-indigenous relations, 85, 85n21
state-level variation of education, of Mexico, 147–56
stationary bandits, 4n6
statist vision of development, 26
status-based authority, 64–5
subdelegate, 83–4
subsidy. *See situado* (subsidy)
Sucre, Bolivia, 240
surveying of vacant land, 197–9, 198n37
Sweden, 21–2, 257
switchmen, ideas as, 254

Talca, Chile, 110
Tamaulipas, Mexico, 130
Tanck Estrada, Dorothy, 99

tariff warfare, 43–4
tax administration, 195n33, 196
tax burden, 162, 172–9
tax capacity, variation in, 179–200
tax collectors, in Mexico, 195
tax ratio, 11n11
tax reform, in Peru, 185–6
tax relief, administrators granting, 184–5
tax state, Civilista, 167–8
tax state development, 158–62, 181–6, 193, 195, 200–1
tax types, 160–2, 163–5, 165–7, 167–8, 168–70, 170–2
taxation, 10–11, 21–2. *See also* Bourbon Reforms; federal taxation; internal taxation; municipal taxation, in Chile
  administration influencing, 180, 180n19
  in Aristocratic Republic, 79–80
  in Chile, 100, 180, 186–92
  in Colombia, 100–1, 180n17, 193–5
  comparative development of, 162–72
  decision on, 179–80
  after guano boom, 181–6
  during guano era, 174–5
  implementing, 181
  in Mexico, 100, 101–2, 193, 195–200
  after nitrate boom, 186–92
  in Peru, 100, 102–3, 180
  during post-independence crisis, 100–3
  revolts and, 183–4, 183n20
  state agents increasing, 191
taxes, 160–2, 161, 169. *See also* Bourbon Reforms; direct taxes; excise tax; head tax; real estate tax
Taylor, Lewis, 76n17
teachers, 130–1, 141
technical expertise, 84–6
Tenenbaum, Barbara, 101
terrain, 30–2
territorial administration, 63n5, 84
Texas, independence declared by, 105
Texas war, 101, 105

textbooks, 131, 131n7, 132–3, 146
textiles, 44
Thies, Cameron G., 18, 206n3
Thomson, Ian, 225
Thorp, Rosemary, 11n13, 76n16
threats, 18, 203, 212, 215n11, 254, 255. *See also* Bourbon Reforms; perceived threat
Thurner, Mark, 75n15, 114–15, 183n20, 183n22
Tilly, Charles, 10, 10n9, 19n18, 59–60, 256, 256n10, 257, 258
timbre, 171–2, 197
tin mining, 240–1
tithe. *See diezmo* (tithe)
tobacco, 45, 90, 93n6, 100, 101, 168
trade, 34n10, 42n15
traditional authority, 116–20
transport, in Colombia, 55
Transport Law, 43
tribute, 85n21
tribute collectors, 75n15
troops, of Spain, 96
Tupac Amarú revolt, 91, 92, 92n4, 114
Tutino, John, 105n15

Uchuraccay, Peru, 106, 106n16
Uhthoff, Luz María, 171–2, 200
United States (U.S.), 33, 39, 49, 50, 138
  colonial rule of, 65n7, 261
  Mexico's war with, 215n11, 224
  Panama and, 214
unpopulated regions, 32n6
uprisings, 111, 183, 183n20, 212–13
urban primacy, 33n9, 56–7
  in Argentina, 237–9
  in Bolivia, 240–1
  in Central America, 245–6
  in Chile, 38–9
  in Colombia, 41–6, 41n12
  definition of, 20, 25, 34
  in Ecuador, 241–2
  elites influenced by, 26
  measurement of, 34–7
  in Mexico, 38, 39–40, 41
  in Paraguay, 242–3
  in Peru, 38, 40–1
  regional economies accompanying, 34
  state-building efforts emergence influenced by, 20, 25, 32–45, 235–46
  in Uruguay, 239
  of Venezuela, 243–4
urbanization, in Mexico, 151
Uruguay, 1–2, 239

vacant land, surveying, 197–9
vaccinations, 1, 2, 2n3, 11n13
Valencia Tovar, Álvaro, 212
Valparaíso, Chile, 31, 38, 39
Vanderwood, Paul, 220
Vatican, 136
Vaughan, Mary Kay, 99, 130
Veliz, Claudio, 63n4
Venezuela, 2, 42n16, 243–4, 259
Veracruz, Mexico, 39, 50, 101
violence, in Chile, 109–13
La Violencia, Colombia, 249
visitadores, 196
voluntary enlistment, 224–7
volunteers, 225
vom Hau, Matthias, 9n8, 59n1
Voss, Stuart F., 153n23, 154
Vu, Tuong, 7

Wagner, Gert, 163n4
Walker, Charles F., 92, 211n8
war, states and, 204–6, 257–8
War of 1000 Days, 55, 214, 230
War of the Pacific, 71n13, 112, 141–2, 144, 203, 228–9. *See also* mobilization capacity
  Bolivia's defeat in, 240
  desertions in, 222
War of the Supremes, 52–3
War to the Death. *See Guerra a Muerte* (War to the Death)
wars, 21–2. *See also* civil wars; mobilization capacity
  army size influenced by, 206, 206n1, 206n2
  Chile and, 18, 52

Index

coercive capacity influenced by, 202
in Colombia, 52–3, 55
as foundational, 94–6
against French, 114
for independence, 94–6
of Mexico, 101, 105, 249
Peru and, 18, 52, 209–11
state and, 204–6, 257–8
weapons, in Colombia, 213
Weber, Eugen, 19n18
Weber, Max, 254
World Bank Governance Indicators, 9, 13n15
World Development Indicators, 11n13
World War I, 191–2
Wright, Thomas C., 188n29

Yaqui, 154–5, 218–19
Yeager, Gertrude M., 140n15
Young, Crawford, 89
Yucatán, 39, 105, 105n15, 220
Yucatán Caste War, 49

Zeitlin, Maurice, 74
Ziblatt, Daniel, 10n9
Zipaquirá, Colombia, 178